ŝtudies in Employment Relations

rs: Rick Delbridge and Edmund Heery

ess School

e employment relationship are central to numerous courses at ·aduate and postgraduate level. Drawing insights from indus- ;, human resource management and industrial sociology, this es an alternative source of research-based materials and texts, y developments in employment research.

·lished in this series are works of high academic merit, drawn range of academic studies in the social sciences.

Relations in the Hospitality and Tourism Industries
ıcas

ıagement (second edition)
:t
eoff White and Janet Druker

e Routledge Research in Employment Relations Series

·rk
/ees reproduce the corporate machine
:abe

t in the Airline Industry
vey

:uropean Labour Identity
the European Works Council
:ichael Whittal, Herman Knudsen and Fred Huijgen

: of People, Things and Services
Transformations
laire A. Simmers and Murugan Anandarajan

formation about this series, please visit: www.routledge.com

The Internet of Peopl
Things and Services

The transformational technologies of
to exert a vast and readily apparent in
Internet penetration is now very high
the context and content of the workpl
and private life is even more porous. N
the technologies to access the Interne
increasing portability. The hardware e
mobile technologies (phones, tablets, w
The increasing mobility and 24/7 acce
revisit the transformations occurring.

Today the Internet consists of billio
and other physical objects with th
interact and exchange information abo
Organizations now use these digital de
and consume Internet-based services
commonly referred to as the Internet of

Information and communications
desktops to laptops to ubiquitous smar
directly over the Internet—the IoPTS
revisit how the Internet transforms our

Claire A. Simmers is Professor Emer
Erivan K. Haub School of Business, Sai

Murugan Anandarajan is Professor
Management, Decision Sciences & MIS
University, USA.

Routledg
Series ed
Cardiff Bu

Aspects of
both unde
trial relati
series prov
reviewing

Books p
from a wid

Employme
Rosemary

Reward M
A critical t
Edited by

Latest in

Power at W
How empl
Darren Mc

Managem
Geraint H

Towards a
The case o
Edited by

The Intern
Workplace
Edited by

For more i

The Internet of People, Things and Services

Workplace Transformations

Edited by Claire A. Simmers
and Murugan Anandarajan

Routledge
Taylor & Francis Group
NEW YORK AND LONDON

First published 2018
by Routledge
605 Third Avenue, New York, NY 10017

and by Routledge
2 Park Square, Milton Park, Abingdon, Oxon, OX14 4RN

Routledge is an imprint of the Taylor & Francis Group, an informa business

Library of Congress Cataloging-in-Publication Data
A catalog record for this book has been requested

ISBN: 978-1-138-74232-1 (hbk)
ISBN: 978-1-315-18240-7 (ebk)

Typeset in Sabon
by Apex CoVantage, LLC

Claire: To my family, especially my husband, Michael; my daughters, Samantha, Jessica, and Christa and my grandchildren, Michael, Brianna, and Nathaniel; the party continues.

Murugan: To Sharmini, Vinesh, Dharman, and Bugsy

Contents

Figures

Tables

Contributors

Murugan Anandarajan is a Professor of Management Information Systems in the Department of Management at Drexel University. His current research interests include artificial intelligence–based classification, artificial life and Internet usage. His research has appeared in journals such as *Behavior and Information Technology*, *Computers and Operations Research*, *Decision Sciences*, *Industrial Data Management Systems*, *Information and Management*, *International Journal of Information Management*, *Journal of Management Information Systems*, *Journal of Global Information Systems*, *Journal of International Business Studies* and the *Omega-International Journal of Management Science*, among others.

Elisabeth E. Bennett, PhD, is presently Associate Teaching Professor of Organizational Leadership Studies at Northeastern University, Boston, MA. Dr. Bennett's research includes virtual human resource development (HRD), organizational culture and informal learning. She co-edited two *Advances in Developing Human Resources* issues on virtual HRD and has written book chapters and articles on the subject. She was formerly director of education research and development in medical education at the Western Campus of Tufts University School of Medicine, and she managed an intranet in university-based continuing education at the University of Georgia where she received her doctorate in Adult Education with an emphasis in Human Resource and Organizational Development. Dr. Bennett served on the board of the Academy of Human Resource Development and presently is a member of the editorial boards for *Human Resource Development Quarterly*, *Adult Education Quarterly*, *Advances in Developing Human Resources* and *New Horizons in Adult Education and Human Resource Development.*

Constant D. Beugré is Professor of Management at Delaware State University where he teaches courses in entrepreneurship and organizational behavior in the undergraduate program and organizational leadership and behavior in the MBA program. He earned a PhD in management from Rensselaer Polytechnic Institute, School of Management and

Technology and a PhD in Industrial/Organizational Psychology from the Université Paris X-Nanterre. Prior to joining Delaware State University, Dr. Beugré was an assistant professor of management and information systems at Kent State University, Tuscarawas Campus. Dr. Beugré was also a visiting fellow at Harvard University. His research interests include organizational justice, entrepreneurial ecosystems and organizational neuroscience. Dr. Beugré has published seven books and more than 70 refereed journal articles, book chapters and conference proceedings. His publications have appeared in academic outlets such as *Organizational Behavior and Human Decision Processes*, *International Journal of Human Resource Management*, *International Journal of Manpower*, *Journal of Applied Behavioral Science*, *Journal of Applied Social Psychology*, *Journal of Business & Psychology* and *Research in the Sociology of Organizations*.

Tomas Blomquist is a professor in Business Administration at Umeå University. He is the director of research at the department and the research profile leader for the business school's research profile on projects and networks. He is currently involved in work on behavioral aspects of coaching in business incubation and interorganizational aspects of business development around digitalization and IoT. Tomas has previously done research with mixed-methods research, and his work is published in several international journals, including *Business Horizons*, *Business Strategy and the Environment*, *Industrial Marketing Management*, *Harvard Business Review* and the *International Journal of Project Management*.

Thomas Calvard is a lecturer in Human Resource Management (HRM) and Organization Studies (OS) at the University of Edinburgh Business School in the UK. He completed his PhD in Organizational Psychology from the University of Sheffield in the UK. He has research interests include diversity, technology and sense making in organizations. He focuses particularly on the disruptive effects that technological and demographic changes can have on the interpretation of diverse viewpoints, perspectives and boundaries in organizations. His research appears in several international, peer-reviewed publications, including *Organization Science, Management Learning* and *The International Journal of Human Resource Management*. His co-authored work in *Organization Science* on the role of automation and limits in the Air France 447 air crash disaster is available for open-access download (http://pubsonline.informs.org/doi/pdf/10.1287/orsc.2017.1138), as well as appearing on *Harvard Business Review (HBR) Online* (https://hbr.org/2017/09/the-tragic-crash-of-flight-af447-shows-the-unlikely-but-catastrophic-consequences-of-automation). Finally, he has recently co-edited a book with Tinu Cornish, *The Psychology of Ethnicity in Organisations*, published by Palgrave in 2017. He also blogs on various HRM topics, including big data and HRM analytics (www.hrzone.com/profile/tomcalvard).

Wendy Campbell is an IT faculty mentor at Western Governors University. Dr. Campbell has been working in IT since the early stages of the Internet through the Internet's astonishing transformation into the Internet of Things. In fact, her first published article was titled: "Is there Life after ArcNet." Dr. Campbell has a Doctorate in IT Security from Northcentral University. She resides in North Ogden, Utah.

Veronica M. (Ronnie) Godshalk is a Professor of Management at the Pennsylvania State University. She is also the BS in Business Program Coordinator for the World Campus online program. Dr. Godshalk teaches courses in management, leadership and strategy. She is the recipient of several teaching awards, including the Teaching & Learning with Technology Fellowship and the Arthur L. Glenn Award for Faculty Teaching Innovation at Penn State. Dr. Godshalk has published many books, articles and chapters, and her research interests include issues surrounding career management, mentoring and entrepreneurship, as well as online pedagogy and technology use. With co-authors Jeff Greenhaus and Gerry Callanan, she is currently working on a fifth edition of *Career Management*. She is an active member in professional associations, such as the Academy of Management. Dr. Godshalk had worked in the computer industry in sales and sales management prior to entering academia, and has been a consultant for several Fortune 500 companies.

David B. Kurz, EdD, is an Assistant Clinical Professor in the Management Department at Drexel University's LeBow College of Business. He has also worked with leading organizations and institutions, advising them in the delivery of effective leadership development and change programs. Dr. Kurz has worked extensively with numerous highly ranked supply chain organizations facilitating their transformations in digital demand planning and end-to-end integration. His work involves implementing programs to improve integration performance across supply chain functions through collaborative learning programs. He holds master's and doctoral degrees from the University of Pennsylvania.

Vivien K. G. Lim is a professor of management in the NUS Business School, National University of Singapore. She received her PhD in Organizational Behavior from Katz Graduate School of Business, University of Pittsburgh. She was Editor-in-Chief of *Applied Psychology: An International Review*. Her research interests focus on the impact of information technology on work, daily commuting, workplace deviance, job insecurity and aging. She has published in *Academy of Management Journal*, *Journal of Applied Psychology*, *Journal of Personality and Social Psychology*, *Journal of Organizational Behavior*, *Journal of Vocational Behavior* and *Human Relations*, among others.

Terri R. Lituchy is the PIMSA Distinguished Chair at CETYS Universidad in Mexico and is also currently teaching at UNC Charlotte. Dr. Lituchy taught one Semester at Sea spring 2016 and has taught courses around the world, on Organizational Behavior, Cross-Cultural Management, International Negotiations and Women in International Business. Dr. Lituchy's research interests are in cross-cultural management and international organizational behavior and her current project, LEAD: Leadership Effectiveness and Motivation in Africa, the Caribbean and the Diaspora, has received many awards as well as grants. Dr. Lituchy has held several leadership and administrative positions, and she has consulted, and conducted training and development programs and workshops for MNCs, NGOs, small businesses and other organizations.

Irina-Marcela Nedelcu is a Masters student in Business Analytics at Drexel University. She holds a Bachelors of Science in Business Administration with concentrations in Business Analytics and Management Information Systems. Her current interests include Machine Learning, Data Visualization and Statistics. She has presented her research findings on smartphone self-protection at the Northeast Decision Science Conference, STAR Scholars Showcast and 16th International Conference of Electronic Commerce. She was the founder and president of the Undergraduate Business Analytics Club (UBAC) and the president of the Management Information Systems Organization (MISO) at Drexel University.

Lisa T. Nelson is a visiting instructor in the Department of Management at the Erivan K. Haub School of Business of Saint Joseph's University. She earned her doctorate in communications and information systems at Robert Morris University. Her research and teaching interests involve topics related to organizational behavior, notably organizational communication, negotiation and conflict resolution, workplace diversity, occupational identity and corporate social responsibility. Currently, she is celebrating the work of management and political theorist Mary Parker Follett (1868–1933), examining applications of Follett's work in organizations in the 21st-century knowledge and service economy.

Kimberly W. O'Connor, JD, is an Assistant Professor of Organizational Leadership at Indiana University-Purdue University Fort Wayne (IPFW) and an attorney licensed in the state of Indiana. She received her doctoral degree from Loyola University School of Law. Her research areas include social media and the law, cybersecurity, employment law and corporate social responsibility. She has been a consultant for social media-related matters in organizations.

James G. Phillips is currently an Associate Professor at Auckland University of Technology. He did his undergraduate training at Adelaide University (honors thesis with Dr. Doug Vickers) and completed his PhD at Flinders University (supervised by Dr. Denis Glencross). After doing some postdoctoral work with Professor George Stelmach on Parkinson's disease and balance in the elderly, he worked for a year at Bendigo College of

Advanced Education. From 1990 to 2010 he worked at the Psychology Department at Monash University collaborating with Professor Bradshaw, Professor Triggs and Professor Blaszczynski. From 2011 to 2013 he worked at Tabor College Victoria. Having identified many of the characteristics of impaired behavior, Dr. Phillips has turned his interests toward remediation. The Internet and mobile phone allow us to take therapeutic interventions beyond the consulting room to provide assistance in "real time" and "on site" rather than "by appointment." Dr. Phillips' recent interests address the trackability and influenceability of behavior online.

Erika Pleskunas is an undergraduate student in Management Information Systems at Drexel University. She has presented her research findings on the IOT and Smartworkplace at STAR Scholars Conference. Her interests include the Internet of Things, data visualization and project management. She is an active member of Alpha Kappa Psi, the professional co-ed business fraternity, and is currently doing a co-op for Johnson & Johnson in the IT Supply Chain.

Carol Portillo earned her PhD in Business Technology Management from Northcentral University. Dr. Portillo has over 18 years of experience in the high-tech industry serving in positions in operations, sales management and channel marketing. With over 15 years of university-level teaching experience, Dr. Portillo has instructed both graduate and undergraduate courses in consumer behavior, marketing management, services marketing and advertising. Dr. Portillo is currently an adjunct faculty at St. Edward's University, in Austin, Texas, and has taught at St. Mary's University, San Antonio, Texas, and Concordia University in Austin. Dr. Portillo's research interests are in the area of online consumer purchasing behavior and Internet purchasing behavior. Dr. Portillo is currently serving on the Pflugerville Education Foundation as a board member.

Rashimah Rajah is a Research Associate at the Koblenz University of Applied Sciences, RheinAhrCampus, Germany. Her research interests are job connectedness, positive psychology, job crafting and emotions in leadership. She has published in *Leadership Quarterly*, *Ivey Business Publishing*, and the *Handbook of Research on Crisis Leadership in Organizations*. She graduated with a PhD in Business Management from the National University of Singapore. She was the recipient of the President's Graduate Fellow Scholarship from 2011 to 2013 for outstanding research as a PhD student.

Ted Saarikko currently holds a post-doctoral position at the University of Gothenburg where he is engaged in an interdisciplinary project concerning the transportation of hazardous materials in terms of business incentives, information systems interoperability and legal restrictions. Prior to defending his doctoral thesis from Umeå University in late 2016, Ted has earned degrees in Computer Science, Japanese language studies and IT Management. He is also affiliated with the Swedish Center for Digital Innovation.

Ted's research focuses mainly on the development of digital platforms, in particular IoT platforms, and how we may leverage them to create distinct value propositions for a range of different actors. Other research interests include affordance theory, entrepreneurship and digital innovation.

Gordon B. Schmidt is an associate professor and current chair of the Organizational Leadership Department at Indiana University Purdue University Fort Wayne (IPFW). His primary research area is how social media (Facebook, Twitter, Instagram, LinkedIn, Reddit) is changing the nature of company–employee relations today. He co-edited a book on how social media is used in selection and recruitment processes by organizations. He's done research on the law related to people fired for social media posts and the nature of organizational social media policies that are created to tell employees or students what online behaviors are inappropriate. He also has done research related to the gig economy and crowdsourcing sites like Amazon Mechanical Turk, where people online are hired to do tasks for organizations. He also does research related to virtual leadership, corporate social responsibility, job apathy, leadership in lean production, motivation and office gossip. He has acted as consultant for social media–related matters in organizations.

Claire A. Simmers, PhD, is a professor emeritus in the management department at Saint Joseph's University in Philadelphia, PA, USA. She has experience in public and private sectors and publishes in the area of sociotechnical interfaces in the Internet-connected workplace, including the impact of technology and the generational mix in the workplace, human capital contributions to competitive advantage and sustainability. She has over 80 scholarly works in her profile and almost 900 citations. She has been a member of the Academy of Management for over 20 years and has served in various leadership positions in the International Theme Committee.

Ulrika H. Westergren is an associate professor at the Department of Informatics, Umeå University, Sweden, and a faculty member of the Swedish Center for Digital Innovation. Ulrika specializes in information technology and organizational change, and her work covers topics such as servitization processes, emergent forms of organizing, digital innovation and value creation. Currently she is focusing on viable business models for firms that are operating within an Internet of Things ecosystem and on IoT for societal benefit. Ulrika's work is published in journals such as *Business Horizons*, *Information and Organization*, *Information Systems and E-business Management Journal* and *Information Systems Journal*. Ulrika holds an AB in International Relations from Bryn Mawr College and a PhD in Information Systems from Umeå University.

1 Introduction

The Internet of People, Things and Services (IoPTS): Workplace Transformations

Claire A. Simmers and Murugan Anandarajan

Introduction

In 2006, we published a volume on the Internet and workplace transformations (Anandarajan, Teo, & Simmers, 2006). At that time, unknown to us, that volume was the midpoint of our journey in examining the interrelationships between user behavior and information and communication technologies (ICT) in the workplace. Our work began as the Internet was becoming more widely used in the business setting, and we investigated factors that influenced end-user adoption of the Internet in the workplace (Anandarajan, Simmers, & Igbaria, 2000). We extended our research by examining the multidimensionality of positive and negative personal Internet usage in the workplace, and we saw the personal and the work increasingly overlapping, enabling unprecedented accessibility to unlimited information on a 24-hour, seven-day-a-week basis. We were no longer bound to our physical location; through the Internet, we could be anywhere in the world. The troubling and promising ways the Internet transformed our workplaces were due to the vastness of information, the disaggregation of work and location, and the rapid worldwide adoption.

Our attention again shifted in sync with ICT advancements, with the increasing portability of devices. We were no longer tethered to desktop devices, but had laptops, tablets, and smart phones owned by the organization, or just as likely owned by the individual. This convergence and overlapping of devices and ownerships allowed for further extension of the 24/7 workplace, as work could be accessed on any device at any time and any place. The information world was in our pockets.

Layered onto hardware portability are advancements in the interconnectivity of the workplace. We are now able, primarily through the "cloud", to link our portable devices to anyone and anything in a spider web of connectivity increasingly known as the Internet of People, Things and Services (Eloff, Eloff, Dlamini, & Zielinski, 2009). IoPTS is about linking the physical world and the digital world through sharing common protocols facilitating interoperationality. This is a world of autonomous communication between intelligent devices that are sensitive to a person's presence and respond by performing specific services that enhance a person's lifestyle (Piccialli &

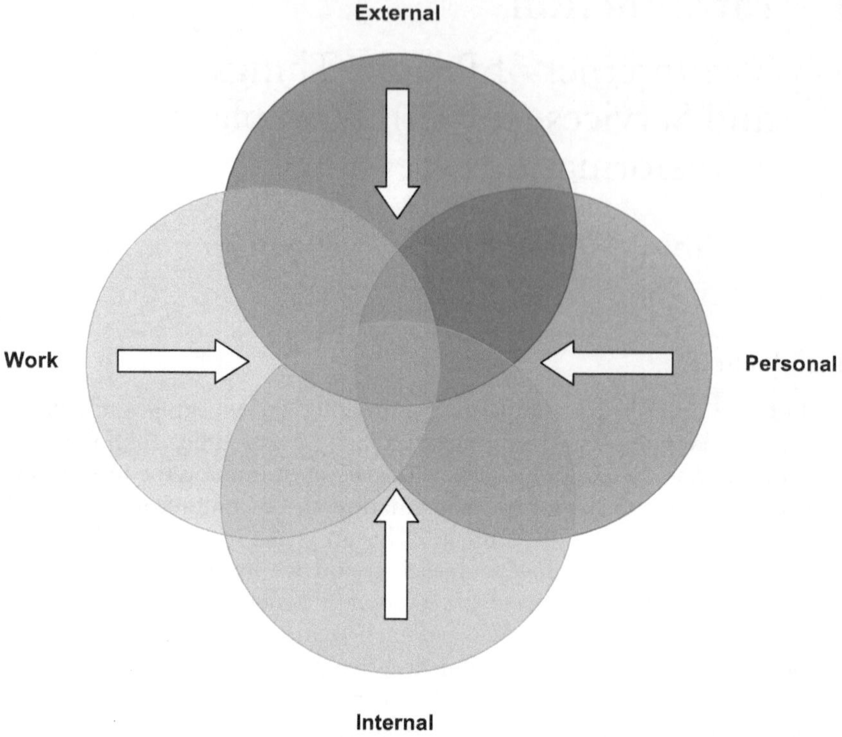

Figure 1.1 IoPTS Producing Increasing Convergence in the Workplace

Chianese, 2017). There are countless applications; more are introduced daily, and even more are planned for the future. Energy efficiency, healthcare, transportation coordination, household appliances, wearables, and self-driving cars are just a few examples (Gershenfeld & Vasseur, 2014). This level of interconnectivity smashes the already blurred boundaries between work and personal lives that we explored in the 2006 volume (Anandarajan, et al., 2006)). Additionally, the porousness of an organization's internal and external boundaries increases; the impacts of the increasing convergence between these four forces are what we explore in this volume. This dynamism is illustrated in Figure 1.1, which shows the increasing convergence (represented by the four arrows) of the spheres of work and personal with the internal and external boundaries of the organization.

Background

Since our 2006 volume, worldwide Internet usage continued to grow. Penetration (defined as the number of users divided by the total population) rose from 1.5% in Africa in 2005 to 31.2% in 2017 and from 67.4% in North

America in 2005 to 88.1% in 2017. There are now 3.9 billon Internet users worldwide, which represents over half the world's population (51.7%) (World Internet Users Statistics, 2017). Internet usage and penetration is only half of the story in the IoPTS world; device connectivity is the more important statistic. The headline in a recent report reads "Gartner Says 8.4 Billion Connected 'Things' Will Be in Use in 2017, Up 31 Percent From 2016" (2017, February 7). This number is forecasted to reach 20.4 billion by 2020 with total spending on endpoints and services to be almost $2 trillion in 2017 (Gartner, 2017).

How will IoPTS affect the workplace? We are just beginning to investigate the impacts; it is a workplace where automation continues to grow rapidly (Corsello, n.d.). Challenges such as retrofitting buildings and homes, data management, and digital security will bring opportunities to those who can provide these types of services (Anderle, 2016). Careers and career paths are already changing as robots and artificial intelligence begin to become realities in the workplace (Ward, 2017). Although "things" will be increasingly providing "services", the role of "people", although shifting, will not only continue, but will become more indispensable. Qureshi and Syed (2014) examined the benefits and challenges of robots in the workplace. Future workers in most professions will need to be educated and trained to work in tandem with robots. Not only will people need education and training on the "things" and how to use the "services", but a recurring theme in this volume is that people will have to take increasing responsibilities in the IoPTS workplace. These responsibilities will be to set their own behavior boundaries in their personal lives and help develop those of others in their organizational lives.

In the pre-Internet workplace, the bilateral psychological contracts summarized employees' beliefs and discernments regarding the implicit and explicit promises and responsibilities comprising the relationship between employee and organization. They were transactional (focusing on tangible compensation requirements) and relational (involving socioemotional elements, such as trust, fairness, motivation, and commitment) (Robinson, Kraatz, & Rousseau, 1994). A new psychological contract evolved in the 1990s, emanating largely from increasing usage of the Internet and other information and communication technologies. This new psychological contract was based on shorter-term employment, employee responsibility for career development, commitment to the work performed rather than to the employer, and the diminishing importance of hierarchy (Ehrlich, 1994). In the IoPTS workplace, the psychological contract continues to evolve, becoming multifoci (Alcover, Rico, Turnley, & Bolino, 2016). Alcover et al. (2016) proposed that the traditional psychological contract based on a bilateral relationship between the employee and organization had been supplanted by a situation where "employees simultaneously depend on several agents, representing one or more organizations, who assign tasks and goals, supervise work, and provide rewards (or impose sanctions) depending on results"

(2016, p. 5). The relationships may be temporary and experienced from different locations, and may include interactions with nonhumans (robots or computers).

We take the multiple-foci psychological contract's approach (Alcover et al., 2016) one step further, proposing that these nonstandard work arrangements will be the standard work arrangements as the IoPTS becomes increasingly ubiquitous. However, there is a paucity of research on what will be motivating those in the IoPTS workplace to fulfill obligations and commitments in the performance of work and how the necessary levels of trust, security, and privacy critical in the IoPTS workplace will be attained (Eloff et al., 2009). This volume is a collection of conceptual and empirical work, providing a rich resource as well as an agenda for future scholarly endeavors.

Part 1: IoPTS Workplace—People

Part 1 has five chapters exploring ways people and the IoPTS interact in the workplace. In the chapters we are reminded that people are still central in the relationships among "things" and "services" but that the fissure between the positives of efficiency and connectivity and the challenges of disassociation and multiple exchange relationships continues to widen. All the authors make strong arguments that people have a major role and heightened responsibility to lessen this fissure rather than placing their reliance on the "things".

In Chapter 2, Lisa Nelson points out that despite the many positive effects, there are three prevalent negative effects: 1) increased disassociation among organizational users and between users and the organization, 2) decreased information quality due to inaccuracy and equivocality, and 3) deteriorating social skills because of user overreliance on technology. Nelson then reaches out to the past for guidance from Mary Parker Follett, an insightful management theorist of the early 20th century. Follett's three most important contributions to organizations—the concepts of circular response, integration, and the law of the situation—are suggested by Nelson as a basis for more humanism in the IoPTS workplace.

In Chapter 3 Constant Beugré argues for the central role of cognition, interpretation, and sense making, all inherent to "people" functionalities. As immense quantities of data are accumulated in the IoPTS, data sense making is necessary if the decision-making process is to have meaning. The mere availability of data is not enough to provide a competitive advantage. What is important is how organizations make sense of the data they collect. As Beugré explains in this chapter, analytics is more a cognitive process than a mere computation of numbers, however accurate they may be. To improve the use of analytics, it is important to combine the use of data with a deep understanding of the domain in which the data are collected and analyzed.

Veronica Godshalk, in Chapter 4, continues with a conceptual warning that the enormity of reach in the IoPTS workplace plants an increasing responsibility on "people" to actively manage this new workplace. She contrasts the contribution that IoPTS can make to maintain work patterns over time and multiple employers and applies the *Too Much of a Good Thing* (TMGT) effect. The technology associated with IoPTS allows for constant 24/7 accessibility, invasive employer access to employee data and behavioral scans, and even implantable devices—thus the TMGT effect. The IoPTS also may have detrimental effects on individuals through higher stress, more discrimination in hiring, slower career progression, and work–life imbalance. IoPTS needs to be managed properly through individual and organizational support convergence.

Rashimah Rajah and Vivien Lim in Chapter 5 and Kimberly O'Connor and Gordon B. Schmidt in Chapter 6 continue the discussion of people in the IoPTS workplace. Rajah and Lim discuss the results of their empirical work indicating that cyberloafing (using the Internet at the workplace for personal matters) can have positive effects on productivity through the dimension of helping behavior in organizational citizenship behaviors (OCB). The reasoning is that if individuals can mitigate the 24/7 connectivity characteristic of the IoPTS workplace, with downtimes of their choosing for personal usage, productivity will be enhanced. This continues a theme of employee control and responsibility in the IoPTS workplace. In Chapter 5, O'Connor and Schmidt analyze court cases involving employees' personal use of social media, and they see a trend toward increasing legal protections for employees. They focus on the impact that social media use and the IoPTS has had on certain aspects of the life cycle of employment, such as selection and termination. They examine data privacy protections for workers and discuss the legal issues that organizations may face when monitoring employees or providing them with employer-owned devices. Additionally, they raise questions about the value gained from the use of social media and data monitoring by organizations as they may not be worth the reputational cost. They posit that such data gleaned from IoPTS *could* be helpful, but there is little research suggesting that the data actually *are* useful.

Part 2: IoPTS Workplace—Things

Part 2 contains four chapters focusing on how the "things" in the IoPTS affect various aspects of the workplace. The Internet of Things is a world where physical and digital objects are seamlessly connected and integrated into vast networks. These networks are active participants in business processes (Eloff et al., 2009). All the chapters highlight that the Internet of Things is going to give us the most disruption as well as the most opportunity (Burrus, 2014) and that organizational actions can and must be instrumental in building trust, privacy, and security (Eloff et al., 2009).

In Chapter 7 Ulrika H. Westergren, Ted Saarikko, and Tomas Blomquist investigated 21 Swedish firms, all early adopters of IoT. They conclude that in order for firms to successfully implement IoT into organizational processes they have to 1) change their work practices accordingly; 2) make sure that they have access to all needed competencies, be they internal or external; and 3) create an environment of trust that will leverage privacy concerns.

Chapter 8 by Wendy Campbell and Chapter 9 by Irina Nedelcu and Murugan Anandarajan examine security infrastructure. The Campbell chapter explores the impact of IoT on the IT security infrastructure of colleges and universities in Utah. Her findings suggest there is awareness of the challenges and risks of the IoT environment and that strategies have been initiated to mitigate these challenges while also embracing the opportunities. Nedelcu and Anandarajan take a narrower focus by examining specifically the use of smart phones and what motivates users to express intentions to protect their smart phones. Their results indicated that the desire to self-protect is influenced by perceived severity, response efficacy, and response cost. Companies should implement stronger policies, train employees on ways to engage in self-protective behaviors, and work with security organizations to design effective intervention methods. Training should be divided by operating systems because iOS users tend to rely more on the system and less on self-protection than do Android users.

Chapter 10 by Elisabeth E. Bennett highlights another promising transformation in the workplace shaped by the IoT—the shift toward IoPTS as multiple intranets linked to leverage virtual human resource development (VHRD). VHRD emphasizes learning, strategy, and cultural dimensions with a focus on learning, development, and performance improvement. Important to implement is a concentration on the processes of interacting with the IoT such as learning agility and design thinking.

Part 3: IoPTS Workplace—Services

How do we use the technology of IoT in the workplace to be of service? The six chapters in this section offer ways organizations and nations can or do utilize IoPTS. Effectively using IoPTS to provide services requires organizational approaches that singly or in combination proactively minimize risk and increase opportunity through a better understanding of users' motivations and requirements, new leadership approaches, and improved organizational policies and procedures

Both Chapter 11 by Thomas Calvard and Chapter 12 by James Phillips explore the role of users' motivations and requirements to use the services offered in IoPTS. Calvard outlines how IoPTS will affect the design of performance management systems with the goal of increasing service to both the employees and the organization. He applies the results of the SWOT analysis to recommend that improving performance management practices and policies for managers and employees be accomplished via further skills development and the design of resilient systems based around users' motivations and needs. James Phillips posits that IoT offers a strong potential for health organizations to offer services to influence health behaviors and improve outpatient support for addicts. When considering IoPTS, health organizations need to be aware of users' motivations and behaviors, as their addict clients will more likely filter their communications with the Internet to a greater extent than the general public and that the Internet of Things is not a panacea.

Carol Portillo and Terri R. Lituchy in Chapter 13 examine how online purchasing will continue to change due to the rapid introduction of IoT. Their study analyzed the predictor variables of gender, digital experience (digital native vs. digital immigrant), level of income, and level of education for impacts on the intent to repurchase online. None of the variables affected, positively or negatively, the intention to repurchase online, thus leading them to conclude that psychographic variables such as user motivations and attitudes are more important than demographic variables. With IoPTS, organizations will be better able to individualize products, services, and offers to a full spectrum of consumers.

In Chapter 14, David Kurz argues that if organizations are to provide the service of an integrated, demand-driven supply chain service aligned to organizational strategy, transformational leadership will be required. He discusses two case examples and then introduces a model that isolates the influence and potential impacts of leadership on the digital transformation of supply chains. The argument is that the digital supply chain, led by technologies such as IoT and advanced analytics, will require enhancements in the management layer's mind-set and attitudes, integration behaviors, and skills in order to offer supply chain services that will realize an organization's competitive advantage.

Chapter 15 by Erika Pleskunas and Murugan Anandarajan continues the theme of this section, which is that organization-wide changes are required to take advantage of the IoPTS technologies to offer enhanced services, whether in human resource management, patient self-regulation, online repurchasing, supply chains, or protections against security breaches. Pleskunas and Anandarajan propose a framework offering guidance on protection from security breaches.

Murugan Anandarajan and Claire Simmers in Chapter 16 discuss how the future workplace will include cross-cultural work forces, global interdependencies, skilled workers from emerging countries improving productivities from within their own borders, remote workers' increased flexibility to meet labor needs, and cultural diversity contributing toward businesses offering products and services. However, IoPTS is still in its infancy in multiple countries, as many of the required factors are in the beginning stage of development; each country has its own unique set of IoPTS capacity and readiness characteristics. The purpose of this chapter is to develop an IoPTS adaption score to classify a country's progress in adopting and using IoPTS.

In *The Internet of People, Things and Services (IoPTS): Workplace Transformations* we offer a more thorough look at how IoPTS is altering the workplace. We have shown the interconnections of people, things, and services in a variety of settings, discussing what currently exists, but more importantly, providing guidance on how to manage what is coming. IoPTS will come—the question before us, on which some guidance is provided in this volume, is how to maximize the constructive aspects while minimizing the threats. The conclusion that is reached from reading the chapters in this book is that keeping People is paramount. IoPTS is the answer.

References

Alcover, C. M., Rico, R., Turnley, W. H., & Bolino, M. C. (2016). Understanding the changing nature of psychological contracts in 21st century organizations: A multiple-foci exchange relationships approach and proposed framework. *Organizational Psychology Review*, *1*, 1–32.

Anandarajan, M., Simmers, C.A., & Igbaria, M. (2000). An exploratory investigation of the antecedents and impact of Internet usage: An individual perspective. *Behaviour and Information Technology*, *19*(1): 69–85.

Anandarajan, M., Teo, T., & Simmers, C. A. (Eds.). (2006). *The internet and workplace transformation: Advances in management information systems series*. New York: M.E. Sharpe.

Anderle, M. (2016, April 8). *Infographic: How the Internet of Things is transforming the workplace*. Retrieved November 10, 2017, from https://blog.dell.com/en-us/infographic-how-the-internet-of-things-is-transforming-the-workplace/

Burrus, D. (2014). *The Internet of Things is far bigger than anyone realizes*. Retrieved November 19, 2017, from www.wired.com/insights/2014/11/the-internet-of-things-bigger/

Corsello, J. (n.d.). *What the Internet of Things will bring to the workplace*. Retrieved November 10, 2017, from www.wired.com/insights/2013/11/what-the-internet-of-things-will-bring-to-the-workplace/

Ehrlich, C. J. (1994). Creating an employer-employee relationship for the future. *Human Resource Management*, *33*, 491–501.

Eloff, J. H. P., Eloff, M. M., Dlamini, M. T., & Zielinski, M. P. (2009). *Internet of People, things and services: The convergence of security, trust and privacy*. The Proceeding of 3rd Companion Able Consortium Workshop IoPTS, Brussel, 8.

Gartner. (2017, February 7). *Gartner says 8.4 billion connected 'things' will be in use in 2017, up 31 percent from 2016*. Retrieved November 10, 2017, from www.gartner.com/newsroom/id/3598917

Gershenfeld, N., & Vasseur, J. P. (2014). As objects go online: The promise (and pitfalls) of the Internet of things. *Foreign Affairs*, *93*(2), 60–67.

Piccialli, F., & Chianese, A. (2017). The Internet of Things supporting context-aware computing: A cultural heritage case study. *Mobile Networks and Applications*, *22*(2), 332–343.

Qureshi, M. O., & Syed, R. S. (2014). The impact of robotics on employment and motivation of employees in the service sector, with special reference to health care. *Safety and Health at Work*, *5*(4), 198–202.

Robinson, S. L., Kraatz, M. S., & Rousseau, D. M. (1994). Changing obligations and the psychological contract: A longitudinal study. *Academy of Management Journal*, *37*, 137–152.

Ward, M. (2017, October 5). *AI and robots could threaten your career within 5 years*. Retrieved November 14, 2017, from www.cnbc.com/2017/10/05/report-ai-and-robots-could-change-your-career-within-5-years.html

World Internet Users Statistics. (2017, November 3). Retrieved November 9, 2017, from www.internetworldstats.com/stats.htm

Part 1

IoPTS Workplace—People

2 Moving From the IoT to the IoP

Applying Mary Parker Follett's Circular Response, Integration, and Law of the Situation to the Role and Responsibilities of the User in the IoPTS Workplace

Lisa T. Nelson

Users as Participants in the Internet of People, Things and Services

Information and communication technology (ICT) is pervasive in organizations for purposes of sharing, managing, and storing knowledge to increase efficiency, performance, decision making, and productivity (Knight, Pearson, & Hunsinger, 2008). Individual users in firms and organizations interact over ICT with each other and with internal and external constituents (e.g., customers, suppliers, and vendors). *Users* are defined here as "firms or individual consumers that expect to benefit from using a product or a service" (von Hippel, 2005, p. 3).

As ICT has become increasingly democratized, individuals find they "are living in a mobile-device-focused society (most people could not live without a mobile phone)" (Zhang, Wang, Vasilakos, & Ma, 2013, p. 91). ICT "has decentralized communication by allowing each individual to be not only an information consumer but a producer as well" (Malone, as cited in Hand & Ching, 2011, p. 364), implying that transactional relationships can also occur. Users of ICT, then, become active participants in what is known today as the *Internet of people, things and services* (IoPTS). The IoPTS is generally defined as "the vision where people, things (physical objects) and services are seamlessly integrated into the networks of networks as active participants that exchange data about themselves and their perceived surrounding environments over a web-based infrastructure" (Eloff, Eloff, Dlamini, & Zielinski, 2009, p. 1). The IoPTS "are three fundamental concepts that form the backbone of the Future Internet" (Aitenbichler et al., as cited in Weber, Martucci, Ries, & Mühlhäuser, 2010, n.p.).

First, the *Internet of people* (IoP) encourages interfacing and interactions between humans and machines, empowering "users with service-independent ubiquitous access" (Weber et al., 2010, n.p.) without using a special app or going through a third party. Luis Molina, founder and CEO of Fermat, identifies the IoP as a way "to use the digital tools at our disposal to build a new and more human-friendly cyberspace alongside the corporate and government-run cyberspace we have now" (Lyons, 2017, p. 4).

Next, the *Internet of things* (IoT) "relates to interconnected physical devices, usually in the form of embedded systems and sensors with one or more network interfaces that are used to collect, forward, compute, or display data" (Weber et al., 2010, n.p.). The IoT "increasingly pervades our daily lives" (Miranda et al., 2015, p. 3), imposing "12.6 million connected devices, including people, processes, data, and things" (Cisco IoT Connections Counter, as cited in Miranda et al., 2015, p. 3). The "things" in the IoT are both physical, as in tangible devices, and virtual, as existing in the world of data and information (Jadhav, 2014). The IoT consists of networks of programs and devices—everything from smartphones, to coffee makers, to home heating and cooling systems, to televisions, to many industrial machines—that connect to the Internet and to each other (Hancock & Hancock, 2016; Miranda et al., 2015). Ideally, the IoT enables more user control over home and work, making both better and easier (Judge & Powles, 2015).

The *Internet of services* (IoS) may be understood to be at the intersection of the IoT and the IoP. Intended to be "the global marketplace of the future" (Weber et al., 2010, n.p.), the IoS deals primarily with the use of web-connected (i.e., Web 2.0) devices and service-oriented architectures (SOA) that enable organizations to manage and share knowledge and data (Schroth & Janner, 2007) in the conveyance of goods and services to consumers. "The objective of the IoS is to set up a fully-fledged digital equivalent of the existing service-based economy. Thus, IoS allows people and software-based entities to engage in service-based economic activities, such as negotiation, bidding, and contracting" (Weber et al., 2010, n.p.).

Problems in Organizations: Negative Effects of ICT on Users in the IoT

IoT devices and methods of use, although convenient and encompassing, can actually have a destructive impact on users in organizations. Three prevalent negative effects described here are increased disassociation among organizational users and between users and the organization, decreased information quality due to inaccuracy and equivocality, and deteriorating social skills because of user overreliance on technology.

Organizational User Disassociation

Organizational user disassociation may lead to deleterious impacts on organizational users' relationships and productivity by putting employee citizenship, productivity, trust, and commitment at risk. Workplaces are social spaces; in fact, telecommuting managers and employees may feel isolated simply from being off-site (see Cooper & Kurland, 2002). Machines and devices connected via the Internet "talk to" and transact with each other, disconnecting human users from active, direct participation in the communication processes, as the machines and devices "speak for" them.

Decreased Information Quality Due to Inaccuracy and Equivocality

Also, although the purpose of each technological innovation appears to be to improve efficiency, organizational users can intentionally or unwittingly compromise efficiency by sabotaging the quality of their communication. Perceived quality of communication, and the information therein, is "a combination of timeliness, usability, and accuracy" (Byrne & LeMay, 2006, p. 151); clarity may also be considered. Accuracy may be understood to include truthfulness and trustworthiness and is a critical aspect of informational justice in the workplace (see Bies & Moag, as cited in Colquitt, LePine, & Wesson, 2017).

At times, users may choose a medium that is too "lean," meaning inappropriate or insufficient for the purpose or situation; this can lead to information equivocality. Also, as seen in today's public discourse, sound bites can be seen as "drive-by" modes of communication, where nuance and reciprocation, if present at all, are undermined. This phenomenon is a characteristic of texting and tweeting and is a reminder that efficiency (speed and brevity) in communication does not necessarily equate to effectiveness.

Overreliance on ICT Leading to Deteriorating Social Skills

Organizational users may also exacerbate disassociation and information inaccuracy and equivocality by becoming overreliant—or overdependent—on ICT, intentionally forgoing appropriately "richer" media, such as face-to-face or phone, in favor of leaner forms that enable us to avoid others. Social avoidance might be purposeful to assuage any social anxiety or rationalized for the sake of efficiency or to assuage any social anxiety. An example is "hiding behind email" rather than getting up and walking down the hall (if the option is available), which reduces face-to-face communication intentionally to avoid human interaction.

"[O]ne of the most frequently expressed concerns about virtual spaces is that traditional social mechanics that facilitate communication are lost" (Akkirman & Harris, as cited in Bennet, Owers, Pitt, & Tucker, 2009, p. 139), despite attempts at increasing engagement via ICT. Jason Perlow (2017), senior technology editor for ZDNet, argues that technological tools "are not particularly helpful in developing our interpersonal relationships and how we interact with people in the real world" (para. 3). Perlow warns, "The more disconnected from face-to-face relationships we become, the more our soft skills atrophy" (para. 4). An argument can also be made that overreliance is a byproduct of an individual's intent to be more efficient and timely.

Purpose and Contribution: Looking for a Human-Oriented Solution

Society, and organizations therein, is arguably past the point of ditching devices, "things," and the technologies behind them. So what can be done to address the problems of organizational user disassociation, information inaccuracy and equivocality, and deteriorating social skills? The prescription here calls for a turning (or reversion) of our attention from devices (the IoT) to the human users (the IoP): "We need to stop obsessing over 'smart' objects, and start thinking smart about people" (Judge & Powles, 2015, para. 8). The rationale for moving from an IoT to an IoP is that reverting the focus to people alleviates organizational users' isolation and, in turn, increases their empowerment through increased citizenship and belonging. The IoS, then, further empowers users by providing the means for users to engage and to conduct transactions directly and without third-party interference

One suggestion for enacting the move from the IoT toward an IoP is to incorporate characteristics of "humanness" in technology and devices by making smartphones more user oriented, adding human context that allows for sociability, personalization, proactivity, and predictability (Miranda et al., 2015). A second suggestion is to make devices more intuitive in functionality; "what if these objects showed us—actually showed us, through their design features, their data flows and their legally-binding background conditions—how our information is being used, who can access it, where it is going, and why?" (Judge & Powles, 2015, para.18). Notice that these two suggestions actually are technology oriented in design, development, and implementation, with the hope of ultimately increasing features and benefits to humans via programmed human-like characteristics.

A third suggestion emphasizes the role and responsibility of the human using the technology. Innovations in technology should not mean that the role of the human user is increasingly minimized, especially in a knowledge economy. ABB Group (NASDAQ Stockholm and NYSE: ABB), a Swiss-based robotics multinational, has become a leader in advancing the IoPTS by "put[ting] humans in charge," because humans are still needed "to control, monitor, and make decisions" (ABB Group, 2016, p. 7). Despite automation and artificial intelligence, humans are still needed to intuit, to perceive and appropriately adjust to nuance, and to inject morality (Tufekci, 2016). Advancing the IoPTS should be fueled by an approach to creating technological devices and products that human users, inside and outside organizations, can control through their distinctly human responses and methods—and not the converse.

Encouraging User Responsibility in the IoPTS Through the Work of Mary Parker Follett

The overarching question pursued by this chapter is as follows: *How might the reorientation of technology to a more human focus be accomplished in order to aid employee users in maximizing their use and outcomes of their interactions and transactions in the IoPTS?*

A human-oriented prescription may be found in the work of management theorist and political scientist Mary Parker Follett (1868–1933). First presented nine decades ago, Mary Parker Follett's work remains fresh and relevant. Leadership scholar Warren Bennis (1995) remarks, "Just about everything written today about leadership and organisations comes from Mary Parker Follett's writings and lectures" (p. 144).

Three of Follett's most salient contributions to today's organizations—*circular response*, *integration*, and the *law of the situation*—offer the means for users to revert the focus of technology to the human parties and to cultivate a democratic space in which they may interact and transact. Circular response and integration are "Follett's process-oriented and humanistic methods of going beyond understanding to seek common interests, actively promote cooperation and emphasize relationships in conflict resolution" (Héon, Damart, & Nelson, 2017, p. 482). A circular response toward integration should respect the totality of the situation occurring between and surrounding engaged parties; the law of the situation, therefore, is concerned with making intentional choices appropriate for the context and for desired outcomes.

Although devices and networks may be seen as "nonhuman," technological environments, such as the IoPTS, should not be viewed in the same manner. Technological environments are conducive to Follett's humanistic approach, because they are environments for human activity. According to Zeynep Tufekci (2014), humanness has not been entirely obscured by technology: "[W]hat's leading to dramatic [societal] consequences is not that people or human nature has radically changed because of technology; rather, it's that the environment in which these mundane acts are taking place has been radically altered by technology" (p. 16).

Newman and Guy (1998) coined the term "Follett's web" to describe "the premise of the theoretical approach which centers on the web of human relationships through which individuals find meaning and identity" (p. 287). This web metaphor applies to today's Web 2.0, which comprises three technological spaces relevant to the IoPTS: (1) web-based applications (O'Reilly, as cited in Schroth & Janner, 2007), (2) the "diverse media and devices for the consumption of Internet based applications" (Schroth & Janner, 2007, p. 36), and (3) "the realization of rich user experiences" (p. 36). "Follett's web" entails humans exchanging information with each other (the IoP), via devices that are interconnected to and over the Internet (the IoT), in the course of conducting transactions (the IoS). "Follett's web" may also resemble a participatory environment that may assume and cultivate dynamic cultures of its own; social media is one example (Hand & Ching, 2011). Mobile social networks (MSNs) and online social networks (OSNs) rely on collaboration, interaction, and feedback (Zhang et al., 2013)—all activities that Follett would recognize as human activities.

Follett's Circular Response, Integration, and the Law of the Situation

Two of Follett's most important works, *The New State: Group Organization, the Solution of Popular Government* (1918) and *Creative Experience* (1924), serve as requisite reading for those desiring to learn about her humanistic, process-oriented, integrative philosophy. *The New State* lends insight into Follett's ideas on democracy and democratic spaces; Follett views workplaces as democratic spaces. *Creative Experience* defines and expands on her conception and application of circular response and integration. The law of the situation is featured in Follett's conference papers, which are compiled in Henry Metcalf and Lyndall Urwick's (1941) *Dynamic Administration: The Collected Papers of Mary Parker Follett.*

Circular Response

Follett devised the concept of *circular response* as a psychological phenomenon to assist us in studying social situations, which include workplace decision making, problem solving, conflict resolution, leadership, and team building. Circular response serves as the foundation for the integrative process, providing the process with its mechanics. Circular response is a coactive, reciprocal process of creating and re-creating our environment through our interactions with each other, as well our responses to each other and to our environment.

> Response is not merely the activity resulting from a certain stimulus and that response in turn influencing the activity; it is because it is response that it influences that activity, that is part of what response means. Cause and effect, subject and object, stimulus and response: these are now given new meanings.
>
> (Follett, 1924/2013, p. 60)

Follett analogizes circular response to a tennis match with two tennis players (Melé & Rosanas, 2003): Player A serves the ball. Player B returns the serve; the way she does so depends on how Player A served the ball. Now, Player A returns; the way she does so takes into consideration her original serve *and* the way Player B returned it. Follett (1924/2013) describes this interinfluencing behavior thusly:

> In human relations, as I have said, this is obvious: I never react to you but to you-plus-me; or to be more accurate, it is I-plus-you reacting to you-plus-me. 'I' can never influence 'you' because you have already influenced me; that is, in the very process of meeting, by the very process of meeting, we both become something different. It begins even before we meet, in the anticipation of meeting.
>
> (pp. 62–63)

The conscious individual is the life source of circular response, and individuals, together, interact with and interinfluence each other dynamically. Individuals need to commit to circular response, but they are not subjugated to it. An individual's development is critical to the process, and individual interests are considered as the collective evolves and works toward common goals and a common will.

> Under the right conditions, a sustained circular response via dialogue in the pursuit of common goals—which themselves may evolve as the process continues—will tend to produce unforeseen solutions that fulfill and/or transcend the initial goals of the participants.
>
> (Shapiro, 2003, p. 589)

Integration

A dynamic, ongoing, unifying process, *integration* proceeds from circular response; the two concepts may be phrased as "circular response toward integration." Integration is key to people understanding one another, leading with and not over others, resolving conflict (Armstrong, 2002), and co-creating an environment by coordinating to fulfill interests.

> The most familiar example of integrating as the social process is when two or three people meet to decide on some course of action and separate with a purpose, a will, which was not possessed by anyone when he came to the meeting but is the result of the interweaving of all. In this true social process there takes place neither absorption nor compromise.
>
> (Follett, 1919, p. 576)

Integration does not subjugate the individual or the process of one's individuation relative to the collective. In fact, integration stresses an individual's responsibility and role.

Integration occurs via experimentation, using the frictions of conflicts and differing interests to achieve a common will by creating something new through "unifying" (Urwick, 1935, p. 166). The process is dynamic, because conflict, unity, and change are never static. More importantly, integration is evolutionary in how it can put conflict, which is unavoidable, to good use in achieving unity and higher states of integration (Metcalf & Urwick, 1941).

Follett views "community as the process of unifying our differences" (Feldheim, 2004, p. 346), "be[ing] responsible for a functional whole" (Metcalf & Urwick, 1941, p. 80), and creating "a collective responsibility" (p. 81). She emphasizes that individual interests coordinate in an integrative unity to become shared interests:

> When you have made your employees feel that they are in some sense partners in the business, they do not improve the quality of their work,

> save waste and time and material, because of the Golden Rule, but because their interests are the same as yours.
>
> (p. 82)

The Law of the Situation

Follett's *law of the situation* states that individuals should adhere and respond to the facts and aspects of a situation in which they find themselves. The law "is based on the complex, reciprocally related interactions that are constantly changing and evolving, providing repeated opportunities to achieve a healthy process or new synthesis, which is integration" (Feldheim, 2004, pp. 344–345). A leader adhering to the law of the situation does not demand obedience but rather cooperation; "one person does not simply give orders to another person, but both should agree to take orders from the situation" (Phelps, Parayitam, & Olson, 2007, p. 7). Facts and data prevail, and "[t]he necessities of the situation govern" (Héon et al., 2017, p. 480). The law of the situation is remarkable not just in its respect for science but also in its focus on the people involved in the situation.

Follett (as cited in Metcalf & Urwick, 1941) argues that "every social process has three aspects: the interacting, the unifying, and the emerging" (p. 198). The unifying, or one's joint understanding with another of the total situation, is a product of the continual interaction; the emerging represents an evolving situation and new understanding thereof, arrived at through "reciprocal adjustment" (p. 200). "The reciprocal influence, the interactive behavior, which involves a developing situation," Follett asserts, "is fundamental for business administration as it is for politics, economics, jurisprudence, and ethics" (p. 201).

How Follett's Concepts Serve Users

A deeper look at how Follett's concepts can assist ICT users in the IoPTS in assuming the responsibility of alleviating user isolation, improving information quality, and avoiding the deterioration of users' communication skills is presented here. Theoretical understanding of where Follett's concepts serve users the most is assisted by explications of *media richness theory*, *social presence*, and *psychological hermeneutics*.

Enriching Lean Media

Media richness theory argues that richness and leanness are fixed, with face-to-face being the richest medium (Daft & Lengel, as cited in Lee, 1994; Huang, Watson, & Wei, 1998). Media richness is important to address with regard to communication quality for three reasons. First, richness of communications media is related to team cohesiveness and agreeability, which in turn affect performance. Research exists to explain reasons for medium choice in team processes (Daft & Lengel, 1984; Snyder & Lee-Partridge, 2013) and the impact of those choices on both on-site and dispersed teams (see Andres, 2006). Task and job complexity, team interdependence, and job pressures, as examples, all influence choices individuals and teams make regarding communication (Fulk, 1993). Additionally, communication via ICT is leaner than that of face-to-face (Knight et al., 2008), and the lack of richness can increase equivocality and negatively affect learning and usability. Finally, evidence suggests that a relatively lean medium of communication, namely email, *can* be used to convey rich information (Huang et al., 1998; Lee, 1994), implying that humans, when relegated to using relatively lean media, can consciously and intentionally add or maximize richness.

Ideally, individuals should use devices and modes of communication with the intent to control the content; in this manner, the human should focus on the message more than the medium (see McLuhan, 1964), despite any limitations the medium imposes. Users should become familiar with any and all means the device affords to enrich media by refining content.

Social Presence

A concept "rooted" in media richness theory (Shen, 2012, p. 201), *social presence* "is defined as the extent to which a medium allows a user to experience others as being psychologically present" (Fulk, Steinfield, Schmitz, & Power, as cited in Shen, 2012, p. 201).

Increasing social presence can be done by "stimulating the imagination of interaction with other humans (e.g., through socially rich text, and picture content, personalized greetings, human audio and video, intelligent agents) or by providing means for actual interaction with other humans" (Hassanein & Head, as cited in Shen, 2012, p. 201). Social presence is shown to be correlated with trustworthiness of information on web sites (Hess, Fuller, & Campbell, 2009) and has become increasingly important in e-commerce transactions (Shen, 2012) and in education (Lau, 2012).

Perlow (2017), in pointing out that technological tools can cause the deterioration of social skills, adds that these tools "also reinforce bad habits and amplify our negative personality traits" (para. 4). ICT users with deteriorating social skills may also exacerbate poor quality of communication and further weaken inherent relationships already existing because of inappropriate mode choice. Dana Carney (2012), in an article in *Forbes*, observes,

> As revolutionizing as technology has been, it's also become an all too convenient way to avoid the real work of meaningful communication when it matters most. What we often don't appreciate as we choose the easy option over the right one, is just how profoundly it can undermine our success . . . in work, love and life.
>
> (para. 3)

Regarding adding socially rich text to a web site, for example, Follett (as cited in Metcalf & Urwick, 1941) likely would advise taking care to use appropriate language (or modes that enable appropriate language). Her concern with language is evident in her discussions about resolving conflict:

> I don't quite see why we are not more careful about our language in business, for in most delicate situations we quite consciously choose that which will not arouse antagonism. You say to your wife at breakfast, 'Let's reconsider that decision we came to last night.' You do not say, 'I wish to give you my criticism of the decision you made last night.'
>
> (p. 47)

As Follett was a pragmatist and astute observer of human nature, she likely would concede that careful language choice is a skill that, although aspirational, is not a prevalent social skill, even though it can be learned. Absent language precision, "likes," emoticons, emojis, symbols, .gifs, and retweets, as relatively lean examples, aim to establish some social presence and personality of the user, convey positive or negative response, and influence others.

Commencing Follett's circular response is a way to attempt to enrichen media. Integration, then, may be viewed here as the accomplishment of media enrichment. Richer media, then, increases social presence, reduces information inaccuracy and equivocality, and requires the flexing of interpersonal social skills. Follett (1924/2013) posits that the point of reducing information inaccuracy and equivocality is not to get parties to agree or to "do away with difference but to do away with the muddle" and create the potential for agreement:

> If I think that I am looking at a black snake and you think it is a fallen branch, our talk will merely be chaotic. But after we have decided it is a snake, we do not then automatically agree what to do with it. You and I may respond differently to 'black snake': shall we run away, or kill it, or take it home and make a pet of it to kill the mice? . . . We have not done away with difference, but we have provided the possibility for fruitful difference.
>
> (p. 6)

How might circular response toward integration and adhering to the law of the situation play out in the IoPTS? Simple, familiar examples are easily found on sites such as eBay.com and other online auction sites and other neighborhood social media sites such as Nextdoor.com, "the private social network for your neighborhood" (Nextdoor.com, 2017). No human third party is present; buyers and sellers conduct transactions themselves, as is characteristic of transactions in the IoS. Even ostensibly simple transactions have the potential to expand and protract into—and, appropriately, be treated as—interest-based, integrative processes via the overall IoPTS.

Psychological Hermeneutics in Receiving and Interpreting Information

ICT users, as message receivers, may enact conscious and intentional human influence on their communication methods and processes through the use of psychological hermeneutics (Lee, 1994). Information systems scholar Allen S. Lee (1994) argues that email, for example, a relatively lean communication medium, can be enrichened by receivers as well as senders. He clarifies, "[R]ichness is not an invariant property of a communications medium, but an emergent property of the interaction between the communications medium and its organizational context" (p. 144).

Psychological hermeneutics illustrate human cognitive involvement from conception and sending to receipt and interpretation of an email message. Examining the role and responsibility of the receiving user is germane to applications of Follett's circular response, integration, and law of the situation, because circular response toward integration does not have to begin with the initiator of the interaction. A receiving user may contribute to enriching the communication via active listening and seeking clarification. A receiver, as a full participant in the integrative process, is as duty bound as anyone else in working to discover and then obeying the law of the situation. Follett, however, likely would eschew the labels of *sender/initiator* and *receiver/respondent* in favor of *coinfluencers*, who co-create a common understanding of meaning in the social construction.

Implications for Users in the IoPTS

The relevance of Follett's work to the IoPTS hinges on Follett's belief in which she "cannot emphasize too strongly (sic) the significance of finding the same underlying principles in every field of human activity" (as cited in Metcalf & Urwick, 1941, p. 201). According to Byrne and LeMay (2006), "[a] correlation exists between communication satisfaction and important organizational outcomes" (p. 152). Intense, creative, process-oriented collaboration poses five main implications for users in organizations and in the IoPTS. The implications presented here relate to trust, feedback processing, employee satisfaction and well-being, organizational attitudes toward time, and online communities of practice.

Trust

"Trust is increasingly playing an important role in modern ICT infrastructures and will more so be the case in IoPTS. Trust is in principle a human action" (Eloff et al., 2009, p. 4) that can be viewed in two ways—first, as the trust users have in devices and networks (see Jadhav, 2014) and, second, as the trust between users interacting via devices and networks. Trustworthiness, and, for that matter, reputation of a user, is particularly critical, because it helps other users to determine with whom they should interact or conduct transactions (Zhang et al., 2013).

Cultivating human skill in communicating is key to enhancing trust both within an organization and between organizations and external stakeholders. Facilitating social interaction within the IoPTS removes an obstacle to rich communication between individuals and groups, "so that interactions are perceived as taking place between people and not things, connected to the Internet" (Miranda et al., 2015, p. 4). The general idea here is to "reduce uncertainty and equivocality of [the] environment" (Allen & Griffeth, 1997, p. 1240) for users by creating trustworthy online environments more conducive to rich interactions and positive transactions.

Follett's circular response and integrative process assists in the development of trust between users by enabling participants to actively mitigate equivocality of the information, which, in turn, promotes informational justice in organizations and between users. Follett addresses trust in the contexts of loyalty to and fellowship within a group—or rather "the consciousness of belonging to a group" (Rosanas & Velilla, 2003, p. 51) and "loyalty to a collective will" (Follett, as cited in Rosanas & Velilla, 2003, p. 51), where an individual's success is related to the success of the group. Steve Denning (2015), in the *Harvard Business Review*, invokes Follett's philosophy when he stresses trust in managing a customer service culture:

> When the goal is the inherently inspiring goal of delighting customers, managers don't need to make employees do their job. With managers and workers sharing the same goal—delighting customers—the humanistic management practices of trust and collaboration become not only possible but necessary.
>
> (p. 4)

Organizations should invest in resources, including time, to maximize richness, to maintain a human presence, and to build interlocking networks in both active and passive communication. One way to do this is by taking greater care in crafting content on web sites and by diversifying media (e.g., corporate intranet, corporate web site, Twitter feed, Facebook page). Organizations and individual users can also capitalize on the flexibility, increasing ease of use, and affordability of smart devices with Internet capability and location technology; these devices prime virtual communities for reconnection "with physical space, and bind[ing] the rich social context tightly with the local environmental context of interacting people to provide personalized services" (Zhang et al., 2013, p. 92). Multimedia (e.g., videos, chat) can enliven web sites to make them more active. Finally, organizations should build trust with stakeholders via loyalty to standards of ethics and professionalism in their communication.

Active Listening

A "rarity in organizations," active listening on the part of receivers has "been replaced with a functionalist, instrumental type of listening that is more connected with coercion and manipulation than with meaning-making and understanding" (Tyler, 2011, p. 144). Accuracy is linked with active listening in the sense that "very rarely do we permit ourselves to understand precisely what the meaning of [the speaker's] statement is" (Rogers, as cited in Tyler, 2011, p. 146).

Active listening is helpful in building trust via leaner forms of communication, such as phone or voice over Internet (de Ruyters & Wetzels, as cited in Park, Chung, Gunn, & Rutherford, 2015). Regarding the IoPTS, a concern regarding rapport might be whether or how "participants learn a range of textual strategies for initiating, fixing, and reorienting (probing, repairing, and realigning) the other participant in a service encounter" (Clarke & Nilsson, 2008, p. 138). If so, then Follett's integration and circular response can influence outcomes of interactions and transactions in the IoPTS; fulfilling the service transaction would entail a progression toward aligning participant interests through integration in order to "achieve the joint construction" (p. 138).

Information Credibility

Follett (1924/2013) recognizes the importance of credible scientific data for analysis and experimentation, as well as the difficulty in gathering accurate information. The difficulty in acquiring the most accurate information is "very great as evidenced by the frequency with which experts disagree. Two experts talking together do not always impress us with their unanimity" (p. 7). Additionally, "facts do not remain stationary" (p. 9) and may "change value over time" (Follett, as cited in Boje & Rosile, 2001, p. 102)—implying that situations may demand adjustments in the integrative process in order to avoid information inaccuracy and equivocality.

Follett likely would remind managers that a major credibility issue in the IoPTS involves establishing professional standards (see Rosanas & Velilla, 2003) and metrics.

> The assessment of trust and reputation within IoPTS contexts and the proliferation of trustworthy services for end users require the definition of common metrics. Metrics are fundamental for defining a uniform and coherent set of service-level agreements (SLAs), that allow a fair competition between services providers, thus fostering innovation and the introduction of new services. Furthermore, common metrics also allow the interoperability between services and communication platforms, which are key aspects in the IoPTS.
>
> (Weber et al., 2010, n.p.)

Feedback Processing

Authentic human interactions and transactions, Follett argues, are nonlinear relationships, because "organizations, and life and behavior within them, are not comprised of linear relationships between variables (e.g., people, actions, concepts, etc.)" (Héon et al., 2017, p. 486). Furthermore, human interactions and transactions, as nonlinear relationships, are dynamic in that they are subject to contingencies. According to Mendenhall, Macomber, and Cutright (2000), Follett's integrative circular response foreshadowed modern nonlinear dynamics with regard to interdependence of variables, reciprocity, and feedback.

When applied to the IoPTS, however, the injection of humanness through the integrative process has its limitations with regard to feedback.

> [W]hile an individual will only, in the best case scenario, input to the system a single evaluation of any given product, a smart object would be able to transmit a constant flow of information, producing a continuously updated set of data.
>
> (Solima, Della Peruta, & Del Giudice, 2016, p. 748)

Email is a prime example of this deficiency; "it lacks the capability for immediate feedback, uses only a single channel, filters out significant cues, tends to be impersonal, and incurs a reduction in language variety" (Lee, 1994, p. 145).

Increasing Employee Satisfaction and Well-Being

Workplaces, as complex social environments, comprise a "primary arena for the development of close personal relationships" (Sloan, Newhouse, & Thompson, 2013, p. 343). Increasing diversity in workplaces may affect the development of social ties at work. Evidence suggests connections between social ties and gender and social ties and race, with men, in general, and African Americans reporting fewer social ties at work (Sloan et al., 2013).

Improving social interactions can help reduce an employee's psychological and physiological stress. "People's subjective experience of their connections with others has immediate, enduring, and consequential effects on their bodies" (Heaphy & Dutton, 2008, p. 138). Increasing media richness can positively affect employee satisfaction levels, especially when critical news is disseminated (Byrne & LeMay, 2006). Also, direct social interaction, and workspaces that support it, play a critical role in encouraging ideas and innovation; the late Steve Jobs, for instance, "encouraged staff to get out of their offices and mingle, particularly with those whom they wouldn't ordinarily interact" (Parise, Whelan, & Todd, 2015, p. 21).

Service work, in particular, is often emotionally laborious (Grandey, 2000) and demands emotional intelligence, fact finding, clarifying and filling holes in information, drawing on expertise, and creativity in problem solving. Virtual teams in organizations and, conceivably, individual users in a global IoPTS may need to overcome negative effects of psychic distance, an individual's perception of differences between their culture and another culture (Magnusson, Schuster, & Taras, 2014). Culturally and emotionally intelligent interactions among users may allow collaborations among users that maximize the potential of the IoPTS.

Adjusting Organizational Attitudes Toward Time

Ideally, when seeking to increase team cohesiveness, organizations should provide and encourage the use of richer forms of communication and, more importantly, the time to use them (Knight et al., 2008). Absent an option for a richer form of communication, but with enough time, parties can opt for a leaner mode and intentionally enrichen it via integration and circular response in order to appropriately respond to the situation. A "need-it-done-yesterday" philosophy poses a challenge, as do users' increasingly truncated attention spans.

Integration is not simply achieved; it is an ongoing process that requires commitment and time: "The most important thing to remember about unity is—that there is no such thing. There is only unifying. You cannot get unity and expect it to last a day—or even five minutes" (Follett, as cited in Love, 2013, p. 586). Taking the time to "get things right" may be worth it in preventing rework and wasted resources and building more cohesive, high-functioning on-site and virtual work teams. Follett (as cited in Metcalf & Urwick, 1941) illustrates this point in an anecdote about an "arbitrary foreman," who neglects to take the time to "see that instructions are understood" (p. 274):

> I knew a case where a workman, reacting against such a foreman, deliberately carried out a wrong order instead of taking it back to the foreman and asking about it, and wasted a large amount of material in order that his foreman should be blamed for this waste. Thus the man who demands a blind obedience may have it react on himself.
>
> (p. 274)

A supervisor or a leader should not merely give orders but serve his or her team, Follett recommends. Taking time to integrate involves being open to questioning by employees, responding to them, and clarifying instructions and plans, to ensure not only quality of communication and learning but also the work product.

Communities of Practice and Innovation

Follett's integration requires the competition of ideas and interests among individuals to create high-functioning, innovative, creative communities of practice (Novicevic, Harvey, Buckley, Wren, & Perna, 2007) and innovation. Promoting innovative communities of practice takes the suggestion of making ICT more user oriented by incorporating "humanness" and human-like functionality and combines it with a user's active, purposeful, engaged role.

The promotion of communities of practice and innovation, as a positive byproduct of employing Follett's work in managing in organizations, does not occur without challenges. A potential obstacle is whether or not organizations are up to the challenge to learn about circular response and integration; to promote it as a strategy; and to commit to practice, especially over ICT, until enculturation.

Continual engagement is the life source of innovative communities whether the communities consist of organizations, individuals, or a combination of providers and users. A trend in innovative communities is to "freely reveal" (von Hippel, 2005, p. 11) or share innovations through open-source, Internet-based software projects and physical devices. These projects reflect a "collective or community effort to provide a public good" (p. 11). Specifically regarding IoT, new global platforms are emerging for entrepreneurs to fund, research, create, share, and market product and service solutions (IEEE Spectrum, 2017). If one accepts that collective efforts in technology optimize the cumulative capabilities of individuals, groups, and organizations, then, indeed, a foundation is laid for the success of Follett's integration. Follett's integration can enable entrepreneurs, for instance, to work out issues in developing and marketing IoT solutions. As a result, the idea of democratization of innovation is now a feature of a technology business model for the present and the future.

Conclusion: A More "Human-Like" ICT?

This chapter focused on responding to the problems of employee user disassociation, a lack of information quality due to inaccuracy and equivocality, and deteriorating social skills experienced by users in organizations and in the IoPTS. Mary Parker Follett's concepts of circular response, integration, and the law of the situation were proposed as an intentional, human-oriented response to mitigate these problems by improving human interactions and transactions in the IoPTS. Follett's concepts help us to reorient ICT use away from devices, networks, and systems toward humans by emphasizing the user's responsibility in participating in the IoPTS. Users acquire the social tools to improve their relationships and interactions with others by getting back to the essence of productive and collaborative interpersonal communication.

As the IoPTS evolves, questions emerge. Notably, could ICT, itself, *enact* integration and circular response? What if humans cannot overcome human-oriented issues in communication?

One answer may exist in emerging case studies on *persuasive technologies*, which "are information technologies that change human attitude and behavior" (Sakamoto, Nakajima, & Alexandrova, 2015, p. 11541). Human attitude and behavior are influenced by "[a]ppropriate feedback . . . chosen according to a user's current situation, which is acquired by sensors attached to physical artifacts" (Nakajima & Lehdonvirta, as cited in Sakamoto et al., 2015, p. 11541). Perhaps these technologies could be called, in the Follettian spirit, coinfluencing technologies, where the law of the situation is obeyed by both users and the technology to enliven the full meaning of a topic, problem, issue, situation, etc. Other technological innovations include interfaces that "employ a variety of media-rich, social, and advanced decision-making components, including recommendation agents (RA) designed to help users with their tasks" (Hess et al., 2009, p. 889). Recommendations generated by the technology are dictated by the situation as much as by the user.

Organizations and technological environments such as the IoPTS are democratic spaces that innovate and thrive on participative problem solving; creative, interest-based conflict resolution; and a culture that is strong but still encourages individual difference. Follett would caution, however, that rapid evolution and innovation must be monitored. Her views on evolutionary democracy as applied to ICT, the technological environments in which it is used, and innovations instruct humans to maintain governance over the evolution. Follett's directive responds to the "phenomenal increase in the level of complexity from a governance point of view," a characteristic of the IoPTS (Eloff et al., 2009, p. 1). Here, also, is a reminder about the necessity of humans in intuiting, making complex decisions, and injecting morality—*dynamically integrating*—in a rapidly changing technological environment.

References

ABB Group. (2016). *A new age of industrial production: The Internet of Things, services, and people*. Retrieved from http://new.abb.com/docs/default-source/technology/a-new-age-of-industrial-production—iotsp.pdf

Allen, D. G., & Griffeth, R. W. (1997). Vertical and lateral information processing: The effect of gender, employee classification, and media richness on communication and work outcomes. *Human Relations*, *50*(10), 1239–1260.

Andres, H. P. (2006). The impact of communication medium on virtual team group processes. *Information Resources Management*, *19*(2), 1–17.

Armstrong, H. (2002). Conflict resolution through integration. *Peace Research*, *34*(2), 101–116.

Bennet, J., Owers, M., Pitt, M., & Tucker, M. (2009). Workplace impact of social networking. *Property Management*, *28*(3), 138–148.

Bennis, W. (1995). Commentary: Thoughts on 'the essentials of leadership'. In P. Graham (Ed.), *Mary Parker Follett, prophet of management* (pp. 142–148). Washington, DC: Beard Books.

Boje, D. M., & Rosile, G. A. (2001). Where's the power in empowerment? Answers from Follett and Clegg. *Journal of Applied Behavioral Science*, *37*(1), 90–117.

Byrne, Z. S., & LeMay, E. (2006). Different media for organizational communication: Perceptions of quality and satisfaction. *Journal of Business and Psychology*, *21*(2), 149–173.

Carney, D. (2012). Hiding behind email? Four times you should never use email. *Forbes*. Retrieved from www.forbes.com/sites/margiewarrell/2012/08/27/do-you-hide-behind-email/#5aa429167bf0

Clarke, R. J., & Nilsson, A. G. (2008). Business services as communication patterns: A work practice approach for analyzing service encounters. *IBM Systems Journal*, *47*(1), 129–141.

Colquitt, J. A., LePine, J. A., & Wesson, M. J. (2017). *Organizational behavior: Improving performance and commitment in the workplace*. New York: McGraw-Hill/Irwin.

Cooper, C. D., & Kurland, N. B. (2002). Telecommuting, professional isolation, and employee development in public and private organizations. *Journal of Organizational Behavior, 23*, 511–532.

Daft, R. L., & Lengel, R. H. (1984). Information richness: A new approach to managerial behavior and organization design. In L. L. Cummings, & B. Staw (Eds.), *Research in organizational behavior* (Vol. 6, pp. 191–233). Greenwich, CT: JAI Press.

Denning, M. (2015). *The internet is finally forcing management to care about people*. Cambridge, MA: Harvard Business School Publishing.

Eloff, J. H. P., Eloff, M. M., Dlamini, M. T., & Zielinski, M. P. (2009, December). *Internet of people, things and services: The convergence of security, trust and privacy*. The 3rd Companion Able Workshop, IoPTS, Novotel Brussels, Brussels, Belgium, 8. Retrieved from http://hdl.handle.net/10204/4409

Feldheim, M. A. (2004). Mary Parker Follett: Lost and found: Again, and again, and again. *International Journal of Organization Theory and Behavior*, 7(3), 341–362.

Follett, M. P. (1918). *The new state: Group organisation, the solution for popular government*. New York: Longmans, Green, and Company.

Follett, M. P. (1919). Community is a process. *The Philosophical Review, 28*(6), 576–588.

Follett, M. P. (1924/2013). *The creative experience*. New York: Longmans, Green, and Company.

Fulk, J. (1993). Social construction of communication technology. *Academy of Management Journal, 36*(5), 921–950.

Grandey, A. A. (2000). Emotional regulation in the workplace: A new way to conceptualize emotional labor. *Journal of Occupational Health Psychology, 5*(1), 95–110.

Hancock, B., & Hancock, L. N. (2016). Somebody's watching: The ever-growing Internet of Things. *Phi Kappa Phi Forum, 96*(3), 12–15.

Hand, L. C., & Ching, B. D. (2011). 'You have one friend request': An exploration of power and citizen engagement in local governments' use of social media. *Administrative Theory & Praxis, 33*(3), 362–382.

Heaphy, E. D., & Dutton, J. E. (2008). Positive social interactions and the human body at work: Linking organizations and physiology. *Academy of Management Review, 33*(1), 137–162.

Héon, F., Damart, S., & Nelson, L. A. T. (2017). Mary Parker Follett: Change in the paradigm of integration. In D. Szabla, W. Pasmore, M. Barnes, & A. Gipson (Eds.), *The Palgrave handbook of organizational change thinkers* (pp. 471–492). New York: Springer International.

Hess, T., Fuller, M., & Campbell, D. (2009). Designing interfaces with social presence: Using vividness and extraversion to create social recommendation agents. *Journal of the Association for Information Systems, 10*(12), 889–919.

Huang, W., Watson, R. T., & Wei, K. K. (1998). Can a lean e-mail medium be used for rich communication? A psychological perspective. *European Journal of Information Systems*, 7(4), 269–274.

IEEE Spectrum. (2017). *The democratization of innovation for the Internet of Things*. Retrieved from http://spectrum.ieee.org/computing/networks/the-democratization-of-innovation-for-the-internet-of-things

Jadhav, N. (2014). Internet of Things: The next frontier of a networked community. *Telecom Business Review: SITM Journal*, *7*(1), 33–38.

Judge, J., & Powles, J. (2015, May 25). Forget the Internet of things: We need an Internet of people. *The Guardian*. Retrieved from www.theguardian.com/technology/2015/may/25/forget-internet-of-things-people

Knight, M. B., Pearson, J. B., & Hunsinger, D. S. (2008). The role of media richness in information technology-supported communication in group cohesion, agreeability, and performance. *Journal of Organizational and End User Computing*, *20*(4), 23–44.

Lau, R. Y. K. (2012). An empirical study of online social networking for enhancing university students' learning. *International Journal of e-Education, e-Business, e-Management and e-Learning*, *2*(5), 425-428.

Lee, A. S. (1994). Electronic mail as a medium for rich communication: An empirical investigation using hermeneutic interpretation. *MIS Quarterly*, *18*(2), 143–157.

Love, J. (2013). A society of control: The people and the individual. *Public Administration Quarterly*, *37*(4), 576–593.

Lyons, T. (2017, May). *The book of Fermat*. Fermat. Retrieved from http://fermat.org/downloads/book-of-fermat.pdf

Magnusson, P., Schuster, A., & Taras, V. (2014). A process-based explanation of the psychic distance paradox: Evidence from global virtual teams. *Management International Review*, *54*(3), 283–306.

McLuhan, M. (1964). *Understanding media: The extensions of man*. New York: McGraw-Hill.

Melé, D., & Rosanas, J. M. (2003). Power, freedom, and authority in management. *Philosophy of Management*, *3*(2), 35–46.

Mendenhall, M. E., Macomber, J. H., & Cutright, M. (2000). Mary Parker Follett: Prophet of chaos and complexity. *Journal of Management History*, *6*(4), 191–204.

Metcalf, H. C., & Urwick, L. (Eds.). (1941). *Dynamic administration: The collected papers of Mary Parker Follett*. New York: Harper Brothers.

Miranda, J., Mäkitalo, N., Garcia-Alonso, J., Mikkonen, T., Canal, C., & Murillo, J. M. (2015). From the Internet of Things to the internet of people. *IEEE Internet Computing*, *19*(2), 40–47.

Newman, M. A., & Guy, M. E. (1998). Taylor's triangle, Follett's web. *Administrative Theory and Praxis*, *20*(3), 287–297.

Nextdoor.com. (2017). *The private social network for your neighborhood*. Retrieved from https://nextdoor.com/

Novicevic, M. M., Harvey, M. G., Buckley, M. R., Wren, D., & Perna, L. (2007). Communities of creative practice: Follett's seminal conceptualization. *International Journal of Public Administration*, *30*(4), 367–385.

Parise, S., Whelan, E., & Todd, S. (2015). How Twitter users can generate better ideas. *MIT Sloan Management Review*, *56*(4), 20–25.

Park, J., Chung, T., Gunn, F., & Rutherford, B. (2015). The role of listening in e-contact center customer relationship management. *The Journal of Services Marketing*, *29*(1), 49–58.

Perlow, J. (2017, January 19). How social media is crippling democracy, and why we seem powerless to stop it [web log comment]. *ZDNet*. Retrieved from www.zdnet.com/article/how-weaponized-social-media-is-crippling-democracy-and-why-were-helpless-to-stop-it/

Phelps, L. D., Parayitam, S., & Olson, B. J. (2007). Edwards Deming, Mary P. Follett and Frederick W. Taylor: Reconciliation of differences in organizational and strategic leadership. *Academy of Strategic Management Journal*, *6*, 1–14.

Rosanas, J. M., & Velilla, M. (2003). Loyalty and trust as the ethical bases of organizations. *Journal of Business Ethics*, *44*(1), 49–59.
Sakamoto, M., Nakajima, T., & Alexandrova, T. (2015). Enhancing values through virtuality for intelligent artifacts that influence human attitude and behavior. *Multimedia Tools and Applications*, *74*(24), 11537–11568.
Schroth, C., & Janner, T. (2007). Web 2.0 and SOA: Converging concepts enabling the internet of services. *IT Professional Magazine*, *9*(3), 36–41.
Shapiro, M. (2003). Toward an evolutionary democracy: The philosophy of Mary Parker Follett. *World Futures*, *59*(8), 585–590.
Shen, J. (2012). Social comparison, social presence, and enjoyment in the acceptance of social shopping websites. *Journal of Electronic Commerce Research*, *13*(3), 198–212.
Sloan, M. M., Newhouse, R. J. E., & Thompson, A. B. (2013). Counting on coworkers: Race, social support, and emotional experiences on the job. *Social Psychology Quarterly*, *76*(4), 343–372.
Snyder, J., & Lee-Partridge, J. E. (2013). Understanding communication channel choices in team knowledge sharing. *Corporate Communications: An International Journal*, *18*(4), 417–431.
Solima, L., Della Peruta, M. R., & Del Giudice, M. (2016). Object-generated content and knowledge sharing: The forthcoming impact of the Internet of Things. *Journal of the Knowledge Economy*, *7*(3), 738–752.
Tufekci, Z. (2014). The social internet: Frustrating, enriching, but not lonely. *Public Culture*, *26*(172), 13–23.
Tufekci, Z. (2016, June). *Machine intelligence makes morals more important* [Video file]. Retrieved from www.ted.com/talks/zeynep_tufekci_machine_intelligence_makes_human_morals_more_important
Tyler, J. A. (2011). Reclaiming rare listening as a means of organizational re-enchantment. *Journal of Organizational Change Management*, *24*(1), 143–157.
Urwick, L. (1935). The problem of organization: A study of the work of Mary Parker Follett. *Bulletin of the Taylor Society and of the Society of Industrial Engineers as Members of Federated Management Societies*, *1*(5), 163–169.
von Hippel, E. (2005). *Democratizing innovation*. Cambridge, MA: MIT Press.
Weber, S. G., Martucci, L. A., Ries, S., & Mühlhäuser, M. (2010). Towards trustworthy identity and access management for the future internet. *Proc. 4th International Workshop on Trustworthy Internet of People, Things & Services (IoPTS)*, *29*.
Zhang, B., Wang, Y., Vasilakos, A. V., & Ma, J. (2013). Mobile social networking: Reconnect virtual community with physical space. *Telecommunication Systems*, *54*(1), 91–110.

3 The Internet of Things and Cognitive Analytics

Constant D. Beugré

Introduction

Today, we live in a world where technological devices (from smart phones to assisting-living devices and smart watches) are ubiquitous and where almost everything can become a computer and be linked to the Internet, leading to the concept of the Internet of Things (IoT). This interconnectivity allows the Internet of Things to collect all kinds of data about human social life (Ma, 2011; Ning & Wang, 2011; Atzori, Iera, & Morabita, 2014; Borgia, 2014; Yang, Zhang, & Vasilakos, 2014). As a result, "data are more deeply woven into the fabric of our lives than ever before" (Bi & Cochran, 2014, p. 250). However, the mere availability of data is not sufficient to improve decision making for individuals as well as organizations. What is important is how decision makers integrate data and knowledge to address particular issues. Indeed, "the value of any analytics effort lies largely in whether it can help decision making" (Kiron, Prentice, & Ferguson, 2014, p. 32).

The goal of the chapter is to call attention to the role of cognitions, interpretation and sense making in using big data analytics. The Internet of Things provides the opportunity to collect vast amounts of data and analytics and improves the ability to analyze the data collected. However, to make sense of the data available, one needs knowledge and expertise. In addition, experience and intuition still remain 'relevant' when individuals make decisions. Improving data-driven decisions requires that decision makers possess knowledge in the domains in which the data are collected and analyzed. Thus, the present chapter emphasizes the role of human cognition, interpretation, understanding and sense making (Daft & Weick, 1984; Weick, 1993; Starbucks, 1996; Mezias & Starbuck, 2003) in analytics and the Internet of Things. It uses the construct of cognitive analytics (Beugré, 2015) to emphasize the importance of integrating these concepts in analytics. Doing so is particularly important because "the gap between relevant analytics and users' strategic business needs is significant" (Kohavi, Rothleder, & Simoudis, 2002, p. 45). The significance of this gap is related to a variety of factors, including cycle time, analytical time and expertise, business goals and metrics, goals for data collection and transformation, distributing analytics results and integrating data from multiple sources

(Kohavi et al., 2002). Although organizations consider analytics important, they often lack adequate strategies to leverage its advantages (Barton & Court, 2012; Davenport, 2014; McAfee, & Brynjolfsson, 2012).

A cognitive analytics perspective has implications for research and practice. From a research perspective, such an approach could lead to both inductive and deductive methodologies. For example, without formulating explicit hypotheses, scholars could analyze existing data to draw inferences and develop theories. They could also test these theories using big data analytics. A cognitive analytics approach could also add to the organizational science literature on analytics. Although the use of big data and analytics is increasing in today's corporate environments, "there is very little published management scholarship that tackles the challenges of using such tools, or better yet, that explores the promise and opportunities for new theories and practices that big data must bring about" (George, Haas, & Pentland, 2014, p. 321). The relative scarcity of organizational research on big data and analytics is astonishing because topics such as human cognition, decision making, sense making, knowledge and learning are essential in understanding and using the vast amounts of data organizations gather and analyze.

From a practical perspective, a cognitive analytics perspective could allow organizations to integrate the three concepts of the Internet of Things, big data and analytics. In fact, the Internet of Things system can be depicted as a "collection of smart devices that interact on a collaborative basis to fulfill a common goal" (Sicari, Rizzardi, Grieco, & Coen-Porisini, 2015, p. 146). As such, it allows the collection of a large amount of data through various wearable and computer devices (Gubbi, Buyya, Marusic, & Palaniswami, 2013; O'Leary, 2013a; Riggins & Wamba, 2015). Managers may focus more on the value rather than the mere collection and analysis of data to the extent that analytics is more a tool than an end in itself. As such, it is helpful when it is properly used. As Shah, Horne, and Capella (2012, p. 23) put it, "investment in analytics can be useless, even harmful, unless employees can incorporate that data into complex decision making."

The present chapter is divided into four sections. The first section describes the concept of the Internet of Things and delineates it. The second section presents a brief overview of big data analytics. The third section discusses the construct of cognitive analytics. Finally, the fourth section explores directions for future research and provides guidelines on how organizations and managers could apply the construct of cognitive analytics.

The Internet of Things

The Internet of Things refers to the integration of several wireless technologies (Eloff, Eloff, Dlamini, & Zielinski, 2009; Gubbi et al., 2013, Li, Xu, & Zhao, 2015). "The words 'Internet' and 'Things' mean an inter-connected world-wide network based on sensory, communication, networking, and information processing technologies" (Li et al., 2015, p. 244). The word 'things' refers to physical objects, such as a phone, a tablet or a watch. To be included in the Internet of Things, these objects must have functionalities to communicate with human agents or with other objects. Hence, these objects must be considered 'smart objects.' The Internet of Things is characterized by its "comprehensiveness in terms of people, services, and things that generate information populating massive databases" (Eloff et al., 2009, p. 8).

> The core concept of the IoT is that everyday objects can be equipped with identifying, sensing, networking and processing capabilities that will allow them to communicate with one another and with other devices and services over the Internet to achieve some useful objective.
> (Whitmore, Argawal, & Xu, 2015, p. 261)

The Internet of Things will continue to generate massive amounts of data that need analysis before generating value for individuals as well as organizations (O'Leary, 2013a; Riggins & Wamba, 2015).

Ashton (2009) coined the term 'Internet of Things' (IoT) to refer to such technologies that he believes have the potential to change the world. "The IoT builds on three pillars related to the ability of smart objects: (i) to be identifiable (anything identifies itself), (ii) to communicate (anything communicates), and (iii) to interact (anything interacts)—either among themselves, thus building networks of interconnected objects, or with end-users or other entities in the network" (Miorandi et al., 2012, p. 1498). The Internet of Things can provide applications in several sectors, including environmental monitoring, health care, inventory and product management, smart homes and workplaces, security and surveillance, to name but a few. It can also provide assistance to disabled people, helping them to live better and more productive lives. The Internet of Things is "going to create a world where physical objects are seamlessly integrated into information networks in order to provide advanced and intelligent services for human-beings" (Yang et al., 2014, p. 120).

According to Miorandi, Sicari, Pellegrini, and Chlamtac (2012), the term 'Internet of Things' is used as an umbrella keyword for covering various aspects related to the extension of the Internet and the Web into the physical realm by widespread deployment of spatially distributed devices with embedded identification, sensing and/or actuation capabilities. Ma (2011) contends that the Internet of Things has the following three characteristics. The first is that ordinary objects, such as cups, tables, screws, foods and automobile tires, are instrumented and can be individually addressed by embedding chips and bar codes. The second characteristic is that autonomic terminals are interconnected. This implies that the instrumented physical objects are connected as autonomic network terminals. The third is that the pervasive services are intelligent and represent an extensively interconnected network, thereby letting every object participate in the service flow to make the pervasive service intelligent. Ma (2011) also identified four layers of the Internet of Things (see Table 3.1): 1) object-sensing layer, 2) data exchange

Table 3.1 The Architecture of the Internet of Things

Layers	*Characteristics*
Object-sensing layer	Handles sensing the physical objects and obtaining data.
Data exchange layer	Handles transparent transmission of data.
Information integration layer	Handles recombination, cleaning and fusion of uncertain information acquired from the networks. Integrates the uncertain information into usable knowledge.
Application service layer	Provides content services for various users

layer, 3) information integration layer and 4) application service layer. The object-sensing layer handles sensing the physical objects and obtaining data; the data exchange layer handles transparent transmission of data; the information integration layer handles recombination, cleaning and fusion of uncertain information acquired from the networks and integrates the uncertain information into usable knowledge; the application service layer provides content services for various users.

It is worth acknowledging that the core concepts of the IoT are not new. In fact, the idea of communication between machines themselves and between machines and humans is not also new. What is new, however, is that the IoT has expanded the notion of communication between technological devices of all kinds. As Whitmore et al. (2015) note, "what the IoT represents is an evolution of the use of these existing technologies in terms of the number and kinds of devices as well as the interconnection of networks of these devices across the Internet" (2015, p. 262). In this regard, the Internet of Things is a technological revolution in computing and communications and one of the main drivers of big data analytics.

Big Data Analytics

Although the two terms big data and analytics are often used in the same phrase, they are different (McAfee & Brynjolfsson, 2012). "Big data refer to large and varied data that can be collected and managed" (George, Osinga, Lavie, & Scott, 2016, p. 1493), whereas analytics refers to "the extensive use of data, statistical and quantitative analysis, explanatory and cognitive models, and fact-based management to drive decisions and actions" (Davenport & Harris, 2007, p. 7). Big data is characterized by high volume, high velocity and high variability (Tien, 2013; Davenport, 2014). The combination of the two terms gives rise to big data analytics, which is defined as technologies and techniques that a company can employ to analyze large-scale, complex data for various applications intended to augment firm performance in various dimensions (Kwon, Lee, & Shin, 2014, p. 387).

Big Data

Although size is one of the key attributes of big data, other attributes, such as velocity, variety and value, are equally important. Volume refers to the magnitude of the data, whereas velocity indicates the speed with which data are collected, stored and analyzed. Variety indicates the multidimensional nature of data sources. For example, data are generated from several sources, including online transactions, emails, videos, images, logs, posts, search queries, health records, social networking interactions, science data, sensors, mobile phones, home appliances and any other technologies that can communicate with humans or other technologies. The Internet of Things adds a multitude of data sources throughout organizations and society (Loebbecke & Picot, 2015). Big data can also be structured, unstructured or semi-structured.

Value refers to the extent to which the data can be used to benefit decision makers. One attribute of value is the veracity of the data; because there are a variety of data sources, it is important to assess data reliability. Zakir, Seymour, and Berg (2015) note that big data analytics reflect the challenges of data that are too vast, too unstructured and too fast moving to be managed by traditional methods (p. 81). The data collected must be "aggregated, fused, processed, analyzed, and mined in order to extract useful information to enable intelligent and ubiquitous services" (Yang et al., 2014, p. 120). Relying on big data and analytics requires the organization to change its decision-making culture (Barton & Court, 2012; McAfee & Brynjolfsson, 2012).

Analytics

Analytics is defined as a group of approaches, organizational procedures and tools used in combination with one another to gain information, analyze that information and predict outcomes of solutions to business problems (Bose, 2009). It has been applied to several areas of organizations, including decision making, finance, human resources management, marketing and supply chain management (Davenport & Harris, 2007; Davenport, Harris, & Morrison, 2010). Analytics is transforming how decisions are made in organizations (Davenport, 2006, 2014; Davenport & Harris, 2007; Davenport et al., 2010; McAfee & Brynjolfsson, 2012; Barton & Court, 2012; Chen, Chiang, & Storey, 2012).

To realize the benefits of analytics, managers need to master the data and the analysis. Analytics can help an organization "better understand its business and markets" and "leverage opportunities presented by abundant data and domain-specific analytics" (Chen et al., 2012, pp. 1166–68). Indeed, insight must be translated into strategic decisions that can benefit the organization. Sharma, Mithas, and Kankanhalli (2014) propose that the first-order effects of business analytics are likely to be on decision-making processes and that improvements in organizational performance are likely to be an outcome of superior decision-making processes enabled by business analytics. "Insights do not emerge automatically out of mechanically applying analytical tools to data. Rather, insights emerge out of an active process of engagement between analysts and business managers employing the data and analytic tools to uncover new knowledge" (Sharma et al., 2014, p. 4). Lavalle, Lesser, Shockley, Hopkins, and Kruschwitz (2011) note that top-performing organizations "make decisions based on rigorous analysis at more than double the rate of lower performing organizations" and that in such organizations analytic insight is being used to "guide both future strategies and day-to-day operations" (p. 22).

Cognitive Analytics

Hogarth and Soyer (2015) note that the usefulness of an analysis depends not only on how well it is executed, but also on how well the results are understood by the intended audience. This requires that the results be communicated to decision makers in an effective manner such that "simulated experience exploits humans' natural ability to transform complicated information into actionable knowledge" (Hogarth & Soyer, 2015, p. 51). Managers increasingly express interest in the use of big data and analytics because of market complexity and the availability of better analytics tools and data (Kiron et al., 2014). Although analytics is now considered an important tool for businesses, the mere availability of data is not enough to provide a competitive advantage.

What is important is how organizations make sense of the data they collect. As a consequence, "big data's power does not erase the need for vision or human sight" (McAfee & Brynjolfsson, 2012, p. 66). In this regard, analytics is more a cognitive process than a mere computation of numbers, however accurate they may be. To improve the use of analytics, it is important to combine the use of data with a deep understanding of the domain in which the data are collected and analyzed.

To explore the challenges facing the effective use of big data analytics, I discuss the concept of cognitive analytics. As indicated earlier, this perspective draws from the concepts of interpretation and sense making (Weick, 1995; Mezias & Starbuck, 2003). "Interpretation is the process of translating these events, of developing models for understanding, of bringing out meaning, and of assembling conceptual schemes among key managers" (Daft & Weick, 1984, p. 286). Likewise, the basic idea of sense making is that reality is an ongoing accomplishment that emerges from efforts to create order and make retrospective sense of what occurs (Weick, 1993, 1995). Hence, sense making emphasizes the tendency for people to try to make things rationally accountable to themselves and others. For example, people do not discard their current beliefs and methods as long as they produce reasonable results (Kuhn, 1962). As a consequence, the use of data is not likely to reduce the reliance on personal experiences, intuition and perceptions. Hence, the literature on big data analytics and the IoT must also incorporate decision makers' cognitions. In a study on the implementation of analytics at a Fortune 500 financial services company, Barbour, Treem, and Kolar (2017) found that practitioners needed to manage existing relationships or form new relationships with experts who possessed the data they needed, who could help them make sense of them and who could, at times, collaborate with them to generate interpretations.

Figure 3.1 describes the link between the Internet of Things, big data analytics and decision making. As illustrated in the figure, data can be collected from several devices that are included in the Internet of Things. These objects can communicate with one another and/or with humans. Interactions between objects and between objects and humans generate data. As discussed earlier, the data generated are characterized by four elements: volume, velocity, variety and value. The third box in the figure relates to the analysis of the data collected. Generally, descriptive as well as predictive analytical tools could be used to analyze the data collected and display the results. However, to make sense of the analysis, it is important for decision makers to have an understanding of the domain in which data are collected and analyzed (cognitive analytics).

The construct of cognitive analytics used in this chapter includes two dimensions: human and technological. The first dimension relates to human cognition and the brain's ability to process information. In this regard, cognitive analytics is construed as a mechanism through which people make sense of the data analyzed. This sense-making process requires an understanding of the meaning of the data as well as the patterns identified. An illustrative example is one of a marketing manager. To make sense of data related to customers, not only must the marketing manager analyze the data but he or she must also have a deep understanding of the market and customers. Lack of such knowledge would render the data unnecessary or insufficient; thus, "big data, no matter how comprehensive or well analyzed, needs to be complemented by big judgment" (Shah et al., 2012, p. 25). This big judgment requires people be well informed about making effective data-driven decisions. The human aspect of cognitive analytics includes three elements: 1) ability to process information, 2) knowledge and expertise and 3) heuristics and cognitive biases.

The second dimension of cognitive analytics deals with technological tools and their capacity to reproduce functions of the human brain. Here, cognitive analytics relies on technological systems to generate hypotheses,

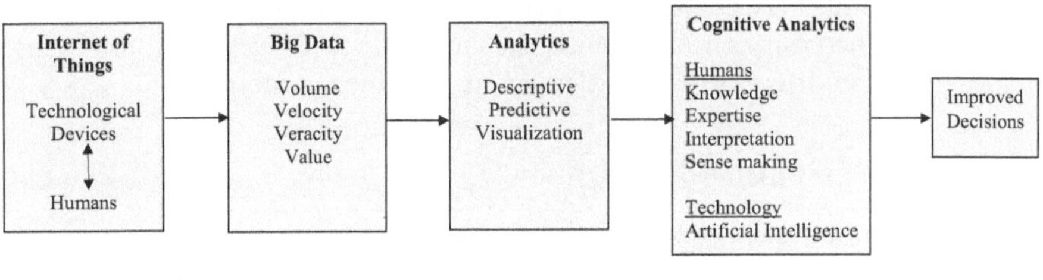

Figure 3.1 The Internet of Things and Cognitive Analytics

drawing from a wide variety of potentially relevant information and connections (Ronanki & Steier, 2014). The main technological aspect of cognitive analytics is represented by artificial intelligence. Cognitive analytics takes the view that data analysis is necessary, but not sufficient, to improve decisions. The use of cognitive analytics requires that people become not only experts in their particular areas but also experts in analytical tools. Hence, it implies a combination of the Internet of Things (to collect data), analytics (to analyze the data) and cognitions (to make sense of the data).

Making sense of the data generated requires the availability of qualified personnel; according to McAfee and Brynjolfsson (2012), "the power of big data does not erase the need for vision or human insight" (p. 66). However, as Manyika et al. (2011), from the McKinsey Global Institute, report, the United States faces a shortage of 140,000 to 190,000 people with deep analytical skills as well as a shortage of 1.5 million managers and analysts to analyze big data and make decisions based on the findings. The best data scientists are also comfortable speaking the language of business and helping leaders reformulate challenges in ways that big data can tackle; it is important to combine domain expertise with data science (McAfee & Brynjolfsson, 2012). It is also equally important to combine the Internet of Things and analytics with cognitions, experience and intuition.

Implications for Research and Practice

This chapter presented the perspective that the Internet of Things has the capacity to generate vast amounts of data that can be analyzed by organizations and individuals to improve decisions. In this regard, the Internet of Things and big data analytics can add value to organizations and individuals. The Internet of Things and big data can help to improve decision making and strategies in organizations (McAfee & Brynjolfsson, 2012), while facilitating personal augmentation (Wilson, Shah, & Whipple, 2015). However, decision makers need to master the data and their analysis if they want to reap the potential benefits of this tool. Indeed, analytics can help an organization "better understand its business and markets" and "leverage opportunities presented by abundant data and domain-specific analytics" (Chen et al., 2012, pp. 1166–68). Insight must be translated into strategic decisions that can benefit the organization or the individual decision maker. The cognitive analytics perspective provides opportunities for research not only on the link between the Internet of Things and big data analytics, but also on the necessity to emphasize the importance of expertise and sense making. It also offers opportunities for management practice.

Implications for Further Research

A cognitive analytics perspective provides opportunities for research on two dimensions: the human dimension and the technological dimension. In considering the human dimension, organizational scholars could focus on the role of expertise, knowledge, cognitions and heuristics in research on the Internet of Things and big data analysis. For example, they could explore the extent to which expertise in a particular domain leads to better decisions. Particularly, they could determine whether organizations that have data scientists with deep knowledge in business and management tend to make better use of big data analytics than those organizations that do not have such data scientists. It is also important to consider whether patterns found in data are really significant, meaningful and relevant; the volume of the data may render minor relationships statistically significant. However, a clear understanding of the domain may help differentiate truly significant and relevant relationships from data noise.

The human dimension may also consider the role of cognitive biases in data-driven decisions. It is important to acknowledge that the availability of data does not compensate for human errors and biases. Kahneman, Lavalo, and Sibolly (2011) noted that when making decisions managers often faced three types of biases: confirmation bias, anchoring bias and loss aversion bias. Confirmation bias leads managers to look for information and trends that validate previously held assumptions. Anchoring bias leads decision makers to weigh heavily one piece of information over another, and loss aversion bias leads decision makers to be more cautions in weighing options. To some extent, acknowledging these biases may help managers reduce them.

The technological dimension of cognitive analytics provides opportunities for further research on the role of artificial intelligence in improving decision making. It is obvious that artificial intelligence is replacing humans in making certain decisions (Simon, 1995; Pomerol, 1997; Nemati, Steiger, Iyer, & Herschel, 2002). Simon (1995) contends that cognitive mechanisms involved in scientific discovery are a special case of general human capabilities for problem solving. This reasoning led to the development of artificial intelligence as both a science and a set of tools to improve decision making (Simon, 1995; Nemati et al., 2002). For example, machine learning is a concept in which computers can learn new things based on the data they analyze and can act on these learnings. Machine learning systems use previously acquired information to make sense of new data. These systems can improve the ability to analyze and use data efficiently and effectively. Artificial intelligence allows delegation of difficult pattern recognition and learning. As such, it contributes to the volume, velocity and variety of data (O'Leary, 2013b). Hence, exploring the reliability of such decision-making tools could be a particularly fruitful research avenue for organizational scholars. As a consequence, big data analytics will be needed to make sense of this large amount of data. Hence, organizational scholars must pay particular attention to the relationship between the Internet of Things and big data analytics.

Implications for Practice

A cognitive analytics perspective of the Internet of Things and big data analytics provides guidelines for management practice, policy making and the betterment of individual lives. From a managerial perspective, cognitive analytics could help organizations recruit data scientists who combine both the skills required to analyze the data and knowledge needed to put this analysis into context. Doing so could help improve decision making. From the policy-making perspective, a cognitive analytics perspective could help policy makers understand that analysis and data are only tools. As such, only a deep understanding and knowledge of societal trends and problems could help make sound policies. Data and analysis can help, but by themselves they cannot substitute for lack of knowledge, expertise and sound judgment.

At the individual level, a cognitive analytics perspective could help citizens improve their personal lives. For example, data related to personal health could be beneficial to citizens only if these citizens themselves understand the meaning of the data and are willing to integrate them in their daily routines. Doing so is important because over the next decade, big data will change the landscape of social and economic policy and research (George et al., 2014). Similarly, the Internet of Things will become more ubiquitous in the future and numerous data will be collected through various wearable devices. Collecting and analyzing this data could prove a useful means for managers and individuals to make informed decisions. For example, in 2016, AT&T started a Smart City Initiative aimed at deploying Internet of Things solutions to cities across the United States (Frost & Sullivan White Paper, 2016). One of the main objectives of this initiative is to improve the quality of life, transportation and personal security in cities. Likewise, utility companies such as Enel in Italy and Pacific Gas and Electric (PG&E) in the United States, are deploying 'smart' meters that provide residential and industrial customers with visual displays showing energy usage and the real-time costs of providing it (Chui, Loffler, & Roberts, 2010).

However, we must acknowledge that the ubiquitous nature of the IoT is also raising concerns for privacy and security (Weber, 2010; Roman, Zhou, & Lopez, 2013; Jing et al., 2014). For example, Jing et al. (2014, p. 2482) note that the "IoT not only has the same security issues as sensor networks, mobile communications networks and the Internet, but also has its specialties such as privacy issues, different authentication and access control network configuration issues, information storage and management." Indeed, "applications of IoT can bring convenience to people, but if it cannot ensure the security of personal privacy, private information may be leaked at any time" (Jing et al., 2014, p. 2482). To address the security challenges, companies are turning to several technological mechanisms, such as virtual private networks and transport layer security (Weber, 2010). However, protecting the Internet of Things is a complex task because the threats that can affect it are numerous and include attacks that target diverse communication channels, physical threats, denial of service and identity fabrication, to name but a few (Roman et al., 2013). These challenges must be successfully navigated for the Internet of Things to live up to its promises of improving our lives.

Conclusion

Drawing on insights from cognitive science (Simon, 1980), this chapter developed a model of cognitive analytics to explore the relationship between the Internet of Things, big data analytics and decision making. Central to this model is the role of cognition, interpretation and sense making. Although a cognitive analytics perspective of the Internet of Things and big data analytics is promising, there is a paucity of management research addressing this topic (George et al., 2014, 2016). Hence, the chapter calls for further research on the role of cognition, interpretation and sense making in using big data and analytics in the age of the Internet of Things.

References

Ashton, K. (2009, June 22). That 'Internet of Things' thing. *RFID Journal*, 1.

Atzori, L., Iera, A., & Morabita, G. (2014). From smart objects to social objects: The next evolutionary step of the Internet of Tings. *IEEE Communications Magazine*, *52*(1), 97–105.

Barbour, J. B., Treem, J. W., & Kolar, B. (2017). Analytics and expert collaboration: How individuals navigate the relationships when working with organizational data. *Human Relations*, *71*(2), 256–284.

Barton, D., & Court, D. (2012, October). Making advanced analytics work for you. *Harvard Business Review*, 79–83.

Beugré, C. D. (2015). *The quest for management research on big data and analytics*. Symposium Organized at the 78th Annual Meeting of the Academy of Management, Vancouver, Canada, August 7–11.

Bi, Z., & Cochran, D. (2014). Big data analytics with applications. *Journal of Management Analytics*, *1*(4), 249–265.

Borgia, E. (2014, December). The Internet of Things vision: Key features, applications, and open issues. *Computer Communications*, *54*, 1–31.

Bose, R. (2009). Advanced analytics: Opportunities and challenges. *Industrial Management & Systems*, *109*(2), 155–172.

Chen, H., Chiang, R. H. L., & Storey, V. C. (2012). Business intelligence and analytics: From big data to big impact. *MIS Quarterly*, *39*(4), 1165–1188.

Chui, M., Loffler, M., & Roberts, R. (2010, March). The Internet of Things. *McKinsey Quarterly*. Retrieved August 28, 2017, from www.mckinsey.com/industries/high-tech/our-insights/the-internet-of-things

Daft, R. L., & Weick, K. E. (1984). Toward a model of organizations as interpretation systems. *Academy of Management Review*, *9*(2), 284–295.

Davenport, T. H. (2006). Competing on analytics. *Harvard Business Review*, *84*(5), 1–10.

Davenport, T. H. (2014). *Big data at work: Dispelling the myths, uncovering the opportunities*. Boston: Harvard Business Review Press.

Davenport, T. H., & Harris, J. G. (2007). *Competing on analytics: The new science of winning*. Boston: Harvard Business Review Press.

Davenport, T. H., Harris, J. G., & Morrison, R. (2010). *Analytics at work: Smarter decisions, better results*. Boston: Harvard Business Review Press.

Eloff, J. H. P., Eloff, M. M., Dlamini, M. T., & Zielinski, M. P. (2009). Internet of people, things and services: The convergence of security, trust and privacy. *3rd Companion Able Workshop—IoPTS, Novotel Brussels*, Brussels, 2 December 2009. Retrieved August 12, 2017, from http://hdl.handle.net/10204/4409

Frost & Sullivan White Paper. (2016). *Smart cities need telecommunications service providers: Smarter solutions provide opportunities to manage resources, create better quality of life*. Retrieved August 28, 2017, from www.business.att.com/content/whitepaper/iot-frost-sullivan-smart-cities-white-paper.pdf

George, G., Haas, M. R., & Pentland, A. (2014). Big data and management. *Academy of Management Journal*, *57*(2), 321–326.

George, G., Osinga, E., Lavie, D., & Scott, B. (2016). Big data and data science methods for management research. *Academy of Management Journal*, *59*(5), 1493–1507.

Gubbi, J., Buyya, R., Marusic, S., & Palaniswami, M. (2013). Internet of Things (IoT): A vision, architectural elements, and future directions. *Future Generation Computer Systems*, *29*(7), 1645–1660.

Hogarth, R. M., & Soyer, E. (2015). Using simulated experience to make sense of big data. *MIT Sloan Management Review*, *56*(2), 48–54.

Jing, Q., Vasilakos, A. V., Wan, J., Lu, J., & Qiu, D. (2014). Security of the Internet of Things: Perspectives and challenges. *Wireless News*, *20*(8), 2481–2501.

Kahneman, D., Lavalo, D., & Sibolly, O. (2011, June). Before you make that big decision. *Harvard Business Review*, 51–60.

Kiron, D., Prentice, P. K., & Ferguson, R. B. (2014). Raising the bar with analytics. *MIT Sloan Management Review*, *55*(2), 28–33.

Kohavi, R., Rothleder, N. J., & Simoudis, E. (2002). Emerging trends in business analytics. *Communications of the ACM*, *45*(8), 45–48.

Kuhn, T. S. (1962). *The structure of scientific revolutions*. Chicago: University of Chicago Press.

Kwon, O., Lee, N., & Shin, B. (2014). Data quality management, data usage experience and acquisition intention of big data analytics. *International Journal of Information Management*, *34*(3), 387–394.

LaValle, S., Lesser, E., Shockley, R., Hopkins, M. S., & Kruschwitz, N. (2011). Big data, analytics and the path from Insights to value. *MIT Sloan Management Review*, *52*(2), 21–32.

Li, S., Xu, L. D., & Zhao, S. (2015). The Internet of Things: A survey. *Information Systems Frontiers*, *17*(2), 243–259.

Loebbecke, C., & Picot, A. (2015). Reflections on societal and business model transformation arising from digitization big data analytics: A research agenda. *Journal of Strategic Information Systems*, *24*(3), 149–157.

Ma, H. D. (2011). Internet of Things: Objectives and scientific challenges. *Journal of Computer Science and Technology*, *26*(6), 919–924.

Manyika, J., Chui, M., Brown, B., Bughin, J., Dobbs, R., Roxburgh, C., & Byers, A. H. (2011). Big data: The next frontier for innovation, competition, and productivity. *McKinsey Global Institute*. Retrieved March 15, 2017, from file:///C:/Users/cbeugre/Downloads/MGI_big_data_full_report.pdf

McAfee, A., & Brynjolfsson, E. (2012, October). Big data: The management revolution. *Harvard Business Review*, 61–68.

Mezias, J. M., & Starbuck, W. H. (2003). Studying the accuracy of managers' perceptions: A research odyssey. *British Journal of Management*, *14*(1), 3–17.

Miorandi, D., Sicari, S., Pellegrini, F. D., & Chlamtac, I. (2012). The Internet of Things: Vision, applications, and research challenges. *Ad Hoc Networks*, *10*(7), 1497–1516.

Nemati, H. R., Steiger, D. M., Iyer, L. S., & Herschel, R. T. (2002). Knowledge warehouse: An architectural integration of knowledge, management, decision support, artificial intelligence and data warehousing. *Decision Support Systems*, *33*(2), 143–161.

Ning, H., & Wang, Z. (2011). Future Internet of Things architecture: Like mankind neural system or social organization framework? *IEEE Communications Letters*, *15*(4), 461–463.

O'Leary, D. E. (2013a). Big data, the Internet of Things and the Internet of signs. *Intelligent Systems in Accounting, Finance and Management*, *20*(1), 53–65.

O'Leary, D. E. (2013b). Artificial intelligence and big data. *IEEE Intelligent Systems*, *28*(2), 96–99.

Pomerol, J. C. (1997). Artificial intelligence and human decision making. *European Journal of Operations Research*, *99*(1), 3–25.

Riggins, F. J., & Wamba, S. F. (2015). Research directions of the adoption, usage and impact of the Internet of Things through the use of big data analytics. *Systems Sciences 46th Hawaii International Conference*, 1531–1540.

Roman, R., Zhou, J., & Lopez, J. (2013). On the features and challenges of security and privacy in distributed Internet of Things. *Computer Networks*, *57*(10), 2266–2279.

Ronanki, R., & Steier, D. (2014). *Cognitive analytics*. Retrieved December 16, 2014, from http://dupress.com/articles/2014-techtrends-cognitive-analytics

Shah, S., Horne, A., & Capella, J. (2012, April). Good data wont' guarantee good decisions. *Harvard Business Review*, 23–25.

Sharma, R., Mithas, S., & Kankanhalli, A. (2014). Transforming decision making processes: A research agenda for understanding the impact of business analytics on organizations. *European Journal of Information Systems*, *23*(4), 433–441.

Sicari, S., Rizzardi, A., Grieco, L. A., & Coen-Porisini, A. (2015). Security, privacy and trust in Internet of Things: The road ahead. *Computer Networks*, *76*(15), 146–145.

Simon, H. A. (1980). *The sciences of the artificial*. Cambridge: MIT Press.

Simon, H. A. (1995). Artificial intelligence: An empirical intelligence. *Artificial Intelligence*, *77*(1), 95–127.

Starbucks, W. H. (1996). Unlearning ineffective or obsolete technologies. *International Journal of Technology Management*, *11*(7/8), 725–737.

Tien, J. M. (2013). Big data: Unleashing information. *Journal of Systems Science and Systems Engineering*, *22*(2), 127–151.

Weber, R. H. (2010). Internet of Things: New security and privacy challenges. *Computer Law & Security Review*, *26*(1), 23–30.

Weick, K. E. (1993). The collapse of sensemaking in organizations: The Mann Gulch disaster. *Administrative Science Quarterly*, *38*(4), 628–652.

Weick, K. E. (1995). *Sensemaking in organizations*. Thousand Oaks, CA: Sage Publications.

Whitmore, A., Argawal, A., & Xu, L. D. (2015). The Internet of Things: A survey of topics and trends. *Information Systems Frontiers*, *17*(2), 261–274.

Wilson, H. J., Shah, B., & Whipple, B. (2015, October). How people are actually using the Internet of Things. *Harvard Business Review*, 1–6.

Yang, Z., Zhang, P., & Vasilakos, A. V. (2014, June). A survey on trust management for Internet of Things. *Journal of Network and Computer Applications*, *42*, 120–134.

Zakir, J., Seymour, T., & Berg, K. (2015). Big data analytics. *Issues in Information Systems*, *16*(2), 81–90.

4 Sustainable Careers and IoPTS

May the Internet of People, Things and Services Be Too Much of a Good Thing for Career and Human Resource Management?

Veronica M. Godshalk

Introduction

This chapter will explore how the Internet of People, Things and Services (IoPTS) provides both opportunities for advancing employees' careers and potential concerns that employees and human resource managers will need to attend to as the IoPTS inevitably becomes a common part of the career and technology landscape. The Internet has increased our ability to interact with other people and to share career-related information and services globally. We are enabled to work collaboratively over long distances and increase our scope of learning. But what will the IoPTS enable with regard to possible effects on organizations' human resource management processes (HRM) and individuals' career management? The IoPTS will allow individuals to pursue *sustainable careers*, in that they will maintain work patterns over time and across multiple social spaces or contexts (work, home, and leisure). These patterns will be characterized by individual agency and will provide meaning to each career actor (Greenhaus & Kossek, 2014; Van der Heijden & De Vos, 2015). This sustainable career theoretical framework allows us to more broadly view the effects of IoPTS on both organizational and individual career management. Because sustainable careers consider varied social contexts, career longevity, and employability, it honors the concept of boundarylessness, in that self-directed career actions and agency supersede the organization's structural boundaries. Sustainable careers also build on boundaryless career theory in that it considers independence from, rather than dependence on, organizational structures for career building (Arthur & Rousseau, 1996). Additionally, sustainable career theory expounds on protean career theory in that the central decision maker is the individual, recognizing his or her ownership and meaning attached to a career (Hall, 2002). Because sustainable careers incorporate this multidimensional approach, with its unique foci on work continuity and social space, it is applicable to helping us understand the context within which IoPTS affects both individual careers and organization's HRM processes.

Sustainable career theory recognizes today's highly individualistic socio-economic climate and simultaneously notes the broader life context, organizational, and societal context (Baruch, 2015) and therefore considers the impact of technology like IoPTS as part of a career ecosystem. Sustainable career theory also considers the organization's HRM role as HR practitioners respect the needs of employees. Because continuity in work patterns is desirable, albeit not necessarily within one employer, today's HRM takes a long-term approach regarding individual employability. This blends the best interests of employers, workers, and society in a balanced fashion. Sustainable careers create flexibility and promote well-being (DeHaaw & Greenhaus, 2015; DePrins, De Vos, Van Beirendonck, & Segers, 2015; Vinkenburg, Van Engen, & Peters, 2015). Career sustainability is not just being employed, but "maintaining employability by accessing opportunities for career and personal development" (Richardson & Kelliher, 2015, p. 117). IoPTS is a technological innovation that supports career sustainability.

This sustainable careers framework will be offered to help explain how IoPTS plays a role within the HRM and individual career management ecosystem. We will review several IoPTS examples that will both positively and negatively affect individuals and organizations. The *Too Much of a Good Thing* (TMGT) effect will also be introduced and applied in order to investigate what may happen when high usage levels of the otherwise benign IoPTS occur. Will the IoPTS be *too much of a good thing* for human resources management? Might IoPTS be *too much of a good thing* leading to unexpected and undesired career outcomes and having disconcerting effects on one's career? We will consider both the TMGT effect and IoPTS on individuals' careers and organizations' HRM. The chapter is designed to provide insight to both individuals managing their careers and HRM professionals concerned with organizational-wide career management practices. Future research opportunities are offered, along with practitioner realities.

The IoPTS Model

The IoPTS is defined as an Internet of people (IoP), things (IoT), and services (IoS) where people, things or physical objects, and services are seamlessly integrated into a network of networks, otherwise known as the "Internet of everything." This environment enables actors to exchange digital data about themselves and their surrounding environment over a web-based infrastructure (ABI Research, 2014; Eloff, Eloff, Dlamini, & Zielinski, 2009). Conceptually, the IoPTS can be viewed as overlapping constructs each to another, allowing both individuals and employers to access and share various types of information and make data-based decisions. The IoPTS is positioned on the framework of sustainable careers because as that theory suggests, we need to consider the social space career actors are working within toward employability, and today's employers and employees face IoPTS at every turn. Figure 4.1 represents those relationships. Examples of IoPTS' integration with and impact on HR and career management functions are noted throughout the chapter.

At the model's intersection of all segments is the need for high levels of security, trust, and privacy. When personal or organizational information is shared via IoT or IoS devices, these systems require a high level of security, as these data usually need to be maintained with high levels of privacy and trust. The International Standards Organization (ISO) has developed and defined standards for information security, which are discussed elsewhere (Eloff et al., 2009). With regard to career management, an example of needed trust includes HR performance evaluations, where employees trust HR professionals to treat evaluative information with respect and to disclose only to necessary management; an example of privacy would be employee's health or salary information, which would be accessible by HR professionals, but is not necessarily needed by others in the firm. It would be expected that in the IoPTS career ecosystem, high data security is ever present, and high levels of trust and privacy would be indicative of how 21st-century organizations maintain and share digital information. Security, trust, and privacy are central to the IoPTS environment, and HRM and information technology professionals need to work closely together to monitor career-related data.

The model posits that each segment of the IoPTS—the IoT, IoP, and IoS—overlap each other such that the "Internet of everything" is more amorphous

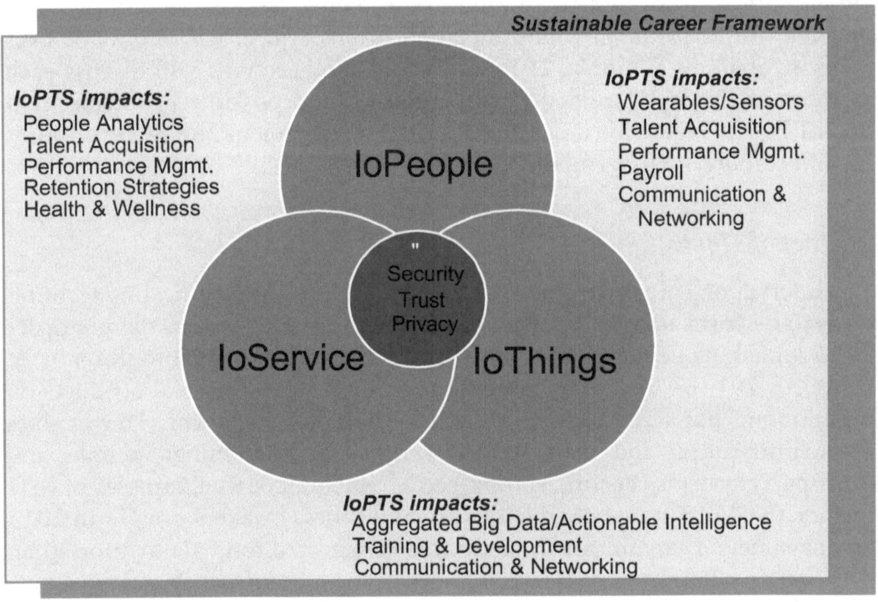

Figure 4.1 Relationship Between IoPTS and HRM and Careers

than discrete. In fact, CEO Mark Hurd of Oracle noted the overlap when he commented:

> CEOs must demonstrate a commitment to employees by becoming champions for HR systems that empower every employee to fully understand his or her job, how it ties into the corporate framework, what's expected of them, what training is available, and how they can use an embedded social network to communicate, collaborate and excel.
>
> . . . The challenge will be daunting, but it can be met with world-class HR technology. As companies begin replacing up to 30 percent of their workforce, they will need thousands of new types of data-native workers to exploit the Internet of Things in the service of the Internet of People.
>
> (Hurd, 2014)

Although the IoT clearly exists from an HR perspective, wearable tracking devices that some employees wear have sensors (*things*) that allow individuals to gather data about *people*. Similarly, the IoP appears to be a distinct concept, yet data are collected via (IoT) *things* and inputted into systems to provide (IoS) *services*, such as people-related analytics within organizations. With these data, the IoS becomes empowered to aid with actionable intelligence as the aggregated data it provides allow HR professionals to become strategic partners within the organization, putting a human touch on analyzing data for top executives (Ajilon, 2016). Today the IoT is providing data to IoSs, and these data are allowing services to optimize our machines—these human-cognizant applications will affect our work lives (Wilson, Shah, & Whipple, 2015). The following sections will discuss each segment of the IoPTS and the opportunities (and possible problems) that the IoPTS will create for individuals' career management and organizations' human resource management.

Internet of Things

The Internet of Things (IoT) is a web-based architecture connecting technologies to perform actions as a way of stitching together various data in order to do something new with that information (Holdowsky, Mahto, Raynor, & Cotteleer, 2015). The IoT represents the connecting of physical products on a multipoint basis and exposing them to digital applications. This enables the IoT to collect and share data directly with other things, people, and third-party systems (Bersin, Mariani, & Monahan, 2016). Examples of IoTs include the 45 million wearable devices and fitness trackers bought in 2015 by consumers. Demand for these devices is expected to grow by more than 45 percent annually through 2019, becoming one of the fastest-growing technology markets. Although most of us are familiar with the Fitbit and Garman wearable devices, analysts suggest that IoT wearable technology will not only demonstrate value in personal fitness, but may also play a huge role in business applications, potentially as much as 60 percent of the market (Bersin et al., 2016). Some human resource management examples include:

- IoT sensors are being used in factories to determine if machines are at properly maintained temperature and humidity environments.
  (Bersin et al., 2016)

- Sensors in lanyards act as identification badges, allowing employees access to various buildings and rooms within the workplace.
  (Bersin et al., 2016)

- The National Basketball Association (NBA) has been using IoT technologies to track and screen player performance and gather statistics.
  (Bersin et al., 2016; Li & Li, 2017)

- The IoT can provide performance data to employers and HR managers, simplifying the entire performance evaluation and appraisal process and making it streamlined and accurate.
  (Pocket HCM, 2016)

- Radio-frequency identification devices (RFID) have long been implemented in retail settings to minimize theft occurring in brick-and-mortar stores. Of those who had implemented RFID for inventory accuracy and replenishment, upwards of 40 percent of those retailers reported gross margin gains of 5 percent or more.
  (Kambies, Raynor, Pankratz, & Wadekar, 2016)

Some individual career examples include:

- Employees working shifts can clock in and out at exact times and can be automatically tracked, leading to error-free calculations of work hours and resulting in accurate payroll processing. Similarly, shift workers can be notified via a text on a smart phone when it is time to clock out.
- Smart phones have a location awareness sensor; map applications can tell you traffic is normal between two locations and how long it will take to reach your (work/interview) destination.
- Healthcare applications utilizing sensors in patient wearables can communicate over the Internet via a server accessible by healthcare professionals who are remotely monitoring multiple older patients with chronic conditions. Smart phones are also being used by people who are not acutely ill and who want to find some location-based information, such as the local hospital or pharmacy.
  (Boulos, Wheeler, Tavares, & Jones, 2011)

Finally, a controversial IoT example often in the news is the issue of police officers facing performance evaluations based on wearables. In Rialto, California, use of physical police abuse was reduced by over 50 percent when officers wore body cameras. Additionally, as more citizens are wearing digital eyewear like Google Glass, public safety will now have another (bystander) perspective from which to gather data. Today, civilians equipped with their smart phone camera or cameras posted on their property are taking videos of unnecessary police abuse, break-ins, and other possibly illegal incidents. With these data points, law enforcement no longer has to rely only on police wearables for data, because perspectives may have been recorded from many angles. And any footage that may have been tampered with or lost will no longer hinder investigations if recordings of an event are in the hands of multiple citizens (Mann & Wassom, 2014; Mims, 2014).

These examples all denote the ability for data to be gathered via various IoT devices that share information with people or systems. Based on the analysis of these data, HR professionals can then work with employees to improve performance. Data can also be used to allow access to healthy work environments and assure accurate payroll processes. Also, using smart phones and location sensors, HR professionals could potentially search for qualified job applicants using IoT technologies and acquire needed talent, marrying people who need jobs with jobs. However, the police wearable example is one in which the data can have damning consequences for police who are unfairly provoked or when the entire scene is not visible from the wearable. In these instances, HR professionals need to gather truthful evidence from numerous sources, which may not include digital sources (i.e., bystanders' sworn testimony, defendants, and peers).

Internet of People

The Internet of People (IoP) was originally conceptualized as "people equipped with human-implantable RFID tags will become part of the ubiquitous network" (Eloff et al., 2009, p. 1).

However, the IoP is increasingly overlapping with IoT such that data are gathered from a variety of sensors, and organizations may capture data that is in both the employees' and management's best interests. These data are allowing companies to gather people analytics (Bersin, Collins, Mallon, Moir, & Straub, 2016). They may be descriptive, predictive, or prescriptive in nature (ABI Research, 2014). The idea of gathering data about employee performance is over 100 years old, stemming back to industrial psychologists and Frederick Taylor in the late 19th century. However, the idea of gathering data from devices employees may wear or attach to themselves is new and allows for gathering data on employee engagement, workplace health and wellness, performance, and other work-related activities. HR professionals are finding ways to use people analytics to understand data that were previously unavailable to managers and employees, allowing companies to use a greater range of information, which may help improve the business' performance (Bersin, Collins, Mallon, Moir, & Straub, 2016).

Some examples of the use of people analytics includes data gathered from analyzing "high-performing job applicants, identifying characteristics of high-performing sales and service teams, predicting compliance risks, analyzing engagement and culture, and identifying high-value career paths and leadership candidates" (Bersin et al., 2016a:1). HR managers note that 77 percent of all organizations are moving towards greater use of people analytics (Bersin et al., 2016a). In fact, specific HRM use cases include the following focused on improving productivity, hiring, and retention:

- The profiles of top insurance salespeople have been analyzed, and it is now passé to screen candidates for grade point average or academic pedigree because those data are no longer a strong indicator of future sales performance.
- Data from the characteristics of top salespeople in software companies, retail banks, and manufacturers were analyzed to reveal that personal networks, internal interactions with other employees, and the time salespeople spend with their customers predicted positive results much more accurately than the amount of sales training received or experience.
- A technology company has developed a recruiting analytics model that accurately predicts candidates who are likely to become "toxic employees," defined as those who are more likely to lie, cheat, or commit crimes, and has dramatically reduced this population from its hires by scrutinizing data from the interview process.
- Several companies are collecting data from LinkedIn and other social networks and are creating predictive models to forecast high-potential employees who may also be highly likely to leave the organization.
- Companies are gathering data regarding office environments that have larger shared workplaces, more natural light, and more interoffice collaboration, as these workplaces result in higher levels of retention and productivity.

(Bersin et al., 2016a)

Many of these IoP data-gathering attempts can cause employees to feel that the employer is acting like Big Brother. An example is Humanyze, a company that is gathering employee behavioral data from its customers via a smart badge, built to look like a smart phone with a microphone, accelerometer, Bluetooth connection, and other tools typically found in a smart phone. This device measures how employees moved throughout the day, with whom they interacted, what their tone of voice was, how they listened (or if they did not listen but spoke over others), and other types of interactions that happen every day. Humanyze also asked their customers to provide key performance metrics, such as sales or customer service completion times, to compare against the behavioral data (Miller, 2015). For these processes to work, companies need to take privacy into account. Employees must know in advance exactly what is being tracked and analyzed. Managers must assure employees that they only collect aggregated data, not statistics on specific individuals. Finally, these studies should make employee participation optional. In that way, IoP analytics will include data from employees who do not feel they have been pressured into contributing (Wilson, 2013). With so much data potentially available from employees' wearables, HR professionals could aim to create more pleasant and efficient work environments by looking at productivity data, patterns of communication, how teams work effectively together, and employee need trends. But there are real obstacles to enlisting workers into this effort, beginning with the fact that employees aren't necessarily comfortable giving management unrestricted access to their private thoughts, location, motivation to perform, time allocated to work, and other nuggets of behavioral data. Just as in Frederick Taylor's time, employers continue to be interested in people analytics data and are beginning to look at new and innovative ways to help quantify what we do at work (Bersin, Mariani, & Monahan, 2016).

Employees also need to consider the benefits, as well as the costs, associated with IoP data gathering. From a career management standpoint, the IoP can assist in quantifying successes in the workplace, communicating that data in career portfolios, in addition to interacting with colleagues around the globe. IoPs may support a sustainable career and employability. Certainly, the costs of giving HR management access to deep levels of personnel data may compromise trust and privacy.

Internet of Services

The Internet of Services (IoS) is defined as "next-generation services provided over the Internet" (Eloff et al., 2009: 2). An overlap between the IoT and the IoS allows employers to gather data from IoT sensors to create actionable intelligence that HR professionals may use in the future. IoS may allow organizations to create service ecosystems whereby resources (tangible things or intangible knowledge, skills, and abilities of employees) can be combined and integrated to enhance a business's viability. Various service providers may in fact be independent entities "in the sense that they remain autonomous and have full control on their own resources (such as human resources, financial resources, production processes, strategic planning, etc.)" (Kutsikos, Konstantopoulos, Sakas, & Verginadis, 2014, p. 238). These IoSs with shared interests and goals may craft contractual agreements so that they cooperate with each other, and their customers, through exchange of necessary data to satisfy end users' needs.

An example of the overlap between IoS and IoT includes software companies using technology that will enable people (and machines) to make more informed decisions by analyzing and creating heuristics with the help of big data. A company named Parsable has developed an interesting set of mobile applications for front-line and field workers in the oil and gas services industry. This technology is able to provide immediate feedback on needed training, safety, and logistic support via applications on mobile smart phones to improve worker performance and drive productivity (Boese, 2015). Parsable is an example of a service provider offering data back to an industry that is not often thought of as advanced in using high-tech tools, yet this shows how IoS can provide actionable intelligence (Willer, 2016) to factory floor and HR professionals.

An example of the overlap between IoS and IoP includes wellness solution providers, such as VirginPulse and Limeade, which encourage employee wellness engagement holistically and are supplemented with innovative technologies. Embedded technology, along with expertise in motivation, competition, and team building, is offered as these companies help to deliver service solutions that drive improved individual health and wellness outcomes, as well as company productivity and results (Boese, 2015). Organizations that integrate VirginPulse and Limeade solutions into their workforce report improvements in retention, absence rates, and overall employee engagement, which research suggests positively affect organizational performance (Goetzel, Guindon, Turshen, & Ozminkowski, 2001). These applications certainly support a sustainable career and work–life balance. Another example is a future IoS offering of holoportation that Microsoft Research is developing. Holoportation is a virtual or augmented reality that will allow people to communicate in 3D, making Skype and other forms of videoconferencing look ancient (Willer, 2016). Holoportation may allow HR professionals to interview candidates at a distance and see and hear both verbal and nonverbal cues. It may also allow groups of individuals around the world to work together by communicating and networking as if in the same space.

These IoS examples create intriguing possibilities, but also share the concern of trust and privacy of the employees' data. Employees don't want something as simple as their need for training (knowledge deficiencies) or as complicated as their health status to be in the hands of individuals who might exploit that information. Additionally, the use of holoportation for interviewing candidates may cause some communication issues or possible virtual discrimination (based on age, gender, ethnicity, ability to use technology, etc.). In these cases, IoS may cause concern for employees and their career management actions.

Will IoPTS Be TMGT?

Although there are many opportunities that accrue to both organizations and individuals to manage careers, the technology associated with IoPTS allows for constant 24/7 accessibility, invasive employer access to employee data and behavioral scans, as well as real-time analysis and action, cost savings, and efficiency. So will IoPTS become *too much of a good thing* in the future? As we see from the stress literature, excessive amounts of a variable may result in conditions in which stressors result in lower levels of accrued benefits or enhanced concerns, and therefore may have detrimental effects on one's career and the organization. The *Too Much of a Good Thing* effect will be discussed so that we can understand under what conditions IoPTS results in positive outcomes for both individuals and organizations and when increasing amounts of IoPTS becomes too much to handle.

To achieve happiness and success, Aristotle once advised individuals to nurture values at the mean between deficiencies and excesses (Grant & Schwartz, 2011). Accordingly, much of the psychological research has focused on demonstrating well-being and performance as a result of positive traits and experiences. Although this focus on a linear relationship has disguised the possibility of a nonmonotonic, inverted, U-shaped phenomenon, other researchers have noted positive relationships may reach context-specific inflection points after which the relationship turns asymptotic and often negative, resulting in an overall pattern of inverted curvilinearity. This phenomenon has been called the *Too Much of a Good Thing* (TMGT) effect (Pierce & Aguinis, 2013). Several studies in the human resource, organizational behavior, and psychology fields have brought credence to this inverted U-shaped phenomenon, and results have consistently found job performance and work satisfaction were highest when employees reported moderate levels of stress (Boswell, Olson-Buchanan, & LePine, 2004; Champoux, 1992; Janssen, 2001; Takeuchi, Wang, & Marinova, 2005; Xie & Johns, 1995). Figure 4.2 graphically describes this phenomenon, noting where moderate levels may create greatest benefits, after which point negative outcomes may be experienced.

Given this phenomenon and its resultant outcomes, it is contended that IoPTS can have both positive and negative effects on career management. Stated differently, in addition to positive outcomes associated with IoPTS,

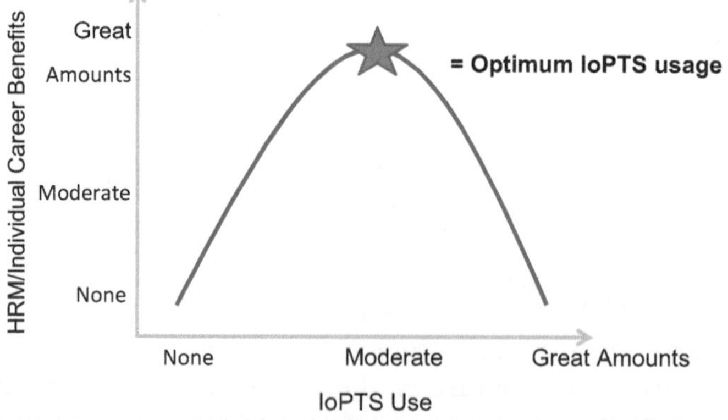

Figure 4.2 Relationship of IoPTS With HRM/Career Management and TMGT Effect

this desirable environment may lead to unanticipated negative consequences when IoPTS use reaches high levels. Stress researchers have demonstrated that each person has an optimal tipping point, above and below which the person does not perform as well as he or she does at the inflection point (Baruch, 2009; Cohen, 1980; Schuler, 1980).

When increasing levels of stress are experienced from moderate IoPTS usage, the individual may experience positive outcomes. For example, when individuals use the IoTs for communicating, networking, and advancing one's career (smart phones using social network media applications) in moderate amounts, IoTs can result in eustress and create many positive career experiences (job opportunities; learning about corporate cultures; connecting with colleagues, friends, and family; etc.). HR professionals, using IoSs, can access data on employee performance and, when gathered with employee knowledge and in moderate amounts, can result in incredible learning experiences on part of both the individual and the organization.

As the individual experiences excessive levels of stress associated with IoPTS usage, which may become intolerable and create distress, he or she moves across the tipping or inflection point of the inverted U-shaped curve, resulting in less desirable career and organizational outcomes. Furthering the examples noted earlier, excessive IoPTS usage may result in the following situations. When employers require employees to work and answer calls or emails using smart phones on personal time, this IoT usage may become extreme (i.e., employees feeling they are working 24/7), causing employees to experience work-related stress and other emotional and physical concerns, which may negatively affect one's career (Baruch, 2009; Boswell et al., 2004; Xie & Johns, 1995). Individuals might experience bias in future promotional opportunities, because management may construe lack of interest in working 24/7 as lack of interest in furthering one's career. In fact, legally, employers may have to pay employees for work activity on personal time, otherwise known as suffer or permit to work (Sova, 2013). Similarly, when HR professionals use excessive amounts of data from IoSs, personnel decision making may become stymied and "analysis paralysis" may result (Boss, 2015). Additionally, HR professionals may cross the line of trust and privacy, exploiting personnel data from IoSs and causing untold harm to individuals and their careers.

The question becomes under which conditions individuals experience optimal stress from IoPTS use, compared to others who may be experiencing distress. For each individual, either the beneficial effects of IoPTS exist (outweighing negative outcomes) or the hazardous effects of IoPTS exist (outweighing positive outcomes). Certainly, one's individual differences associated with career aspirations, age, gender, race, or career stage may affect IoPTS usage, either enabling eustress or creating distress. Studies, particularly those from the work–life integration and the job demands-resources literatures (Bakker & Demerouti, 2007; Greenhaus & Powell, 2003; Kain & Jex, 2010; Warner & Hausdorf, 2009), suggest work demands may be handled if met with sufficient resources, thereby also affecting these relationships. In sum, research may lead to practical conclusions for employees embracing IoPTS usage, and therefore should investigate the relationship between IoPTS use and an individual's responsibility for managing career management outcomes and the stress that may lead to positive, as well as negative, outcomes. It is clear that IoPTS usage will become more rampant, not less, and researchers need to provide guidance as to how practitioners can manage it. Future research opportunities should also investigate the inverted U-shaped relationship between IoPTS usage and organizational outcomes, and the following will discuss possible opportunities.

Future Opportunities with IoPTS, HRM, and Career Management

The Internet of People, Things and Services will create numerous opportunities for HR professionals and for individuals to manage their careers. In this section, we will review practitioner and research possibilities with regard to IoPTS usage and its effect on human resource management and organizational concerns. We will also discuss how the IoPTS environment will affect individual career management.

Practitioner Realities and Research Possibilities: IoPTS and HRM

What we know is that IoPTS has already enabled HR practitioners to do the following tasks with greater ease and in greater scale. Table 4.1 discusses the organizational benefits and concerns associated with IoPTS usage for HR professionals. These undertakings mean that HR practitioners continue to need to work closely with information technology professionals to use IoPTS to:

- Acquire human resources, noting 20 percent of the time job seekers do not submit applications due to poor e-recruiting application websites.
(Sceulovs & Shatrevich, 2015)

- Reward human resources through informed performance management systems.
- Enhance professional development because most training programs can be offered with minimal time needed away from work or costs of travel.
- Provide human resources with greater, more accurate, and timely information sharing.
- Retain human resources via enabled sharing of performance information so that individuals know where they stand in the organization and what opportunities might become available to them in the future.
(Ensher, Nielson, & Grant-Vallone, 2002)

So let's look specifically at how IoPTS will continue to affect HR management. IoTs allow HR to disseminate job opportunities, and IoSs enable HR to do quicker and more thorough reviews of potential job candidates. IoSs are

Table 4.1 IoPTS Usage in HRM

Benefits	*IoPTS Usage for Human Resource Management*	*Concerns*
Highly efficient	Acquire human resources via IoT and IoS	Depersonalized and possibly discriminatory
Enhanced performance management system	Reward human resources via IoP and IoS	Security risk
Training and development via videoconferencing from around globe	Enhanced professional development via IoS and IoT	Greater employability may increase intention to leave
Performance data sharing	Retain human resources via IoS	Security risk

available for HRM so that the onslaught of resumes received can be processed via software looking for key words on resumes. These resume robots parse data received in the resume, categorize meaning attached to data (such as contact info and work experience), attach keywords based on job description, and score resumes based on relevancy (Pinola, 2011).Then the HR professional receives an update based on those meeting the greatest number of criteria.

The upside of this capability is that the life of an HR professional is enhanced because more candidates can be efficiently scrutinized. However, there are disconcerting issues associated with IoSs influencing hiring decisions. First, the process is highly depersonalized. HR managers may easily weed out potential prospects based on these electronic submissions, with little or no personal contact. More experienced candidates may not get a chance to share why they are job searching. Young college graduates may be lucky enough to be interviewed on the phone, but with few visual cues may not sound "the part" or project potential. Interviewing skills over the phone are not taught in school, and graduates may have a difficult time learning how to interact and sell themselves in an IoPTS environment. More importantly, who the HR manager is and how to contact that person prior to an interview may never be discovered, because job application systems allow for the air of anonymity to exist.

Second, the IoPTS environment where job seekers submit applications electronically may create a discriminatory situation. HR managers may not consider more experienced prospects by parsing years of experience noted on resumes, guessing age, or making salary guesstimates. Older prospects may be discriminated against due to their lack of comfort with submitting job applications online (if that is the only way to apply for jobs). Studies note that electronic submissions may be ignored if it is perceived that the applicant's name is different from the majority of company employees (Employers' replies to racial names, 2016). Applicant names, such as Bertha or Edith (applicant believed to be old), Baadir (Muslim), Imani (African), or Jose (Hispanic), may not be evaluated due to perceived ethnicity or age. If a school is clearly of a particular religion, candidates may not be considered, as was the practice in Northern Ireland where companies did not hire individuals who attend Catholic colleges, thinking they too were Catholic (No names, no bias? Anonymising job applications to eliminate discrimination is not easy, 2015). Social media sites are available noting whether a candidate is gay or straight, and HR managers might investigate, then discriminate (Valentino-DeVries, 2013). Individuals who have extensive gaps in their employment history may not be considered, and the gap may be due to unemployment, family needs, or being previously incarcerated (Stinson, 2014). Finally, the IoSs allow for automated personality tests, either online or over the phone, which weed out 30 percent of candidates. Studies suggest that these tests may not be accurate, particularly for people with disabilities and mental illnesses. Other research confirms that these personality tests have little connection with performance (Weber & Dwoskin, 2014).

These concerns should be actively monitored by HR professionals and researchers so that the IoPTS does not tip over the point of being highly effective and efficient and produce discriminatory concerns. Researchers do have the opportunity to look at these situations, as well as the many that the IoPTS usage will create, including the reductions in cost and time, transfer of administrative workload from HR professionals to employees, the effect of increase in data provided to employees, the need to integrate HR into other systems within the organization particularly IT, and the increased emphasis on HR as a strategic partner with all other business functions (Ensher et al., 2002). Researchers might also investigate how effective IoPTS usage is in acquiring, rewarding, retaining, and providing professional development opportunities for employees. Researchers will need to investigate at what point the IoPTS usage becomes *too much of a good thing*, or not, for HRM.

Practitioner Realities and Research Possibilities: IoPTS and Individual Career Management

Individuals also need to manage their careers wisely within the IoPTS environment. As noted, traditional career management is changing, and practitioners need to manage their sustainable careers within the new IoPTS ecosystem. Although the human-aware IoS systems available are providing digital services that are increasingly part of our lives at home (i.e., systems that change lighting or music in your home or buy products from Amazon), these systems will soon define our personal career space at work in the future too (Wilson et al., 2015).

Table 4.2 discusses the individual benefits and concerns associated with IoPTS usage for career management. Some specific areas practitioners need to pay attention to include:

- Appreciate the selection process has changed and is automated by IoSs.
- Practice new interviewing skills that will include use of IoTs, such as videoconferencing.

- Understand that performance management data may be more easily gathered by IoTs and feedback will be offered more frequently and based on these data.
- Realize that compensation will be tied closely to performance management IoSs and that benefit management will be the employees' responsibility using these HR systems.
- Request training and development opportunities as often as possible, as many are offered via IoT systems, such as videoconferencing.
- Recognize that other career development opportunities may exist, but at a distance, such as e-mentoring. Networking at a distance may become commonplace via IoP.
- Understand that the excessive use of computers (IoT) may create physical strains. Yet computer use also allows for flexibility in time and workplace locations, possibly providing for work–life balance,

(deJanasz & Godshalk, 2013; Ensher et al., 2002; Ensher & Murphy, 2007; Godshalk, 2007; Sceulovs & Shatrevich, 2015)

These issues suggest that information offered to the employee within the IoPTS ecosystem can only aid in informed career management decision making (Greenhaus, Callanan, & Godshalk, 2010). Job seekers will need to understand how to maneuver within the IoSs involved in resume gathering. Information can be shared and accessed from smart phones (IoTs) so that employees looking for work know fairly instantaneously when jobs are

Table 4.2 IoPTS Usage in Individual Career Management

Benefits	*IoPTS Usage for Career Management*	*Concerns*
Eases application process	Appreciate selection processes using IoS	Depersonalized and possibly discriminatory
Improved professional development	Enhance interviewing skills using IoT	Young/older candidates might not be prepared
More accurate/ unbiased data	Enhance performance management systems via IoT	Security risk
More accurate/ unbiased data	Compensation tied to performance management systems via IoS	Security risk
Improved professional development	Training and development available via IoT	Greater employability may increase intention to leave
Enlarged professional network	Other career development opportunities via IoP and IoT	Greater employability may increase intention to leave
Flexibility	Computer strain due to IoT	Physical and emotional strain

posted. Smart phone users report 94 percent use a smart phone to browse for jobs, whereas 50 percent say they have filled out a job application via a phone (Smith, 2015).

College students will need to rely on more experienced counselors to understand what a resume in the IoPTS environment looks like and what is most effective in presenting yourself to organizations. Much like what we are seeing in healthcare, employees will need to manage their career progression either alone or with the aid of trusted advisors. Gone is the day when employees should rely on the company exclusively for career progression, and employability should be the goal given a sustainable career environment (DeHaaw & Greenhaus, 2015). IoTs will provide the ability to easily interact with others and learn about career opportunities. Whether that information is shared verbally through smart phones, Skype or Google Hangout conversations, or other Voice over Internet Protocols (VoIP), or via email, texting, or instant messaging, job seekers can readily interact with colleagues and HR professionals around the globe. Job seekers have the ability to compare one job in a company to others of interest and can gather real data by interacting with current or past employees of a given company. Networking via the IoTs will be the primary mode of communication. Whereas our "old school" approach to networking has been to be a part of the "old boys club" and to be physically present at events, given the IoPTS, we will be using various technologies to network. A word of caution regarding networking—it will take much time until IoPTS virtual networking formally replaces the "old school" method.

The IoPTS has created an environment where the availability of open jobs, job descriptions, salary/benefit information, corporate financial performance, company management profiles, and culture can easily be determined. IoS websites, such as LinkedIn and Glassdoor, allow job seekers to both look for jobs and investigate companies that may have posted jobs (Who Is Managing Your Career on the Internet?, 2016). Current or past employees may also share information about opportunities at various companies and suggest whether or not the job opportunity is as attractive as the offering the company asserts. These same individuals may be able to share who key decision makers are within the company.

Communication availability using IoTs allows employees to increase their scope of productivity and learning capabilities. Companies like Google have found that employees can learn and be productive even when teams have members at remote locations (He, 2013). As more workplaces become knowledge-based environments, companies will experience the tension of allowing employees to work together effectively, while allowing them to do their jobs from almost anywhere. The IoPTS creates these remote working environments, which may enhance career opportunities. Opportunities for career growth may not be available at the local office, but the IoPTS may allow career opportunities to exist at other locations, without the need to physically relocate to company facilities. These are all benefits of managing one's career within the IoPTS.

The IoPTS also may have detrimental effects on individuals. As mentioned previously, researchers might investigate whether discrimination has become more common (or at least more measurable) or not, as HR professionals actively use IoSs to weed out job seekers. Additionally, much has been written in the work–life balance literature about negative effects of working from home and lower advancement potential (Almerm, Cohen, & Single, 2004; Leslie, Manchester, Park, & Mehng, 2012; Rogier & Padgett, 2004). Researchers might consider the effects of IoTs on flexible work schedules and locations and possible detrimental effects on career progression. Another research opportunity will be how efficient the IoPTS usage is in seeking and securing jobs. Also, performance management data, which are more easily gathered by IoTs, should be investigated to see what effects this actionable intelligence has on individual careers. Finally, much has been written about the physical strains associated with constant computer usage, and researchers may continue to investigate those who work from home and possible health outcomes (Baruch, 2009; Warr, 2007). Researchers will need to investigate at what point IoPTS usage becomes *too much of a good thing* with regard to employee health, wellness, performance, and career development and advancement potential. Both employees and employers will gain much from this shared knowledge, and a sustainable career workforce will be enabled.

Conclusion

The chapter has reviewed the IoPTS and its effects on both HR management and employees' career management. The chapter contributes a model, based on sustainable career theory, identifying segments of the IoPTS and career-related capabilities gleaned from each. The importance of sustainable career theory is that it considers work continuity and social space important for employability, which calls for the inclusion of IoPTS usage and its relevance to career management. The TMGT phenomenon was also introduced as a possible guideline within which both opportunities and disconcerting concerns of IoPTS usage should be considered. Many examples were offered regarding IoPTS usage and possible outcomes from the organizational (HRM) perspective and the individual's sustainable career management perspective.

What we know about the IoPTS is that it is relatively new and growing, and it will create an inordinate amount of opportunities. But it also will create an environment within which the employee might experience significant career change. The TMGT phenomenon tells us that employees might experience extreme levels of stress, and hence fewer benefits, if they experience IoPTS in uncomfortable amounts. This phenomenon can be managed properly when various individual and organizational supports come together. But many questions are associated with IoPTS usage and outcomes for which we do not yet have answers. HR practitioners are currently dealing with IoPTS and effects on the organization and employees. So this area is ripe, and future researchers are encouraged to investigate IoPTS and its effects on HR management and sustainable career management.

References

ABI Research. (2014, May 7). *Internet of Things vs. internet of everything: What's the difference?* Retrieved February 14, 2017, from www.abiresearch.com/whitepapers/internet-of-things-vs-internet-of-everything/

Ajilon. (2016, June 9). *HR and the Internet of Things*. Retrieved February 14, 2017, from http://blog.ajilon.com/human-resources/hr-and-the-internet-of-things/

Almerm, E. D., Cohen, J. R., & Single, L. E. (2004). Is it the kids or the schedule?: The incremental effect of families and flexible scheduling on perceived career success. *Journal of Business Ethics*, *54*(1), 51–65.

Arthur, M. B., & Rousseau, D. M. (1996). *The boundaryless career: A new employment principle for a new organizational era*. New York: Oxford University Press.

Bakker, A., & Demerouti, E. (2007). The job demands-resources model: State of the art. *Journal of Managerial Psychology*, *22*(3), 309–328.

Baruch, Y. (2009). Stress and careers. In C. L. Cooper, J. C. Quick, & M. Schabracq (Eds.), *International handbook of work and health psychology* (3rd ed., pp. 197–220). West Sussex, UK: Wiley/Blackwell.

Baruch, Y. (2015). Organizational and labor markets as career ecosystem. In A. De Vos, & B. I. J. M. Van der Heijden (Eds.), *Handbook of research on sustainable careers* (pp. 364–380). Cheltenham, UK: Edward Elgar.

Bersin, J., Collins, L., Mallon, D., Moir, J., & Straub, R. (2016a, February 29). *People analytics: Gaining speed*. Retrieved February 14, 2017, from http://dupress.com/articles/people-analytics-in-hr-analytics-teams/

Bersin, J., Mariani, J., & Monahan, K. (2016b, May 24). *Will IoT technology bring us the quantified employee? The Internet of Things in human resources*. Retrieved February 14, 2017, from https://dupress.deloitte.com/dup-us-en/focus/internet-of-things/people-analytics-iot-human-resources.html#endnote-sup-3

Boese, S. (2015, February 13). *From the 'Internet of Me' to reimagining the workforce, major HR technology trends are transforming the way modern business gets done*. Retrieved February 14, 2017, from www.hreonline.com/HRE/view/story.jhtml?id=534358323

Boss, J. (2015, March 20). *How to overcome the 'Analysis Paralysis' of decision-making*. Retrieved February 25, 2017, from www.forbes.com/sites/jeffboss/2015/03/20/how-to-overcome-the-analysis-paralysis-of-decision-making/#353858bc1be5

Boswell, W. R., Olson-Buchanan, J. B., & LePine, M. A. (2004). Relations between stress and work outcomes: The role of felt challenge, job control, and psychological strain. *Journal of Vocational Behavior*, *64*, 165–181.

Boulos, M. N. K., Wheeler, S., Tavares, C., & Jones, R. (2011). How smartphones are changing the face of mobile and participatory healthcare: An overview, with example from eCAALYX. *BioMedical Engineering OnLine*, *10*, 24–38.

Champoux, J. E. (1992). A multivariate analysis of curvilinear relationships among job scope, work context satisfactions, and affective outcomes. *Human Relations*, *45*(1), 87–111.

Cohen, S. (1980). After effects of stress on human performance and social behavior: A review of research and theory. *Psychological Bulletin*, *98*, 82–108.

DeHaaw, S., & Greenhaus, J. H. (2015). Building a sustainable career: The role of work-home balance in career decision making. In A. De Vos, & B. I. J. M. Van der Heijden (Eds.), *Handbook of research on sustainable careers* (pp. 223–238). Cheltenham, UK: Edward Elgar.

deJanasz, S. C., & Godshalk, V. M. (2013). The role of e-mentoring in proteges' learning advancement and satisfaction. *Group & Organization Management*, *38*(6), 743–774.

DePrins, P., De Vos, A., Van Beirendonck, L., & Segers, J. (2015). Sustainable HRM for sustainable careers: Introducing the 'Respect Openness Continuity (ROC)' model. In A. De Vos, & B. I. J. M. Van der Heijden (Eds.), *Handbook of research on sustainable careers* (pp. 319–334). Cheltenham, UK: Edward Elgar.

Eloff, J. H. P., Eloff, M. M., Dlamini, M. T., & Zielinski, M. P. (2009). *Internet of People, things and services: The convergence of security, trust and privacy*. Proceedings of the Third International Workshop IoPTS, Brussels, 1–8.

Employers' replies to racial names. (2016, June 20). Retrieved February 28, 2017, from www.nber.org/digest/sep03/w9873.html/

Ensher, E. A., & Murphy, S. E. (2007). E-mentoring: Next-generation research and strategies. In B. R. Ragins, & K. E. Kram (Eds.), *The handbook of mentoring at work: Theory, research and practice* (pp. 299–322). Thousand Oaks, CA: Sage Publications.

Ensher, E. A., Nielson, T. R., & Grant-Vallone, E. (2002). Tales from the hiring line: Effect of the internet and technology on hiring processes. *Organizational Dynamics*, *31*(3), 224–244.

Godshalk, V. M. (2007). Social implications of e-mentoring: Why might e-mentoring work? In F. Li (Ed.), *Social implications and challenges of e-business* (pp. 31–45). Hershey, PA: Idea Group.

Goetzel, R. Z., Guindon, A. M., Turshen, J. I., & Ozminkowski, R. J. (2001). Health and productivity management: Establishing key performance measures, benchmarks, and best practices. *Journal of Occupational & Environmental Medicine*, *43*(1), 10–17.

Grant, A. M., & Schwartz, B. (2011). Too much of a good thing: The challenge and opportunity of the inverted U. *Perspectives on Psychological Science*, *6*(1), 61–76.

Greenhaus, J. H., Callanan, G. A., & Godshalk, V. M. (2010). *Career management* (4th ed.). Thousand Oaks, CA: Sage Publications.

Greenhaus, J. H., & Kossek, E. E. (2014). The contemporary career: A work-home perspective. *Annual Review of Organizational Psychology and Organizational Behavior*, *1*(1), 361–388.

Greenhaus, J. H., & Powell, G. N. (2003). When work and family collide: Deciding between competing role demands. *Organizational Behavior and Human Decision Processes*, *90*, 291–303.

Hall, D. T. (2002). *Careers in and out of organizations*. Thousand Oaks, CA: Sage Publications.

He, L. (2013, March 29). *Google's secrets of innovation: Empowering its employees*. Retrieved February 28, 2017, from www.forbes.com/sites/laurahe/2013/03/29/googles-secrets-of-innovation-empowering-its-employees/#6df609747eb3/

Holdowsky, J., Mahto, M., Raynor, M. E., & Cotteleer, M. (2015, August 21). *Inside the Internet of Things (IoT), Deloitte University Press*. Retrieved February 14, 2017, from http://dupress.com/articles/iot-primer-iot-technologies-applications/

Hurd, M. (2014, May 30). *The Internet of Things is really the Internet of People*. Retrieved February 24, 2017, from https://blogs.oracle.com/oraclehcm/the-internet-of-things-is-really-the-internet-of-people

Janssen, O. (2001). Fairness perceptions as a moderator in the curvilinear relationships between job demands, and job performance and job satisfaction. *Academy of Management Journal*, *44*(5), 1039–1050.

Kain, J., & Jex, S. (2010). Karasek's (1979) job demands-control model: A summary of current issues and recommendations for future research. In P. L. Perrewé, & D. C. Ganster (Eds.), *New developments in theoretical and conceptual approaches to job stress* (pp. 237–268). Bingley, UK: Emerald Publishing Group.

Kambies, T., Raynor, M. E., Pankratz, D. M., & Wadekar, G. (2016, January 14). *Closing the digital divide: IoT in retail's transformative potential the Internet of Things in the retail industry*. Retrieved February 14, 2017, from https://dupress.deloitte.com/dup-us-en/focus/internet-of-things/iot-retail-strategies.html#endnote-1

Kutsikos, K., Konstantopoulos, N., Sakas, D., & Verginadis, Y. (2014). Developing and managing digital service ecosystems: A service science viewpoint. *Journal of Systems and Information Technology*, *16*(3), 233–248.

Leslie, L. M., Manchester, C. F., Park, T. Y., & Mehng, S. A. (2012). Flexible work practices: A source of career premiums or penalties? *Academy of Management Journal*, *55*(6), 1407–1428.

Li, B., & Li, Y. (2017). Internet of Things drives supply chain innovation: A research framework. *International Journal of Organizational Innovation*, *9*(3), 71–92.

Mann, S., & Wassom, B. D. (2014, December 23). Body cameras for police officers: What about for ordinary citizens? *Forbes*. Retrieved February 24, 2017, from www.forbes.com/sites/realspin/2014/12/23/body-cameras-for-police-officers-what-about-for-ordinary-citizens/3/#46905f028ad5

Miller, R. (2015, February 24). *New firm combines wearables and data to improve decision making*. Retrieved February 14, 2017, from https://techcrunch.com/2015/02/24/new-firm-combines-wearables-and-data-to-improve-decision-making/

Mims, C. (2014, August 18). What happens when police officers wear body cameras. *Wall Street Journal*. Retrieved February 24, 2017, from www.wsj.com/articles/what-happens-when-police-officers-wear-body-cameras-1408320244

No names, no bias? Anonymising job applications to eliminate discrimination is not easy. (2015, October 31). Retrieved February 28, 2017, from www.economist.com/news/business/21677214-anonymising-job-applications-eliminate-discrimination-not-easy-no-names-no-bias/

Pierce, J. R., & Aguinis, H. (2013). The too-much-of-a-good-thing effect in management. *Journal of Management*, *39*(2), 313–338.

Pinola, M. (2011). *How can I make sure my resume gets past resume robots and into a human's hands?* Retrieved February 28, 2017, from http://lifehacker.com/5866630/how-can-i-make-sure-my-resume-gets-past-resume-robots-and-into-a-humans-hand

Pocket HCM. (2016, May 3). *How IoT can be a game-changer for HR?* Retrieved February 24, 2017, from http://blog.pockethcm.com/how-iot-can-be-a-game-changer-for-hr/

Richardson, J., & Kelliher, C. (2015). Managing visibility for career sustainability: A study of remote workers. In A. De Vos, & B. I. J. M. Van der Heijden (Eds.), *Handbook of research on sustainable careers* (pp. 131–145). Cheltenham, UK: Edward Elgar.

Rogier, S. A., & Padgett, M. Y. (2004). The impact of utilizing a flexible work schedule on the perceived career advancement potential of women. *Human Resource Development Quarterly*, *15*(1), 89–106.

Sceulovs, D., & Shatrevich, V. (2015). Internet of Things as a framework for e-recruitment's business model? Retrieved February 28, 2017 from www.inase.org/library/2015/books/MCSI.pdf, 125–131.

Schuler, R. S. (1980). Definition and conceptualization of stress in organizations. *Organizational Behavior and Human Performance*, *25*, 184–215.

Smith, A. (2015, November 19). *Searching for work in the digital era*. Retrieved February 28, 2017, from www.pewinternet.org/2015/11/19/searching-for-work-in-the-digital-era/

Sova, K. (2013). *Yes, you do have to pay employees for checking e-mail outside of work*. Retrieved February 25, 2017, from http://sovalaw.com/blog/2013/08/21/yes-you-do-have-to-pay-employees-for-checking-e-mail-outside-of-work/

Stinson, J. (2014, August 25). *Hiring bias against the unemployed: Should there be a law?* Retrieved February 28, 2017, from www.pewtrusts.org/en/research-and-analysis/blogs/stateline/2014/08/25/hiring-bias-against-the-unemployed-should-there-be-a-law/

Takeuchi, R., Wang, M., & Marinova, S. V. (2005). Antecedents and consequences of psychological workplace strain during expatriation: A cross-sectional and longitudinal investigation. *Personnel Psychology*, *58*(4), 925–948.

Valentino-DeVries, J. (2013, November 20). *Bosses may use social media to discriminate against job seekers: Firms use data they find early in job process, new study finds*. Retrieved February 28, 2017, from www.wsj.com/articles/SB10001424052702303755504579208304255139392/

Van der Heijden, B. I. J. M., & De Vos, A. (2015). Sustainable careers: Introductory chapter. In A. De Vos, & B. I. J. M. Van der Heijden (Eds.), *Handbook of research on sustainable careers* (pp. 1–20). Cheltenham, UK: Edward Elgar.

Vinkenburg, C. J., Van Engen, M. L., & Peters, P. (2015). Promoting new norms and true flexibility: Sustainability in combining career and care. In A. De Vos, & B. I. J. M. Van der Heijden (Eds.), *Handbook of research on sustainable careers* (pp. 131–145). Cheltenham, UK: Edward Elgar.

Warner, M. A., & Hausdorf, P. A. (2009). The positive interaction of work and family roles. *Journal of Managerial Psychology*, *24*(4), 372–385.

Warr, P. B. (2007). *Work, happiness and unhappiness*. Mahwah, NJ: Lawrence Erlbaum Publishers.

Weber, L., & Dwoskin, E. (2014, September 29). *Are workplace personality tests fair? Growing use of tests sparks scrutiny amid questions of effectiveness and workplace discrimination*. Retrieved February 28, 2017, from www.wsj.com/articles/are-workplace-personality-tests-fair-1412044257/

Who Is Managing Your Career on the Internet? (2016, June 20). Retrieved February 28, 2017, from http://highlyeffectivejobsearch.com/who-is-managing-your-career-on-the-internet/

Willer, P. (2016, May 6). *How the Internet of Things will impact HR*. Retrieved February 24, 2017, from www.eremedia.com/tlnt/how-the-internet-of-things-will-impact-hr/

Wilson, H. J. (2013, October 20). *Wearable gadgets transform how companies do business: Companies are decking employees out with devices that help them do their jobs better*. Retrieved February 14, 2017, from www.wsj.com/articles/wearable-gadgets-transform-how-companies-do-business-1382128410

Wilson, H. J., Shah, B., & Whipple, B. (2015, October 28). *How people are actually using the Internet of Things*. Retrieved July 18, 2017, from https://hbr.org/2015/10/how-people-are-actually-using-the-internet-of-things

Xie, J. L., & Johns, G. (1995). Job scope and stress: Can job scope be too high? *Academy of Management Journal*, *38*(5), 1288–1309.

5 Cyberloafing in the Realm of IoPTS

Examining Individual Neutralization and Organizational Citizenship Behavior

Rashimah Rajah and Vivien K. G. Lim

Introduction

Having and providing Internet access at the workplace is no longer perceived as providing organizations with a competitive advantage; the Internet has become so ingrained in organizational functions that it is seen as a necessity. The Internet is used as a means to keep up with current affairs, conduct research on products or ideas for innovation, and to communicate with clients and fellow colleagues (Yellowlees & Marks, 2007). With the advent of the Internet of People, Things and Services (IoPTS), physical objects and services are seamlessly integrated into networks as active participants (individuals) exchange data about themselves over a web-based infrastructure (Eloff, Eloff, Dlamini, & Zielinski, 2009). As individuals relay data about themselves on various platforms, we observe the convergence of a physical and digital identity as a participant of the IoPTS network is identified through their activities on various platforms such as online banking, online shopping, and social media sites.

Indeed, individuals also tend to have a *single* digital identity despite being registered on different platforms as various services are integrated to provide individuals with customized service. Cookies are stored on buying platforms like Amazon and Skyscanner, and advertisements similar to the items searched for would appear on search engines like Google. Social media platforms are connected with an individual's email account and digital phonebook such that users are confronted with online friend requests or friend suggestions from people they might know personally in real life, but who would otherwise not be able to find them on the social media site like Facebook. Facebook even cooperates with Transferwise, a company dealing with international money transfers, to allow users to use the Facebook Messenger app to transfer money across borders (Kahn, 2017).

With increasing ease of running errands from the comfort of one's own chair, or rather, mobile devices, the boundaries at the workplace become blurred. Whereas in the past employees would have to be physically away from the office to engage in nonwork activities such as shopping and banking, employees can now do them using the company's Internet resources while being physically at work. This phenomenon is known as *cyberloafing*. Cyberloafing refers to using companies' Internet access for personal purposes (Lim, 2002). The most common forms of cyberloafing are checking and sending non–work-related *email* at the workplace, *browsing* non–work-related websites (e.g., entertainment and sports news), and *interacting* for non–work-related purposes on social media platforms like Facebook.

The objectives of the chapter are four-fold. First, we examine cyberloafing in the context of IoPTS. As briefly highlighted earlier, the advent of IoPTS *encourages* cyberloafing at the workplace due to the convergence of employees' physical and digital identities, making it easier for employees to engage in nonwork activities during working hours. What are the challenges for management as a result of this? How can an organization deal with cyberloafing in the complex IoPTS workplace? Is *more* IoPTS needed to solve this very issue that arises out of IoPTS? Second, we categorize the cyberloafing behaviors engaged in by employees and in doing so operationally define cyberloafing in the IoPTS environment. By *IoPTS environment* we refer to the fact that services for individuals are integrated on various platforms and on different objects. For instance, an individual has a Facebook account that can be accessed on both work computers as well as personal mobile devices, and within Facebook he or she has access to contacts from other apps like the push-messaging service WhatsApp and also Transferwise, as mentioned previously. We also take into account security, privacy, and trust concerns that arise out of IoPTS and how they are related to cyberloafing. Third, we examine if cyberloafing behavior leads to positive organizational outcomes. In this chapter, we focus on organizational citizenship behavior (OCB) as a positive outcome of cyberloafing. Fourth, we examine if there are psychological processes that can strengthen or attenuate the relationships between cyberloafing and OCB. Implications for management are discussed.

Literature Review on Cyberloafing

Cyberloafing refers to the act of employees using their companies' Internet access for personal purposes during work hours (Lim, 2002; Lim & Teo, 2005). Examples of cyberloafing include browsing non–job-related websites (e.g. social networking, sports, news and entertainment), checking and sending personal emails, and other activities such as online shopping and online gaming. Cyberloafing is a common phenomenon in today's organizations, as firms increasingly have high-speed access to the Internet that is necessary for research, execution, and communication. Not only is the Internet more available in the workplace, there are also few restrictions as to which websites employees can surf. This is because the vast information that can be found on the World Wide Web is needed for work and for companies to remain updated and competitive (Lim & Teo, 2005). As such, it is considerably easier for employees to abuse this relatively free access to the Internet for their own personal matters during work hours.

Cyberloafing has been conceptualized as a form of workplace deviance (Lim, 2002). According to Robinson and Bennett (1995), workplace deviance refers to voluntary behavior that violates significant organizational norms, and in so doing, threatens the well-being of the organization or its members or both. Examples of deviant behaviors at the workplace include littering the work environment, coming in late without permission, and falsifying receipts in order to get more reimbursement from the company. Some research on cyberloafing identifies it as a deviant form of workplace behavior, evident through the financial losses suffered by organizations as a result of cyberloafing.

When employees are cyberloafing at work, such as having other non–work-related websites open in other browsers or being busy with personal activities on their mobile devices, they are essentially juggling multiple mental tasks at the same time. In a review of studies on the impact of different media technologies on cognitive capabilities, Greenfield (2009) found that individuals who engaged in multitasking performed worse in the tasks assigned. For example, participants who were asked to understand CNN news stories recalled significantly fewer facts from the stories shown earlier when they were in the multitasking condition (Bergen, Grimes, & Potter, 2005). In an experimental study with a university setting, half of the students in a classroom were allowed to use Internet-connected laptops during a lecture, whereas the other half had to keep their computers shut (Hembrooke & Gay, 2003). The study found that students who browsed the Internet performed significantly worse on a subsequent test relating to the lecture's content.

Similarly, processing distracting information at work through browsing websites, visiting social networking sites, and receiving and sending personal emails exacts a cognitive cost that depletes cognitive resources necessary to perform tasks at work (Greenfield, 2009). Clearly, cyberloafing is costly to the organization as the company's Internet resources are misused and employees' productivity levels are negatively affected. Several organizations attempt to counter this problem by blocking URLs for pornography content, game sites, social networking sites, entertainment sites, shopping or auction sites, and sports sites (SurveilStar.com, 2008). Organizations are also increasingly using Internet surveillance programs and putting in place explicit policies regarding usage of the Internet (Bequai, 1998). In Singapore, starting in 2017, Internet access for civil service employees was banned nationwide (The Straits Times, 2016).

In the era of smart phones and IoPTS, cyberloafing becomes even harder to control. With a growing Gen Y population in the workforce, concerns about the use of the company's Internet for non–work-related purposes become bigger due to the widespread adoption and use of social media by Gen Y (Sultan, Rohm, & Gao, 2009). Personal ICT devices are used for personal purposes that go undetected because companies cannot monitor those forms of computer-mediated communications at the workplace. With the advent of generous mobile data packages, employees do not usurp the company's Internet resources. Their personal mobile subscriptions allow them to use their own resources when surfing the Web for personal purposes during work hours. However, by reducing the amount of man hours available for work-related matters through such distracting activities, engagement in cyberloafing remains an issue pertinent to the management of IoPTS.

It is important to note at this juncture that the focus is not on curbing cyberloafing. In fact, cyberloafing has been found to be positively related to employees' well-being and productivity, as it acts as a form of "mental break" before employees return their attention to work matters (Lim & Chen, 2009). One of the earliest works on the positive side of cyberloafing also highlighted that personal web usage can be a way to blend personal and work life and a way for employees to contribute to continuous learning (Anandarajan & Simmers, 2005). The question is then one that is focused on how we can manage cyberloafing in the workplace given the IoPTS environment.

IoPTS and Cyberloafing

Although the level of engagement in cyberloafing can be encouraged through the advent of IoPTS, cyberloafing does not come without its issues. For instance, concerns among users with regard to security, trust, and privacy arise as a result of the regular exchange of participants' data on multiple networks (Eloff et al., 2009). Integration of different apps and platforms for a customized experience include obtaining data that are not necessarily given with consent. For example, after Facebook bought WhatsApp for US$19 billion in February 2014 (Covert, 2014), WhatsApp users were confronted with concerns regarding the privacy of their identity, as the option to keep their WhatsApp account and contacts separate from those in Facebook was an *opt-out* possibility, not opt-in (WhatsApp, n.d.). What this means is that unless users explicitly state that they do not wish to share their WhatsApp account information with Facebook, this "seamless integration" is done automatically without express consent.

In the context of the workplace, using these apps poses an even higher threat with regard to security, trust, and privacy, because cyberloafing activities might be subject to monitoring by their superiors. In certain firms, surveillance methods need to be in place to protect company assets, safeguard propriety information, and avoid costly litigation which can stem from inappropriate electronic communications in the workplace (Chory, Vela, & Avtgis, 2016). Governance frameworks in companies are also essential in supporting interoperability and reducing liability. Yet governance can "easily become excessive, fostering an environment in which people are continuously monitored and controlled" (Roman, Najera, & Lopez, 2011, p. 54). This affects employees on all three aspects of security, trust, and privacy because employees lose confidentiality of their Internet activities at the workplace (security), their personal information and data are collected (trust), and they lose their "right to be let alone" (privacy) (Eloff et al., 2009). In the realm of IoPTS, however, managers are conflicted between setting up governance frameworks necessary to protect company's data while giving employees sufficient autonomy and privacy to ensure job satisfaction among their workers.

Despite concerns regarding security, trust, and privacy when using the Internet at the workplace, studies have found that many employees continue to use the companies' Internet access for personal purposes (Claybaugh & Nazareth, 2009). In the UK, the costs of wastage due to personal Internet usage have been estimated to be £38,000 per year for an organization and approximately £11.2 billion per year for the UK economy (Bloxx, 2008). A study by SurveilStar.com showed that 30% of the companies surveyed were losing more than a day's work per week from such cyber activities (SurveilStar.com, 2008). The CEO of Yahoo, Marissa Meyer, also rolled out a ban on telecommuting because it was feared that employees loaf when they are working from home, rendering Yahoo to lose its competitive advantage (Forbes, 2013). Although Meyer's ban was criticized by advocates of remote work, this move exemplifies the challenges faced by management in striking a balance between distraction and productivity as a result of IoPTS.

The ubiquity of cyberloafing can be explained by the following reasons. First, trust anchors have been introduced in IoPTS to manage users' digital identities and access control. These trust anchors enable transaction-based privacy protection, provider-independent access to transaction data, flexible third-party accountability, and user-friendly, end-to-end secure communication (Weber, Martucci, Ries, & Mühlhäuser, 2010). This allays several concerns among users regarding security, trust, and privacy. Employees then trust that personal information exchanged during work through cyberloafing would be kept within that encrypted network and not be released to their superiors.

Second, the boundaries regarding which activities count as cyberloafing and which ones count as actual work are becoming increasingly blurred. Nowadays, the use of personal devices at the workplace is, to an extent, sanctioned by the organization. It is not unusual in certain industries for employees to be contacted on their personal mobile number for work-related queries (e.g., within virtual teams) (Sarker & Wells, 2003). Fitbits and wellness apps are installed in personal devices as part of HR initiatives (Peppet, 2014), and a portion of employees even receive an ICT device paid for (including monthly bills) by the company to increase their levels of connectedness to job matters (Sheridan, 2012).

These boundaries become even blurrier when employees use their personal social media accounts for work purposes. For instance, companies create Facebook accounts to reach out to a wider audience, generate sales, and portray their desired image to the online community (Shih, 2010). There are even individual positions and entire teams dedicated to managing organizations' social media platforms. Do these behaviors fall under cyberloafing?

Are employees usurping companies' resources when they are using their individual Facebook accounts to promote the company's social media posts during working hours? Also, when the company provides an ICT device to increase an individual's connectedness to work matters during his or her personal time, is it acceptable to install personal apps and check personal emails on that device?

IoPTS innovations exist to combat cyberloafing. For example, there are apps that utilize the "Pomodoro technique." The "Pomodoro technique" is a time management strategy where one uses a timer to break his or her work into focused time blocks (usually 25 minutes) separated by a 5-minute break. After four consecutive working time blocks, individuals take a longer break, around 15 or 20 minutes (Kennedy, 2017). This can help cyberloafing employees focus on work matters for specific periods of time, while scheduling their cyberloafing activities as part of an official break. This is especially relevant to employees who view cyberloafing not as a deviant work behavior, but as a well-deserved mental break after periods of high concentration on work tasks (Lim & Chen, 2009).

"Slack" is another example of an innovation that motivates employees to work together on a common platform and keep focused on their project goals. "Slack" integrates apps, services, and resources for employees to collaborate with the fun factor of using apps during cyberloafing but with clearly work-related objectives (Slack, n.d.). Apps and programs that utilize the "Scrum" technique, an incremental agile software development framework for managing product development (Scrum Alliance, n.d.), are also possible solutions to combat cyberloafing and distraction at work. In the "Scrum" system, teams have a set amount of time—a sprint—to complete their work. Team members also meet daily to assess their progress (Scrum Alliance, n.d.). With clear deadlines and work objectives, and also preset times for concentration and breaks, organizations can deal with cyberloafing in the complexities of an IoPTS workplace. However, is the answer to the result of IoPTS—cyberloafing—*more* IoPTS?

This chapter examines cyberloafing from an organizational behavior perspective and offers management alternative possibilities in dealing with cyberloafing. Instead of having restrictive policies, blocking certain websites, or employing more IoPTS to manage cyberloafing, we explore the possibility of allowing cyberloafing to happen without active intervention as we focus on the possible positive effects cyberloafing has on productivity and the workplace—organizational citizenship behavior (OCB).

Cyberloafing and OCB

Although many scholarly works identify cyberloafing as a form of workplace deviance, an increasing amount of attention is focused on the positive effects of cyberloafing. For example, Lim and Chen (2009) found that cyberloafing can serve as a form of rest-and-recovery mechanism. Taking time off work to browse websites for personal purposes helps to refresh and revitalize employees' minds, which in turn may help to increase productivity. Cyberloafing was akin to taking a traditional physical break from work such as walking to the pantry to get coffee or simply taking a walk outside. In a similar vein, Dijksterhuis, Bos, Nordgren, and van Baaren (2006) found that distractions or breaks in attention enable the unconscious mind to handle large amounts of information and to integrate them into an evaluative summary judgment, unavailable in conscious deliberation.

Given the prevalence of cyberloafing at the workplace, it would be interesting to examine if such behavior can bring benefits to organizations. We ground our research in theories of neutralization and compensatory behavior to explore the link between cyberloafing and positive outcomes like OCB.

At the organizational level, organizational justice has been found to be an antecedent of cyberloafing; lower organizational justice has a significant impact on cyberloafing (Blau, Yang, & Ward-Cook, 2006; Lim, 2002). Employees who received unfair treatment attempted to "pay back" by using company resources (i.e. the Internet and man hours) for personal purposes instead of for work. Such mechanisms are prevalent in works relating to workplace deviance, or counterproductive work behavior (CWB) as well, where employees vent their frustrations with the injustice at the workplace by engaging in deviant acts (Fox, Spector, & Miles, 2001; Jones, 2009).

At the individual level, other than addiction to the Internet (Young, 1998, 2004), cyberloafing behavior has been explained by neutralization techniques engaged in by workers to justify their counterproductive work behavior. Lim (2002) used the metaphor of the ledger, an extension of neutralization theory, to explain how individuals rationalize their deviant actions to the point where such behaviors now become acceptable in their minds. Neutralization occurs when guilt resulting from committing delinquent acts is reduced through a form of a priori rationalization (Sykes & Matza, 1957). There are different types of neutralization, which include denial of harm (minimization), denial of victim, denial of responsibility, and appeal to norms (normalization) (Mitchell and Dodder, 1983). In the context of this study, we will be examining two types of neutralization, in particular, minimization and normalization. These two neutralization techniques were chosen because they have been shown in past research to have a significant impact on cyberloafing (Lim & Teo, 2006).

Although it appears that CWB has only detrimental effects on the company where workers purposefully become less productive and where the organization's resources are misused or misappropriated, several scholars have noted the parallel between workplace deviance and OCB (Miles, Borman, Spector, & Fox, 2002). OCB refers to the act of engaging in behaviors that are beyond one's job scope and role requirements (Organ, 1988). OCB can be divided into two categories: OCB-individual (OCB-I) and OCB-organization (OCB-O). OCB-I refers to helping behavior displayed to other individuals within the company. Examples include passing information to fellow colleagues or going out of one's way to help a coworker (Moorman & Blakely, 1995). OCB-O refers to acts of OCB aimed toward the organization. Examples include preserving organizational resources and adhering to the organization's norms and rules.

Studies have generally found that CWB is negatively related to OCB (Bukhari & Ali, 2009). This is because CWB is generally associated with negative affect, whereas OCB is related to positive affect (Spector & Fox, 2002). Employees engage in counterproductive work behavior, when they are experiencing negative affect, to alleviate that negative mood or emotion; OCB is typically observed as an extension of an individual's positive affect, who then goes out of his or her way to help fellow colleagues.

However, recent research suggests that OCB can result from negative affect as well. Scholars propose that individuals who are experiencing negative affect are generally motivated to alleviate this mood state. OCB helps these individuals alleviate negative affect so they feel more positive about themselves when helping others (Cialdini & Fultz, 1990). Ilies, Fultmer, Spitzmuller, and Johnson (2009) found that individuals with negative affect tend to perform OCB to assuage that negative emotion. Thus, CWB like cyberloafing is related to OCB through the following mechanism: Individuals who engage in CWB tend to be in a negative mood state. Simultaneously, to relieve themselves from that negative affect, they perform OCB to feel better. Therefore, although we concur that CWB may not necessarily *lead* to OCB, the common factor of negative affect that individuals may experience means that individuals who cyberloaf are also more likely to simultaneously engage in OCB.

Another mechanism through which CWB is related to OCB is guilt. This is because engaging in CWB, like cyberloafing, can invoke guilt, and in turn, individuals may seek to alleviate this guilt by engaging in OCB (Perrewé & Zellars, 1999). Because of the guilt individuals feel after cyberloafing at work, they may be compelled to remedy the situation by engaging in extra-role behaviors such as OCB. However, such a proposition holds when employees believe that their act of deviance was unjustified. For example, when workers are unable to find reasons for displaying counterproductive work behavior, such as wasting time on non–work-related websites even though organizational justice is high, they tend to compensate for such unjustified behavior by performing OCB, such as assisting their coworkers at work (Spector & Fox, 2010). However, when cyberloafers are able to justify their behaviors through neutralization techniques and when this feeling of guilt is no longer present, the literature suggests that they will be less likely to engage in OCB (Spector & Fox, 2010).

Extending the works on neutralization and cyberloafing, we propose that employees engage in cognitive compensatory techniques such as minimization of harm and normalization to justify this deviant behavior (Fointiat, 1998).When guilt associated with cyberloafing is mitigated or alleviated, individuals who cyberloaf will be less compelled to engage in organizational citizenship behaviors to make up for their cyberloafing activities. Thus, we put forth the following hypotheses:

H1: Cyberloafing is positively related to OCB-I and OCB-O.
H2a: Neutralization techniques (minimization and normalization) moderate the relationship between cyberloafing and OCB-I such that the relationship becomes weaker when neutralization is high.
H2b: Neutralization techniques (minimization and normalization) moderate the relationship between cyberloafing and OCB-O such that the relationship becomes weaker when neutralization is high.

Before proceeding to examine the relationships between cyberloafing and OCB, we will first expand the construct definition of cyberloafing by analyzing the various forms or categories of cyberloafing in the context of smart phones and IoPTS. The traditional definition of cyberloafing referring to the "act of employees using their companies' Internet access for personal purposes during work hours" is reconstructed to include Internet access that does not only belong to the company and to include personal ICT devices that are not owned by the company, by virtue of the fact that engagement in cyberloafing activities can now occur using personal handheld devices. For the purposes of this chapter, we redefine cyberloafing as the act of using ICT devices and Internet access for personal purposes during work hours.

Blanchard and Henle (2008) identified two major types of cyberloafing: minor cyberloafing (e.g., sending and receiving personal email at work) and serious cyberloafing (e.g., online gambling, surfing adult-oriented web sites). Although these scholars provided a useful framework, we adopted Blau et al.'s (2006) classification of cyberloafing instead, as it is more comprehensive. We tested Blau, Yang, and Ward-Cook's (2006) categorization of cyberloafing in Study 1 to see if cyberloafing activities in the context of IoPTS can be classified into the proposed categories: 1) browsing-related, 2) non–work-related email, and 3) interactive cyberloafing, extracting the different activities that fall under the definition of cyberloafing in the context of IoPTS. Using the results from Study 1, we tested the following research model, taking into account the different types of neutralization techniques (minimization and normalization) and OCB (OCB-individual and OCB-organization) Figure 5.1 depicts the relationships among variables in our study.

Method: Study 1

Sample and Instrument

We conducted Study 1 to test our proposed cyberloafing instrument and to examine if the items indeed fall into the three dimensions of interactive,

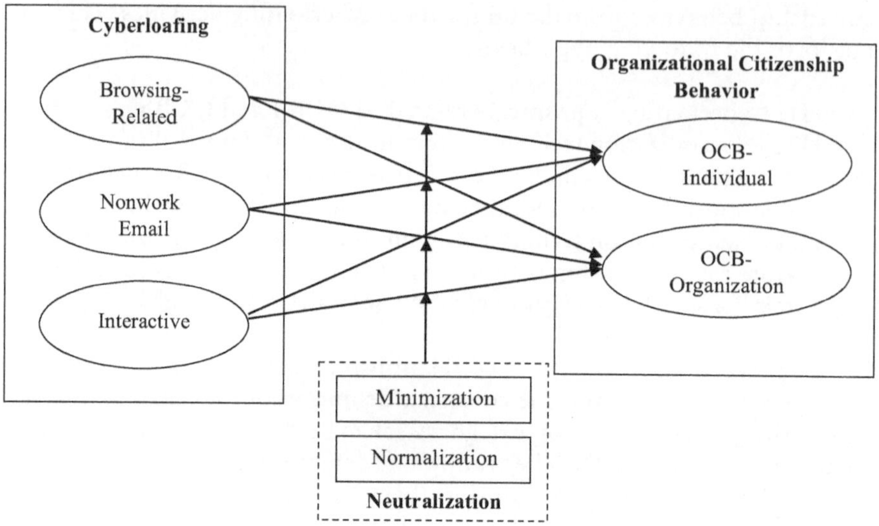

Figure 5.1 Research Model Illustrating the Relationships Between the Variables

email, and browsing-related cyberloafing as per our research model. To test this, we distributed survey questionnaires that comprised only the cyberloafing items. The survey questionnaires were administered to 114 undergraduates studying at a large tertiary institution in Singapore. Respondents were then given course credit for participation in the pilot study. Sixty-two percent of the subjects were female, and the mean age was 22 years (SD = 1.75).

A 20-item cyberloafing scale developed by Lim (2002) was used to assess cyberloafing. Items were scored from 1 (Never) to 6 (Constantly). When developing the scale, the context of IoPTS was taken into consideration such that these activities can be done not only using the institution's Internet access and computers, but also through personal ICT devices with Internet access. For instance, even in the case where social media sites like Facebook and YouTube are blocked by the organization's firewall systems, we still included the item to account for individuals who may be engaging in such activities using their personal ICT devices and their personal mobile data subscription, given that they are engaging in such cyberloafing activities during work hours in the office. The institution where this study was conducted is not known for blocking many external web sites other than those containing pornographic or explicit content. Because the item measuring respondents' tendency to visit such web sites previously had low base rates due to social desirability concerns (Lim, 2002; Lim & Teo, 2005), the item related to explicit content was excluded in this study.

Respondents were asked to put themselves in the situation where they were in a class or lecture and were told to respond to how often they engaged in cyberloafing while they were in class. As highlighted earlier, cyberloafing was not only confined to the context of the institution's Internet access and resources, but could also be carried out using individuals' personal ICT devices like smart phones and personal laptops. Although we note that the student sample is not entirely representative of the working population, this method of conducting the study was carried out for the following reason. We argue that the classroom setting, which requires students to pay attention and focus on academic work, is analogous to the work context, where employees are supposed to be paying attention to work rather than engaging in non–work-related activities during work hours. The university also provides encrypted Internet access to matriculated students, and similar concerns regarding security, trust, and privacy are prevalent among students as they are among employees who are given Internet access at work. Cyberloafing in class, therefore, has comparable similarities to cyberloafing at work.

Results: Factor Analysis

The initial cyberloafing instrument consisted of 20 items. We conducted factor analysis with Varimax rotation, and after removing items that loaded on more than one factor, we were left with 16 items, which loaded appropriately in line with Blau et al.'s (2006) categorization of cyberloafing into three dimensions: browsing-related, non–work email, and interactive cyberloafing. Items that had factor loadings of less than 0.4 were also removed from the instrument. The factor analysis results are as follows. Three items loaded on one factor (browsing-related), three items loaded on a second factor (email), and the rest loaded on a third factor (interactive).

These items have content validity as well, because they were cross-checked with Blau et al.'s (2006) initial definitions of the three dimensions, and the items had content similarity with the definitions. For example, the items "Browsing general news sites" and "Browsing sports-related web sites" loaded on the browsing-related factor. The items "Visiting social networking sites, e.g., Facebook, Twitter, and Instagram" and "Playing online games" loaded on the interactive factor and fit with Blau et al.'s (2006) categorization, as these activities involve communication, engagement, and participation from other individuals, rendering the term "interactive." The three items related to checking, sending, and receiving personal emails also corresponded to the email dimension of cyberloafing. Through Study 1, we found the cyberloafing items and categories prevalent in today's context of IoPTS. The resultant 16-item cyberloafing measure was then used in Study 2 to test our hypotheses.

Method: Study 2

Sample

Survey questionnaires were completed by 120 working adults, who were full-time employees and worked for an organization with Internet access at the point of filling in the survey. Females comprised 59% of the respondents. The mean age was 28 years (SD = 9.83).

Measures

Cyberloafing

After conducting factor analysis for the initial instrument, a final 16-item cyberloafing scale was used for Study 2. The scale tapped on the different dimensions of cyberloafing mentioned earlier (interactive, email, and browsing-related). Sample items include "Browsing general news sites," "Visiting social networking sites (e.g., Facebook, Twitter, Instagram)," and "Sending non–work-related email."

It is important to examine not only the different types of cyberloafing activities that employees engage in, but also how frequently they do so. Subjects responded to how often they engaged in each activity in the list by indicating their response using a scale from 1 (Never) to 6 (Constantly). In view of the fact that some companies block specific web sites and that individuals may not have access to them, a "Not Applicable" (N/A) option was also included in the scale. Of course, this N/A option did not have to be used if employees cyberloafed using their personal ICT devices and where such web sites were not blocked by their subscription packages. The composite cyberloafing score was calculated by averaging all 16 items, taking into account the N/A responses such that scores are not necessarily lower when several sites are blocked. The internal reliabilities for browsing-related, non-work email, and interactive cyberloafing were .60, .92, and .87, respectively. Other than browsing-related, where the Cronbach's alpha was slightly lower due to the small number of items, the other internal reliabilities surpassed acceptable research standards.

Organizational Citizenship Behavior

Respondents reported the types of OCB they engaged in on a 14-item OCB scale (Moorman & Blakely, 1995). Seven of these items measured OCB-individual (OCB-I), which involves helping or displaying extra-role behavior to other employees or coworkers in the company. Items measuring OCB-I include "Helping others who have been absent," "Assisting the supervisor with his or her work when not asked," and "Going out of the way to help new employees." The other seven items measured OCB-organization (OCB-O), which refers to extra-role behaviors that benefit the organization. Example items are "Giving advance notice when unable to come to work," "Conserving and protecting organizational property," and "Taking undeserved work breaks (reverse coded)."

Respondents indicated the frequency of engaging in such acts by using a scale from 1 (Never) to 6 (Every time). By having an even-numbered scale, we minimize response bias, as we eliminated the middle point of "Sometimes." To this end, respondents were compelled to take a stand on whether they tended to engage in such acts frequently or if they did so occasionally. The Cronbach's alpha for OCB-I was .82, whereas that for OCB-O was .61. One reason for the slightly low figure for OCB-O could be attributed to the fact that three out of seven items in the scale had to be reverse-coded, which may affect how subjects responded to the scale. Nonetheless, because the OCB-O scale adopted for this study is widely used and has been previously validated, we proceeded to retain the OCB-O scale in its entirety.

Although instances of cyberloafing and OCB were self-reported, which may lead to method variance, a study by Kelloway, Loughlin, Barling, and Nault (2002) found that such method variance for measures of CWB and OCB indicated that the presence of such an influence does not compromise the substantive interpretation of these scales. Besides, such measures are best provided by the employee or the individual because supervisors' perceptions of cyberloafing and OCB may not be accurate, especially when these behaviors tend to be covert in nature. Although we acknowledge the possibility of method variance in our measures, due to the fact that these two constructs have been found to be distinct from each other and that employees themselves are the best sources of information for behaviors that they engage in covertly, we argue that there is scientific support to our methodology (Kelloway et al., 2002).

Neutralization

To measure neutralization, we included scales on minimization (denial of harm) and normalization (appealing to norms, i.e., "everyone else is doing it"). Logically, these two neutralization techniques are most prominent in the context of cyberloafing because, on one hand, harm is done to the company in terms of productivity costs. On the other hand, as studies have previously shown, cyberloafing is perceived to be a common and normal thing to do in organizations. Other forms of neutralization are not relevant in this context, because it is not possible to deny responsibility, for instance, as employees engage in such acts voluntarily. They are not instructed to do so by their superiors, and there is also no tangible "victim" in the case of cyberloafing—different from contexts of stealing from someone else or hurting someone physically.

Minimization

The scale used by Aquino and Becker (2005) for their study on neutralization in lying behavior was adapted for this study. Four items measured minimization, which included "It is a harmless act that will not hurt any other party" and "Such activities do not cause anyone harm." The inter-item reliability score was .82.

Normalization

Normalization items were also adapted from Aquino and Becker's (2005) scale. Six items measured normalization, including "I was following a standard practice/norm in the company" and "Other people engage in such activities all the time." The inter-item reliability score was .82.

Results

Table 5.1 shows the means, standard deviations, and correlations of the measured constructs, including their respective internal reliabilities. Cronbach's alphas exceeded acceptable research standards, which renders more confidence in our findings.

Regression analyses were conducted to test for the main effects of the different types of cyberloafing on OCB-I and OCB-O. Age, gender, and income were controlled for in these regressions. This is in line with previous research, which found these factors to affect the extent of cyberloafing. For example, Lim and Chen (2009) found that men were more likely to cyberloaf than women, and Ugrin, Pearson and Odom (2007) found that younger individuals were more prone to cyberloaf. Although income was not found to have an impact on empirical factors according to the study by Akman and Mishra (2010), research findings that employees tend to cyberloaf more when they feel overworked and underpaid (Lim & Teo, 2005) may result in individual income being a confounding factor. As such, we controlled for income as well. Table 5.2 shows our results for Hypothesis 1.

Regression analyses suggest that other than the positive association between nonwork email and OCB-O ($\beta = .239$, $p < .05$), none of the other relationships in Hypothesis 1 were supported. To test for interaction effects as posited in Hypothesis 2, the relevant variables were centered and hierarchical linear regressions were conducted. Control variables were added in the first step, the independent variables were added in the second step, the moderator variables were added in the third step, and the product term of the relevant centered variables were added in the fourth and final step. Table 5.2 shows the results from the moderated regression analyses. From these regression analyses, six interaction effects were significant.

None of the interaction effects was in the direction predicted. Instead, under conditions of high cyberloafing activity, individuals who engaged in more neutralization techniques (minimization and normalization) also engaged in more OCB.

Discussion and Implications for Management

In the realm of IoPTS, despite concerns on security, trust, and privacy, cyberloafing seems to continue to be prevalent in today's organizations. In particular, cyberloafing activities are categorized under browsing-related,

Table 5.1 Means, Standard Deviations, and Correlations

	Variables	*Mean*	*SD*	*1*	*2*	*3*	*4*	*5*	*6*	*7*	*8*	*9*	*10*
1	**Age**	27.8	9.83										
2	**Gender**	1.59	0.49	–.27**									
3	**Income**	3.52	1.57	.12	–.04								
4	**Browsing-Related**	1.63	1.06	–.01	–.24*	.02	(.60)						
5	**Nonwork Email**	2.82	1.45	–.21*	.17	.09	.36*	(.92)					
6	**Interactive**	1.32	1.00	–.31**	.15	–.20*	.47**	.50**	(.87)				
7	**Minimization**	3.43	0.86	–.18*	.12	–.06	.20*	.46**	.33**	(.82)			
8	**Normalization**	3.19	0.86	–.17	.04	–.03	.20*	.17	.20*	.51**	(.82)		
9	**OCB-I**	3.68	0.80	.17	–.04	.22*	–.01	.01	.00	.05	.18*	(.82)	
10	**OCB-O**	4.00	0.64	.19*	.03	.07	.00	.08	–.15	–.12	–.05	.25**	(.61)

Figures in parentheses denote internal reliabilities.

Table 5.2 Regression Analyses of Cyberloafing and OCB

Variables	*OCB-Individual*		*OCB-Organization*	
	β *Step 1*	*β* *Step 2*	*β* *Step 1*	*β* *Step 2*
Age	.142	.160	.202*	.176
Gender	.053	.034	.099	.122
Income	.205*	.217*	.038	–.036
Browsing-Related		–.047		.090
Nonwork Email		.000		.239*
Interactive		.081		–.313*
R^2	.066	.070	.043	.106
ΔR^2		.004		.063*

*p < .05.

Moderated regression analyses of cyberloafing, neutralization, and OCB

Variables	*OCB-Individual*			*OCB-Organization*		
	β *Step 1*	*β* *Step 2*	*β* *Step 3*	*β* *Step 1*	*β* *Step 2*	*β* *Step 3*
Age	.106	.158	.140	.222*	.192*	.163
Gender	.061	.042	.120	.093	.121	.129
Income	.198*	.208*	.215**	.045	–.044	–.052
Browsing-Related		–.080	–.040		.083	.083
Nonwork Email		.019	.094		.327**	.388
Interactive		.062	.013		–.311**	–.295
Minimization		–.063	–.080		–.222*	.227
Normalization		.269**	.210*		.090	.066
Browse × Mini			–.343*			–.287*
Browse × Norm			.433**			.383**
Email × Mini			.063			.067
Email × Norm			.196			.294*
Interactive × Mini			–.117			.197
Interactive × Norm			.048			–.337*
R^2	.054	.114	.255	.051	.143	.238
ΔR^2		.060	.051**		.091*	.096*

**Correlation is significant at the 0.01 level.
*Correlation is significant at the 0.05 level.

nonwork email, and interactive cyberloafing. With the ubiquity of personal ICT devices like smart phones with personal mobile data subscriptions, employees now find even more opportunities to engage in cyberloafing activities at work. This phenomenon, however, is not something that can be easily curbed in organizations. Marissa Meyer's ban on telecommuting was seen as an unfavorable move by economic critics (Time, 2014), and having rules controlling employees' behavior is an unsuccessful way of retaining talent, encouraging the best employees to quit (Bradberry, 2016). This chapter thus focuses on how we can better manage cyberloafing behavior by paying attention to the possible positive effects of cyberloafing (i.e., OCB).

In Study 2, Hypothesis 1 was partially supported. Nonwork email was positively associated with OCB-O. Individuals who used the company's resources for personal emails tended to perform extra-role behavior for the organization. The other posited relationships, however, were not supported. A plausible explanation for this is that personal email is clearly not related to work. Employees thus feel guilty and compensate by engaging in OCB.

For the other cyberloafing activities, less guilt could be involved. One could argue, for instance, that browsing and interactive cyberloafing is related to work, as one can browse the Internet for work-related research and information, and one could engage in social media to help market the company's products to a wider audience. As such, individuals who check and send personal emails during work hours may feel more compelled to compensate the organization for their loafing behavior, compared to those who engage in browsing and interactive cyberloafing activities.

It is interesting to note in this study that there was only one negative relationship between cyberloafing and OCB that was statistically significant, namely that between interactive cyberloafing and OCB-I. The other relationships, such as browsing-related and OCB-I and OCB-O, email and OCB-I, and interactive and OCB-O, were not negative. This is contrary to previous research done on CWB, where there is usually a moderately negative relationship between the two constructs. One reason for this is that cyberloafing may bring about more positive outcomes to the organization compared to other forms of CWB such as losing one's temper at work or property theft.

Another noteworthy finding is that instead of OCB decreasing with higher neutralization, the interaction effect was in the opposite direction as per our initial prediction. The higher the neutralization, the more the employees who cyberloafed tended to engage in OCB. We predicted that neutralization techniques will moderate the relationships between cyberloafing and OCB such that the positive relationships will be weaker when neutralization is high than when it is low. This is because neutralization techniques—such as denial of harm to the company or appeal to norms—represent a *cognitive* compensatory technique, whereas OCB is a *behavioral* compensatory technique. We predicted that individuals who cyberloaf will engage in less behavioral compensation when they engage in cognitive compensation and rationalize their actions.

However, our findings suggested that the positive relationships become stronger when neutralization is high. Cognitive compensatory behaviors alone do not appear to sufficiently reduce the dissonance from voluntarily reducing one's productivity by using the organization's resources for non–work-related purposes. Our findings suggested that individuals engaged in both cognitive neutralization techniques and behavioral compensatory acts, in the form of OCB, to justify their cyberloafing behaviors. It appears that *both* cognitive and behavioral manifestations of compensatory techniques operate in tandem in our context. A plausible explanation is that individuals cannot distinguish one type of compensatory technique from the other, and thus tend to engage in both to make amends for their deviant behavior of cyberloafing at work.

So what implications does our work have on managing cyberloafing with the complexities of IoPTS? The preliminary answer seems to be let market forces rule. Employees are typically agentic individuals who comprehend the detrimental effects cyberloafing can have on a company's bottom line. Although cyberloafing may be easier than before with the advent of IoPTS, employees' psychological processes seem to be developing in such a way that the negative effects of technology are offset by their own initiatives at bringing balance back to productivity in the workplace. OCB is increasingly included in performance appraisals in organizations, but employees who cyberloaf are not necessarily less productive according to standard key performance indicators. So let employees have their Fitbits. Let employees run errands on their smart phones. Their compensatory behavior would make up for their lapses of concentration at work.

Conclusion

To the best of our knowledge, this study presents an initial attempt at examining the relationship between cyberloafing and OCB in the context of IoPTS. In a time where technology and the Internet are so ingrained in our workplace, this piece of research studying the outcomes of cyberloafing is not only timely, but also crucial, in helping to further the understanding of underlying psychological processes individuals engage in when cyberloafing (Johns, 2006).

This research suggests that increasing levels of cyberloafing lead to increasing levels of OCB, and it therefore should be studied as a positive construct instead of being defined as a type of workplace deviance. Although Lim and colleagues (Lim, 2002; Lim Teo, & Loo, 2002; Lim & Teo, 2005) conceptualized cyberloafing in their initial efforts to examine this phenomenon, in her more recent work (e.g., Lim & Chen, 2009), Lim did find that cyberloafing can indeed lead to gain in work. In line with Lim and Chen (2009), our findings showed that cyberloafing is related to a positive organizational construct, and managers and practitioners may wish to consider this while formulating the organization's Internet policies. Although cyberloafing may lead to waste of resources and may appear to be unproductive, we argue that there may be a flip side to the coin, where it can be related to positive outcomes that benefit the firm as well.

Future directions for research include studying the different levels of cyberloafing (minor vs. major, short spurts over time vs. long durations), using different devices (firm's computers vs. personal handheld devices) and examining if the aforementioned relationships between cyberloafing, OCB, and neutralization techniques still hold. In addition, OCB in the context of IoPTS should be examined. Perhaps individuals compensate for their cyberloafing behavior in the IoPTS environment through more IoPTS innovations such as initiating discussions on "Slack" for a more productive work environment as we deal with the challenges of the Internet of People, Things and Services.

References

Akman, I., & Mishra, A. (2010). Gender, age and income differences in Internet usage among employees in organizations. *Computers in Human Behavior*, *26*, 482–490.

Anandarajan, M., & Simmers, C. A. (2005). Developing human capital through personal web usage in the workplace: Mapping employee perceptions. *Communications for the Association for Information Systems*, *15*, 776–791.

Aquino, K., & Becker, T. (2005). Lying in negotiations: How individual and situational factors influence the use of neutralization strategies. *Journal of Organizational Behavior*, *26*, 661–679.

Bequai, A. (1998). Employee abuses in cyberspace: Management's legal quagmire. *Computers & Security*, *17*, 667–670.

Bergen, L., Grimes, T., & Potter, D. (2005). How attention partitions itself during simultaneous message presentations. *Human Communications Research*, *31*, 311–336.

Blanchard, A. L., & Henle, C. A. (2008). Correlates of different forms of cyberloafing: The role of norms and external locus of control. *Computers in Human Behavior*, *24*, 1067–1084.

Blau, G., Yang, Y., & Ward-Cook, K. (2006). Testing a measure of cyberloafing. *Journal of Allied Health*, *35*, 9–17.

Bloxx. (2008). *Productivity, internet abuse, and how to improve one by eliminating the other*. Retrieved from www.bloxx.com/assets/downloads/bloxx_whitepaper_productivity.pdf

Bradberry, T. (2016, June 26). This is why good employees quit. *World Economic Forum*.

Bukhari, Z. U., & Ali, U. (2009). Relationship between organizational citizenship behavior and counterproductive work behavior in the geographical context of Pakistan. *International Journal of Business and Management*, *4*, 85–92.

Chory, R. M., Vela, L. E., & Avtgis, T. A. (2016). Organizational surveillance of computer-mediated workplace communication: Employee privacy concerns and responses. *Employee Responsibilities and Rights Journal*, *28*(1), 23–43.

Cialdini, R. B., & Fultz, J. (1990). Interpreting the negative mood-helping literature via 'mega'-analysis: A contrary view. *Psychological Bulletin*, *107*, 210–214.

Claybaugh, C. C., & Nazareth, D. L. (2009). *Measuring severity of internet abuse in the workplace: Creation of a Thurston scale*. AMCIS 2009 Proceedings, Paper 593. Retrieved from http://aisel.aisnet.org/amcis2009/593

Covert, A. (2014, February 19). Facebook buys WhatsApp for $19 billion. *CNNTEch*.

Dijksterhuis, A., Bos, M. W., Nordgren, L. F., & van Baaren, R. B. (2006). On making the right choice: The deliberation-without-attention effect. *Science*, *311*, 1005–1007.

Eloff, J. H. P., Eloff, M. M., Dlamini, M. T., & Zielinski, M. P. (2009). *Internet of people, things and services-the convergence of security, trust and privacy*. Proceedings of the Third International Workshop IoPTS, Brussels.

Fointiat, V. (1998). Rationalization in act and problematic behavior justification. *European Journal of Social Psychology, 28*, 471–474.

Forbes. (2013, February 25). Back to the stone age? New Yahoo CEO Marissa Meyer bans working from home.

Fox, S., Spector, P. E., & Miles, D. (2001). Counterproductive work behavior (CWB) in response to job stressors and organizational justice: Some mediator and moderator tests for autonomy and emotions. *Journal of Vocational Behavior, 59*, 291–309.

Greenfield, P. M. (2009). Technology and informal education: What is taught, and what is learned. *Science, 323*, 69–71.

Hembrooke, H., & Gay, G. (2003). The laptop and the lecture: The effects of multitasking in learning environments. *Journal of Computing in Higher Education, 15*, 46–64.

Ilies, R., Fultmer, I. S., Spitzmuller, M., & Johnson, M. D. (2009). Personality and citizenship behavior: The mediating role of job satisfaction. *Journal of Applied Psychology, 94*, 945–959.

Johns, G. (2006). The essential impact of context on organizational behavior. *Academy of Management Review, 31*, 386–408.

Jones, D. A. (2009). Getting even with one's supervisor and one's organization: Relationships among types of injustice, desires for revenge, and counterproductive work behaviors. *Journal of Organizational Behavior, 30*, 525–542.

Kahn, J. (2017, February 21). Facebook Messenger now lets you send money with TransferWise. *Bloomberg Technology*.

Kelloway, E. K., Loughlin, C., Barling, J., & Nault, A. (2002). Self-reported counterproductive work behaviors and organizational citizenship behaviors: Separate but related constructs. *International Journal of Selection and Assessment, 10*, 143–151.

Kennedy, S. (2017, March 16). The 12 best Pomodoro timer apps to boost your productivity. *Zapier*.

Lim, V. K. G. (2002). The IT way of loafing on the job: Cyberloafing, neutralizing and organizational justice. *Journal of Organizational Behavior, 23*, 675–694.

Lim, V. K. G., & Chen, D. J. Q. (2009). Cyberloafing at the workplace: Gain or drain at work? *Behavior and Information Technology, 31*(4), 343–353.

Lim, V. K. G., & Teo, T. S. H. (2005). Prevalence, perceived seriousness, justification and regulation of cyberloafing in Singapore: An exploratory study. *Information and Management, 42*, 1081–1093.

Lim, V. K. G., & Teo, T. S. H. (2006). Cyberloafing and organizational justice: The moderating role of neutralization technique. In M. Anandarajan, T. S. H. Teo, & C. A. Simmers (Eds.), *The Internet and Workplace Transformation* (pp. 241–258). Armonk, New York: M.E. Sharpe Inc.

Lim, V. K., Teo, T. S., & Loo, G. L. (2002). How do I loaf here? Let me count the ways. *Communications of the ACM, 45*(1), 66–70.

Miles, D. E., Borman, W. E., Spector, P. E., & Fox, S. (2002). Building an integrative model of extra role work behaviors: A comparison of counterproductive work behavior with organizational citizenship behavior. *International Journal of Selection and Assessment, 10*, 51–57.

Mitchell, J., & Dodder, R. A. (1983). Types of neutralization and types of delinquency. *Journal of Youth and Adolescence, 12*, 307–318.

Moorman, R. H., & Blakely, G. L. (1995). Individualism-collectivism as an individual difference predictor of organizational citizenship behavior. *Journal of Organizational Behavior, 16*, 127–142.

Organ, D. W. (1988). *Organizational citizenship behavior: The good soldier syndrome*. Lexington, MA: Lexington Books.

Peppet, S. R. (2014). Regulating the Internet of Things: First steps toward managing discrimination, privacy, security and consent. *Texas Law Review, 93*, 85–176.

Perrewé, P. L., & Zellars, K. L. (1999). An examination of attributions and emotions in the transactional approach to the organizational stress process. *Journal of Organizational Behavior, 20*, 739–752.

Robinson, S., & Bennett, R. (1995). A typology of deviant workplace behaviors: A multi-dimensional scaling study. *Academy of Management Journal, 38*, 555–572.

Roman, R., Najera, P., & Lopez, J. (2011). Securing the Internet of Things. *Computer, 44*, 51–58.

Sarker, S., & Wells, J. D. (2003). Understanding mobile handheld device use and adoption. *Communications of the ACM, 46*(12), 35–40.

Scrum Alliance. (n.d.). *What is scrum?* Retrieved from www.scrumalliance.org/why-scrum

Sheridan, K. (2012). *The virtual manager: Cutting-edge solutions for hiring, managing, motivating, and engaging mobile employees*. New York: Career Press.

Shih, C. (2010). *The Facebook era: Tapping online social networks to market, sell, and innovate*. New York: Pearson Education.

Slack. (n.d.). *Slack: Where work happens*. Retrieved from https://slack.com/

Spector, P. E., & Fox, S. (2002). An emotion-centered model of voluntary work behavior: Some parallels between counterproductive work behavior and organizational citizenship behavior. *Human Resource Management Review, 12*, 269–292.

Spector, P. E., & Fox, S. (2010). Theorizing about the deviant citizen: An attributional explanation of the interplay of organizational citizenship and counterproductive work behavior. *Human Resource Management Review, 20*, 132–143.

The Straits Times. (2016, June 8). Singapore public servants' computers to have no internet access from May next year. Retrieved from www.straitstimes.com/singapore/singapore-public-servants-computers-to-have-no-internet-access-from-may-next-year

Sultan, F., Rohm, A. J., & Gao, T. T. (2009). Factors influencing consumer acceptance of mobile marketing: A two-country study of youth markets. *Journal of Interactive Marketing, 23*(4), 308–320.

SurveilStar.com. (2008). *Prevent e-mail and internet abuses with SurveilStar*. Retrieved from www.surveilstar.com/anti-internet-email-abuse-with-monitoring-software.html

Sykes, G. M., & Matza, D. (1957). Techniques of neutralization: A theory of delinquency. *American Journal of Sociology, 22*, 664–670.

Time. (2014, June 5). Telecommuting: What Marissa Mayer got right: And wrong. Retrieved from http://time.com/money/2791618/telecommuting-what-marissa-mayer-got-right-and-wrong/

Ugrin, J. C., Pearson, J. M., & Odom, M. D. (2007). Profiling cyber-slackers in the workplace: Demographic, cultural, and workplace factors. *Journal of Internet Commerce, 6*, 75–90.

Weber, S. G., Martucci, L. A., Ries, S., & Mühlhäuser, M. (2010). *Towards trustworthy identity and access management for the future internet*. Paper presented at the 4th International Workshop on Trustworthy Internet of People, Things & Services

(IoPTS) Tokyo, Japan. Retrieved from https://pdfs.semanticscholar.org/85a5/3bf1b6a2f47b0ad4b9473da80d12ea700dc0.pdf

Whatsapp. (n.d.). *Whatsapp FAQ: How do I choose not to share my account information with Facebook?* Retrieved from https://faq.whatsapp.com/general/26000016

Yellowlees, P. M., & Marks, S. (2007). Problematic internet use or internet addiction? *Computers in Human Behavior*, *23*, 1447–1453.

Young, K. S. (1998). Internet addiction: The emergence of a new clinical disorder. *CyberPsychology and Behavior*, *1*, 237–244.

Young, K. S. (2004). Internet addiction: A new clinical phenomenon and its consequences. *American Behavioral Scientist*, *48*, 402–415.

6 Social Media, Data Privacy, and the Internet of People, Things and Services in the Workplace

A Legal and Organizational Perspective

Kimberly W. O'Connor and Gordon B. Schmidt

Introduction

This rise of social media is part of the general trend of a world where people, things, and services are connected through the Internet at all times, an internetworking system known as the Internet of People, Things and Services (IoPTS) (Eloff, Eloff, Dlamini, & Zielinski, 2009). Currently, there are 2.46 billion social media users worldwide. By 2021, it is estimated that the number will grow to over 3 billion. Statisticians further predict that there is no end in sight to the increasing number of social media users due to the ease of access to social media through smartphones and mobile applications ("apps") (Statista, 2016).

Massive amounts of data are generated by social media users daily (Conner, n.d.). For example, Facebook reports that 350 million images are uploaded on its site every 24 hours (Smith, 2016). Twitter reports that people or brands send more than 340 million tweets per day (Conner, n.d.). Each image, status update, or tweet carries with it metadata, such as the user's location or time of day, among other pieces of information (Vidsys, 2017). This metadata translates into real-time intelligence, which may be collected and used by organizations, law enforcement, or the government, among others (Vidsys, 2017; Department of Justice, 2013).

Recent statistics indicate that workers, as well as employers, are among those using social media in both positive and negative ways. For example, digital platforms can be used by employers for recruitment and marketing, to enhance worker productivity, and to foster industry connectivity, along with many other beneficial uses. At the same time, employers may be concerned that employees are using social media for non–work-related purposes or that they are posting content that may reflect poorly on the organization (Olmstead, Lampe, & Ellison, 2016). Likewise, because of the ease of connectivity, employees may compromise an organization's proprietary information when they log on to their work accounts through an unsecured network. These concerns, and many others, have led a number of organizations to enact workplace social media policies to govern employees (O'Connor, Schmidt, & Drouin, 2016).

Having a social media policy in place, however, may not be sufficient to change worker behavior, and potential legal issues may arise. For example, court cases involving issues such as worker protections, antidiscrimination laws, and free speech rights, as well as the National Labor Relations Act (NLRA) have occurred when employees have been disciplined for their social media behaviors (Schmidt & O'Connor, 2015; O'Connor et al., 2016). Cases involving invasion of privacy, as well as violations of state and federal electronic communications laws, have also occurred when confidential employee information has been shared inadvertently by an organization.

With regard to data privacy, we currently live in an environment of pervasive computing (Kang & Cuff, 2005), with individuals connected to the Internet actively and passively through various objects that communicate information. Pervasive computing applies not to just cell phones or computers, but also to everyday devices that are embedded with microprocessors (Rouse, 2016). These devices include objects such as appliances, GPS-enabled devices, Apple Watches, fitness devices, and the like. The information that is constantly generated and gathered by these devices presents legal issues related to the ownership of the devices and/or the ownership of the information produced (Ackerman & Mainwaring, 2005). However, solid infrastructure regarding data security and legality of content is often several steps behind the implementation of the technology itself (Eloff et al., 2009). This is problematic when employers use this information to make employment-related decisions, as relatively few legal protections exist to protect workers.

This issue is only more complicated by smart devices, which are so central to the IoPTS and are increasingly common in the workplace. Smart devices may reveal significant information about employees' behavior to an organization, whether it is intentional or not. For example, GPS-enabled devices may inform employers that employees are not at a work location when they are supposed to be. Timestamps on social media posts may reveal that workers are "surfing the Net" when they should be working on organizational tasks (also known as "time theft"). Information from wellness program devices such as Fitbits may reveal medical issues to an organization that an employee may not even be aware of. All of these examples present situations where employers may be gathering data from smart devices, which in turn could be used to make workplace decisions. This becomes especially problematic when the information gained relates to classes of workers that are protected by law, such as those who are protected by Title VII antidiscrimination laws, the Americans with Disabilities Act (ADA), or the Genetic Information Nondisclosure Act (GINA), among others.

In this chapter, we will explore the transformative effect that social media and workplace data privacy concerns have had with regard to the Internet of People, Things and Services. We will focus on the impact that social media use and the IoPTS have had on certain aspects of the life cycle of employment, such as selection and termination. We will also examine data privacy protections for workers, as well as discuss the legal issues that organizations may face when monitoring employees or providing them with employer-owned devices. Finally, we conclude with suggestions about relevant organizational policy implementation and needed future research.

Use of Social Media and Data-Driven Analytics in Selection: Legal Issues and Cases

Employers have an interest in hiring the best candidates, in large part so that their companies are best represented to the public. Because of this, collecting information about a candidate via social media has become one of the primary tools of the employment screening process (Schmidt & O'Connor, 2016). In a 2015 study by Jobvite, 96% of recruiters reported that they have used social media websites to screen applicants, with Facebook, LinkedIn, and Twitter being recruiters' social media of choice. Sixty-nine percent of employers say they have declined an applicant based on the information they have found on social media (Reppler, 2011).

Employers also report looking beyond profile pages when screening candidates. They may read applicants' status updates, look at their pictures, review their friends list, and see what pages they have liked. Some of this information might be intentionally posted by the user, whereas some might be posted inadvertently due to the connectivity of the devices used. For example, in 2011 it was discovered that sexual activity tracked by Fitbit users actually showed up in Google search results. This was due to the fact that Fitbit's tracker and online profile settings were defaulted to public, and users were recording their sexual activity as calorie-burning exercise. Unless users affirmatively deactivated the public setting, anyone (including employers) could find their recorded sexual activity in search engine results. Fitbit has since changed its setting to avoid this particular issue, but this case illustrates that IoPTS devices may reveal information users are not aware of and would prefer not be revealed (Rao, 2011).

Data-driven analytics is a new human resources (HR) phenomenon where digitally stored data is used to make personnel decisions. Data can be gathered from just about anything that is stored digitally, from emails, to Internet searches and social media searches, to wearable devices (Peck, 2013; Ahmed, 2016). One of the many advantages of data-driven analytics is "predictive analysis," meaning that employers can predict which candidates will be top performers in a company and which employees are most at risk for leaving (Biro, 2017). There are a number of processes and/or algorithms that organizations can employ to select (or deselect) candidates, and there are currently very few regulations regarding these methods.

In 2016, the Equal Opportunity Employment Commission (EEOC) put forth a five-year Strategic Enforcement Plan that, in part, focuses on the use of data-driven selection analytics for hiring and firing (EEOC, n.d.). The EEOC is concerned that discriminatory practices may be linked to data-driven analytics because the very foundation of this practice is to differentiate between various types of people and make distinctions that separate "desirable" people from "undesirable" people for HR purposes (Gumbus & Grodzinski, 2016). Employers should expect the EEOC to employ a heightened level of scrutiny regarding future complaints about such practices. Until then, there exists very little oversight. Thus, the potential for an organization to violate existing Title VII antidiscrimination laws by deselecting a candidate due to race, religion, gender, national origin, or any other type of protected class characteristic certainly exists.

Although cases of discrimination in selection are difficult to prove because most applicants do not know that they have been deselected in this manner, there are a handful of documented instances of employer discrimination through social media use and/or Internet searches of candidates. One Title VII selection case that dealt with online information being used in selection was *Gaskell v. University of Kentucky* (2010). In *Gaskell*, the leading candidate for the observatory director position at the University of Kentucky was deselected due to his religious beliefs. The university's search committee used the Internet to search Gaskell's name and found an article that he had published called, "Modern Astronomy, the Bible and Creation," which argued that theories of evolution could be reconciled with Christian beliefs about creation. After discovering the article, the university subsequently hired a less qualified candidate. Gaskell sued, and the case was settled after an internal email surfaced where a search committee member wrote, "Clearly this man is complex and likely fascinating to talk with, but potentially evangelical. If we hire him, we should expect similar content to be posted on or directly linked from the department web site." Passing Gaskell over due to his religious beliefs is Title VII discrimination. The University of Kentucky settled the case with Gaskell for $125,000 (*Gaskell*, 2010). As this case illustrates, employers need to be aware that they are subjecting themselves to potential liability when using the Internet as a selection tool (Delarosa, 2014).

Social Media Policies Governing Selection

In an effort to avoid discrimination in selection, employers may want to consider implementing a policy governing the methods they use during selection. Such a policy should address which social media sites the employer wants to be searched, how the information that is gleaned is assessed, which personnel are placed in charge of the search, and how the gathered data are stored by the organization, among other considerations. Organizations will likely also want to specify what information should be examined and which should be ignored due to legal concerns, relevance, or even just lack of predictivity. Policies can help prevent employer liability by establishing a well-thought-out plan that prevents the utilization of arbitrary selection methods (Schmidt & O'Connor, 2016).

According to a recent survey, a reported 80% of companies currently have a social media policy in place that addresses their workers' personal social media use (Rubenstein, 2014). The wording of workplace social media policies, however, varies greatly between organizations. For example, some employers have strict social media policies, which may even include language that requires employees to post disclaimers that distance their personal opinions from that of their employers' (Lopez, 2014). On the other hand, some organizations encourage employees to freely post opinions and/or facts about their workplaces for recruiting and marketing purposes (Holtz, 2016).

Research by O'Connor et al. (2016) indicates that employees are often woefully underinformed as to the parameters of their employer's social media policy. Training workers on social media policies is crucial in order to avoid potential legal issues. Best practices for employers may likely involve educating the workforce early and often throughout the employees' career and using a variety of training methods to do so. Training methods may include a combination of face-to-face training, videos, or written and signed handbook policies, among others (O'Connor et al, 2016).

The National Labor Relations Board (NLRB) has also provided guidance on social media policy language for organizations. Most importantly, the language of a policy must not be overbroad and must not infringe upon employees' rights to communicate with one another about the terms and conditions of their employment (Schmidt & O'Connor, 2015). Unfortunately, there is little existing guidance for organizations with regard to the language of IoT-related policies, even though security breaches and privacy concerns are often more pronounced in IoPTS than in social media. This is due to the widespread nature of cyberattacks, which are projected to involve IoT 25% of the time by 2020 (Ashford, 2016). IoPTS workplace policies should therefore consider issues such as encryption, securing the data from smart devices, remote access and network protection, and privacy, among other considerations (Saha, 2017).

Disciplinary Action by Employers for Employees' Personal Social Media Use

Poorly trained employees may not only lack understanding of their workplace policies, but they also likely do not understand what legal protections may or may not apply to protect their personal social media use. A common misperception is that First Amendment protections mean that employees' personal expressions online are protected speech that is free from employer discipline. However, private-sector employees actually cannot rely on First Amendment protections because the government is not their employer, though their speech regarding working terms and conditions is generally protected under the NLRA (O'Connor et al., 2016; National Labor Relations Board, 1935). Public-sector employees, however, enjoy some First Amendment protection for the things they post, as long as it qualifies as a matter of "public concern," which is defined as matters "relating to any matter of political, social, or other concern to the community" (*Connick v. Meyers*, 1983; O'Connor & Schmidt, 2015).

Many legal cases involving employee discipline (across all professions) have been the result of the rapidly evolving social media phenomenon, with the term "Facebook Fired" being used by the popular media to describe such situations (Hidy & McDonald, 2013; O'Connor & Schmidt, 2015; Drouin, O'Connor, Schmidt, & Miller, 2015). In fact, a 2012 SHRM survey reported that 33% of companies had disciplined someone in the previous 12 months for a social media–related policy violation (Society for Human Resource Management, 2012). Problems typically arise for the employee or job candidate when unprofessional conduct or negative content is seen by recruiters, colleagues, supervisors, or the public (O'Connor et al., 2016).

This prevalence means there are several practical considerations for organizations dealing with social media discipline issues. Foremost among these are employee morale and public perception of discipline cases. Because social media consists of a highly connected, global network of people, special consideration must be given by organizations as to how these cases are handled. Poor handling of termination cases can result in a demoralized workforce and/or public backlash in the form of decreased sales or boycotts (Schmidt & O'Connor, 2015). It is therefore of paramount importance to the organization that in disciplinary cases, the employee's privacy is protected.

Protecting Employee Privacy

Data gleaned from social media may also be used to harass users or to violate their privacy. For example, personal information may be revealed through hacking into a social media account, or even hacking into full websites. One prominent example was when iCloud was hacked, and hundreds of private celebrity photos (some of which were nudes) were released online across a number of social media sites (Arthur, 2014). Intentionally violating someone's privacy is the primary objective behind the concept of "doxxing," or revealing the personal information of someone else on the Internet (McMahon, Bressler, & Bressler, 2016). Often doxxing is used to harass someone who takes a particular stance or position that upsets a group of Internet users.

Similar privacy issues stem from "citizen journalism," which is the collection, analysis, and dissemination of news information by everyday Internet users. Take the 2013 Reddit example, where social media users wrongly identified and accused an innocent man of the Boston Marathon bombing (Evans, 2015). Or, more recently, when Twitter users misidentified a University of Arkansas engineering professor as among the white nationalists at a rally in Charlottesville, Virginia (Pogue, 2017). At the same rally, Twitter users also *correctly* identified other attendees, which resulted in at least one protestor losing his job (Ortutay, 2017). Similarly, the prominent use of facial recognition technology on many social media sites complicates the legal landscape, as an individual may now be identified solely based upon a mathematical formula used for what someone looks like. But because the technology has not been perfected yet, misidentification of users is still a reality (Security Center, n.d.). Taken together, these examples and others certainly should give rise to individuals' privacy and security concerns when it comes to personal information or harassment via the Internet.

Employee privacy in the workplace is an increasingly critical issue for both employer and employee to understand, given the connectivity of the IoPTS world. Though the law recognizes that employees have a right to privacy, that right is often outweighed by the employers' right to protect the workplace and everyday business operations. There are, however, very specific and limited circumstances where an employee's privacy is protected by law. Specifically, an employee's personal information (Social Security number, home address, driver's license number, etc.), protected health information under the Health Insurance Portability and Accountability Act of 1966 (HIPAA), I-9 Immigration form, and disability information all must be kept confidential by the employer (Halpern, 2010).

This issue of employee privacy is especially important as it relates to employer-issued IoT devices that can collect, store, and exchange data (Peyton, 2015). With employer-provided IoT devices now widespread, employers are able to monitor nearly every aspect of an employee's workday, as well as their off-duty conduct. Although employees may feel that their privacy has been usurped by the abundance of information available to their employer through these devices, monitoring employee communications and locations is generally allowed under the law, with limited exception.

Worker privacy becomes an even more complex issue in the IoT world, especially if the employer chooses to take adverse legal action against an employee based upon information about the employee's activity or whereabouts outside of work hours (Ortutay, 2017). For example, an employee might claim that the employer disapproved of some protected or legal activity outside the workplace that the employer learned of through an IoT device or social media. Technological advances in IoPTS have made data more readily available and easier to collect now than ever before, with three out of four companies reporting that they engage in employee monitoring practices (Findlaw, n.d.). Monitoring employees, though, presents organizations with a variety of potential legal issues, as well as concerns for privacy, security, and trust (Eloff et al., 2009). A lot of these issues depend heavily on which device is used to gather the data and how the information is stored.

Tracking Employees: Employer-Owned Global Positioning System ("GPS") Devices

Employers have many reasons why they may want to track an employee's location. These reasons may be for customer service purposes, establishing delivery and drop-off times, safety concerns, efficiency, and performance quality, as well as ensuring compliance with company policies (Barron, n.d.). GPS devices use satellites to reveal an individual's or object's location in real time, and the information gathered is sent and stored in a server for employers to access when needed. Both public-sector and private-sector employers have been able to use GPS devices to track their employees' whereabouts for the last several years. The increased use of GPS devices has brought to the forefront the debate between the employer's right to monitor employees and the employees' right to privacy. Several cases have been litigated, which all establish the legality of GPS technology in the workplace, with only limited restrictions (Rosenburg, 2010).

For example, in *Cunningham v. New York Dept. of Labor* (2013), a state employee was accused of falsifying time records and other information related to work travel. As part of the employer's investigation, a GPS device was installed on the employee's personal vehicle. The employee was ultimately terminated after the GPS device revealed that the employee was indeed engaging in misconduct. He later sued and won his case, arguing that the evidence gathered from the GPS device should be excluded under the Constitution, which prohibits unreasonable searches under the Fourth Amendment.

The *Cunningham* case establishes the precedent for the right of a public-sector employer to install a GPS tracking device to monitor its employees during working hours without a warrant. However, the employee in *Cunningham* prevailed because the court concluded that the employer made no attempt to avoid tracking the employee outside business hours, which amounts to a violation of the Fourth Amendment (*Cunningham*, 2013). The law is different, though, with regard to nongovernmental workers. The Fourth Amendment does not apply to private-sector employers, though some states have made it illegal for private-sector employers to place a location-tracking device on an employee's vehicle without the employee's consent or knowledge. If these state law protections do exist, they only apply to situations in which the vehicle is owned by the employee. If the vehicle is company owned, GPS or other tracking devices are generally legal and permissible (Barron, n.d.).

Several cases to support private-sector employers who have GPS-installed devices on company vehicles have made their way through the court system. Employees have used the tort theories of "unreasonable intrusion" and "invasion of privacy," among others, to make their claims. However, courts have consistently held that private-sector employers may monitor the employee's location both during working and nonworking hours if the vehicle is employer owned. This is also the case when employees have not consented to the tracking device and/or have no knowledge that the tracking device is even there (Rosenburg, 2010).

Employees may well be concerned that employer location monitoring may supply employers with information that may be negatively used against them. However, GPS tracking should not be the sole disciplinary measure used by employers. GPS devices can malfunction, transmit incorrect information, or paint a picture that is factually erroneous. Employers should therefore develop a clear policy for monitoring and understand the law on monitoring as it applies to their workplace (Darcy, 2016). As stated, for public-sector employers, the location monitoring must be limited to working hours only. For private-sector employers, state law protections or tort claims regarding employee privacy may apply.

Worth noting here is that an organization may not necessarily set out to track an employee's movement, but such information may be available to the organization anyway. An emerging device that may fall into this category is the subdermal microchip. Though five states (California, Missouri, North Dakota, Oklahoma, and Wisconsin) have already enacted employee microchip protection laws in an effort to prohibit private-sector employers from requiring microchip implantation in their employees as a condition of employment, at least one U.S. employer has already offered this technology to their employees.

Three Square Market ("32M") is a Wisconsin-based company that recently made headlines when it asked their 85 employees to get microchipped. Though implantation of the microchip was voluntary on the employees' part, 41 of the 85 employees agreed to it. The microchip, which was implanted into employees' hands, allows them to log into computers, use copiers and snack machines, and open office doors (Esack, 2017). 32M says that the device will not be used to track employees' movements, and to do so would likely violate Wisconsin state law (Bacheldor, 2006; Robertson, 2017). But could other companies use a subdermal microchip for this purpose in the future? Absolutely. That is unless more microchip protection laws are enacted. The 32M case illustrates that concerns about the overall lack of security, trust, and privacy infrastructures are indeed legitimate, as employers' use of technological advances is outpacing legal protections for workers (Eloff et al., 2009).

Mobile Devices and Mobile Apps

A smartphone is a mobile phone that performs many functions of a traditional computer, typically having such features as a touch screen, Internet access, a high-resolution camera, information on the owner's exact location, and texting capabilities, among other functions. Smartphones are an increasingly common part of the technology-driven workplace, with many employers choosing to provide their workforce with these devices. Employer-owned smartphones are particularly common in industries such as healthcare and financial services, where employees need to be easily accessible to the employer. There is no question, though, that smartphones pose a security risk to the employer. Because of their mobility, it is likely that employees will use their devices on a variety of networks, some of which may be unsecured. Corporate data that are stored on mobile devices can quickly become out of the employer's control and can result in data breaches (McLellan, Sherer, and Fedeles, 2015).

Bring your own device (BYOD) policies are common, with one estimate being that half of all employers will have this policy in place by 2017 (McGlaun, 2013). BYOD policies mean that the employee purchases their own smartphone and uses it for both work and personal life. Employees therefore have freedom to choose their own devices, and employers save on technology costs. Some employers even offer to pay or partially pay for the employee's device and/or monthly data plan. It sounds like a win-win situation; however, BYOD policies present additional legal issues. For example, courts will generally consider the employee the owner of the device, but allow the employer to access and monitor the data. At this time there are no federal or state statutes that regulate BYOD policies or practices (McLellan et al., 2015). There is little regulation otherwise, aside from the employers' risk of invasion of privacy lawsuits or possible violation of the Computer Fraud and Abuse Act, which makes it illegal for an individual to access a protected computer without or exceeding authorization (Cooney, 2016). Often, employers will affirmatively obtain their employees' consent to monitoring as part of the cost-sharing BYOD arrangement. Some jurisdictions will allow employer access policies to be implemented through tacit consent and "pop-up" windows (McLellan et al., 2015).

Some employers also have the policy that they will remotely wipe or brick your BYOD device if you are terminated or resign. In *Rajaee v. Design Tech Homes* (2014; DLA Labor Dish, 2015), an employer remotely wiped the iPhone of a sales rep following his resignation. This deleted both his personal and work-related data and restored the phone to its original factory settings. The ex-employee sued, claiming that his employer caused damage to electronically stored information and intentionally accessed electronic information without his authorization, which he claimed violated federal law. However, the court rejected the employee's claims, holding that even though he lost all of his personal photos, videos, contacts, and passwords, it does not amount to a "loss" under the law (DLA Labor Dish, 2015). Employees should therefore back up any personal data when their employer participates in a BYOD program.

Some employers may require that certain mobile apps are downloaded onto employees' work devices. These apps may have "surreptitious monitoring capabilities." Surreptitious monitoring capabilities mean that some apps have particular capabilities of monitoring and tracking that are unbeknownst to the user. These can potentially be used by the employer to track the location of an employee or to intercept communications from an employee's smartphone. Whether or not surreptitious monitoring by the employer is illegal depends on the ownership status of the device, as well as the nature of the information being accessed (Cooney, 2016).

In May 2015, a woman sued her employer after she was terminated for deleting a GPS tracking app from an employer-owned smartphone. The employee allegedly deleted the app in an effort to maintain some measure of off-duty privacy, because her employer required that employees leave their smartphones turned on at all times (*Arias v. Intermex Wire Transfer*, 2015). Although the case settled out of court, the litigation still identifies several issues faced by employers wishing to track employees through company-issued, GPS-enabled smartphones. These issues include potential lawsuits for wrongful termination, invasion of privacy, unfair business practices, retaliation, and other claims (Austermuehle, 2016). This case is also important because it illustrates the issue of whether an employee should have a "reasonable expectation of privacy" with regard to movements outside of work, or whether the employer can establish a valid interest in knowing an off-duty employee's whereabouts (Trinh, 2015).

Wellness Programs, Wearables, and Data Privacy

Employers have an interest in maintaining a healthy workforce, as health-related work loss totals cost employers approximately $260 billion per year (Mitchell & Bates, 2011). The Affordable Care Act also compels most companies to provide health insurance to employees. Therefore, when organizations are able to maintain a healthy workforce, it can help better manage costs in healthcare, sick pay, family medical leave, disability pay, and health-related turnover.

As the epidemic of "lifestyle diseases," or chronic diseases attributable to inactivity, poor nutrition, tobacco use, and alcohol consumption, has gripped the United States, wellness programs offered by employers have gained popularity (Mattke et al., 2013). As of 2016, 60% of large companies (those with over 1,000 employees) offered wellness programs, and 51.1% of companies with between 500 and 1,000 employees did as well. Though smaller companies are less likely to offer wellness programs, the overall percentage of employers in the United States who participate in such programs is 18.4%. It is also expected that this percentage will continue to grow (Craver, 2017).

Wellness programs come in a variety of forms. Employers may offer gym memberships, weight management, health screenings, health coaches, stress management, and/or smoking cessation programs, just to name a few options. Wearable electronics, such as Fitbits, are also gaining popularity as part of employer-sponsored healthcare or lifestyle programs. For example, among employers with an active fitness program, 25% offer wearables to their employees, and 7% of those employers collect the data from the wearables to assess employee health (Haggin, 2016).

Collecting data from wearable technology presents many potential risks for both employee and employer. For example, researchers at Symantec, a California information-management company, recently confirmed that hackers can easily track the location of many health monitors. Low-cost wearables are also often not encrypted (Austen, 2015). Encryption provides a layer of cybersecurity whereby data are translated into secret codes that require a password in order to decrypt the text (Beal, n.d.). Without encryption, data from wearables, such as the user's name, address, telephone number, and date of birth, are highly susceptible to hackers. Yet even if a particular wearable is encrypted, the smart device that links to it may not be. Again, this is a weak point that hackers can target, just as they did when Fitbit user accounts were hacked in 2016 (Austen, 2015; Ahmed, 2016).

Employers face many potential areas of legal liability if employees' personal information is exposed in a cyberattack. Claims for damages may be brought under federal and/or state law and include potential liability for negligence, invasion of privacy, breach of express or implied contract, or misrepresentation. And as this area of the law expands, additional causes of action may arise (Caswell, Langevin, & Hofmann, 2015). Employers who encourage or require their workforce to wear devices and do not keep employees' information secure may have trouble avoiding liability when that information is compromised (Ahmed, 2016).

An unsettled legal issue is whether employers have a duty to disclose serious medical conditions that are uncovered by the employer's wellness program. For example, assume that in the course of vision screening at work, the employee has a retinal scan that indicates that the employee may be diabetic. Does the employer have a duty to disclose that information to the employee? The answer is "maybe" as cases related to wellness screening are working their way through the legal system.

For example, in *Whitman v. Interactive Health Solutions* (2017), the husband of a bridal store employee (hereinafter, the "plaintiff") was eligible under his wife's wellness plan for "comprehensive biometric screening" (*Whitman*, 2017). Good results from the screening meant that his wife would receive a discount on their health insurance premiums. As part of the screening, the plaintiff gave blood in 2011 to a third-party wellness company, Interactive Health Solutions (IHS), so that he could receive the overall summary of his health. The health report he received read, "Congratulations! You achieved your goal" (*Whitman*, 2017). However, the blood work actually indicated that he had signs of advanced kidney disease, a critical health condition that required prompt medical attention. However, no one from IHS notified the plaintiff of the medical condition. The blood work report was also never sent to a physician to read. It was only sent directly to the plaintiff, and as a layman, he did not understand any of the report beyond the congratulatory statement.

In 2012, the plaintiff again gave blood to IHS as part of the wellness program. Like the year before, he received a report that read, "Congratulations! You achieved your goal" (*Whitman*, 2017). By this time, the blood work actually showed advanced kidney disease nearing or at the stage of kidney failure. IHS again failed to contact the plaintiff about his serious medical condition. Though the full report was sent to the plaintiff and not to a physician, he again relied on the statement that he had achieved his health goal. But by 2013, the plaintiff started feeling ill. He went to the doctor, who ordered blood work. Upon receiving the results, the doctor called the plaintiff and told him to go directly to the emergency room because his kidneys had failed. The plaintiff then required a kidney transplant.

Though the *Whitman* case settled out of court for an undisclosed sum in May 2017, it is a case of first impression, meaning that this case is the first of its kind. Had it progressed to trial, the issues for the court to decide would have been whether the third-party wellness provider, IHS, should have been held liable for negligence for 1) failing to notify the plaintiff of the need for medical attention or 2) failing to send the report for a physician to review. Likewise, the court would have had to decide if the bridal store also owed a duty to the plaintiff. Guidance regarding the duties and liabilities attached to employer-sponsored wellness programs is most certainly forthcoming, as cases similar to *Whitman* will undoubtedly soon work their way through the legal system (*Whitman*, 2017).

Email Privacy and the Workplace

The Electronic Privacy and Communications Act of 1986 (EPCA) has a "business use" exception to the general rule that the employer has to have consent to intercept wire, oral, or electronic communication. The business use exception permits a company to monitor its phone and email systems (Londin, 2013). This means that employers do not need an employee's consent to intercept email as long as they have a valid business reason for doing so. Additionally, if the employee is using the employer's equipment or email to send and receive messages, the employer has the right to intercept them. This is known as the "provider" exception to the EPCA. Some employers take the step of also getting the employee's signature on an acknowledgement stating that their emails will be monitored at work. Monitoring emails in this circumstance is permitted under what is known as the "consent" exception (Bussing, 2011).

The issue becomes whether the employee's personal email account is private from the employer. The answer depends largely upon whether the employee opens personal email accounts on employer-owned devices. Courts have generally concluded that there is implied consent on the part of employees who choose to open and/or send personal email at work. Employees should also be aware that even if they are using a password to open their personal accounts, the password may get stored and is likely visible to the organization's monitoring software. Similarly, deleted personal emails may also get stored or permanently backed up by the employer's digital storage system (Privacy Rights Clearinghouse, 2017). Therefore, it is wise for an employee to assume that personal email accounts viewed on employer-owned devices are not private. Employees should not have a reasonable expectation of privacy with regard to personal email accounts in these circumstances (Bussing, 2011).

Some courts have extended the EPCA's exceptions to employee-owned devices that are simply used at the workplace. For example, in *Sitton v. Print Direction* (2011), an employer did not violate an employee's privacy right by printing out personal emails left open at work on the employee's personal laptop. The court held that because the employee was on the employer's premises and on company time and the employer had legitimate concerns that the employee was running another business from the employer's worksite, printing and reading those emails was permissible under the law (*Sitton*, 2011). Notably, a result like this will likely vary based on jurisdiction due to state laws that may also apply. It is therefore important for employees to understand the laws regarding email privacy on personal devices in the jurisdiction where they reside (Bussing, 2011).

Workplace Policies Regarding Data Collection and Data Usage

Employers should develop specific policies related to monitoring, whether it is GPS, email, wearables, wellness programs, or otherwise. The policy should articulate what is acceptable workplace use versus personal use of the devices (Alaniz, 2008). The policy should also clearly state what the employer's right to access, monitor, and wipe devices is and whether the employer will be accessing personal information.

Employers need to be familiar with the laws regarding privacy, as well as any additional legal protections that may apply to data collection or data usage (Austermuehle, 2016). Employers also need to designate which workers will have access to collected and stored data. They will need to be specific about how such employees should use data and for what purposes. Likewise, employers need to explain how the company will protect the employee's personal information (Lannon & Schreiber, 2016).

Employees need to be trained on the policy. This includes the policy language, rationale of the policy, and the practical application and meaning. Providing examples of acceptable versus nonacceptable uses is also advisable, as is educating employees about their legal rights and obligations regarding data collection and data usage. Policies need to be applied consistently so that employers can avoid potential liability for discriminatory practices. Employees also need to be trained on policies early and often during the duration of their employment, especially when policies are rewritten or changed by the organization (O'Connor et al., 2016).

Future Research Directions and Conclusion

A number of fruitful future research directions arise in the areas of social media, data privacy, and IoPTS. One overriding question across all the applications discussed in this chapter is how organizational actions are perceived by employees and by the public. Organizations likely do not want to take actions that are looked at negatively, yet little research so far has examined these perceptions. Drouin et al. (2015) examined perceptions related to termination decisions and found that many legal applications of social media data use in termination decisions were looked at unfavorably. Sayre and Dahling (2016) looked at reactions to social media monitoring and found that participants viewed the use of monitoring as "more fair and less invasive" when the organizations gave workers a justification for its use. Both academic and internal organizational research may want to examine reactions to different organizational uses of social media and IoPTS data. Research in this area may very well lead organizations to the conclusion that the value gained from the use of social media and data monitoring may not be worth the reputational cost.

Another major area in need of research across social media data usage is effectiveness of use. Although rationales have been created about how such data use *could* be helpful, there is little research suggesting that use actually is useful. For example, in one of the few published empirical studies of the use of social media in the selection, Van Iddekinge, Lanivich, Roth, and Junco (2016) found that social media data are not predictive of work performance and may potentially lead to adverse impact situations. Also, in their volume on social media in selection, Landers and Schmidt (2016), caution organizations in their use of social media data in the selection process. For any of the applications, empirical work is needed to examine if it is beneficial to organizations and what that data actually predict.

One important research area will always be examining and considering new technologies and their impact. Many of the issues of today related to the IoPTS were technologically impossible just a few years ago. As such, researchers and practitioners need to keep pace with new technologies as they arise. Especially difficult is determining which technologies will take hold and become widespread versus which will only be brief fads. Organizations will also need to keep abreast of new legal cases, as they will change what organizational practices are legal and appropriate.

In conclusion, in the rapidly evolving Internet world of IoPTS, social media and other data privacy issues have had a transformative impact on the workplace. They have also presented organizations with many issues, both positive and negative, to consider. Specifically, with regard to selection and termination of employment, social media has played an increasingly prominent role in organizations. Likewise, data management and employee privacy are vital, as wellness programs, GPS tracking, and mobile devices are often offered to employees. In this chapter, we explored these issues in depth, with a focus on IoPTS, the legal issues social media and data management present, and their impact on the workplace.

References

Ackerman, M. S., & Mainwaring, S. D., (2005). Privacy issues and human-computer interaction, in L. F. Cranor & S. Garfinkel (Eds.), *Security and Usability*. (pp 381-399), Sebastopol, CA: O'Reilly.

Ahmed, D. (2016). *Wearable tech: Where data privacy collides with employment law*. Retrieved from www.cybersecuritytodayblog.com/2016/10/24/wearable-tech-where-data-privacy-collides-with-employment-law/

Alaniz, R. (2008). *The advantages and pitfalls of employee monitoring*. Retrieved from www.fleetfinancials.com/channel/gps-telematics/article/story/2008/07/the-advantages-and-pitfalls-of-employee-monitoring.aspx

Arias v. Intermex Wire Transfer, 15-cv-01101 (E.D. CA, 2015).

Arthur, C. (2014). Naked celebrity hack: Security experts focus on iCloud backup theory. *The Guardian*. Retrieved from www.theguardian.com/technology/2014/sep/01/naked-celebrity-hack-icloud-backup-jennifer-lawrence

Ashford, W. (2016). IoT to play a part in more than a quarter of cyber attacks by 2020, Says Gartner. *ComputerWeekly.com*. Retrieved from www.computerweekly.com/news/450288414/IoT-to-play-a-part-in-more-than-a-quarter-of-cyber-attacks-by-2020-says-Gartner

Austen, K. (2015). The trouble with wearables. *Nature*, *525*(7567), 22–24.

Austermuehle, E. (2016). *Monitoring your employees through GPS: What is legal, and what are the best practices*. Retrieved from www.greensfelder.com/business-risk-management-blog/monitoring-your-employees-through-gps-what-is-legal-and-what-are-best-practices

Bacheldor, B. (2006). Wisconsin governor signs 'chip implant' bill. *RFID Journal*. Retrieved from www.rfidjournal.com/articles/view?2385

Barron, S. (n.d.). *Monitoring employees in the modern workplace: Can a GPS lead to TMI?* Retrieved from http://hrprofessionalsmagazine.com/monitoring-employees-in-the-modern-workplace-can-a-gps-result-in-tmi/

Beal, V. (n.d.). *Encryption*. Retrieved from www.webopedia.com/TERM/E/encryption.html

Biro, M. (2017). *The time for data-driven HR is now*. Retrieved from http://converge.xyz/the-time-for-data-driven-hr-is-now/

Bussing, H. (2011). *Employee privacy: What can employers monitor?* Retrieved from www.hrexaminer.com/employee-privacy-what-can-employers-monitor/

Caswell, T., Langevin, J., & Hofmann, Z. (2015). *Looking at the angles of liability after a cyberattack*. Retrieved from www.martindale.com/insurance-law/article_Zelle-LLP_2199360.htm

Conner, M. (n.d.). Data on big data. *Marcia Conner Blog*. Retrieved from http://marciaconner.com/blog/data-on-big-data/

Connick v. Meyers, 461 U.S. 138, (1983).

Cooney, M. (2016). *Smartphone tracking apps raise security, privacy, and legality questions*. Retrieved from www.networkworld.com/article/3068627/security/smartphone-tracking-apps-raise-security-privacy-and-legality-questions.html

Craver, J. (2017). *The state of wellness programs in 2016*. Retrieved from www.benefitspro.com/2017/01/09/the-state-of-wellness-programs-in-2016

Cunningham v. N.Y. Dep't of Labor, 2013 WL 3213347, N.Y. Slip Op. 04838 (2013).

Darcy, J. (2016). *Read this before you use GPS to track employees*. Retrieved from www.paychex.com/articles/human-resources/read-this-gps-track-employees

Delarosa, J. (2014). From due diligence to discrimination: Employer use of social media vetting in the hiring process and potential liabilities. *Loyola of Los Angeles Entertainment Law Review*, *35*, 249.

Department of Justice. (2013). *Using metadata as the foundation for a government-wide FOIA library*. Retrieved from www.justice.gov/oip/blog/using-metadata-foundation-government-wide-foia-library

DLA Labor Dish Editorial Board. (2015). *What recent case law can teach you about BYOD workplaces?* Retrieved from www.labordish.com/2015/03/what-recent-case-law-can-teach-about-byod-workplaces/

Drouin, M., O'Connor, K. W., Schmidt, G. B., & Miller, D. A. (2015). Facebook fired: Legal perspectives and young adults' opinions on the use of social media in hiring and firing decisions. *Computers in Human Behavior*, *46*, 123–128.

EEOC, (n.d.). *The Age Discrimination in Employment Act*. Retrieved from https://www.eeoc.gov/laws/statutes/adea.cfm.

Eloff, J. H. P., Eloff, M. M., Dlamini, M. T., & Zielinski, M. P. (2009). *Internet of People, things and services: The convergence of security, trust and privacy*. 3rd Companion Able Workshop-IoPTS, Novotel Brussels, Brussels, Belgium.

Esack, S. (2017). Bionic workforce alarms pa: Lawmaker, who offers bill to prevent microchip implants. *Harrisburg Bureau*. Retrieved from www.mcall.com/news/nationworld/pennsylvania/mc-nws-pa-microchip-worker-bill-20170804-story.html

Evans, S. J. (2015). 'It almost became its own beast': Moderator of Reddit's 'find Boston bombers' thread tells of how millions of users descended on the subreddit in the days after the attack: And even identified the wrong suspect. *Daily Mail.com*. Retrieved from www.dailymail.co.uk/news/article-3035378/It-beast-Moderator-Reddit-s-Boston-Bombers-thread-tells-millions-users-descended-subreddit-days-attack-identified-wrong-suspect.html

Findlaw. (n.d.). *Monitoring employees*. Retrieved from http://smallbusiness.findlaw.com/employment-law-and-human-resources/monitoring-employees.html

Gaskell v. University of KY. (2010). Civil Action No. 09-244-KSF. (E.D. KY Jan 12, 2010).

Gumbus, A., & Grodzinski, F. (2016). Era of big data: Danger of discrimination. *ACM SIGCAS Computers and Society*, *45*(3), 118–125.

Haggin, P. (2016). *How should companies handle data from employees' wearable devices?* Retrieved from www.wsj.com/articles/how-should-companies-handle-data-from-employees-wearable-devices-1463968803

Halpern, J. (2010). *Why is confidentiality important?* Retrieved from www.halpernadvisors.com/why-is-confidentiality-important/

Hidy, K. M., & McDonald, M. S. E. (2013). Risky business: The legal implications of social media's increasing role in employment decisions. *Journal of Legal Studies in Business*, *18*, 69–88.

Holtz, S. (2016). Social media at work: Enable your employees to be company advocates. *Monster*. Retrieved from http://hiring.monster.com/hr/hr-best-practices/workforce-management/employee-performance-management/social-media-at-work-us.aspx

Kang, J., & Cuff, D. (2005). Pervasive computing: Embedding the public space. *Washington & Lee Law Review*, *62*, 93–146.

Landers, R. N., & Schmidt, G. B. (2016). Social media in employee selection and recruitment: An overview. In *Social media in employee selection and recruitment*. Cham, ZG: Springer International Publishing.

Lannon, P., & Schreiber, P. (2016). *BYOD policies: What employers need to know*. Retrieved from www.shrm.org/hr-today/news/hr-magazine/pages/0216-byod-policies.aspx

Londin, J. (2013). *Workplace privacy laws: 10 things all employers need to know*. Retrieved from www.rocketlawyer.com/blog/a-peek-at-workplace-privacy-laws-10-things-all-employers-need-to-know-915192

Lopez, C. (2014). *The opinions expressed in this post are my own and not necessarily those of my employer: Disclaimers and the NLRB's continuing (and confusing) assault on employer social media policies*. Retrieved from www.laborandemploymentlawcounsel.com/2014/05/the-opinions-expressed-in-this-post-are-my-own-and-not-necessarily-those-of-my-employer/

Mattke, S., Liu, H., Caloyeras, J. P., Huang, C. Y., Van Busum, K. R., Khodyakov, D., & Shier, V. (2013). Workplace wellness programs study. *Rand Health*. Retrieved from www.dol.gov/ebsa/pdf/workplacewellnessstudyfinal.pdf

McGlaun, S. (2013). 50% of workers will be required to use their own smart phones on the job. *The Daily Tech*. Retrieved from www.dailytech.com/Report+50+of+Workers+Will+Be+Required+to+Use+Their+Own+Smartphones+on+the+Job+by+2017/article31469.htm

McLellan, M. L., Sherer, J. A., & Fedeles, E. R. (2015). Wherever you go, there you are (with your mobile device): Privacy risks and legal complexities associated with international 'bring your own device' programs. *Richmond Journal of Law and Technology*, *21*, 11–15.

McMahon, R., Bressler, M. S., & Bressler, L. (2016). New global cybercrime calls for high-tech cyber-cops. *Journal of Legal, Ethical and Regulatory Issues*, *19*(1), 26–37.

Mitchell, R., & Bates, P. (2011). Measuring health-related productivity loss. *Population Health Management*, *14*(2), 93–98.

National Labor Relations Board. (1935). *National labor relations act*. Retrieved from www.nlrb.gov/resources/national-labor-relations-act

O'Connor, K. W., & Schmidt, G. B. (2015). Facebook fired: Legal standards for social-media based termination of employment of K-12 public school teachers. *Sage Open*. Retrieved from http://sgo.sagepub.com/content/5/1/2158244015575636

O'Connor, K. W., Schmidt, G. B., & Drouin, M. (2016). Helping workers understand and follow social media policies. *Business Horizons*, *59*(2), 205–211.

Olmstead, K., Lampe, C., & Ellison, N. B. (2016). Social media and the workplace. *Pew Research Center*. Retrieved from www.pewinternet.org/2016/06/22/social-media-and-the-workplace/

Ortutay, B. (2017). Social media harnessed to expose white nationalists at rally. *ABC News*. Retrieved from www.laboremploymentperspectives.com/2016/10/03/worker-privacy-and-security-in-an-internet-of-things/

Peck, D. (2013). They're watching you at work. *The Atlantic*. Retrieved from www.theatlantic.com/magazine/archive/2013/12/theyre-watching-you-at-work/354681/

Peyton, A. (2015). A litigator's guide to the Internet of Things. *Richmond Journal of Law and Technology*, *22*, 1.

Pogue, D. (2017). Internet shaming: When mob justice goes virtual. *CBS News*. Retrieved from www.cbsnews.com/news/internet-shaming-when-mob-justice-goes-virtual/

Privacy Rights Clearinghouse. (2017). *Workplace privacy and employee monitoring*. Retrieved from www.privacyrights.org/printpdf/67553

Rao, L. (2011). Sexual activity tracked by Fitbit shows up in Google search results. *Techcrunch*. Retrieved from https://techcrunch.com/2011/07/03/sexual-activity-tracked-by-fitbit-shows-up-in-google-search-results/

Reppler. (2011). Managing your online image across social networks. *The Reppler Effect*. Retrieved from http://blog.reppler.com/2011/09/27managing-your-online-image-across-social-network

Robertson, A. (2017). A Wisconsin company will let employees use microchip implants to buy snacks and open doors. *The Verge*. Retrieved from www.theverge.com/2017/7/24/16019530/three-sqaure-market-implant-office-keycard-biohacking-wisconsin

Rosenburg, K. (2010). Location surveillance by GPS: Balancing an employer's business interest with employee privacy. *Washington Journal of Law, Technology & Arts*, *6*, 143.

Rouse, M. (2016). Pervasive computing (ubiquitous computing). *IoT Agenda*. Retrieved from http://internetofthingsagenda.techtarget.com/definition/pervasive-computing-ubiquitous-computing

Rubenstein, A. (2014, April 29). Employee misuse of social media on the rise, survey says. *Law 360*. Retrieved from www.law360.com/articles/532775/employee-misuse-of-social-media-on-the-rise-survey-says

Saha, B. (2017). IoT workplace policy. *Mobiloite Workplace Blog*. Retrieved from www.mobiloitte.com/blog/iot-workplace-policy

Sayre, G. M., & Dahling, J. J. (2016). Surveillance 2.0: How personality qualifies reactions to social media monitoring policies. *Personality and Individual Differences*, *90*, 254–259.

Schmidt, G. B., & O'Connor, K. W. (2015). Fired for Facebook: Using NLRB guidance to craft appropriate social media policies. *Business Horizons*, *58*(5), 571–579.

Schmidt, G. B., & O'Connor, K. W. (2016). Legal concerns when considering social media data in selection. In R. Landers, & G. B. Schmidt (Eds.), *Social media in employee selection and recruitment* (pp. 265–287). Cham, ZG: Springer International Publishing.

Security Center. (n.d.). *How facial recognition software works*. Retrieved from https://us.norton.com/internetsecurity-iot-how-facial-recognition-software-works.html

Sitton v. Print Direction, Inc., 312 Ga. App. 365 (2011).

Smith, K. (2016). Marketing: 47 Facebook statistics for 2016. *Brandwatch Blog*. Retrieved from www.brandwatch.com/blog/47-facebook-statistics-2016./

Society for Human Resource Management. (2012, January 12). *An examination of how social media is embedded in business strategy and operations*. Retrieved from www.shrm.org/hr-today/trends-and-forecasting/research-and-surveys/pages/2anexaminationofhowsocialmediaisembeddedinbusinessstrategyandoperations surveyfindings.aspx

Statista. (2016). *Number of social media users worldwide from 2010 to 2021 (in billions)*. Retrieved from www.statista.com/statistics/278414/number-of-worldwide-social-network-users

Trinh, L. (2015). *Woman fired for deleting 24 hour tracking app*. Retrieved from http://blogs.findlaw.com/law_and_life/2015/05/woman-fired-for-deleting-24-hour-tracking-app.html

Van Iddekinge, C. H., Lanivich, S. E., Roth, P. L., & Junco, E. (2016). Social media for selection? Validity and adverse impact potential of a Facebook-based assessment. *Journal of Management*, *42*(7), 1811–1835.

Vidsys. (2017). Social media's important role in the Internet of Things. *Vidsys Blog*. Retrieved from www.vidsys.com/general/social-medias-important-role-internet-things/

Whitman v. Interactive Health Solutions, Inc., No. 15L004421, (Cir. Ct. Cook Cty., 2017).

Part 2

IoPTS Workplace—Things

7 Initiating the Internet of Things

Early Adopters' Expectations for Changing Business Practices and Implications for Working Life

Ulrika H. Westergren, Ted Saarikko and Tomas Blomquist

Introduction

The Internet of Things (IoT) is estimated to grow at an exponential rate in the coming years. As things get connected, a myriad of opportunities arise—the intelligent home that knows you and your preferences and offers a day-to-day personalized experience; the smart car that not only helps a person drive in an eco-friendly way, it stays in touch with the manufacturer for software updates and sets an appointment with a technician if any service or repairs are needed; and connected health care, with physicians monitoring patients through online systems where diagnosis and treatment are facilitated by the continuous access to context-aware data. A sensor-infused world, where things and humans seamlessly interact, can thus provide us with needed information and enable us to make better choices. Undeniably the IoT brings with it the potential for new and enhanced forms of value creation, increased efficiency, and new revenue streams. However, there is also a vulnerability built into any connected system. Security breaches cover the entire scale from irritating, as in someone remotely turning on one's lights when they should be turned off, to detrimental, as in someone tampering with the breaks or navigation system of a connected car, and in addition, the IoT raises issues of privacy concerns as collected data can be used to pinpoint individual behaviors and habits. Indeed, there are many forecasts and future visions regarding the development, dissemination, and economic influence of the IoT (see for example: Manyika et al., 2013; Porter & Heppelmann, 2014; Burkitt, 2014). However, less is known about how the IoT will affect working life, both in terms of new work practices and impending consequences for individual workers. In this chapter, we therefore ask the question: What hopes and expectations are associated with IoT introduction and use in firms, and how do early adopter business professionals intend to make strategic use of the IoT in organizational processes? We present a study of 21 Swedish firms that are all actively engaging with the IoT to create new business models, modes of working, and ways of interacting with both customers and staff. We use the technological frames perspective

(Orlikowski & Gash, 1994) to capture business professionals' assumptions, expectations, and knowledge about the IoT. By identifying technological frames and studying and capturing firms' sense-making processes, we can learn about possible implications of IoT within organizations and thereby increase our understanding of the transformational impact of the IoT on working life.

Related Research

The term "Internet of Things" was first used to describe the act of furnishing physical objects with a digital identity—usually via radio-frequency identification (RFID) (Borgia, 2014; Gama, Touseau, & Donsez, 2012). Today the IoT has come to be associated with technological breakthroughs such as wireless technologies, cloud computing, and virtual reality (Ferretti & Schiavone, 2016).

Although the IoT does not represent a single technology or set of standards, the idea of connected products and services imbued with a moderate "intelligence" may be characterized as an innovation in so far as it marks a departure from existing practices. As such, it conforms to the definition of an innovation offered by Rogers (2003, p. 12):

> An innovation is an idea, practice, or object that is perceived as new by an individual or other unit of adoption. [. . .] 'Newness' of an innovation may be expressed in terms of knowledge, persuasion, or a decision to adopt.

An innovation is not merely a certain object or a specific technology, but also the manner in which that object or technology is perceived by different actors across different contexts.

Rogers (2003) argues that time is a relevant factor in the diffusion of an innovation, outlining five broad categories of adopters based on the timeliness of adoption: innovators, early adopters, early majority, late majority, and laggards. The availability of communication channels and influence exerted by social systems are directly related to the decision to adopt or reject an innovation. As majority adopters embrace an innovation when it is *in vogue*, their decision is reinforced by a social system of like-minded others and whose message is supported by well-developed communication channels. On the other hand, innovators and early adopters have to take an active part in shaping their respective social system, establishing communication channels and (especially in the case of early adopters) often putting pressure on their peers to follow suit. However, time is also relevant in relation to the maturity of connected devices and our ability to understand their repercussions. Reviews by Atzori, Iera, and Morabito (2010) and Borgia (2014) show how the requisite interfaces and standards that enable IoT interoperability and mobility have only recently gained sufficient technological maturity to stimulate wider interest. Fully standardized interfaces between networks, devices, and software applications are nigh impossible to attain given the wide range of domains in which IoT is poised to make an entry. The speed of progress in digital technology multiplies complexity and increases the need for firms to find staff with appropriate skills (Bullen, Abraham, & Galup, 2009). Because the IoT does not comprise a discrete set of technologies, the time prospective adopters have to gain knowledge, form an opinion of, and implement the IoT varies greatly depending on what type of solution is warranted.

With the evolution of the IoT through the development of cloud computing, miniaturization, smart sensors, and mobile technology, objects can not only be identified and located, they can collect, process, and transmit context-aware data through time and space (Greengard, 2015). This in turn creates new opportunities and challenges for firms and their employees, and both technological issues—for example, technology standards and issues of privacy, security, and control (Vermesan & Friess, 2013)—and organizational issues, such as value creation, business model innovation, and interorganizational and intraorganizational collaboration (Saarikko, Westergren, & Blomquist, 2016; Saarikko, Westergren, & Blomquist, 2017), need to be addressed. Most of the IoT research to date has focused on the technological advancements and not on the organizational aspects of the emerging IoT (Whitmore, Agarwal, & Da Xu, 2015). Digital technology has already had a profound impact on working life, as various devices and software have facilitated communication, improved efficiency, enabled mobility, and increased productivity (Shehadi & Karam, 2014). Moreover, digital technology has enabled telework and distance learning, connecting people to globally available resources and supporting knowledge sharing and cross-functional cooperation (Coenen & Kok, 2014). However, we know little about what implications the IoT will have for working life, as it offers unprecedented access to data about products, processes, and people. As a consequence organizations will be forced to make strategic choices about data management linked to expected economic returns and anticipated value creation, as well as to the firm's overall strategy, including organizational culture and resources (Porter & Heppelmann, 2014; Dodgson, Gann, & Salter, 2008). Technological advancement has also opened up security breaches, as transactional data may be accessed, manipulated, and transmitted beyond the borders of the firm (Miller & Wells, 2007). In addressing security issues, managers must strive to find a balance between trust, security, and privacy concerns (Eloff, Eloff, Dlamini, & Zielinski, 2009), as digital technology also makes it easier to track and monitor employees, something that can lead to a culture of distrust and an increase in stress-related health care claims (Miller & Wells, 2007; Lugaresi, 2010; Onley, 2005). The potential impact of the IoT on working life is great, and thus so is the opportunity to learn from firms who are early adopters of the IoT and who have already identified and started to address some of these issues.

Theoretical Framework

We use the technological frames framework introduced by Orlikowski and Gash (1994) to investigate how business professionals view the introduction of the IoT within organizations and what strategic implications they see. Technological frames are defined as

> that subset of members' organizational frames that concern the assumptions, expectations, and knowledge they use to understand technology in organizations. This includes not only the nature and role of the technology itself, but the specific conditions, applications, and consequences of that technology in particular contexts.
>
> (Orlikowski & Gash, 1994, p. 178)

The main idea is that people's cognitive processes, both individually and collectively, have a profound impact on how technology is designed, implemented, and used within any given context. This makes it an especially relevant framework to apply when studying the Internet of Things, considering that although the technological development regarding connectivity has already come quite far, firms are still figuring out how to use the IoT to create business value and enhance strategy and what consequences this will have for work practices. By studying and capturing their sense-making process, we can learn about possible implications of IoT within organizations.

The technological frames framework is divided into three domains (Figure 7.1): 1) *nature of technology*, which refers to people's understanding of technology, its functionality, and its possibilities; 2) *technology strategy*, which refers to people's views on what technology might add to their organization and what the reason is for technology adoption; and 3) *technology-in-use*, which refers to people's views on how technology will be used within the organization and what consequences this will bring. A common way of applying the framework is to study different groups within an organization and compare technological frames between groups. In this way both common ground and potential tensions can be discerned. In our study, we apply the technological frames framework *within and between* firms to see

Figure 7.1 The Technological Frames Framework

if there are congruent and incongruent frames within specific organizations and between the different firm groups.

By applying this framework, we create an understanding for individuals' thoughts on how the emerging IoT will transform workplaces and what the implications will be for working life, thereby highlighting the transformational potential of the IoT from an organizational point of view.

Methodology

This chapter is based on a qualitative case study (Klein & Myers, 1999; Walsham, 1993) performed in 2015–2016. Qualitative research is characteristically well suited to capture people's intentions, expectations, and thoughts regarding different phenomena (Mason, 2002), and the empirical inquiry within case study research examines a present phenomenon in depth and within its actual setting (Yin, 2009). Together the authors performed semi-structured interviews with 28 representatives in strategic positions from 21 different firms to learn about their thoughts and strategies for adopting and implementing IoT into their business processes and what their experiences were of the implications of embracing the IoT from an organizational perspective. Most interviews (21) were done over the phone, but some (7) were in person, and all lasted an average of 47 minutes per interview. Table 7.1 provides a list of firms and respondents.

Selected firms were early adopters of IoT and thus were actively implementing the IoT into their business processes. They also represented a wide variety of industries. Inspired by Burkitt (2014) we studied three separate categories of firms: product-oriented (PO) firms, delivering specific products for either a business or consumer market; service-oriented (SO) firms, offering service provision to both other businesses and to consumers; and technology-oriented (TO) firms, creating IoT devices, sensors, and other technology that enable connectivity and the collection and transmission of data. The TO firms in our study were actively developing technological solutions for the IoT. Whereas they could be considered innovators within a more general technology innovation context, we have chosen to regard them as early adopters within the IoT paradigm, as they are adapting and applying existing skill sets to a new context.

The data analysis was performed in two stages. First we performed an in-case analysis for each firm (Eisenhardt, 1989) where we coded the data from the interviews into the three different categories of firms and the three main theoretical concepts: nature of technology, technology strategy, and technology-in-use. In the second stage, we performed a cross-case analysis searching for common patterns and divergent stances between cases and within the different types of firms. At this point we also looked for congruent and incongruent frames within and between firm groups. The results are presented in the next section. All company names have been fictionalized in order to protect privacy.

Table 7.1 Interview Respondents

Type of firm	*Name of firm*	*Industry*	*Role of respondent*	*No. of interviews*
Product-oriented	P01	Heavy machinery	Responsible for IoT solutions; responsible for IoT service development; division manager, IT	3
	P02	Heavy machinery	After-sales manager; division manager, IT	2
	P03	Animal control	CEO	1
	P04	Professional appliances	Responsible for IoT solutions; after-sales manager	2
	P05	Professional appliances	Responsible for IoT solutions	1
Service-oriented	S01	Facility management	Innovation manager	1
	S02	Payments solutions	CTO	1
	S03	Transportation	Manager IoT solutions	1
	S04	Resort management	CIO (interviewed twice)	2
	S05	Facility management	IoT strategist	1
	S06	Facility management	System technician	1
Technology-oriented	T01	Telecommunications	IoT business developer	1
	T02	Connectivity and cloud solutions	CEO; CTO	2
	T03	Connectivity and cloud solutions	CEO	1
	T04	Connectivity and cloud solutions	CEO	1
	T05	Smart sensors	CTO	1
	T06	Smart sensors	CTO	1
	T07	Smart sensors	CTO	1
	T08	Interface design	CEO	1
	T09	IoT solutions designer	CEO	1
	T10	Information security consultants	IoT strategist; information security consultant	2

Results

The results section is structured around the three concepts from the technological frames framework: nature of technology, technology strategy, and technology-in-use. Specific quotes show the reasoning within select firms, whereas most findings are applicable to all firms within a certain category.

Nature of Technology

Nature of technology refers to people's understanding of technology, its functionality, and its possibilities. In this section, we see how the different groups of firms have one major thing in common: the belief that data are the key to new business value.

Product-Oriented Firms

All respondents mention the collection and use of data as the main possibility with the IoT. Connected environments and products make it possible to learn more about customers and tailor better offerings, and they also provide an opportunity to collaborate with others in order to create entirely new and innovative solutions. In terms of current needs, much of the brand identity is imbued in the firm's respective products and their performance in the field. As such they are keen to both ensure that products are durable and that any errors that occur may be promptly rectified. The firms featured in this study all consider the IoT a vital component in addressing the latter issue. That is, the ability to extract data straight from products directly translates into the ability to remotely and continuously supervise them after the point of sale and provide support to customers as needed. However, respondents also agreed that a lot of data is being collected without a specific focus, but in the hopes of coming up with new solutions to existing problems:

> We gather a whole lot of data, really. We don't actually use it anywhere near as much as we could. But we're trying to become smarter and smarter.
>
> (Division manager, IT, P02)

Looking to future potential, continuous access to products provides the opportunity to conduct long-term analysis on performance over time for the product as whole as well as individual components. The resulting insights can provide invaluable input for future product development, informing designers of common errors that need to be addressed or features that are rarely used (and thus perhaps not necessary). As access to data is growing increasingly interesting, product-oriented firms are also becoming more aware of the inadequacies of existing legal frameworks. Although ownership of physical products is clearly regulated, ownership of data is not. Here we may discern several distinct perspectives, ranging from P01 and P04 that assert exclusive ownership of product data, to P02 and P05 that want access to data but consider it impractical or impossible to claim exclusive privilege for fear of alienating customers. Regardless of perspective, we may anticipate that data access and ownership will become a standard part of future sales contracts—something that P02 has already introduced.

Service-Oriented Firms

The study also included different types of service-oriented firms, ranging from payment solutions to the management of individual facilities and even large tourist resorts. Among the more ambitious firms may be noted S01, S03, and S05 where S01 and S03 operate large and relatively heterogeneous organizations that directly interact with and serve thousands of customers daily, and S05 is a specialist consultant in architecture, infrastructure, and city planning. Differences notwithstanding, they all see a significant potential for IoT to provide better information through which to enhance internal processes as well as offer more compelling services for their respective customers. In a broad sense, service-oriented firms are interested in the ability of sensors to provide real-time information that can be used to plan and perform service-related tasks based on actual conditions rather than guesses and rough estimates.

Whereas most of the service providers were generally keen on the idea of gathering as much data as they could with the aid of an ever more advanced set of tools, bringing these ideas into practice is not all that simple. A specific challenge is the lack of technology standards, which makes it difficult to create systems that can be easily integrated with others:

> [W]e see an incredible range of possibilities with IoT. The current limitation is basically to get a hold of a horizontal platform [that can handle multiple systems]. Alternatively, there are a lot of different systems in the market these days, but individually they do not provide the overall benefit needed to outweigh the costs of managing and supporting [multiple] systems.
>
> (Innovation manager, S01)

The firms in our study not only discuss how to keep the balance between security and privacy, but also finding the balance between using data to provide value and overusing data and risk being perceived as intrusive. The service providers included in our study were all very clear on the fact that they did not want to bear the risk of violating any laws by recording personal data—nor did they want to shoulder the responsibility for warding off unauthorized access to sensors for illicit surveillance. Their response to this issue was to utilize sensors that are deliberately unspecific. For instance, sensors can be made smart enough to detect *if* there is a person in any given space, but too dumb to detect *who* it is.

Technology-Oriented Firms

The technology-oriented firms featured in our study differ in that they do not perceive the IoT as a means to improve their own internal processes, but to market their skills and experience in the form of a technical infrastructure (T01, T02, and T03), technical components (T05, T06, and T07), or data management and interface design (T04 and T08) that may be put to fruitful use by customers. As such, although their areas of expertise differ substantially, these actors do have a firm grasp of what the IoT entails in terms of how hardware and software are intermingled in practice. Some of them represent mature companies that have been working with different technologies and approaches for connectivity in remote locations since long before IoT became a household term. The most extreme example, T01, traces its roots back some 150 years and has been working with different technologies for communication since the days of the telegraph. Less extreme, but nonetheless with a long history, T05 has been working with different technologies for tracking wildlife since the 1970s and the days of analogue radio transmitters. To them, the IoT is not so much a new paradigm or even a novelty, but rather a possibility to repackage their respective skill sets to form new market offerings to a broader range of customers. The other firms are more recent and have developed their business models in direct response to the combination of ever cheaper and more capable hardware and the growing acceptance of sensors and connected devices from prospective customers. T02 and T04 were both established less than 10 years ago and have both developed market offerings that are intended to make the complexity of IoT more manageable and thus more palatable for customers that lack the requisite skill set (or interest) themselves.

Technology Strategy

Technology strategy refers to people's views on what technology might add to their organization and what the reason is for technology adoption. In this section we see how initial expectations of the IoT are tied to the generation and analysis of data, with potential to influence new work practices, create enhanced business offerings, and nurture strategic collaborations.

Product-Oriented Firms

The PO firms saw possibilities of connecting their products and staying in touch with them after the point of sale, using data to tailor service and maintenance offerings, and for product development purposes. When errors do occur, error reports can be automatically compiled and transmitted to support staff that dispatch service technicians who then have access to accurate data regarding the problem (enabling them to bring the correct tools and spare parts) as well as the location of the product courtesy of GPS technology. Interestingly, firms like P02, who manufactures heavy machinery used in remote locations, and P04, who manufactures appliances for use in hotels (among other places), offer fairly similar perspectives regarding the need to include location data, ostensibly with the aim of promoting complete and accurate error reports. Moreover, connected products afford the opportunity to preempt breakdowns by sending automated warnings when a component is not operating within acceptable parameters. Alternatively, support staff can manually check performance and anticipate problems or schedule preventive maintenance based on insight into the product's maintenance history or upcoming work schedule. Over time, these capabilities can be harnessed to cultivate more intimate relationships with customers based on continuous interactions rather than intermittent contacts based on sale of new products.

However, PO firms are also susceptible to external pressures that strongly encourage adoption of IoT. One tangible example voiced by both P01 and P05 is the risk of their products being retrofitted with third-party hardware, thus circumventing the product developer entirely and permitting other actors to build services based on their products. The long-term consequence of this practice is that entire new product-based business ecosystems may arise that the product-oriented firms are unable to affect or even extract profit from. In this scenario, the product-oriented firm would be permanently demoted to the less profitable role of hardware supplier while other actors reap the profits from value-adding services or other attractive features.

Another reason for PO firms to adopt the IoT is that customers are becoming more demanding with regard to IT-related features. Users demand similar features in their workplace tools to the ones they are able to utilize in their private lives. Just as employees who are always reachable may feel pressured to respond to calls or emails outside of working hours, developers such as P05 feel the pressure to develop features that are not derived from product functionality as much as user expectations and overall technology trends. Wireless connectivity and digital displays are not integral to the ability of a chain saw to fell a tree, yet such features are starting to appear because their absence would make the product seem dated or even obsolete to an ever more tech-savvy user demographic.

Service-Oriented Firms

The SO-firms featured in this study were mainly looking to create more efficient services based on contextual data, but also saw possibilities in combining data from various sources to develop entirely new services. The ability to provide better service at lower costs is a common theme found among all firms as services are traditionally associated with manual labor in some sense—if not physically demanding then at least necessitating a physical presence. For instance, S01 offers, among other things, cleaning services for various facilities such as hotels and offices. Although the act of cleaning itself requires human intervention, knowing where cleaning is necessary does not. In fact, a significant amount of time is wasted as personnel have to manually inspect different areas to check if they need attention, if soap dispensers need to be filled, or if more paper towels are needed. These activities are essentially an unproductive use of human resources that could be applied elsewhere. Hence, with the use of sensors, cleaning can be conducted as needed rather than based on a schedule. If, for instance, a restroom has not been used since it was last cleaned, then one may surmise that it does not require attention and move on to other areas that do.

In addition to monitoring the need for service intervention, the same principle can be applied to monitoring the whereabouts and behavioral patterns of customers. Firm S03 is active in public transportation and sees significant potential in utilizing sensors that monitor where travelers board and depart their vehicles. More reliable and comprehensive insights can serve to inform planning for the addition of more bus lines or bus stops in order to satisfy unmet commuter needs or to eliminate bus stops that are rarely used. Firm S04 has similar interests where they, as managers of a vast sprawling resort, are very keen to see where customers begin their day and where queues tend to form during different times of the day. If queues regularly form at certain points, then it may be wise to provide more amenities (for example, restrooms) at those locations. Alternatively, if lines form because customers are waiting to buy a travel pass needed to access facility attractions, then management should consider building additional kiosks either nearby to better handle the load or at another location in order to better distribute visitors across the entire facility.

The use of technical aides such as sensors provides S01 with access to more reliable and comprehensive data regarding operational costs. These data can in turn be compared with other similar facilities and provide valuable input for future negotiations of service contracts. The better you are able to estimate the costs associated with maintaining a given facility, the better equipped you are to fend off competition and pick lucrative customers. The behavior of visitors or customers is also relevant in relation to the operation of the facilities themselves. For instance, S06 operates facilities that include offices, meeting rooms, lecture halls, storage rooms, and even laboratories. Given the sheer size and diversity of their facilities, operational costs could run quite high if lighting, heating, and ventilation were to be run at 100% around the clock. However, by equipping rooms with sensors that detect occupancy, individual rooms may be put into a "sleep mode" when not in use—switching lights off and reducing ventilation and heating until someone enters.

Technology-Oriented Firms

The technology-oriented firms all saw data as their new main currency—creating solutions to generate, access, maintain, and secure bits and bytes. The TO firms also saw the emergence of new opportunities to apply existing skill sets. Regardless of their particular niche, TO firms all see their potential markets widening considerably over the coming years and evolving from selling hardware and software to selling highly valued functions and services. This new role holds significant potential for entering new markets as well as new business areas, but success is contingent upon the ability to formulate compelling value propositions. A broad market offering holds great potential, but also requires the would-be provider to educate prospective customers regarding the relevance, applicability, and potential value of their offering—or maybe even IoT as a concept. Several of the firms featured in this study solved the issue by forming partnerships with different actors that could complement them in terms of supplying complementary skills or domain knowledge.

T03 offers a technical platform that may be employed to enable IoT solutions across a range of different applications. Using their technical baseline, they may occupy a similar role in the value chain across multiple industries with little or no modification. However, they initially faced difficulties marketing their platform, as customers did not readily see its value or relevance. T03 responded by gradually formulating partnerships with firms that supply niche solutions that convey a clear sense of value to different types of customers. One of the more salient illustrations of this point is their partnership with a firm that specializes in algorithms for energy-efficient driving. As the idea of reducing fuel consumption (up to 10%) provides a tangible financial incentive, the partnership has enabled T03 to establish a strong presence in public transportation and logistics where even small improvements in fuel economy translates into substantial savings.

Technology-in-Use

Technology-in-use refers to people's views on how technology will be used within the organization and what consequences this will bring. Although the IoT will be applied in many different contexts, the firms agree that in many cases new skills and competencies are required and that this will have consequences for how work is organized and what their customers come to expect from them.

Product-Oriented Firms

Overall, the PO firms say that the realization of products in an IoT paradigm requires tighter collaboration between organizational units that traditionally work in relative isolation. Physical hardware and digital complements are both essential to IoT-enabled products, yet have different development cycles as well as life spans. A physical product may take years to develop, test, and manufacture, whereas digital additions (for example, in the form of services that enhance or complement the product) can be developed in a matter of months. Furthermore, a physical product may be in active use for years or even decades. Digital services, on the other hand, may be added throughout its life span, serving to optimize the product itself or adapting it to new usage patterns by customers. Our study demonstrates two approaches to promoting the necessary collaboration across functional divisions. One approach is illustrated by P05, which has formed competence center where executive staff meet and coordinate efforts. This has proven to be a good way to "jump-start" an IoT initiative and demonstrate management support in an organization without overturning established structures. Another, more grassroots-oriented approach, is demonstrated by P01 who is working to co-locate key personnel from different departments in the same office in order to encourage mutual understanding and enable impromptu meetings. Again, this facilitates interdisciplinary understanding without the requirement for major organizational upheavals. All respondents claim that their IoT process started with one or two engaged individuals who saw the opportunities with IoT and convinced others to join. However, they also say that once IoT became a pronounced strategic priority that is when it really took off. PO firm representatives state that implementing IoT requires a major cultural change within their organizations.

> If you want to move from being a product supplier to a service provider, then you cannot believe that the organizational structures that were in place in the first stage will continue to live in the second.
>
> (Division Manager IT, P01)

Service-Oriented Firms

Service provision is generally a complex business where providers are constantly trying to match resources with requirements. More often than not, the routines set in place to accommodate service requirements are educated guesses based on past experience. Failure to find the right balance is commonplace and results in a less-than-satisfactory customer experience. What IoT provides is the range of tools needed to efficiently supervise the facilities that are under the service provider's care and *know*, rather than guess, where attention is required. Even when not directly compelled by legal restrictions, IoT may be employed to streamline internal processes and respond to service requirements more rapidly.

Rather than invest in advanced, dedicated IoT solutions, S04 has opted for a more basic approach to incorporating technology to extract relevant information from their operations. Their use of RFID tags is the most basic application of an IoT technology featured in this study, yet it is also the most mature, having been in active use for two decades. Furthermore they believe that the vast majority of data is only relevant to the particular context in which it was created.

> We do not have an ambition that we must, at any price, see everything in one interface or have all the data in one place, we don't. Instead, it is more relevant for us to benefit from a certain type of data in the

> right place. But not necessarily so that we need to gather everything in one system, look at it in one interface, no. Absolutely not! We're not a nuclear power plant, you know.
>
> (CIO, S04)

This view of data differs from the PO firms, who were keen to gather as much data as possible over extended periods. By stressing the contextual relevance of data, SO firms are able to tailor solutions that fit their specific needs and provide them with appropriate information that can be used to create more efficient work processes and gain a better understanding of customer preferences and behaviors.

Technology-Oriented Firms

The IoT represents a rather complex field where hardware, software, infrastructure, and business models evolve asynchronously, yet somehow have to be harnessed and forged into a coherent offering in order to gain market appeal. Technology-oriented firms essentially need to consider the ways and means for converting their technical proficiency into tangible and readily conveyable utility for potential customers. One approach, which was discussed in the previous section, is to adopt a partner strategy and cooperate with different actors in different industries. The study suggests that this approach is preferable for firms that develop the general infrastructure that connects different devices or sensors. However, it is not the only route available, as IoT infrastructure solutions may be aimed at particular industries as well. T02 have chosen to specialize in solutions for retrofitting buildings even though their offering that includes both sensors and technical infrastructure could just as well be applied in other areas. However, their devotion to a particular industry enables T02 to fixate on a finite set of concerns and tweak their offering with that in mind. As such, they are able to push the integration of hardware, software, etc., in such a way that it promotes efficiency, functionality, and convenience in a way that is tailored for a particular domain.

> Where we win it is because we have, we have the lowest installation costs and the simplest installation. We have such a fast project turnaround that in a few hours we can deliver data into their cloud. Otherwise, there will be a project that takes six months. I worked on a project back in August, where we met the CEO of a British company one day, and within four weeks we had a full installation that was up and running in their office. From that first meeting to delivery and installation and them receiving data into their application.
>
> (CTO T02)

Other companies, such as T05 and T07, take the idea of specialization even further and offer IoT-based products that are very specific in both form and function. T05 offers solutions for tracking wildlife, which usually takes the form of different collars that are fitted around the animal's neck and periodically transmit location and other relevant data. T07 has developed a rock bolt used to construct mine shafts or tunnels equipped with sensors that can detect and transmit shifts in pressure that provides an early warning system that a collapse may be imminent. This product conforms to the extreme requirements placed on both durability (being fired into solid rock) and longevity (extremely low power consumption). Although the underlying technology may very well be applicable in other situations, the product itself is highly adapted to one specific domain. Table 7.2 provides a summary of the results.

Discussion

This study sought to identify technological frames and capture firms' sensemaking processes as they were asked to reflect on their implementation and adoption of IoT. Through this we can learn about possible implications of IoT within organizations and thereby increase our understanding of the transformational impact of the IoT on working life. We show that different types of firms can be grouped together in three broad categories: product-oriented, service-oriented, and technology-oriented firms. Each group had different reasons for adopting IoT. TO firms saw the opportunity to be market leaders; SO firms saw an opportunity to create more efficient processes, thus creating both internal and external value; PO firms saw the investment in IoT as part of an ongoing strategy to move from products to services and into new markets based on product knowledge. We found that there were three recurring topics that all firms reflected upon and that had bearing on their respective adoption processes. We label these as changing work practices and working together with others; skills, competencies, and new demands on frontline staff; and privacy, security, and trust. Next we discuss these findings in relation to the literature.

Changing Work Practices and Working Together with Others

Due to the rapid development of technology, digital innovation strategy contains a high degree of uncertainty (Dodgson et al., 2008). We see that in order to manage uncertainty firms are turning to agile work practices, with short sprints, and fast delivery. The respondents, regardless of type of firm, all see the potential for improving work practices as one of the major benefits of the IoT. They also recognize the importance of technology champions, while realizing that a successful implementation requires the support of top management. This entails working closer with end users and with cross-functional teams. Indeed Porter and Heppelmann (2015) have gone so far as to say that continuing the practice of having different divisions run as functional silos that operate in relative isolation from one another is

Table 7.2 Summary of Results

Theoretical construct / Type of firm	Nature of technology	Technology strategy	Technology-in-use
	People's understanding of technology, its functionality, and its possibilities	*People's views on what technology might add to their organization and what the reason is for technology adoption*	*People's views on how technology will be used within the organization, and what consequences this will bring*
Product-oriented firms	IoT provides the opportunity to move from products to services. Continuous access to data creates opportunity to monitor products after point-of-sale.	Data can be used to tailor service- and maintenance offerings. Collected data can also be used for product development purposes. Warding off threats from competitors/retrofitters and meeting customer demands.	IoT will require tighter collaborations between different organizational units. Implementing IoT requires a cultural change within the firms.
Service-oriented firms	Opportunity to create more efficient processes and thereby more internal and external value. Base services on actual data and facts instead of estimates and guesses.	Use contextual data to create more efficient services. Combine data points to develop entirely new services. Learn from customer behaviors and use data to develop a service edge.	IoT will automate processes, save time and increase productivity. Firms may better understand customer preferences and behaviors. The use of IoT will promote the image of the firms as an innovative service provider.
Technology-oriented firms	Opportunity to be market leaders. Repackage skill sets to reach new customers.	Regarding data as the new currency. Apply existing skill sets in new contexts. Access to external competence and partnerships with others.	Technological proficiency must be converted into tangible and readily conveyable utility for customers. Either adopt a partner strategy and branch out or adapt to a specific industry and integrate technology for a particular domain.

simply not amenable to the successful creation, implementation, and operation of IoT-based products and services. This is especially notable in PO firms, where the development of a successful IoT solution requires internal cooperation between different divisions, such as Research and Development, IT, and Sales and Marketing. Convincing people to work together across established borders is a slow process in the more established PO firms, but is deemed necessary in order to create innovative results. Because many of the PO firms earn a significant amount of money on the aftermarket, we see that organization will change with similar patterns as the SO firms. Their end clients will come to expect that the PO firms start delivering services, keeping track of equipment, and notifying them of current status and needed maintenance.

This study also included different types of service-oriented firms, ranging from payment solutions to the management of individual facilities and even large tourist resorts. As these firms differ substantially in terms of type and scope, it is not surprising that we found a wide range of different views on technology in general and IoT in particular. However, operational diversity and complexity are not necessarily accurate predictors of technology perspective. SO firms expect to create a more efficient organization with an increasing number of business processes based on actual data, rather than educated guesses. They anticipate major changes in work practices, where their staff has access to correct and up-to-date information that is relevant for their specific tasks or duties. TO firms are more experienced in agile work practices, and are used to handling rapid changes in customer requirements. The major difference for them lies in how they do business—from being "just" a technology provider, to becoming part of an ecosystem of firms, a partner among others.

Skills, Competencies, and New Demands on Frontline Staff

The implementation of the IoT also highlights the need for new skills and competencies. Almost all firms state that they need to become better at data analytics, and several are actively recruiting people who match that profile. One of the major opportunities for IoT-enhanced business is the creation of an ecosystem where each participating actor contributes to the benefit of the whole group (Porter & Heppelmann, 2014). A typical IoT ecosystem consists of all three categories of firms: product owners, service providers, and technology developers. As the IoT enables collaboration across firm borders, being able to function in different networks with a variety of people from diverse backgrounds becomes an important personal skill. At the same time, as firms move toward a more open and collaborative environment, competencies might be found in the network instead of within the organization. This creates opportunities for firms to provide niche services, but might also make some current jobs obsolete, or at least likely to be done by someone else.

Firms also express that an interconnected world creates expectations that they have to live up to. For example, when working in an SO firm one will see that customers increasingly expect the service provider to instantly know about their current usage, previous patterns of use, and recurring problems, simply by analyzing their data. The same will also happen for other types of firms as customers will come to expect individual treatment, whether it concerns a product, process, or solution, based on the impression that "these firms have access to our data, therefore they know us, and should be able to figure out what we need." This creates a situation where analytical competency becomes a critical resource for any firm looking to benefit from the IoT, not only because the firms themselves see the merits of data analytics, but because their customers will come to demand it. If frontline staff are not able to deliver services in the way customers come to expect, we will assume that tensions and stress will accrue and the possibility to use the IoT to give a service edge will rapidly disappear.

Previous research shows that with the advent of platforms and application programming interfaces (APIs) that permit interoperability, we are rapidly moving from closed to open systems (Stankovic, 2014) that are expandable as long as one abides by an established set of rules and regulations. However, we are clearly not there yet, and the firms in our study all mention the lack of standards and common interfaces as something that impedes the practical implementation of IoT. For PO firms, adding a technological solution to their products becomes a matter of risk management as they try to determine which solution will become a de facto standard. Betting on the wrong horse might not only prove costly, it might lead to the demise of the entire firm. SO firms, on the other hand, typically cater to a diverse group of customers and face many different systems. For them the challenge is to navigate between various systems and contexts while they continuously innovate and develop their offering. An increased awareness of the possibilities with IoT increases the demand for data that is needed in order to make viable decisions. The need for open APIs will be something that we expect both PO and SO firms will face strongly during the upcoming years.

Privacy, Security, and Trust

The rapid diffusion of new technology creates a myriad of new opportunities, but also challenges, as firms and their employees struggle with a number of related issues, for example, the aforementioned problem of technology standards and issues of privacy, security, and control (Vermesan & Friess, 2013).

The IoT provides ready access to data that can be used for enhancing customer value. The same data can also create uncertainties regarding potential tracking and monitoring of both customers and employees. SO firms and TO firms alike repeatedly point out that simply having access to data does not mean that they intend to exploit it if it puts them in a position of potentially harming the integrity of their customers. The same reasoning must apply to their interactions with their own employees. That is, firms must be transparent about potential privacy issues and find ways to address them in order to create a trustful working environment. Previous research has shown that the use of technology makes it easier to track and monitor employees, something that can lead to a culture of distrust and an increase in stress-related health care claims (Miller & Wells, 2007; Lugaresi, 2010; Onley, 2005). As the IoT evolves and working life gets increasingly connected, these issues will grow in scope. A connected world is full of digital traces, and firms have to be careful to not allow misuse of personal information. Firms that are able to find a balance between security and privacy and gain the trust of employees, customers, and network partners will have a head start vis-à-vis their competitors. Being able to trust clients, suppliers, and staff to ensure the integrity and enforce security of one's IoT ecosystem will be essential. This will affect working life in that firms must design work practices that prevent the loss of data, uphold systems that are resilient, and enforce routines to detect and recover from attacks. Even if one builds the best systems with the best hardware and infrastructure, there is always the possibility that humans will make mistakes, that there are insiders who are leaking information, and that errors are made. If critical and/or sensitive data get lost or get into the wrong hands, the negative impact on the firm is potentially enormous. It is therefore essential that firms have a clear strategy in place that focuses on data protection and security. Furthermore, an awareness of risks and a dedication to protect individuals and organizations must be something that follows the evolution of IoT platforms and their subcomponents.

Conclusions

This study shows that the IoT, although in its early stages, has an anticipated profound impact on business processes and working life. Based on a study of 21 firms representing three different categories—product-oriented, service-oriented, and technology-oriented—we note that although contextual conditions vary, all firms need to strategically manage their IoT processes. Specifically, we conclude that in order for firms to successfully implement IoT into organizational processes, they have to 1) change their work practices accordingly; 2) make sure that they have access to all needed competencies, be they internal or external; and 3) create an environment of trust that will leverage privacy concerns. This requires a deliberate effort on the part of management, and we would therefore strongly recommend potential adopters learn about the IoT, to consider implications and consequences of adopting IoT on a strategic level, and not simply regard it as a technology investment like any other. In addition, new work practices should be firmly established throughout adopter organizations both before and during implementation, and consequences for working life must be discussed. With regard to academia, we hope to inspire researchers exploring the social and organizational implications of the IoT to consider the technological frames present within different individuals and groups of individuals (for example, specific business units) as well as firms and groups of firms to better understand expectations, ongoing strategies, and consequences, before, during, and after technology adoption.

This research was done from a management point of view, and the focus was on early adopters of the IoT. As the IoT continues to evolve, it would also be interesting to study individual workers' technological frames with regard to the IoT and look at other categories of innovation adopters, such as the strategic choices made by the early (and eventually late) majority. We have shown how the implementation of the IoT is bound to have an impact on working life. As more and more products get connected, life as we know it will be transformed, and connectivity will follow us into both our private and professional spheres. Future research should therefore delve even deeper into the issues of privacy and security and the ethical concerns associated with the IoT.

References

Atzori, L., Iera, A., & Morabito, G. (2010). The Internet of Things: A survey. *Computer Networks*, *54*(15), 2787–2805.

Borgia, E. (2014). The Internet of Things vision: Key features, applications and open issues. *Computer Communications*, *54*, 1–31.

Bullen, C., Abraham, T., & Galup, S. D. (2009). IT workforce trends: Implications for curriculum and hiring. *Communications of the Association for Information Systems*, *20*(1), 129–140.

Burkitt, F. (2014). A strategist's guide to the Internet of Things. *Strategy+Business*, *4*(77), 2–12.

Coenen, M., & Kok, R. A. (2014). Workplace flexibility and new product development performance: The role of telework and flexible work schedules. *European Management Journal*, *32*(4), 564–576.

Dodgson, M., Gann, D. M., & Salter, A. (2008). *The management of technological innovation: Strategy and practice*. Oxford: Oxford University Press.

Eisenhardt, K. M. (1989). Building theories from case study research. *Academy of Management Review*, *14*(4), 532–550.

Eloff, J. H. P., Eloff, M. M., Dlamini, M. T., & Zielinski, M. P. (2009). *Internet of people, things and services: The convergence of security, trust and privacy*. Proceedings from 3rd CompanionAble Workshop—IoPTS, Novotel Brussels, Brussels, 2 December 2009.

Ferretti, M., & Schiavone, F. (2016). Internet of Things and business processes redesign in seaports: The case of Hamburg. *Business Process Management Journal*, *22*(2), 271–284.

Gama, K., Touseau, L., & Donsez, D. (2012). Combining heterogeneous service technologies for building an Internet of Things middleware. *Computer Communications*, *35*(4), 405–417.

Greengard, S. (2015). *The Internet of Things*. Cambridge, MA: MIT Press.

Klein, H. K., & Myers, M. D. (1999). A set of principles for conducting and evaluating interpretive field studies in information systems. *MIS Quarterly*, *23*(1), 67–93.

Lugaresi, N. (2010). Electronic privacy in the workplace: Transparency and responsibility. *International Review of Law, Computers & Technology*, *24*(2), 163–173.

Manyika, J., Chui, M., Bughin, J., Dobbs, R., Bisson, P., & Marrs, A. (2013). *Disruptive technologies: Advances that will transform life, business, and the global economy* (Vol. 12). New York: McKinsey Global Institute.

Mason, J. (2002). *Qualitative researching*. Thousand Oaks, CA: Sage Publications.

Miller, C., & Wells, S. F. (2007). Balancing security and privacy in the digital workplace. *Journal of Change Management*, *7*(3–4), 315–328.

Onley, D. S. (2005). Technology gives big brother capability. *HR Magazine*, *50*(7), 99–102.

Orlikowski, W. J., & Gash, D. C. (1994). Technological frames: Making sense of information technology in organizations. *ACM Transaction on Information Systems*, *12*(2), 174–207.

Porter, M. E., & Heppelmann, J. E. (2014). How smart, connected products are transforming competition. *Harvard Business Review*, *92*(11), 64–88.

Porter, M. E., & Heppelmann, J. E. (2015). How smart, connected products are transforming companies. *Harvard Business Review*, *93*(10), 96–114.

Rogers, E. M. (2003). *Diffusion of innovations* (5th ed.). New York: Simon and Schuster.

Saarikko, T., Westergren, U. H., & Blomquist, T. (2016). *The inter-organizational dynamics of a platform ecosystem: Exploring stakeholder boundaries*. Proceedings from 49th Hawaii International Conference on System Sciences (HICSS), IEEE, Koloa, HI, 5167–5176.

Saarikko, T., Westergren, U. H., & Blomquist, T. (2017). The Internet of Things: Are you ready for what's coming? *Business Horizons*, *60*(5), 667–676.

Shehadi, R., & Karam, D. (2014, January 14). *Five essential elements of the digital workplace* [Web log article]. Retrieved from www.strategy-business.com/blog/Five-Essential-Elements-of-the-Digital-Workplace

Stankovic, J. A. (2014). Research directions for the Internet of Things. *IEEE Internet of Things Journal*, *1*(1), 3–9.

Vermesan, O., & Friess, P. (Eds.). (2013). *Internet of Things: Converging technologies for smart environments and integrated ecosystems*. Aalborg: River Publishers.

Walsham, G. (1993). *Interpreting information systems in organizations*. Chichester: Wiley Books.

Whitmore, A., Agarwal, A., & Da Xu, L. (2015). The Internet of Things: A survey of topics and trends. *Information Systems Frontiers*, *17*(2), 261–274.

Yin, R. K. (2009). *Case study research: Design and methods*. Thousand Oaks, CA: Sage Publications.

8 The Impact of the Internet of Things (IoT) on the IT Security Infrastructure of Traditional Colleges and Universities in the State of Utah

Wendy Campbell

Introduction

The Internet has allowed us to communicate, collaborate, educate, and conduct business, regardless of time or place. The speed and availability of Internet-capable devices, such as computers, smartphones, gaming consoles, TVs, and tablets, have made it possible for our society to be connected and stay connected to the Internet 24 hours a day. In addition to people, physical objects are now being connected to the Internet. The Internet of Things can include any physical object that one chooses to track or monitor. These smart "things" are predicted to interact—collect data, relay, and process information with one another without direct human intervention (Chen, 2012). Researchers estimate that more than 50 billion "things" will be connected to the Internet by 2020 (Evans, 2011).

The Internet of Things—Opportunities

The Internet of Things offers many opportunities. Applications for the Internet of Things currently exist in industries such as automotive, transportation, healthcare, and retail. Automobiles have been connected to the Internet for years. Today's automobiles link to smartphones, display real-time traffic alerts, stream audio, and offer emergency roadside assistance at the touch of a button. Many cars, trains, and buses are equipped with sensors to monitor and report on maintenance status and vehicle location. IoT applications have been deployed in air, ground, and sea transportation and can make the transportation of goods and people more efficient. Medical IoT devices, including stationary, wearable, implantable, and ingestible, are now available to patients. These devices monitor various illnesses and send clinical data to healthcare providers. Smart environments include buildings and homes equipped with sensor technology that helps monitor resource consumption, regulate HVAC systems, and detect intrusions. The IoT in retail has helped retailers enhance the customer shopping experience and improve sales—smart shelves can be used to detect when inventory is low, and customers can use smart mirrors that allow them to "try on" clothes virtually—outside of the fitting room.

Traditional colleges and universities are also discovering the benefits of the IoT. The use of the IoT can streamline faculty administration functions, including attendance and progress tracking. IoT implementations in higher education could create personalized, dynamic, and interactive learning environments where students, faculty, and devices can interact with each other (Kiryakova, Yordanova, & Angelova, 2017). Colleges and universities can also use IoT devices to initiate a campus lockdown system, including electronic perimeter security and immediate student, faculty, and police notifications (Lutz, 2014). The potential uses of IoT technology on college and university campuses are endless.

The Internet of Things—Challenges

The Internet of Things will add much more convenience and efficiency to our lives. However, as always, there is a downside. The IoT has triggered a merge between our physical and virtual environments. Cybercriminals now can attack both the virtual (logical) and physical infrastructures of their targets. The Internet of Things is a relatively new research field. Exploratory research studies have been conducted to identify the many challenges, including issues with application standardization (Bandyopadhya & Sen, 2011), scalability (Chen, 2012), and security and privacy (Suo, Wan, Zou, & Liu, 2012; Polk & Turner, 2011). IoT applications lack communications and data security (Suo et al., 2012), as well as authentication and identity management (Polk & Turner, 2011). Current encryption algorithms are designed for devices with significant processor speeds and memory, such as computers, smartphones, and tablets. Given the limited memory and processor speed of IoT devices, the applicability of these encryption techniques is unclear (Polk & Turner, 2011). Authentication will present significant challenges for the Internet of Things (Polk & Turner, 2011). Unlike individuals, IoT devices will be unable to authenticate using biometrics, and due to the vast number of devices, static passwords would be both inefficient and insecure. Individual privacy is also a concern. Individuals have no control over the personal information embedded in object tags. Individuals can be tracked without their knowledge or consent (Weber, 2010). The cost of storing and managing the "big data" created by the Internet of Things is another major challenge (Chen, 2012). Relational database management systems cannot handle the large volume and the unstructured data created by the Internet of Things (Chen, Mao, & Liu, 2014). The increase in "big data" will affect data acquisition, storage, management, and analysis.

IoT systems are very complicated. They are developed using various layers of technology, including edge devices, firmware, protocols, and software, making configurations quite complex. Complex systems are harder to design securely, configure securely, and use securely. Standards supporting the IoT have not yet been fully developed, which increases their complexity. Many IoT devices are vulnerable because they have exposed backdoors, weak passwords, or simply lack adequate security controls (InfoSec Institute, 2017). A Hewlett-Packard Development Company (2014) Internet of Things research study revealed that 70% of the most commonly used IoT devices contain serious vulnerabilities, and 90% of the IoT devices collected at least one piece of personally identifiable information (PII). The data obtained from these insecure objects can be used to acquire confidential student information or used to access and control critical university systems.

The problem is that traditional colleges and universities do not have the IT security infrastructure in place to manage the risks created by the IoT. Thirty-five percent of all security breaches occur in higher education (Coleman & Purcell, 2015; Beaudin, 2015; Security Magazine, 2014). Thirty-six percent of the higher education breaches were perpetrated by hacking or malware, 30% were perpetrated by unintended disclosure, and 17% were perpetrated by mobile device breaches (Coleman & Purcell, 2015; Grama, 2014; Educause, 2014b). In 2015, Harvard University, Penn State University, Auburn University, Washington State University, John Hopkins University, the University of Virginia, the University of Maryland, and the University of Connecticut were all victims of cyberattacks (Simon, 2016; Coleman & Purcell, 2015; Smith, 2015; McCarthy, 2015). Colleges and universities have long struggled with finding a balance between academic freedom and security (Wolff, 2015; Callahan, 2014). However, the security risks of the Internet of Things have the potential to damage students, faculty, and the reputation and security posture of traditional colleges and universities.

IT Security Challenges of Traditional Colleges and Universities

The network environment of a traditional campus is unique and complex. Campus networks extend across broad geographic areas. In addition to the main campus, many colleges and universities have satellite campuses throughout the city or state. Campus networks are fragmented and decentralized, and support a massive, ever-changing user base and require a vast amount of bandwidth. In addition to providing resources for their students and faculty, colleges and universities provide resources to their local communities. Campus network environments promote openness, including research, faculty–student interaction, and peer-to-peer collaboration (Wolff, 2015; Callahan, 2014). To further complicate the security issues, students, faculty, and staff are bringing their own devices on campus and connecting to the campus network. These mobile devices, including notebooks, tablets, and smartphones, are infiltrating college and university campuses. Bring-your-own-device (BYOD) technologies create a security risk because colleges and universities have little or no control over the devices that users introduce to the network (Educause, 2014b). Consequently, the campus network includes an array of network topologies, operating systems, software applications, devices, and local and remote users.

Colleges and universities are prime targets for cyberattacks because of their openness and the amount of personally identifiable information and intellectual property that they create, store, and transmit. Colleges and universities store healthcare records, police reports, financial records, intellectual property, and personal data. Nonetheless, academia has not totally embraced the need for IT security (Wolff, 2015). A study conducted by the Chicago Better Business Bureau found that college students are the most at risk for malware infection because of their use of social media and smartphones (Jedra, 2013). An Experian Simmons study found that more than 98% of college students visit social media networking sites on a daily basis (Griffin, 2015). Colleges and universities are also experiencing an increase in Distributed Denial of Service (DDoS) attacks (Akamai Technologies, 2016). In 2015, the University of Virginia, Pennsylvania State University, University of Connecticut, Washington State University, Johns Hopkins University, University of Maryland, and the University of Southern California, were all victims of DDoS attacks (Johnston, 2016). In the first six months of 2016, the Massachusetts Institute of Technology was targeted with 35 DDoS attacks (Akamai Technologies, 2016). DDoS attacks not only make campus resources unavailable for students, faculty, and staff, but they also create a conduit for the attacker to steal network data and metadata. This data can then be used to breach information systems or steal PII.

Decentralized Physical and Network Security Management

Due to their decentralized structure, traditional colleges and universities not only have challenges with their IT infrastructure, but they also have challenges with their IT leadership and decision-making structure (Educause, 2014a). This decentralization makes it impossible for colleges and universities to develop and enforce cohesive security policies and procedures (Maskari, Saini, Raut, & Hadimani, 2011). Security is divided into two major areas: physical and logical (network). Physical security focuses on the protection of tangible assets reinforced by security guards and physical access controls. Logical security concentrates on the protection of information systems and the digital assets of colleges and universities (Melendez, Luse, Townsend, & Mennecke, 2008). The Internet of Things integrates existing information technology and operations technology networks, including sensors and smart devices (Cisco, 2015). This convergence creates new security challenges. The convergence of information technology (IT) and operational technology (OT) security requires a new approach to security that combines shared devices, data, networks, policies, and priorities.

Convergence is not a new concept for many IT organizations. In the late 1980s to early 1990s, IT organizations struggled with the convergence of voice and data communications. In the not so near past, data and voice communication was managed by different departments. Now, 25 years later, because of the emergence of the Internet of Things, the IT organization is on the brink of another convergence—physical and logical security. Merging physical and logical security is seen by many advocates as a way to reduce costs and improve organizational efficiency and security (Messmer, 2010; Ting, 2010; Zalud, 2010; Jain, 2008). Combining logical and physical security processes and infrastructures simplifies the manageability of the security infrastructure and increases the visibility of resources, which makes it easier for universities to detect, prevent, and recover from security incidents (Carney, 2011).

IoT Security Challenges of Traditional Colleges and Universities

Securing the Internet of Things will be a challenging task for colleges and universities. A limitless connection of "things" has its disadvantages. The increase in the number of objects connected to the Internet increases the number of campus vulnerabilities and subsequently increases the risk of campus exploitation and attack. Devices that were previously immune to exploits and malware are now vulnerable, including security systems, HVAC systems, access doors, and even vending machines. Any device connected to the Internet has the potential of being compromised (Kumar, 2014). These smart devices could create backdoors into the campus systems; they can become a conduit for malware propagation, or they can store personally identifiable information and compromise privacy (Beaver, 2014).

Data Management

The big data created by the Internet of Things will cause issues with data storage, data retrieval, and data analysis. Colleges and universities will need new governance strategies to manage the variety (structured, semi-structured, and unstructured), volume, and velocity of data created by the IoT (Jimenez-Peris, 2015). According to the Cisco Systems Global Cloud Index Report, it is estimated that the Internet of Things will generate 400 zettabytes (ZB) (a trillion gigabytes) of data a year by 2018 (Worth, 2014). The data from these "things" must be processed and analyzed in real time to monitor what they are doing, their operating conditions, their load, and their configuration (Jimenez-Peris, 2015). Existing network infrastructures may be ill equipped to handle the volume and velocity of data created by the IoT. Gartner research director Fabrizio Biscotti suggests that processing large quantities of IoT data in real time will create many challenges for organizations, including in terms of bandwidth, capacity, and analytics (Gartner & Gartner, 2014). The IoT will generate massive amounts of data from globally distributed sources. Furthermore, backing up this enormous volume of data will further compound the bandwidth issue and will create data storage issues. A campus's capacity to back up zettabytes of raw data is likely to be unaffordable and inefficient. Also, the sorting and analysis of large volumes of data will generate significant data processing loads that will overwhelm most campus networks.

Data Security and Privacy

The data produced by the Internet of Things will not only create data management issues, but it may also create privacy issues. Device sensors and RFID tags could generate a vast amount of personally identifiable information. Students, faculty, and staff will have no control over the personal information embedded in object tags and can be tracked without their knowledge or consent (Weber, 2010). Similar to PCs and smartphones, most IoT devices also have embedded operating systems. However, current security models for regularly updating security patches and antivirus signatures and enabling data encryption are not feasible for most IoT devices (Orebaugh, 2014; Polk & Turner, 2011). "Most IoT devices have low capabilities regarding both energy and computer resources. Thus, they cannot implement complex security schemes" (Atzori, Iera, & Morabito, 2010, p. 2801). These limitations will result in IoT devices that are vulnerable to hacking and malware and will increase the risk of campus exploitation and attack.

Theoretical Proposition

The purpose of this survey research study was to investigate the impact of the Internet of Things (IoT) on the IT security infrastructure of traditional colleges and universities in the state of Utah. This study is based on the systems theory perspective of holism. Holism implies that everything is connected, inseparable, and functions a whole; it suggests that the whole is more than the sum of its parts and maintains that complex systems, such as the Internet of Things, should be governed holistically (Matindi & Ngugi, 2014). Many traditional colleges and universities have discovered the benefits of deploying IoT technology on their campuses. However, if not implemented appropriately, IoT devices have the potential to jeopardize the confidentiality, integrity, and availability of campus resources.

The Internet of Things integrates existing IT and OT networks, in addition to sensors, devices, and other smart objects (Cisco, 2015). This convergence creates new security challenges. IT and OT networks are usually managed with different priorities (Cisco, 2015). The priority of IT is to protect the confidentiality, integrity, and availability of information and information systems; the focus of the OT is to ensure university operations and safety. The convergence of IT and OT security requires a new approach to security that combines shared devices, data, networks, and priorities.

Physical security and network security management must be a holistic and collaborative effort to be effective in an IoT environment. Traditional colleges and universities that integrate these once-disparate systems may be more efficient in addressing and mitigating risk. Partnering these two security entities will create a more cohesive and seamless security organization. This collaboration will translate into fewer incidents and more efficient protection for campus resources—buildings, networks, equipment, information, students, and employees. Major transformations are needed in network infrastructures, IT organizational structures, and IT risk management to support the Internet of Things. Based on the earlier theory, the following propositions have been developed:

- P1. The IoT will redefine IT security management in traditional colleges and universities due to the convergence of physical and logical security.
- P2. The IoT will increase IT security risks in traditional colleges and universities.
- P3. The IoT will change traditional campus IT infrastructures due to the influx of big data.

Research Methods

Population and Sample

The target population included 24 traditional colleges and universities in the state of Utah. Utah was selected for this study because of its principal three cities—Provo, Ogden, and Salt Lake City—are among the top 15 in the country with the highest concentration of STEM (science, technology, engineering, and math) sector employment (Bernardo, 2017; Vara, 2015). Utah is considered by some to be the next Silicon Valley (Bernardo, 2017; Feldman, 2017; Rampton, 2017; Vara, 2015). The chief information officer (CIO) from each college and university was invited to participate in the survey. Eleven colleges and universities, representing seven cities across the state of Utah, participated in the study.

Data Collection

This research study involved interaction with human subjects and was governed by basic ethical principles of The National Commission for the Protection of Human Subjects of Biomedical and Behavioral Research. The research for this study was presented to the Northcentral University Institutional Review Board (IRB) for approval. No data collection or research activities had begun before the researcher received written approval for this study from the IRB. The data collected in this study originated from an online survey created using SurveyMonkey. The online survey allowed the researcher to reach geographically diverse Utah populations in a short amount of time. The researcher identified the CIO for each of the colleges and universities in Utah by visiting each school's website. A recruitment email request was sent to participants, including the survey link, inviting them to complete the online survey. A follow-up phone call was placed to each participant. The survey instrument was available for 30 days.

Survey Instrument

The online survey used a combination of questions, including demographic, multiple choice, ordinal scale, interval scale, and open-ended. The online survey included the following questions:

Q1. What is the university's current student enrollment?
Q2. Describe the types of Internet of Things (IoT) devices that have been deployed within your university.
Q3. Who has ownership of the IoT data that are being collected?
Q4. What were the top five IT security risks before the IoT deployment?
Q5. What are the top five IT security risks after the IoT deployment?
Q6. Which department is responsible for monitoring new IoT security risks?
Q7. How have the IT security risks changed since the IoT deployment?
Q8. How has the IT infrastructure changed since the IoT deployment?
Q9. What are the challenges with managing IoT data?
Q10. Describe the integration of physical and logical (network) security after the IoT deployment.

Assumptions

A few assumptions were associated with this study. It was assumed that the participants in this study had an in-depth understanding of information technology, risk management, and university operations. Another assumption was that the participants would respond to survey questions honestly and without bias toward what might be considered the acceptable answer.

Limitations

The limitations of this study included the perceptions and honesty of each participant. The online survey instrument was also a limitation. The email invitation for the survey could have been categorized as spam or junk mail and subsequently ignored or deleted. The topic of IT security was also a limitation. Many participants may have been reluctant to disclose any information about potential campus vulnerabilities.

Results

Demographics

The study consisted of 11 (out of 24) traditional colleges and universities, representing seven cities across the state of Utah. Forty-six percent of the colleges and universities surveyed had a student population of 5,000 to 10,000 (medium), 36% had a student population of 10,000 to 50,000 (large), and 18% had a student population of less than 5,000 (small).

Internet of Things Devices

Seven of the colleges and universities have kiosks installed. Nine have HVAC systems. Ten have security systems. Six have smoke and fire detection systems. IoT devices that are unique to individual colleges and universities include secure door access, digital audio-visual signage, solar panels, IP cameras, and parking meter automated pay systems.

Ownership of IoT data

In three of the colleges and universities, the information technology department has ownership of the IoT data. In three colleges and universities, the operations technology department is the owner of the IoT data. In the remaining five colleges and universities, the information technology department and the operations technology department share ownership of the IoT data.

Risks Before IoT Deployment

The top five risks for the eleven colleges and universities before the IoT deployments included malware, the disclosure of PII, unauthorized access, network intrusion, and social engineering.

Risk After the IoT deployment

The top five risks for the 11 colleges and universities after the IoT deployments included disclosure of PII, network intrusion, unauthorized access, malware, and social engineering.

Monitoring New IoT Risks

In nine of the colleges and universities, the information technology department is responsible for monitoring new IoT risks. In two of the colleges and universities, both the information technology department and the operations technology department have shared responsibility for monitoring new IoT risks.

Changes in IT Security Risks

One university noted that the IT risks had increased significantly. Two colleges and universities reported that the IT risks have slightly increased. Two colleges and universities reported that the IT risks significantly decreased. One university noted that the IT risks slightly decreased. Two colleges and universities indicated that there was no change in the IT risks. One university stated that the risks are the same, but the effect of the risk is different. One university indicated that there was a slight increase due to another attack vector.

Changes in IT Infrastructure

Five colleges and universities indicated that the changes in the IT infrastructure included the integration of physical and network security management. Two colleges and universities indicated that the IT infrastructure changes include a separation of physical and network security management. Four colleges and universities indicated that the IT infrastructure changed to closed networks. Three colleges and universities noted no change to the IT infrastructure. One university indicated the IoT added another layer of complexity and required more resources to maintain and troubleshoot the IT infrastructure.

Challenges with IoT Data Management

Four colleges and universities indicated that data storage and data analytics are challenges. Three colleges and universities stated that data encryption is a challenge. Four colleges and universities indicated that the protection of PII is a challenge. Two colleges and universities reported that bandwidth is a challenge. Six colleges and universities reported that access control is a challenge.

Test of Propositions

Proposition 1

The IoT will redefine IT security management in traditional colleges and universities due to the convergence of physical and logical security.

Shared IoT Data Management

The Internet of Things redefined the IT security management infrastructure of traditional colleges and universities in the state of Utah. Seventy-three percent of the colleges and universities were required to change the way they manage network security. After the IoT implementations, the information technology department and the operations technology department have shared the responsibility of managing the IoT data. For many years in higher education, there has been a trend toward decentralization of IT service delivery. However, with the deployment of the IoT, that trend has changed. IT and OT have shared ownership of the IoT data that are being collected, stored, and analyzed. The monitoring of new IoT risks is also a shared responsibility between IT and OT.

Proposition 2

The IoT will increase IT security risks in traditional colleges and universities.

Change in IT Security Risks

The IT security risks in traditional colleges and universities in Utah did not increase after the IoT deployments. However, the variety and impact of the risks changed. Before the IoT deployment, the top risk was malware. After the IoT deployment, 55% of the schools reported that the top risk was the release of PII. Although the risks did not change, the effect of the risks changed. In addition to the threats to the logical infrastructure, the IoT has created threats to the campus's physical infrastructure systems.

Proposition 3

The IoT will change traditional campus IT infrastructures due to the influx of big data.

Isolated IoT Networks

Utah colleges and universities reported that the influx of big data had created challenges with data storage, data analytics, data encryption, and the protection of PII. The colleges and universities were required to change their IT infrastructures. Fifty-five percent of the colleges and universities reported that they separate the IoT data from the structured data. This data isolation is accomplished by virtual area network (VLAN) or by physical network separation.

Discussion

The research study yielded three major themes regarding the impact of the IoT on the IT security infrastructure of traditional colleges and universities in the state of Utah. The themes included security convergence, network segmentation, and threats to privacy and PII.

Security Convergence

Historically, physical security systems have been in a closed environment and managed by the operations technology (facilities) department. However, with the move to IP-based systems, there is the need to include the IT department (Messmer, 2010). Security convergence is a risk management strategy that merges two distinct security functions: physical security and information security management (Melendez et al., 2008). Physical security includes a different set of threats, vulnerabilities, and risks. Physical security mechanisms protect campus facilities, work areas, equipment, and people. Physical threats fall into many categories such as natural disaster threats (i.e., wind, earthquakes, and floods); environmental threats (i.e., power outages, energy disruptions, and communication failures); and human threats (i.e., violence, theft, and vandalism). Loss from physical threats can be even more devastating to a college or university than IT security threats. Consequently, IT security is ineffective in the absence of physical security, and physical security is ineffective in the absence of IT security.

Colleges and universities in Utah have combined the management of IoT security. This centralized management structure makes it possible for Utah colleges and universities to develop and enforce cohesive security priorities, policies, and procedures. Combining information and physical security processes also simplifies the cost and manageability of the security infrastructure. Research by McCreight and Leece (2016) found that having one standardized security organization can offer significant cost and operating efficiencies—OT and IT departments no longer need to create and maintain their proprietary networks. Convergence also increases the visibility of resources, which makes it easier for Utah colleges and universities to detect, prevent, and recover from security incidents.

Convergence offers colleges and universities the opportunity to restructure their security infrastructure and combine systems, which spare time, money, and bandwidth. Convergence also provides a holistic view of security across the entire campus and can provide colleges and universities with several tangible benefits, including increased operational efficiencies, reduction in risks, and streamlined risk mitigation and incident management strategies (Carney, 2011).

Network Segmentation

The variety, volume, and velocity of the big data created by the IoT have caused issues with data storage, data retrieval, and data analysis. To alleviate these issues, colleges and universities in Utah have created separate networks—physical and virtual networks—to isolate the IoT big data from the structured university data. Physical network segmentation enhances security by only allowing authorized traffic (data and users) that is physically connected to the network to have access to resources. However, many colleges and universities have realized that this same separation can be accomplished by integrating VLAN and virtual private network (VPN) technologies.

VLANs can logically separate IoT traffic from other university traffic on the network. Because VLANs are a logical segmentation, IoT devices on the same VLAN do not have to be physically located together, which saves time, resources, and bandwidth. VPNs can create a secure communication link between geographically distant locations. With the implementation of VPN technology and cryptographic tunneling protocols, it is possible to prevent unauthorized data transmission and data interception to and from IoT devices.

Colleges and universities implementing VLANs and VPNs to separate their IoT have realized the following benefits:

1. ***Enhanced Security.*** IoT data can be separated from the structured data network, decreasing the chances of confidential information breaches.
2. ***Cost reduction.*** Cost savings result from the elimination of running separate networks and the more efficient use of existing bandwidth.
3. ***Enhanced network performance.*** Separating networks into multiple logical groups reduces traffic on the network and enhances performance.

VLAN implementations have helped Utah colleges and universities address scalability, flexibility, security, and network management issues created by the Internet of Things.

Threats to Privacy and Control

IoT devices have low capabilities regarding both energy and computer resources and are unable to support complex security structures, including encryption, antimalware, and intrusion detection. These limitations make IoT devices vulnerable to exploitation and attack, which threatens privacy and control. The IoT has created new threats, vulnerabilities, and attack vectors that malicious actors can exploit to compromise privacy and control. Healthcare providers can improperly diagnose and treat patients based on modified health information or manipulated sensor data (Cloud Security Alliance, 2015). Intruders can gain physical access to homes or businesses through attacks against electronic, remote-controlled door lock mechanisms (Atzori et al., 2010). Malicious actors can steal identities and money based on leakage of sensitive information or by aggregating data from many different systems and sensors (Cloud Security Alliance, 2015). Critical infrastructure systems, emergency vehicles, and the human body can be manipulated, causing injury or death, through unauthorized access to wearable medical devices (Cloud Security Alliance, 2015). Unauthorized tracking of an individual's behaviors, activities, and locations can be collected from sensors without notice or consent of the individual (Miorandi, Sicari, De Pellegrini, & Chlamtac, 2012).

Implications

The results of this research will serve as a standard for colleges and universities to utilize in preparing their campuses for the Internet of Things. Many traditional colleges and universities in Utah have discovered the benefits of the Internet of Things. However, if not implemented appropriately, IoT devices have the potential to jeopardize the confidentiality, integrity, and availability of campus resources. The implications of this study maintain that a holistic approach to IT security management will help colleges and universities address the complex and dynamic issues surrounding the Internet of Things.

IT Governance

Due to the convergence of physical and information security, departmental silos in traditional colleges and universities will start to disappear. Also, the sole IT decision-making role of C-level (chief) executives may be abated in place of an IT governance committee. These committees may include C-level executives, facilities director, IT faculty chair, and IT faculty members, among others. IT governance is a proactive solution to ensure that IT goals are in alignment with organizational goals. IT governance includes all possible combinations of physical and virtual assets, local and remote systems, and internal and external stakeholders. It is an instrument to control and manage the IT resources such as infrastructure technology, people, and the Internet of Things (Bianchi & Sousa, 2016).

Effective IT governance is necessary to ensure that the technologies, policies, and processes do not negatively affect organizational performance. Such governance in higher education was found to be more effective under a delegated model of decision-making authority that empowers IT governance bodies rather than a CIO-centric model (Carraway, 2015). Physical and IT security roles will still be required, but there will be much more communication among those roles and much more integration of solutions, including policies, procedures, and technologies. The implementation of IT governance strategies will help colleges and universities identify IoT risks, analyze the reliability and scalability of the IT infrastructure, and help mitigate the threats created by the Internet of Things.

Cloud Infrastructures

Due to limited bandwidth, budgets, and staffing, colleges and universities may need to consider moving their IoT data to the cloud. The volume of data collected, transmitted, and stored may overwhelm most campus networks and power grids due to the energy consumption of IoT devices. "Cloud infrastructure provides the necessary means regarding hardware capacity and processing power required for processing the enormous amounts of data expected to be generated from the IoT" (Subramanian, Gopal, & Muthusamy, 2015, p. 1).

There are several advantages for colleges and universities to adopt a cloud-computing infrastructure. Cloud providers specialize in particular applications and services, and this expertise allows them to manage upgrades and maintenance, backups, disaster recovery, and redundancy. Cloud computing offers scalability and flexibility when managing the volume, velocity, and variety of data created by the IoT in universities and colleges. Vermesan et al., (2011) suggested that cloud computing is the future of the Internet and that the Internet of Things is expected to be the biggest user of the cloud.

A research study conducted by eCampus News (2015) found that colleges and universities are currently using the cloud to manage a wide range of technology, administrative, and educational systems. However, the adoption of cloud computing presents many challenges in terms of security, privacy, interoperability, control, performance, integrity and reliability, and intellectual property management (Jain & Pandey, 2013). Sixty-eight percent of colleges and universities reported that security is the top challenge with cloud computing (eCampus News, 2015). Privacy and security are always at risk when data are transmitted over the Internet. Once the data leave the campus, the cloud provider has full control over the data. Also, storage costs can be extremely expensive for colleges and universities that have a large amount of data. Successful cloud initiatives will be dependent on explicit service-level agreements, including clauses addressing availability (outages), response time, data ownership, and protection of intellectual property and PII. Colleges and universities need to weigh the costs and benefits of managing the IoT in the cloud. Despite the potential security risks posed by cloud services, some would argue that cloud services might offer more security than on-campus solutions, given the complexity of the Internet of Things.

Conclusion

The purpose of this research survey was to investigate the impact of the Internet of Things (IoT) on the IT security infrastructures of traditional colleges and universities in the state of Utah. Twenty-four traditional colleges and universities were invited to participate in the study. Eleven completed the online survey. The research propositions suggest that physical security and network security management must be a holistic, collaborative effort to secure an IoT environment. The research findings uncovered three themes identified as the IoT Security Triad (see Figure 8.1), which are enumerated in Table 8.1.

1. **Network Segmentation.** Fifty-five percent of the colleges and universities reported that they separate the IoT data from the structured data.
2. **Security Convergence.** Seventy-three percent of the colleges and universities reported the management of IoT data is shared between the information technology department and the operations technology department.
3. **Threats to privacy and security.** Fifty-five percent of the schools reported that the number-one risk after the IoT deployment was the release of personally identifiable information.

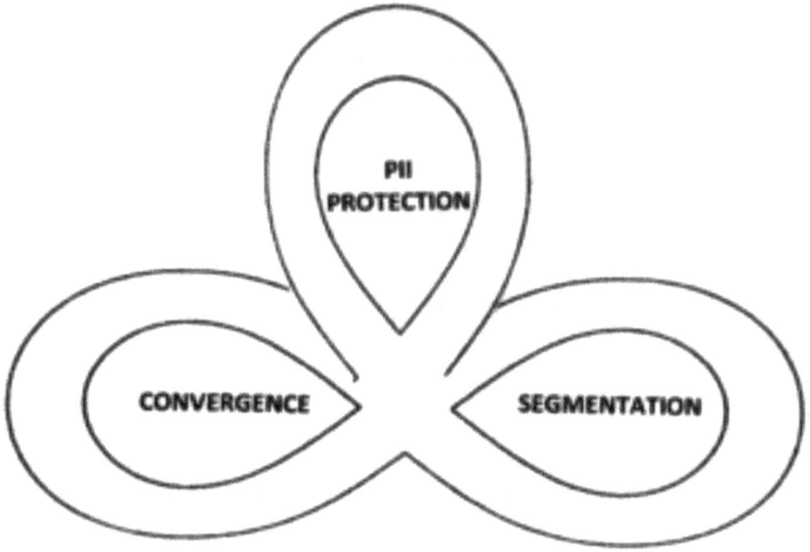

Figure 8.1 IoT Security Triad

Table 8.1 Research Findings

Security Convergence	Establish IT governance committee composed of various stakeholders (facilities management and IT management) to help manage the risks created by the IoT Establish cohesive policies and procedures on how IoT technology is acquired, configured, managed, and maintained Establish security policies, incident response procedures, and business continuity and disaster recovery plans
Data/Network Segmentation	Conduct risk analysis to assess the risk and necessity of each IoT device connected to the network, including type of connection—LAN, WAN, Wi-Fi Implement VPNs and VLANS to isolate IoT data and networks Modify factory default configurations for all IoT devices, including default passwords and unneeded protocols Insist that vendors disclose any backdoors or vendor interfaces to IoT devices Purchase devices that are capable of being secured; IoT devices should be configured to provide the maximum level of security Establish a process for configuration management Implement intrusion detection systems that alert administrators of malicious network activity Conduct periodic technical audits of IoT devices and networks to ensure ongoing effectiveness
Protection of Privacy and PII	Release of information related to the IoT devices should be on a strict, need-to-know basis and only to persons explicitly authorized to receive such information Provide training and information awareness programs to ensure that faculty, staff, and students remain diligent in guarding sensitive network information Minimize the threat from malicious insiders by conducting employee background checks and monitoring

Recommendations for Future Study

The Internet of Things will have similar impacts on other service-related organizations—organizations dedicated to serving large and dynamic populations, including K–12 schools. Similar to colleges and universities, K–12 school networks are relatively large and need to be accessible by students, parents, staff, and outside agencies (Glassberg, 2016). The wireless networks are usually "open to the public," allowing anyone to connect any device to the network. Many school districts have instituted BYOD policies, introducing additional vulnerabilities (Herold, 2016). These accessibility issues make K–12 schools easy targets for hackers. These schools are attractive targets due to the amount of data they collect, including academic records, attendance records, and medical history (Lestch, 2015). Between 2005 and 2014, nearly 800 educational institutions have experienced a data breach; one-third of those breaches occurred at K–12 schools (Pribish, 2015). Security experts suggest that these schools are at risk because they rely more on technology for day-to-day operations and incorporate more mobile devices, applications, online programs, and web-based testing into the classroom (Lestch, 2015). Many K–12 schools struggle with finding a balance between IT security and providing access to the network to support their educational mission (Herold, 2016). Although many schools have seen a significant increase in the number of IoT devices, many K–12 schools still struggle with obtaining affordable access to high-speed Internet and robust wireless connectivity (Schooldude, 2014). Twenty-three percent of school districts do not have enough bandwidth to meet the current needs for digital learning (Education Superhighway, 2016). Consequently, most K–12 schools do not have adequate bandwidth or funding to support and secure the Internet of Things. Many of these schools have already deployed IoT devices, including surveillance cameras, motion detectors, lighting systems, and wireless door locks to enhance campus security and safety (McIntyre, 2016). However, funding to support security improvements may require cutting spending in other areas of the budget, raising taxes, or increasing school fees (Glassberg, 2016).

Recommendations for Security Practitioners

In the next few years, billions of objects will be embedded with microchips, RFID tags, and sensors. It is essential that educational institutions implement a layered defense strategy—deter, detect, deny, delay, and defend to prevent unauthorized access, manipulation, and control of IoT devices. "A defense-in-depth strategy is based on the idea that people, technology, and operational security must be provided to ensure end-to-end defense" (Chapple & Seidl, 2015, p. 197). These strategies must include the protection of PII, network segmentation, and physical and network security convergence.

The primary strategy is to develop a "security-aware" campus culture. Students, faculty, and staff should have a sense of awareness, accountability, and responsibility for IT security. The author recommends the strategies in Table 8.1. As the Internet of Things continues to evolve, issues of trust, identity, privacy, protection, safety, and security (Hudson, 2016) will continue to afflict colleges and universities. The IoT has changed the way colleges and universities in Utah manage their infrastructure, data, and risks. These colleges and universities have discovered that physical security and network security management must be a holistic and collaborative effort to be effective in this environment.

References

Akamai Technologies. (2016). *Akamai's state of the internet report.* Retrieved October 27, 2016, from https://content.akamai.com/PG7010-Q2-2016-SOTI-Connectivity-Report.html?utm_source=GoogleSearch&gclid=CMirzP-R_M8CFUlNfgodR3YAKQ

Atzori, L., Iera, A., & Morabito, G. (2010). The Internet of Things: A survey. *Computer Networks*, *54*, 2787–2805. Retrieved from https://cs.uwaterloo.ca/~brecht/courses/854-Emerging-2014/readings/iot/iot-survey.pdf

Bandyopadhya, D., & Sen, J. (2011). Internet of Things: Applications and challenges in technology and standardization. *Wireless Personal Communications*, *58*(1), 49–69. Retrieved from http://arxiv.org/pdf/1105.1693.pdf

Beaudin, K. (2015). College and university data breaches: Regulating higher education cybersecurity under state and federal law. *Journal of College and University Law*, *41*(3), 657–695.

Beaver, K. (2014). Is your security program ready for the Internet of Things? *Information Security, Insider Edition: Securing the Internet of Things*, 9–11. Retrieved from http://pro.techtarget.com/Global/FileLib/targeted_downloads/ISM_InsideEdition_final.pdf

Bernardo, R. (2017). *2017's best & worst metro areas for STEM professionals.* Retrieved October 9, 2017, from https://wallethub.com/edu/best-worst-metro-areas-for-stem-professionals/9200/

Bianchi, I., & Sousa, R. (2016). IT governance mechanisms in higher education. *Procedia Computer Science*, *100*(2016), 941–946. Retrieved from www.sciencedirect.com/science/article/pii/S187705091632422X

Callahan, M. (2014). *Higher education faces unique cybersecurity challenges.* Retrieved February 3, 2016, from www.edelman.com/post/higher-education-faces-unique-cybersecurity-challenges/

Carney, J. (2011). *Why integrate physical and logical security?* Retrieved July 1, 2015, from www.cisco.com/web/strategy/docs/gov/pl-security.pdf

Carraway, D. (2015). *Information technology governance maturity and technology innovation in higher education: Factors in effectiveness.* Retrieved December 20, 2016, from https://libres.uncg.edu/ir/uncg/f/Carraway_uncg_0154M_11689.pdf

Chapple, M., & Seidl, D. (2015). *Cyberwarfare: Information operations in a connected world.* Burlington, MA: James & Bartlett Learning.

Chen, M., Mao, S., & Liu, Y. (2014). Big data: A survey. *Mobile Networks and Applications*, *19*(2), 171–209. Retrieved from www.ece.ubc.ca/~minchen/min_paper/BigDataSurvey2014.pdf

Chen, Y. K. (2012). *Challenges and opportunities of Internet of Things.* Design Automation Conference (ASP-DAC), 2012 17th, Asia and South Pacific, 383–388.

Retrieved from www.cp.eng.chula.ac.th/~piak/teaching/ads/ads2013/iot/Internet-of-things.pdf

Cisco. (2015). *Technology trends*. Retrieved October 26, 2015, from www.cisco.com/web/solutions/trends/iot/security.html

Cloud Security Alliance. (2015). *Security guidance for early adopters of the Internet of Things*. Retrieved December 23, 2016, from https://downloads.cloudsecurityalliance.org/whitepapers/Security_Guidance_for_Early_Adopters_of_the_Internet_of_Things.pdf

Coleman, L., & Purcell, B. (2015). Data breaches in higher education. *Journal of Business Cases and Applications*, *15*, 1–7. Retrieved from www.aabri.com/manuscripts/162377.pdf

eCampus News. (2015). *Trends in cloud computing in higher education*. Retrieved December 24, 2016, from http://eschoolmedia.com/wp-content/uploads/2016/06/vion0622.pdf

Education Superhighway. (2016). *K-12 connectivity*. Retrieved December 23, 2016, from www.educationsuperhighway.org/the-connectivity-gap/

Educause. (2014a). *Foundations of information security: Institutional implications of safeguarding data*. Retrieved February 3, 2016, from http://net.educause.edu/ir/library/pdf/pub4011.pdf

Educause. (2014b). *Just in time research: Data breaches in higher education*. Retrieved February 27, 2016, from https://net.educause.edu/ir/library/pdf/ECP1402.pdf

Evans, D. (2011). *The Internet of Things: How the next evolution of the internet is changing everything*. Cisco Internet Business Solutions Group (IBSG) White Paper. Retrieved from www.cisco.com/web/about/ac79/docs/innov/IoT_IBSG_0411FINAL.pdf

Feldman, A. (2017). *Silicon slopes vs. Silicon Valley: Four tech unicorns, thousands of startups, no frenzy*. Retrieved October 9, 2017, from www.forbes.com/sites/amyfeldman/2017/04/03/silicon-slopes-vs-silicon-valley-four-tech-unicorns-thousands-of-startups-no-frenzy/#7fe5ab8d3922

Gartner, J., & Gartner, R. (2014). *Gartner says the Internet of Things will transform the data center*. Retrieved September 7, 2015, from www.gartner.com/newsroom/id/2684915

Glassberg, J. (2016). *America's schools have a big cybersecurity problem*. Retrieved December 23, 2016, from www.huffingtonpost.com/entry/americas-schools-have-a-big-cybersecurity-problem_us_57bf0366e4b06384eb3e770b

Grama, J. (2014). *Just in time research: Data breaches in higher education*. Retrieved May 13, 2016, from https://net.educause.edu/ir/library/pdf/ECP1402.pdf

Griffin, R. (2015). *Social media is changing how college students deal with mental health: For better or worse*. Retrieved March 13, 2016, from www.huffingtonpost.com/entry/social-media-college-mental-health_us_55ae6649e4b08f57d5d28845

Herold, B. (2016). *Technology in education: An overview*. Retrieved December 23, 2016, from www.edweek.org/ew/issues/technology-in-education/

Hewlett-Packard Development Company. (2014). *Internet of Things research study*. Retrieved May 11, 2015, from http://h20195.www2.hp.com/V2/GetDocument.aspx?docname=4AA5-4759ENW&cc=us&lc=en

Hudson, F. (2016). *The Internet of Things is here*. Retrieved November 2, 2016, from http://er.educause.edu/articles/2016/6/the-internet-of-things-is-here

InfoSec Institute. (2017). *Security challenges in the Internet of Things (IoT)*. Retrieved April 11, 2017, from http://resources.infosecinstitute.com/security-challenges-in-the-internet-of-things-iot/

Jain, A. (2008). *Identity management: The value of physical & logical convergence.* Retrieved April 16, 2015, from www.siliconindia.com/guestcontributor/guestarticle/217/Identity_Management__The_Value_of_Physical__Logical_Convergence___Ajay_Jain.html

Jain, A., & Pandey, U. (2013). Role of cloud computing in higher education. *International Journal of Advanced Research in Computer Science and Software Engineering, 3*(7), 966–972. Retrieved from www.ijarcsse.com/docs/papers/Volume_3/7_July2013/V3I6-0242.pdf

Jedra, C. (2013). *Study: Millennials indifferent to online risk.* Retrieved March 11, 2016, from www.usatoday.com/story/news/nation/2013/10/16/millennials-cyber-security/2995157/?siteID=je6NUbpObpQ-CFcV.UCA4u97lBWVxmZPYg

Jimenez-Peris, R. (2015). *Big data and cloud challenges from IoT.* Retrieved September 7, 2015, from http://ec.europa.eu/information_society/newsroom/cf/dae/document.cfm?action=display&doc_id=7681

Johnston, L. (2016, January 18). DDoS attacks against universities are on the rise. Retrieved January 26, 2018, from https://www.axiomcyber.com/blog/hacking/ddos-attacks-against-universities-are-on-the-rise/

Kiryakova, G., Yordanova, L., & Angelova, N. (2017). Can we make schools and universities smarter with the Internet of Things? *TEM Journal, 6*(1), 80–84. doi: 10.18421/TEM61-11.

Kumar, A. (2014). Seven IoT risks you must consider. *Information Security, Insider Edition: Securing the Internet of Things*, 3–8. Retrieved from http://pro.techtarget.com/Global/FileLib/targeted_downloads/ISM_InsideEdition_final.pdf

Lestch, C. (2015). *Cybersecurity in K-12 education: Schools face increased risk of cyberattacks.* Retrieved December 23, 2016, from http://fedscoop.com/cybersecurity-in-k-12-education-schools-around-the-country-face-risk-of-cyber-attacks

Lutz, R. (2014). *The implications of the Internet of Things for education.* Retrieved October 13, 2015, from www.systech.com/systech-blog/384-the-implications-of-the-internet-of-things-for-education

Maskari, S., Saini, D., Raut, S., & Hadimani, L. (2011). *Security and vulnerability issues in university networks.* Proceedings of the World Congress on Engineering 2011 Vol. I, WCE 2011, London, U.K., July 6–8, 2011. Retrieved from www.iaeng.org/publication/WCE2011/WCE2011_pp520-524.pdf

Matindi, R., & Ngugi, G. K. (2014). Determinants of procurement performance at Kenya National Highways Authority (KeNHA). *International Journal of Social Sciences and Entrepreneurship, 1*(5), 768–793. Retrieved June 11, 2015, from www.issr-journals.org/links/papers.php?journal=ijias&application=pdf&article=IJIAS-14-313-01

McCarthy, K. (2015). *Five colleges with data breaches larger than Sony's in 2014.* Retrieved May 13, 2016, from www.huffingtonpost.com/kylemccarthy/five-colleges-with-data-b_b_6474800.html

McCreight, T., & Leece, D. (2016). Physical security and IT convergence: Managing the cyber-related risks. *Journal of Business Continuity & Emergency Planning, 10*(1), 18–30. Retrieved from www.ncbi.nlm.nih.gov/pubmed/27729098

McIntyre, E. (2016). *How is the Internet of Things impacting schools?* Retrieved November 4, 2016, from www.educationdive.com/news/how-is-the-internet-of-things-impacting-schools/420209/

Melendez, J., Luse, A., Townsend, A., & Mennecke, B. (2008). *Convergence of physical and logical security: A pre-implementation checklist.* Proceedings of MWAIS

2008, Eau Claire, WI, USA, Association for Information Systems, Atlanta, GA, USA, 23–24 May.

Messmer, E. (2010). *Converging physical and IT security*. Retrieved April 16, 2015, from www.networkworld.com/article/2240602/security/converging-physical-and-logical-security—a-good-idea-or-not-.html

Miorandi, D., Sicari, S., De Pellegrini, F., & Chlamtac, I. (2012). Internet of Things: Vision, applications, and research challenges. *Ad Hoc Networks*, *10*, 1497–1516. Retrieved from www.sciencedirect.com/science/article/pii/S1570870512000674

Orebaugh, A. (2014). What do we need to make IoT security a reality? *Information Security*, 31–33. Retrieved from http://internetofthingsagenda.techtarget.com/opinion/What-do-we-need-to-make-IoT-security-a-reality

Polk, T., & Turner, S. (2011). *Security challenges for the Internet of Things*. Workshop on Interconnecting Smart Objects with the Internet, Prague. Retrieved from www.iab.org/wp-content/IAB-uploads/2011/03/Turner.pdf

Pribish, M. (2015). *Colleges, K-12 schools are information-rich targets for hackers*. Retrieved December 23, 2016, from www.azcentral.com/story/money/business/tech/2015/08/21/colleges-schools-information-rich-targets-hackers/32093511/

Rampton, J. (2017). *Utah, the next Silicon Valley?* Retrieved October 9, 2017, from www.entrepreneur.com/article/297109#

Schooldude. (2014). *The unique challenges facing the IT professional in K-12 education*. Retrieved December 23, 2016, from www.schooldude.com/Portals/0/public%20content/reports%20and%20presentations/technology%20management/sr-2013-it-survey.pdf

Security Magazine. (2014). *35 percent of all security breaches take place in higher education*. Retrieved February 3, 2016, from www.securitymagazine.com/articles/86000-percent-of-all-security-breaches-take-place-in-higher-education

Simon, N. (2016). *2015 Data breaches in the higher education sector*. Retrieved May 13, 2016, from https://bitsighttech.com/blog/data-breaches-higher-ed

Smith, F. (2015). *Putting 2015's higher education cyberattacks into perspective*. Retrieved May 13, 2016, from www.edtechmagazine.com/higher/article/2015/09/putting-2015-s-higher-education-cyberattacks-perspective

Subramanian, S., Gopal, V., & Muthusamy, M. (2015). Security and privacy challenges of IoT-enabled solutions. *ISACA Journal*, *4*. Retrieved December 24, 2016, from www.isaca.org/Journal/archives/2015/Volume-4/Pages/security-and-privacy-challenges-of-iot-enabled-solutions.aspx

Suo, H., Wan, J., Zou, C., & Liu, J. (2012). Security in the Internet of Things: A review. *Computer Science and Electronics Engineering, 2012 International Conference on*, *3*, 648–651. doi: 10.1109/ICCSEE.2012.373

Ting, D. (2010). *Converged security pays dividends*. Retrieved April 16, 2015, from www.networkworld.com/article/2291412/lan-wan/converged-security-pays-dividends.html

Vara, V. (2015). *How Utah became the next Silicon Valley*. Retrieved July 14, 2015, from www.newyorker.com/business/currency/utah-became-next-silicon-valley

Vermesan, O., & Friess, P., Guillemin, P., Gusmeroli, S., Sundmaeker, H., Bassi, A., Jubert, I., Mzura, M., Harrison, M., Eisenhauer, M., & Doody, P. (2011). *Internet of Things: Global technological and societal trends*. Retrieved December 24, from www.internet-of-things-research.eu/pdf/IoT_Cluster_Strategic_Research_Agenda_2011.pdf

Weber, R. (2010). Internet of Things: New security and privacy challenges. *Computer Law & Security Review*, *26*, 23–30. Retrieved from www.sciencedirect.com/science/article/pii/S0267364909001939

Wolff, J. (2015). *Can campus networks ever be secure?* Retrieved February 3, 2016, from www.theatlantic.com/technology/archive/2015/10/can-campus-networks-ever-be-secure/409813/

Worth, D. (2014). *Internet of Things to generate 400 zettabytes of data by 2018.* Retrieved September 7, 2015, from www.v3.co.uk/v3-uk/news/2379626/internet-of-things-to-generate-400-zettabytes-of-data-by-2018

Zalud, B. (2010). *Convergence: Leap and the net will appear.* Retrieved April 16, 2015, from www.securitymagazine.com/articles/80764-convergence-leap-and-the-net-will-appear-1

9 Securing the Smart Phone

A Motivational Model

Irina-Marcela Nedelcu and Murugan Anandarajan

Introduction

Smart phone ownership has grown exponentially in the last decade. According to Pew Research, in 2013, 56% of American adults were smart phone owners (Smith, 2013). This number has substantially increased since 2011, when only 35% of American adults owned smart phones. In addition, people spend more time on their smart phones; in 2013, on average, a person spent 34 hours per month on his or her smart phone, a growth of 8 hours since 2012 (Fingas, 2014).

An increase in the ownership, functionality, and usage of Internet-connected devices has led to higher exposure to cybercrime (DeNisco, 2017). By 2020, it is expected that more than 21 billion devices will be connected with each other. According to the National Communications Association, this will provide hackers with more opportunities to attack phones (Express, 2017). In 2016, smart phone infections increased nearly 400%. This is due to an increase in the number of devices connected to the Internet.

These cybercrimes include identity theft, fraud, and storing illegal information. Research by Frost and Sullivan reveals that over 80 million smart phones were hacked in the United States in 2012 (Iadarola, 2013). Thus, it is critical that smart phone owners take measures to protect themselves against potential criminal activities when using these devices.

To prevent cybercrime institutions such as the Department of Justice and the FBI recommend that people engage in self-protective behaviors such as changing passwords monthly, reading applications' permissions before downloading them, and clearing their phones at least every six months. In 2012, the Pew Research Internet Project determined that only 50% of smart phone users deleted their browsing and search history from their devices; 30% turned off their location when not in use, and 59% had backed up their smart phones (Boyles, Smith, & Madden, 2012). Although these self-protective behaviors have become more common over the last few years, there are still significant gaps between the safeguard recommendations and actual behavior (García Zaballos & González Herranz, 2013).

Smart Phones, IoT, and Security

Currently, smart phones have several sensors that store information gathered from the environment: location, sound, images, etc. This information is shared with other devices, such as other smart phones, PCs, laptops, smart watches, etc. These data are then analyzed, providing insights on preferences and behaviors. New technology increased smart phones capabilities, so they not only collect information (sensory function) but also make suggestions (actuating function). As they store new information from the environment, smart phones can trigger certain actions, which makes them part of the IoT (Internet of Things), a network of interconnected devices that collect and transfer data between each other. Smart phones have IoT applications in four categories: personal IoT (fitness apps), group IoT (control smart homes), community IoT (mapping apps), and industrial IoT (providing personalized marketing material on social media) (Hausenblas, 2014). The use of IoT devices is rapidly growing, and the number of connected devices is expected to reach 21 billion by 2020. This provides attackers more opportunities to target devices to steal information (Express, 2017).

IoT has greatly affected our lives. We now live in a society in which refrigerators order food and devices such as Alexa add items to a grocery list. The drawback of using this technology is that private information about our lives is being shared among devices. Individuals who use IoT devices might not even be aware of the amount of information they are sharing. These data can be hacked and used with malevolent intent (Brill & Jones, 2016).

Smart phones are increasingly used to control IoT devices. However, the infrastructure to protect the data shared between smart phones and other IoT devices is not developed enough (We Live Security, 2017). Usually, IoT devices are made of microcontrollers, which do not provide enough security (Patterson, 2017). This lack of security has only increased the threat of potential attacks. Also, IoT devices are always connected with each other. They are not being turned off, as are other human-controlled devices. This leads to a higher exposer to cybercrime (Dickson, 2015).

Theoretical Model

Research in the area of smart phone security is relatively new. This research study examines the factors that motivate individuals to practice self-protective behaviors to guard against smart phones being compromised. Understanding why smart phone owners do or do not carry out these practices can help guide the development of education and training programs to increase individuals self-protective smart phone behaviors.

We use the Protection Motivation Theory (PMT) (Rogers, 1975) to examine how individuals perceive the seriousness of cybercrime and their vulnerability to it and the cognitive awareness processes individuals experience when they take self-protective measures against potential harm. In this study, we modify the PMT model by introducing two additional moderating variables: independence and the type of operating systems. Independent people often have difficulty in perceiving risks due to their increased self-confidence, and thus, will engage less frequently in self-protective behaviors than those less independent individuals. Additionally, according to Benenson, Gassmann, and Reinfelder (2013), the type of operating system on their smart phones influences how individuals perceive risks, with Apple operating system users less likely to take self-protective measures due to perceptions that the Apple operating system is more secure. Thus, these two variables are connected to the individuals' perceptions of smart phone cybercrime.

The next section describes the theoretical underpinnings of the research study, along with the proposed hypotheses. This is followed by the methodology and data analysis. The fifth section discusses the main results of this research study and how they relate to our theoretical framework. Finally, we provide a conclusion and limitations of the study.

Literature Review

PMT was developed by Rogers (1975) to understand fear appeals, messages that can instigate fear, and how the cognitive process influences behavior change. Fear is defined as a negative emotion that can be expressed psychologically as high arousal (Witte, 1992). Threat is the danger that exists whether the individual is knowledgeable of this or not. When the individual knows about the threat, then he or she perceives the threat. Perceived threat leads an individual to feel fear. Fear motivates the individual to engage in protective behaviors and attitudes to reduce the threat (Norman, Boer, & Seydel, 2005).

Protective behavior is influenced by two independent appraisals: threat appraisal and coping appraisal. Threat appraisal is defined as the intensity with which individuals perceive fear. The way that a person feels about the danger or the risk determines intention (Rogers, 1975). If the threat appraisal creates fear, then a person would appeal to the coping appraisal, which would eventually cause protection motivation (Tanner, Hunt, & Eppright, 1991). These two appraisals sustain, arouse, and direct activities of individuals (Rogers, 1975). Furthermore, changes in intentions lead to changes in actual behaviors. Protection motivation is considered a mediating variable between self-protective behavior and the two independent appraisal processes (Boer & Seydel, 1996).

The threat appraisal process involves perceived severity and perceived vulnerability. Perceived severity is defined as the importance with which individuals perceive the occurrence of a negative event, whereas perceived vulnerability represents the possibility that one will experience harm, with both of them increasing the likelihood of engaging in self-protective behavior (Rippetoe & Rogers, 1987).

Coping appraisal processes represent the responses that may eliminate the threat and the factors that may determine the individual's willingness to engage in a certain behavior (Norman et al., 2005). Coping behavior is a product of three components: response efficacy, self-efficacy, and response cost (Rogers, 1975). Response efficacy is defined as the belief that the recommended practices are adequate in diminishing the dangers. Self-efficacy represents the confidence that individuals have in performing the recommended actions (Norman et al., 2005). Response costs represent the effort, time, money, and complexity that an individual needs to take into consideration when he or she takes protective measures. Response efficacy and self-efficacy are variables that increase the likelihood of pursuing the adaptive response, whereas response cost decreases the likelihood (Prentice-Dunn & Rogers, 1986). Thus, intention is determined by the addition of perceived severity, perceived vulnerability, response efficacy and self-efficacy, and the subtraction of the response cost (Norman et al., 2005). The research model is illustrated in Figure 9.1.

Very few studies have used PMT to study smart phones. For instance, Tu and Yuan (2012) examined the factors that influence users' behavior when it comes to device loss and theft. They examined how coping behavior is affected by the threat appraisal. If smart phone users believe that the threat is high, then they try to diminish it by taking coping action. Herath and Rao (2009) examined the willingness of employees to follow the security policies established by the organizations they work for. This is an important subject because the technological tool itself is not enough to ensure the security of the information that the smart phone contains. Security policies help increase the security of smart phones. The results of the study indicated that perceived severity, response efficacy, and self-efficacy had a positive effect

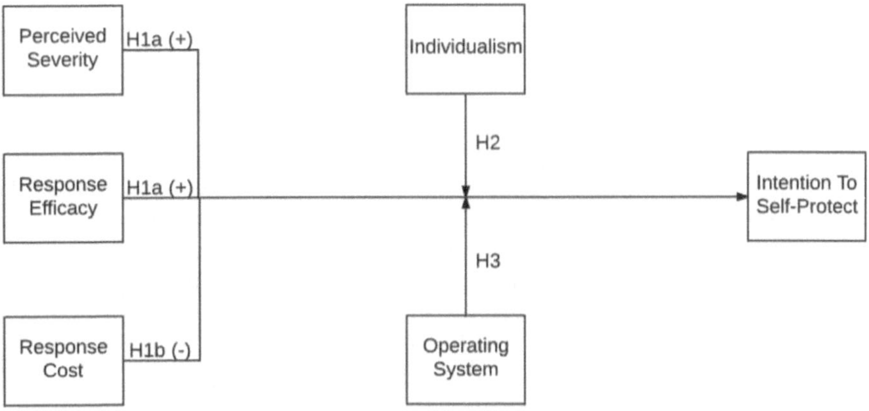

Figure 9.1 Perceived Severity, Response Efficacy, and Response Cost as Predictors for Intention to Self-Protect; Individualism and Operating System as Moderating Variables

on intentions to self-protect. However, response cost has a negative effect on their behavior.

Based on these arguments, we propose the following hypothesis:

> *H1a: Smart phone users' intentions to take safeguard measures are influenced by their coping appraisal; therefore, there is a positive relationship between perceived severity, perceived vulnerability, response efficacy, perceived self-efficacy, and intention to self-protect.*
>
> *H1b: Smart phone users' intentions to take safeguard measures are influenced by their threat appraisal; therefore, there is a negative relationship between response cost and intention to self-protect.*

According to Oltedal, Moen, Klempe, and Rundmo, (2004), the way that people perceive risks is not only influenced by the threats they are exposed to but also by the environment in which they live. According to cultural theory, individuals are not born with certain fears. They choose the targets of their fears as well as the intensity of their fears, as both affect attitudes and behaviors. Douglas and Wildavsky (1982) developed the cultural theory to predict and explain risk perceptions. Of the four views of life (individualism, egalitarianism, fatalism, and hierarchy) individualism is the most relevant to this study. This is the only view that shows a low level of awareness toward all kinds of risks. Risk perceptions of the other views depend on the type of risk. This could be explained by the individualist's high level of self-confidence in individual control. This phenomenon suggests the importance of recognizing whether the risks affect many people or individuals. Individualists are afraid only of risks that put their freedom in danger (Oltedal et al., 2004).

Individualism has been studied before in the context of security. Triandis, McCusker, and Hui (1990), focused on the difference between individualists and collectivists. Individualistic people are more concerned with the pleasure and achievement that they gain by performing a certain action. Unlike them, collectivists value security, integrity, and obedience. Low-individualistic people's behaviors are determined by their collectives.

However, people are very diverse, and explaining their behavior by just looking at their level of individualism would not be enough (Oltedal et al., 2004). Thus, cultural theory cannot predict entirely people's behaviors. Maiyaki (2013) analyzed the moderating effect of individualism on intention. Individualism was split into two groups: low individualism and high individualism. It was found that low individualism has a stronger effect as a moderator on intention than high individualism. Individuals who have a low level of individualism tend to have more positive intentions. This leads them to eventually engage in positive behavior.

Still, we cannot generalize that a person with a certain level of individualism will protect themselves in different situations in the same way. It is recommended that specific variables are used in measuring people's intentions to engage in self-protective behavior when they are using their smart phones. In achieving this, the PMT variables can be used to specifically measure the factors that directly influence people's intentions. Individualism would then be used as a moderator in order to emphasize the results.

Thus, we propose the following hypothesis:

> *H2: The relationship between intention to protect and threat and coping appraisals is stronger for low individualism than for high individualism.*

In 2013, the U.S. Department of Homeland Security and the U.S. Department of Justice reported that 79% of the mobile malware targeted Android, whereas only 0.7% of the malware attacks took aim at iOS; thus, another potential factor influencing the relationship between intention to protect and the two individual appraisals might be the type of operating system that individuals have on their smart phones (Chang, 2013). The two most popular operating systems that now exist on the marketplace are Google's Android and Apple's iOS (Sunnebo, 2013). Thus, in this chapter, we examined the impact the type of system (iOS or Android) has on intention to engage in self-protecting actions.

Just by looking at these numbers, one could state that iOS is safer than Android, but malware attacks are only one kind of security breach. Other major threats are network and web-based attacks, social engineering attacks, resource and service availability abuse, unintentional/malicious data loss, and attacks on the device's data (Symantec, 2011). Even though these two operating systems provide a certain level of security, it is insufficient to protect smart phone owners from becoming victims of cybercrime.

According to Benenson et al. (2013), individuals who own Android smart phones tend to be more aware of their smart phones' security. They are more likely than iOS users to have security applications installed on their smart phones. Also, Android users were more aware of the dangers of installing apps on their phones. Thus, we propose the following hypothesis:

> *H3: The relationship between intention to protect and threat and coping appraisals is stronger for Android smart phone users than iOS smart phone users.*

Methodology

This research study was performed using a cross-sectional survey design. Data was collected from working adults through Amazon Mechanical Turk (AMT). AMT is an online marketplace where individuals have the opportunity to complete Human Intelligence Tasks (HITs) offered by requestors in exchange for payment (www.mturk.com/mturk/welcome). A total of 300 HITs were posted and accepted on AMT in July 2013. Out of those 300 accepted HITs, 252 (84%) of the surveys remained after removing 48 incomplete surveys.

Most instruments used in this study were adapted from validated scales used in past research. The questions that measured coping appraisals (response efficacy, self-efficacy, and response cost) and threat appraisals (perceived vulnerability and perceived severity) were reworded from Rogers' scales (Maddux & Rogers, 1983). The instrument measuring individualism is a short version of the scale proposed by Dake (1991). The questions measuring intention of individuals was developed using the steps recommended by Federal Communications Commission (FCC) to reduce the risk of cybercrime (FCC, 2015).

Table 9.1 summarizes the demographics of the respondents. The age ranged from 18 to over 65 years old (most of them being under 34 years old), and a higher percentage of males (61%) than females (39%) participated in the study. Most of the people surveyed have either Android (54%) or iOS (42%), operating systems and only 4% had a Windows Phone.

Data Analysis and Results

All hypotheses were tested using hierarchical multiple regression. Entered at step 1 were the demographic variables (gender and age) as control factors. Entered at step 2 were the PMT base model, and entered at step 3 and 4 were the hypothesized interaction terms. We centered all continuously measured predictors prior to running the analyses and explored significant interactions (Aiken, West & Reno, 1991).

Table 9.2 presents the regression results. As a group, the control factors did not account for a significant amount of variance in the outcome variables. The addition of the PMT variables to the model in step 2 significantly increased the variance explained in intention to self-protect ($\Delta R^2 = 0.15$, $p < .01$).

Table 9.1 Demographic Breakdown of the Respondents

Business/Industry		Gender		Operating system	
IT	12%	Male	61%	Android	54%
Non-IT	88%	Female	39%	iOS	42%
				Windows Phone	4%
Highest Level of Education				**Age Group**	
High School			7%	18–24 years old	27%
Some College			38%	25–34 years old	46%
Bachelor's Degree			38%	35–44 years old	17%
Some Graduate or Professional Study			4%	45–54 years old	7%
Master's or Professional Degree			10%	55–64 years old	3%
Doctoral Degree			3%		

Table 9.2 Hierarchical Regression Results: Control, PMT, Individualism, and Operating System on Intention to Self-Protect

	Step 1	*Step 2*	*Step 3*		*Step 4*	
			Low individualism	*High individualism*	*iOS*	*Android*
Age	.039	.023	.132	–.107	.025	–.009
Gender	.064	.073	.078	.106	.082	.070
Perceived Vulnerability		.056	.134	–.043	.046	.059
Perceived Severity		.159*	.226*	.083	.171	.145
Response Efficacy		.171**	.171*	.179	.033	.349***
Self-Efficacy		.076	.161	.003	.146	–.010
Response Cost		–.250***	–.205*	–.235**	–.193	–.364***
R^2	.6%	14.9%	25.1%	10.8%	12.9%	24.5%

*Significant at the 0.05 level.
**Significant at the 0.01 level.
***Significant at the 0.001 level.

Hypothesis 1 predicted a positive relationship between perceived severity, perceived vulnerability, response efficacy, perceived self-efficacy, and intention to self-protect and a negative relationship between response cost and intention to self-protect. The relationship between perceived severity and intention to self-protect was supported as the coefficient was significant ($\beta = .159$, $p = .019$). Response efficacy ($\beta = .171$, $p = .007$) and response cost ($\beta = -.250$, $p = .000$) were fully supported as well. The relationships between perceived vulnerability ($\beta = .056$, $p = .396$) and perceived self-efficacy ($\beta = .076$, $p = .248$) and intention to protect were not significant. The R^2 for this base model was 14.9%.

Hypothesis 2 predicted that the relationships found in the PMT base model are moderated by the level of individualism. The respondents were divided into a low and a high group. The respondents who had a mean score of 3.5 or less were considered low-individualistic people. The respondents who scored higher than 3.5 were considered high-individualistic people.

For low-individualistic people, the relationship between perceived severity ($\beta = .226$, $p = .023$), response efficacy ($\beta = .171$, $p = .043$), response cost ($\beta = -.205$, $p = .030$), and intention to protect was fully significant. However, the relationship between perceived vulnerability ($\beta = .134$, $p = .176$), self-efficacy ($\beta = .161$, $p = .100$), and intention to protect was not significant. By using the PMT only for low-individualistic respondents, a higher percentage of the sample can be predicted ($R^2 = 25.1\%$).

For high-individualistic people, only the relationship between response cost ($\beta = -.235$, $p = .009$) and intention to protect was fully significant. However, the relationship between perceived vulnerability ($\beta = -.043$, p = .646), self-efficacy (β = .003, p = .974), perceived severity (β = .083, p = .379), response efficacy (β = .179, p = .057), and intention to protect was not significant. At this point, the PMT can explain the behavior of only 10.8% (R^2) of the high-individualistic respondents.

Hypothesis 3 predicted that the relationships found in the PMT base model are moderated by the type of operating system that respondents have on their smart phones. Android users showed a strong relationship between response efficacy (β = .349, p = .000), response cost (β = –.364, p = .000), and intention to protect. The relationships between perceived severity (β = .145, p = .116), perceived vulnerability (β = .059, p = .512), self-efficacy (β = –.010, p = .911), and intention to protect were not supported as the beta coefficient was not significant. The R^2 for Android users is 24.5%.

Unlike Android users, iOS users do not show any significant relationships between the PMT variables and intention to protect. Thus, the PMT variables had the following values: perceived vulnerability (β = .046, p = .653), perceived severity (β = .171, p = .108), response efficacy (β = .033, p = .743), self-efficacy (β = .146, p = .159), and response cost (β = –.193, p = .059). The R^2 for iOS users is 12.9%.

Discussion

The goal of this study is to examine the factors that motivate people to engage in self-protective behavior when they are using their smart phones. Hypothesis 1 proposed that people's behavior is influenced by the five PMT variables. The results indicate that the desire to self-protect is influenced only by three of these variables: perceived severity, response efficacy, and response cost. The higher level of perceived severity and response efficacy, the more individuals tend to engage in self-protective behavior. This means that whenever they perceive a high risk, they are motivated to protect themselves. In addition, if individuals are confident that the actions that they take are effective, then they engage in this type of behavior. As expected, our results indicate that when the level of response cost is high, motivation to self-protect decreases, potentially increasing the danger. Contrary to our expectations, perceived vulnerability and self-efficacy were not significant.

Hypothesis 2 proposed that individualism acts as a moderator of the PMT model. The results indicated that the same three variables that were significant in the PMT base model are significant for low-individualistic people. Moreover, by looking only at low-individualistic people, we can explain more of the variation in the model. Perhaps this happens because low-individualistic people are more open to the idea of self-protection. We could also assume that these types of people are influenced less easily by their perceptions and abilities and rely more on others or "the system" for protection.

On the other hand, high-individualistic people are influenced only by response cost. As expected, high-individualistic people are self-motivating. Thus, when they decide whether to self-protect or not when they use their smart phones, they focus on the response cost—technology enjoyment trade-off.

Hypothesis 3 proposed that people's behaviors are also influenced by the type of operating system they use. Android users are influenced by response efficacy and response cost. Looking at the five types of security breaches (malware, web/network-based breaches, social engineering, data loss/integrity, and resource/service abuse), the Android operating system is not always providing a lower level of protection. Still, considering what the media is publishing about smart phone security, the Android system becomes associated with a less secure operating system than iOS. Therefore, Android users are more open to the idea of engaging in self-protective behavior because they feel that they cannot rely only on their smart phone's security. Response cost is also significant, which means that Android users are highly influenced by what they have to give up in order to enjoy technology. However, iOS users do not have any significant relationships between the PMT variables and intention to self-protect. As Benenson et al. (2013) noted, iOS users are less aware of their smart phones' security weaknesses so these users rely more on the systems for protection.

As IoT has grown more prevalent, it is important to pay close attention to the way that smart devices are integrated. This integration increases opportunities for cybercrime, as the devices are increasingly linked to all aspects of personal and professional life. Companies, recognizing the need to take actions to decrease the risk of smart phones being vulnerable to attacks could, for example, implement stronger policies, train employees on ways to engage in self-protective behaviors, and work with security organizations to design effective intervention methods for users of operating systems to act as better guardians of their smart phones.

References

Aiken, L. S., West, S. G., & Reno, R. R. (1991). *Multiple regression: Testing and interpreting interactions*. Thousand Oaks, CA: Sage Publications.

Are smartphones threatening the security of our IoT devices? (2017). *We Live Security*. Retrieved November 5, 2017 from https://www.welivesecurity.com/2017/07/28/smartphones-security-iot-devices/

Benenson, Z., Gassmann, F., & Reinfelder, L. (2013, April). Android and iOS users' differences concerning security and privacy. In *CHI'13 extended abstracts on human factors in computing systems* (pp. 817–822). New York: ACM.

Boer, H., & Seydel, E. R. (1996). Protection motivation theory. In *Mark Conner & Paul Norman (Eds.), Predicting Health Behaviour: Research and Practice with Social Cognition Models* (pp. 95–120). Buckingham: Open University Press.

Boyles, J., Smith, A., & Madden, M. (2012). Privacy and data management on mobile devices. *Pew Research Center*. Retrieved November 5, 2017 from http://www.pewinternet.org/2012/09/05/privacy-and-data-management-on-mobile-devices/.

Brill, H., & Jones, S. (2016). Little things and big challenges: Information privacy and the Internet of Things. *American University Law Review*, *66*, 1183.

Chang, J. (2013). Android is target of 79 percent of mobile malware, government report says. *ABC News*. Retrieved November 5, 2017 from http://abcnews.go.com/Technology/android-target-79-percent-mobile-malware-government-report/story?id=20096620.

Cyber criminals 'could target smart phones in bid to hold users to ransom'. (2017). *Express*. Retrieved November 5, 2017 from https://www.express.co.uk/life-style/science-technology/778603/cyber-criminals-hack-smart-phones-televisions-ransom-internet-ready-products.

Dake, K. (1991). Orienting dispositions in the perception of risk: An analysis of contemporary worldviews and cultural biases. *Journal of Cross-Cultural Psychology*, 22(1), 61–82.

DeNisco, A. (2017). Businesses beware: Smartphone malware rises 400% in 2016, *Nokia Reports*. Tech Crunch. Retrieved November 5, 2017 from https://www.techrepublic.com/article/businesses-beware-smartphone-malware-rises-400-in-2016-nokia-reports/.

Dickson, B. (2015). Why IoT security is so critical. *Tech Crunch*. Retrieved November 5, 2017 from https://techcrunch.com/2015/10/24/why-iot-security-is-so-critical/.

Douglas, M., & Wildavsky, A. (1982). Risk and culture: Berkeley. *University of California Press*, 272, 10–15.

Fingas, J. (2014). Two-thirds of Americans now have smartphones. *Engadget*. Retrieved November 5, 2017 from https://www.engadget.com/2014/02/11/two-thirds-of-americans-now-have-smartphones/.

García Zaballos, A., & González Herranz, F. (2013). *From cybersecurity to cybercrime: A framework for analysis and implementation*. Inter-American Development Bank.

Hausenblas, M. (2014). Smart phones and the Internet of Things. *MapR Technologies*. Retrieved November 5, 2017 from https://mapr.com/blog/smart-phones-and-internet-things/.

Herath, T., & Rao, H. R. (2009). Protection motivation and deterrence: A framework for security policy compliance in organisations. *European Journal of Information Systems*, *18*(2), 106–125.

Iadarola, B. (2013). Mobile handset insurance: What's the value for the carrier? *Frost & Sullivan*. Retrieved November 5, 2017 from http://www.frost.com/c/10392/blog/blog-display.do?id=2986198.

Maddux, J. E., & Rogers, R. W. (1983). Protection motivation and self-efficacy: A revised theory of fear appeals and attitude change. *Journal of Experimental Social Psychology*, *19*(5), 469–479.

Maiyaki, A. A. (2013). Moderating effect of individualism/collectivism on the association between service quality, corporate reputation, perceived value and consumer behavioural intention. *Journal of Marketing & Management*, *4*(1).

Norman, P., Boer, H., & Seydel, E. R. (2005). Protection motivation theory. In *Predicting Health Behaviour: Research and Practice with Social Cognition Models* (pp. 81–126). Maidenhead: Open University Press.

Oltedal, S., Moen, B. E., Klempe, H., & Rundmo, T. (2004). Explaining risk perception: An evaluation of cultural theory. *Trondheim: Norwegian University of Science and Technology*, *85*(1–33), 86.

Patterson, S. (2017). Researchers find gaps in IoT security. *Network World*. Retrieved November 5, 2017 from https://www.networkworld.com/article/3200030/internet-of-things/researchers-find-gaps-in-iot-security.html.

Prentice-Dunn, S., & Rogers, R. W. (1986). Protection motivation theory and preventive health: Beyond the health belief model. *Health Education Research*, *1*(3), 153–161.

Rippetoe, P. A., & Rogers, R. W. (1987). Effects of components of protection-motivation theory on adaptive and maladaptive coping with a health threat. *Journal of Personality and Social Psychology*, *52*(3), 596.

Rogers, R. W. (1975). A protection motivation theory of fear appeals and attitude change. *The Journal of Psychology*, *91*(1), 93–114.

Smith, A. (2013). Smartphone Ownership 2013. *Pew Research Center*. Retrieved November 5, 2017 from http://www.pewinternet.org/2013/06/05/smartphone-ownership-2013/.

Sunnebo, D. (2013). Android leads in the US, but iOS and windows are growing faster. *Kantar World Panel*. Retrieved November 5, 2017 from https://www.kantarworldpanel.com/global/News/While-Android-Leads-iOS-and-Windows-Are-Growing-At-A-Faster-Pace.

Symantec analysis of apple's iOS and Google's android platform cites improved security over PCs, but major gaps remain. (2011). *Symantec*. Retrieved November 5, 2017 from https://www.symantec.com/en/ca/about/newsroom/press-releases/2011/symantec_0627_02.

Tanner, J. F., Jr., Hunt, J. B., & Eppright, D. R. (1991). The protection motivation model: A normative model of fear appeals. *The Journal of Marketing*, 36–45.

Ten steps to smartphone security. (2015). *FCC*. Retrieved November 5, 2017 from https://www.fcc.gov/smartphone-security/Android.

Tu, Z., & Yuan, Y. (2012, January). Understanding user's behaviors in coping with security threat of mobile devices Loss and theft. In *System Science (HICSS), 2012 45th Hawaii International Conference on* (pp. 1393–1402). Maui, HI: IEEE.

Triandis, H., McCusker, C., & Hui, C. (1990). Multimethod probes of individualism and collectivism. *Journal of Personality and Social Psychology*, 59.

Witte, K. (1992). Putting the fear back into fear appeals: The extended parallel process model. *Communications Monographs*, *59*(4), 329–349.

10 Intranets of People, Things, and Services

Exploring the Role of Virtual Human Resource Development

Elisabeth E. Bennett

Introduction

Technology continues to transform the workplace with increasingly sophisticated and complex innovations creating the interconnected age. The phenomenon of a growing number of connected devices and Internet-enabled services has been dubbed the *Internet of Things*. Billions of devices are connected through Internet protocols that allow remote communication and operation (McEwen & Cassimally, 2014; Eloff, Eloff, Dlamini, & Zielinski, 2009; Kranz, 2017). Eloff et al. (2009) extended the definition of the Internet of Things to include the Internet of People, Things and Services (IoPTS), which they define as "the vision where people, things (physical objects) and services are seamlessly integrated into the network of networks as active participants that exchange data about themselves and their perceived surrounding environments over a web-based infrastructure" (p. 2). The idea of a *network of networks* means intranets, which are private systems closed except to defined members, and this is important to the conversation. Intranets provide behind-the-scenes control and capture, process, and distribute data collected from IoPTS devices. Security is critical due to the value and sensitivity of that data.

Organizational networks are extending beyond the traditional abode of the workplace to homes and other spaces where people communicate with their organizations, engage in alternative work strategies, and balance work with their personal lives. An IoPTS device that represents leisure to one person, such as tracking miles hiked using a Fitbit, is work to the person who maintains the network in the manufacturer's systems. The smart devices extend the relationship between company and consumer far beyond the point of purchase.

As networks expand, one must view these networks as coming in closer proximity to one another and having competing claims over the devices, data, and people. The modern home with multiple devices connected to Wi-Fi is now considered an intranet of things (Poghosyan, Pefkianakis, Guyadec, & Christophides, 2016), and the future envisions human intranets with wearable, closed systems (Rabaey, 2015). Overlapping of personal and professional lives is profound and is an essential ingredient in this connected Internet of many things (McEwen & Cassimally; Kranz, 2017). This integration of personal and professional is critical to human resource development (HRD), a field that studies people and organizational systems.

Learning, performance, and development are fundamental to HRD, both at the individual level and at group/organizational levels and increasingly occur in IoPTS. Optimizing this technology and the functions of technology-enabled organizations cannot be accomplished without organizational learning (Langer, 2010). HRD provides fundamental support to what exists, but also helps explore future ramifications of a new area of inquiry within HRD, studying technology's role in work and learning. The purpose of this chapter is to address the intersection of IoPTS with virtual human resource development (VHRD), which is a virtual environment predicated on intranets. VHRD emphasizes the learning, strategy, and cultural dimensions of technology, and it can be viewed as an intranet of people, things, and services. The chapter first provides an overview of VHRD and then it extrapolates aspects of IoPTS to VHRD, focusing on intranets as fundamental components of IoPTS, and argues that IoPTS can be conceptualized as the Internet linking multiple intranets. Finally, the chapter addresses guidelines and implications for leveraging VHRD and IoPTS, including learning agility, technology development, and design thinking.

IoPTS and Virtual Human Resource Development

When individuals learn, organizations also learn; new knowledge is embedded into systems, practices, and structures of the organization, including intranets and knowledge management systems (Bennett, 2009; Langer, 2010). One could say the development of IoPTS is a result of organizational learning as the concept becomes reality and organizations adapt to deliver and continually improve connected products. Even employees not involved on a design team will learn and adapt their jobs around new smart products. For example, a pilot program using Bluetooth-enabled sensors alerted nurses to the movement of patients who were at a high risk for falls on the premise that earlier nursing intervention could prevent injury (Balaguera et al., 2017). Though the authors called the pilot a *medical intranet of things*, it is clear that people, patients, and nurses, as well as healthcare IT systems were important to complete the IoPTS intervention. Patient privacy standards demand that this kind of intervention remains in a closed and encrypted system. As with many technological advances, the initial focus is often on the technical aspects rather than on people, which is why HRD is important in the early development stages. Because people are required to change their routines, and organizations expect new performance to accompany technology-based change, it is important to consider these together.

Learning is increasingly accomplished through network technology, whether technology mediates communication from one person to the next, captures information within handbooks and knowledge repositories, or absorbs the experiences and decisions of people who shape technical systems and processes. Development, learning, and performance of people are absolutely critical to IoPTS, which will alter the virtual environment for VHRD. Technical changes brought by IoPTS offer new strategies, technologies, and services that can be used together to expand the virtual nature of work and learning. For example, cameras and microphones can allow a mentor located remotely to watch the performance of a mentee in real time and offer immediate feedback to share expertise, and the performance can be record for future use to train other employees.

IoPTS not only expands the virtual environment of work, but there is a loop effect; problems creatively solved by using IoPTS for talent management add to the knowledge base, which in turn expands the application of IoPTS in new areas. In much the same way users are instrumental in driving development in social media platforms, user experiences will affect future IoPTS HRD applications. Effective talent development often offers a financial incentive for organizations to invest in new technology (Bennett, 2006b), leading to new solutions. VHRD is an example of investment in human resource management software and general networking resources.

Defining Virtual HRD

Predicated on intranets that are virtually unlimited in terms of scalability (Bennett, 2014a), VHRD is defined as a "media rich and culturally relevant web environment that strategically improves expertise, performance, innovation, and community-building through formal and informal learning" (Bennett, 2009, p. 364). Web environment means networked and interconnected rather than the Internet. In this perspective, the environment that makes up a firm's private knowledge system produces workflow, communication, databases, and various software applications that integrate in a seamless manner. The network can include links to external sites and partner applications, though communication is typically controlled behind the scenes. Access has moved from tethered computers to include mobile devices. Several aspects of VHRD need highlighting. First, though, the field of HRD tends to be defined by what it does, such as McLagan's (1989) perspective that HRD integrates career development, organization development, and training, or Swanson and Holton's (2001) view that HRD is designed to "unleash the power of human expertise" (p. 4), VHRD is defined as an environment that typically includes an intranet or virtually networked applications; IoPTS is creating an expansive virtual environment by connecting VHRDs. When people access technology, they metaphorically step within the virtual space and become part of it. To be strategic, the activities and processes in VHRD need to be aligned with the organizational mission at all levels. Through the

VHRD lens, intranets are not just collections of people communicating via technology, but rather a dynamic environment where people interact with the objects, data, and applications residing there. These systems are designed for humans to use, so they may include human characteristics, such as feelings, humor, pride, and insight. An intranet was even given a personal name, IAN or "information as needed", and it was viewed by employees as a colleague rather than as a machine (Bennett, 2006b).

Second, cultural relevance primarily alludes to organizational culture where members share beliefs, assumptions, and values (Deal & Kennedy, 2000; Schein, 2010), central to how an organization functions, overlapping with regional or national culture, all of which have similarities and differences. Shared understandings about what is important create a filter through which people evaluate and act upon new information (Bennett, 2009), which means the data communicated through IoPTS run through a cultural filter. The filter may be composed of tacit knowledge as well explicit knowledge, such as facts, articulated rules, and procedures. When a company manages knowledge, it can also convey and renew the culture by providing members new examples of how cultural values are enacted and modeled, such as intranet protocols (Bennett, 2014b). The potential exists for intranets, and IoPTS, to support or change cultural values and practices (Bennett, 2009). Rich media, such as the inclusion of audio and video, can further foster modeling and adoption of cultural values because greater social and emotional connection can be made person-to-person and person-to-object across distance and time. For example, it is common for leaders to record podcasts about the direction of the company so that employees on all shifts can hear the same message. Media departments set the scene, including the leader's attire, the background, and how people move in and out of the picture. These selections affect what organizational members believe is acceptable behavior. The video could be from yesteryear, posted to reaffirm the founder's vision of a company (Schein, 2010) accompanied with a cultural artifact, such as a golden scoop that represents the value of high quality for an ice cream producer. In Bennett (2006b), a small, digital counter at the top of an intranet home page turned out to be a significant cultural artifact in a hospital that valued protecting people because it alerted the community that a colleague was in an accident. Employees felt a visceral response of sadness for the colleague involved, even if they did not know any of the specifics or the employee. It also triggered a review of safety protocols. In IoPTS, the accident reports can be done through mobile devices, more quickly communicating safety performance data.

Third, improving development and performance at group, organizational, and individual levels requires both formal and informal learning processes. Formal learning is most often discussed in HRD, typically called training or 'courses'. Courses are designed to meet specific learning objectives, and they may be required or voluntary. For example, new employees are oriented to the company and to their jobs often by attending classes online.

Compliance training is easily delivered and tracked electronically, such as a hospital safety course that reports results directly to an employee record database (Bennett, 2006b). Data can be viewed at the individual level but also aggregated to benchmark one department against another. Innovation, however, often requires unpredictable learning, particularly involving creative ideas and new experiences, which may be sparked by informal and unexpected learning. Informal learning is the type adults most often use at work. It is learner directed, although employees may not recognize it as learning because it is so natural to the everyday setting (Schugurensky, 2000). Informal learning has been conceptualized as having modes that vary based on level of consciousness of learning and intention to learn (Bennett, 2012; Schugurensky, 2000). The four modes of informal learning are (1) *self-directed learning*, which is intentional and conscious; (2) *incidental learning* in which a person is conscious of learning but did not intend to learn; (3) *tacit learning*, which is nonconscious and unintentional; and (4) *integrative learning* which is nonconscious but intentional, often involving intuition and tacit processing that becomes conscious through sudden insight or the "aha!" moment (Bennett, 2011a, 2012). Designers of IoPTS, for example, may experience sudden insight when a solution appears to them after work hours even though their minds were focused on a different activity. Engaging the senses in IoPTS may spark more informal learning, such as using visuals and graphics rather than just text that could limit creative thinking.

These three aspects explicate the richness found in VHRD enabled by the complexity in the IoPTS. By defining VHRD as a webbed environment, acknowledging cultural filters, and facilitating formal and informal learning, a greater linkage is possible between people and smart devices that make the virtual environment practically limitless by "webbing in" new applications and extending networks to new areas (Bennett, 2014a). Next, we look at trends in how VHRD has been applied to work in the field, transforming the workplace.

Trends in Virtual HRD

VHRD is still formalizing as an area of inquiry. Due to the focus on VHRD as an environment, many theoretical and practical perspectives can be applied to it, including alternative work strategies (Bennett, 2009), virtual teams (Bennett & Bierema, 2010; Germaine & McGuire, 2014), adult learning (Bennett, 2011b), sociomateriality (Fagan, 2014), talent management (Yoon & Lim, 2010), adaptive game-based learning (Huang, Han, Park, & Seo, 2010), scenario planning (McWhorter & Lynham, 2014), assessment and measurement (Chapman & Stone, 2010; Nafukho, Graham, & Muyia, 2010), boundary crossing in a 24/7 world (Thomas, 2014), 3D applications (Ausburn & Ausburn, 2014), and sustainability (Bennett & McWhorter, 2017a). The growing literature demonstrates many lenses that can be placed on this under-researched area.

Bennett and Bierema (2010) view VHRD as an ecology with harmonies, either with various stakeholder purposes where they align or constraints emerging where they misalign. For example, providing salary increases for achieving new credentials documented through an intranet can harmonize development with management incentives. Additionally, how network access is designed reveals management values and beliefs, and may indicate how much trust an organization has in its members. Constraints placed on an employee's access to information hinder learning and innovation, though these constraints may have a strong rationale. Information is a necessary component of problem solving, and it must be both accessible and valuable (Glassman & Kang, 2010), yet we know some organizations make avenues of information inaccessible. The reason to limit access may be rooted in experience, such as a sentinel event, or cultural beliefs about employees. As noted earlier, cultural relevance shapes the web environment and is one factor in determining access to information within and outside of the organization. For example, some organizations do not allow employees to access YouTube videos through corporate networks for fear employees will waste time on entertainment, yet many instructional videos are available to help solve organizational problems and bring new ideas forward. Any cultural or technological constraints need to be diagnosed and resolved to ensure employees have what they need to do their jobs, and this is often done by HRD practitioners.

HRD as a profession is grappling with how to become partners with technologists designing VHRD environments to promote optimal learning and development, including identifying new skills and knowledge needed to prepare nontechnical professionals for working with sophisticated and complex technologies (Bennett, 2010). This means addressing how to incorporate smart devices, new services, and other IoPTS things to enhance VHRD. Just as there are many levels of employees in an organization—and these levels often equate to information access—a future trend is how to prepare people for the growth of robots in the workplace, which will perform certain types of jobs that were once done by people. At one time, online access to benefits information was a new and novel HR service, but it is now simply expected by employees. The new and novel service now might be posting QR codes that employees scan with mobile applications when they enter the company gym and accrue fitness points for a wellness program, or directly transmit the number of steps on a smart treadmill. Another example is the growing use of GPS locators that monitor employees for time and wage compliance and the resulting need for transparency and other best practices (Cifolelli, 2016). From a cultural standpoint, close monitoring should be carefully justified because it can lead to distrust, disempowerment, and tensions between management and the workforce. HRD has a natural advocacy role (Bennett & McWhorter, 2017a) with an organizational performance role and so it is uniquely positioned to help craft best practices. Next, this chapter looks more closely at IoPTS and how it relates to VHRD.

Integrating the Internet and Intranets of People, Things, and Services

IoPTS is a trend that is expected to grow in the future (McWhorter, 2014) by transforming business models (Kranz, 2017; McEwen & Cassimally, 2014). IoPTS is estimated to have a global economic impact in the trillions of dollars by 2025 (Manyika et al., 2015). Internet-ready sensors that network smart devices promote efficiency in such places as healthcare facilities, transportation, manufacturing, and global supply chains as devices take actions independently in a self-organized, networked way (IBM, 2015; McKendrick, 2015), and there is an emerging sense that organizational learning and decision making may occur independently of humans when artificial intelligence is incorporated (Bennett & McWhorter, 2017b). Strategic decision making incorporates the big data generated by IoPTS (McEwen & Cassimally, 2014), but people are integral to interpretation. The need for analytics will drive new jobs, such as data scientists, but training a wider variety of employees on the concept of IoPTS is needed (Kranz, 2017). Education and training services will prepare the workforce for IoPTS, and these services will increasingly be accomplished through networked technologies.

Reviewing several books on the topic of IoPTS, none of the indexes listed the term intranet (Greenberg, 2015; Kranz, 2017; McEwen & Cassimally, 2014; Rowland, Goodman, Charlier, Light, & Lui, 2015), which suggests that few authors are writing about IoPTS with intranets in mind; however, more recent articles are beginning to discuss the integration of intranets and the Internet (Balaguera et al., 2017; Gadallah, elTager, & Elalamy, 2015; Mani, Byun, & Cocca, 2013). For example, IoPTS allows the tire company, Goodyear, to "network its systems together, enabling Goodyear to easily gather and analyze data from the factory floor while delivering advanced communications capabilities for a variety of plant solutions" (Kranz, 2017, p. 40). The system is not just about individual devices being separately connected to the network, but how they work within a holistic system for tactical and strategic advantage (Kranz, 2017). Though described in Internet terms, the case is clearly an intranet.

Networking now links internal networks with dispersed devices by using Internet protocols and cloud storage, creating a new type of intranet that connects across space and time. In some ways, each smart device may be considered a micro intranet that can be connected to a macro intranet, both private and closed (Gadallah et al., 2015). This indicates that IoPTS can be conceptualized as the Internet providing intranet-to-intranet linkage.

IoPTS allows the flexibility to move between large-scale computing to smaller-scale computing, or fog computing (Kranz, 2017). These *enchanted objects* are designed to work in the real, physical world, such as a sports bracelet that functions in the rain (McEwen & Cassimally, 2014). The sports bracelet that only tracks daily steps and resets every 24 hours is less complex than transmitting that information to one's phone so that software can trend the data over time. Even more complex is evaluating fitness data, including heart rate, for medical recommendations to call emergency services if the potential for heart attack is detected. More complex is not always better, but the level of service will determine how people and things interact. The combination of physical with virtual will create more seamless, natural, and ubiquitous computing, with the many hubs of communication representing a large-scale model of how humans think, where free flowing, scale-free information is paired with inductive reasoning to solve problems in practice (Glassman & Kang, 2010).

IoPTS makes it possible to join people to the network through implantable RFID tags (Eloff et al., 2009), often called the human intranet (Rabaey, 2015). Previously, radio-frequency identification (RFID) was used to track inventory of materials and products, but it is increasingly an aid in recovery of abducted children or for health services. The ultimate form of service might be a personalized, custom, encrypted intranet tailored to each individual. Organizations will need to address the ethical and legal issues of requiring employees to be implanted with tags that open electronic locks but also let managers track employee movements. This Internet–intranet integration ensures that personal and professional boundaries will be increasingly blurred.

Security, privacy, authentication, beliefs, trust, and reputation are all modeled in Eloff et al.'s (2009) IoPTS cube, which demonstrates that organizational culture is endemic to IoPTS as well as VHRD. One of the great threats to IoPTS is heavy-handed control of the Internet, particularly where governments or very large organizations can cut off Internet–intranet links. Recent history has shown that governments can suspend Internet access during social unrest (Yang, 2013). Hacking can render smart devices into zombies for launching denial-of-service attacks, taking advantage of minimal security in home-based intranets (Constantin, 2016). Beyond control and hacking, privacy is a critical concern because technologists mine usage patterns of intranets, often without intrusive sensors, including the residential or home-based intranets (Eloff et al., 2009; Poghosyan et al., 2016). Data and technology transfer across international boundaries will be a growing concern to the public, and nation-states may seek to place restrictions on IoPTS, especially where demographic and technical information affects national security. When IoPTS is considered in totality, organizations can and should balance opportunities with ethical practices.

Guidelines and Implications

Disparate knowledge about the capabilities and dangers of networked devices and the reality of competing cultural assumptions about how these vast network connections should function are intrinsic to the complex phenomenon of IoPTS. Issues such as cultural conflict and feelings of customer betrayal can damage the reputation and branding of the product or service (Eloff et al., 2009). Furthermore, mixed messages can cause unintended cultural change and set an organization up for future problems. It is so important for IoPTS designers to see the learning and customer side of their work, even if technical specifications are their main focus. One cannot assume two organizations have identical values regarding the privacy of their employees, customers, and industry partners. Taking into account VHRD and the enabling role of intranets in IoPTS, this section discusses guidelines and implications.

To begin the discussion, Figure 10.1 represents some of the prevailing themes from this chapter and models how IoPTS and VHRD influence the virtual environments they share. Virtual environments grow and change dynamically as new networks, devices, people, and services are added or disconnected many times in a day. New connections might add industry partners working with the organization or devices that report data periodically to central servers. On the left side of the figure are ways that VHRD influences IoPTS. First, development of employees is often through services that also make use of IoPTS, as some of the earlier examples demonstrate. VHRD professionals become clients of IoPTS and will demand new IoPTS solutions. Second, VHRD develops the intellectual capital of an organization, and thus is instrumental for developing the people that design or support new technologies and services. Third, VHRD has many tools, techniques, and theories that can be applied to innovation and the organizational change cycle. Lastly, VHRD can use its people-advocacy role to develop best practices so that organizations stay on the right side of ethical boundaries and maintain good labor relations.

On the right side of the figure, IoPTS influences VHRD in several ways. First, IoPTS dramatically expands the ways in which networks can grow and integrate new things, and thus it expands the virtual environment in which

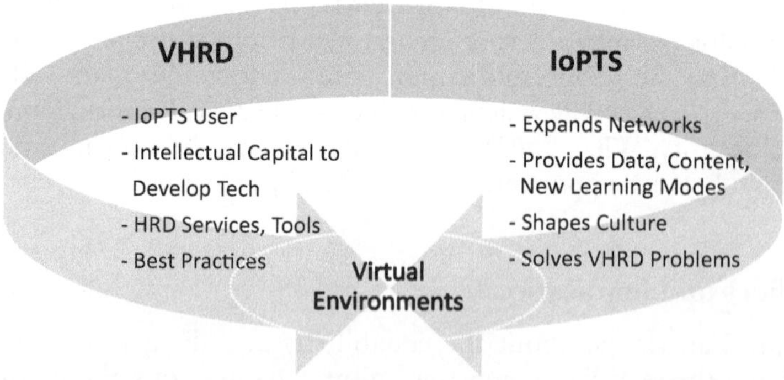

Figure 10.1 How VHRD and IoPTS Mutually Influence Virtual Environments

VHRD resides. Second, expansion of networks provides more data, content, and new modes of learning that have not yet been imagined. In other words, it will provide resources for learning and development. An example might be 3D cameras that upload local scenes in real time for team problem solving or role-play. These technologies have a way of shaping organizational culture in the same way telegraph machines or gramophones represent eras of human history. IoPTS becomes part of the world in which we live, shaping values and how people establish shared understandings, relationships, and histories. Lastly, IoPTS can be applied to solve organization problems as a strategy, including how to connect remotely located industry partners, and thus provides ways to change organizational infrastructure and practices. The ideas represented in Figure 10.1, as well as those presented in this chapter, suggest the need for guidelines.

Strategies for VHRD in IoPTS

Organizational systems and business practices are affected by IoPTS, so in addition to the issues previously discussed in the chapter, enumerated here are some basic strategies:

- Responsible Organization Certifications: As IoPTS evolves, the public will grow savvier about security and privacy. Much like other industry and trade standards, it is anticipated that consumers, and employees, will want to know that a particular device or service is trustworthy. Industry-wide policies will be developed for responsible use of IoPTS devices and certified, perhaps with a seal of approval from a third-party association. Corresponding training programs can certify IoPTS professionals.
- New Roles and Partnerships: IoPTS will drive new partnerships in supply chain management as well as new roles for employees, such as solution integrators who help build an ecosystem on behalf of the end user (Papert & Pflaum, 2017). Numerous other roles include those who finance IoPTS initiatives, whether it is venture capital or public subsidies through research institutions, and how partnering organizations share information and complete subprocesses. Cooperation can present a good business case for cost sharing, which will require business agreements (Tilanus, Ran, Faeth, Kelaidonis, & Stavroulaki, 2013).
- Designs for Individual and Organizational Learning: IoPTS presents new opportunities for both individual and organizational learning through technological advances. Employees and partners need to engage in a learning process to understand how to match the organizational mission with the potential of IoPTS. Where updates and advances are not communicated to the wider organization but kept closed to only a small in-group, out-group employee efforts may be counterproductive to the strategy of IoPTS. In fact, integrating technology with the

wider organization tends to optimize the work (Langer, 2010). Additionally, IoPTS has the capability to personalize learning and provide near-instantaneous feedback on performance. An important question to ask is: How can people learn from this system or device?

- Sociocultural Influence: The wider social context of the organization and the larger society will influence IoPTS through acceptance or resistance to adoption, as well as through embedding values and assumptions into component design. Adoption increases technology development capacity (Bashir, Ali, Asrar, & Babar, 2015); that is, the more people who are exposed to new technologies, the greater knowledge and skills they have to participate in the future of IoPTS. It is important to understand the cultures of partnering organizations and make assumptions explicit to avoid misunderstandings about design or business agreements. Conversely, shared values around privacy and security are powerful for ensuring against breaches and fostering mutual trust. Sociocultural factors will determine how privacy issues are handled, as well as the openness of the IoPTS architecture.

Learning is an innate and fundamentally human characteristic that will be more critical in the future than it is now. Within VHRD, organizations move away from thinking that learning and development are synonymous with formal and subject-based training. Rather, informal, everyday learning through experiences in IoPTS will be as important as formal modes, and IoPTS can provide on-demand learning resources to supply new information. Beyond this, employees need to be selected and trained for higher-order thinking to contribute to the advancement of IoPTS, given that technology will increasingly handle lower-order and repetitive tasks. Next we will look at specific implications for IoPTS and VHRD.

Implications

A general implication of this chapter is that organizations need to reinforce learning, development, and innovation in everyday practices. Employees and managers might assume characteristics of network leadership in which people lead by following, which creates space for the development of social-professional networks and allows for emerging qualities of group motivation and action (Kubiak & Bertram, 2005). Network leadership can generate a diversity of ideas and healthy collaboration needed for IoPTS. More specific implications for IoPTS include learning agility, technology development, and designing thinking.

Learning Agility

With an increased emphasis on informal learning, building greater capacity for quickly integrating experience with new information will be highly valued as organizations adopt IoPTS. In other words, employees and leaders will need learning agility (Bennett & McWhorter, 2017a; Hallenbeck, 2016). Learning that occurs outside of the organization forms new experiences for the individual but must be transferred to the organization (Bennett, 2010). For example, new learning in a university course only becomes part of organizational learning when it is applied to the work setting. Until then, it only exists as potential. Likewise, people need to acquire new learning; otherwise, knowledge and skills can decay over time. Today's challenge is not to "codify and dispense critical information, but to develop milieus and settings where individuals can learn through their own experiences" (Glassman & Kang, 2010, p. 1412) by recognizing that learning is not a series of hierarchical and deductively derived logic statements, but rather one that uses abduction. Abduction involves induction as well as deduction. In other words, it is induction that is the precursor to deductive logic systems. Everyone has a "semi-unique" (p. 1413) form of knowing through personal experience. The key is to adapt quickly to new conditions that demand learning.

Induction and intuition are human traits for learning and problem solving—ones that machines cannot easily replicate as of yet. There is no doubt that machines can follow extant deductive logic trees faster than humans, based on raw computing speed. However, machines have not yet replicated the human capacity for feeling, aesthetics, or intuitive powers where ideas not normally associated together or stored near in memory suddenly fuse to create a key insight (Bennett, 2011a). Adequate support for learning must also be provided for personalized learning (Robinson & Sebba, 2010), and low levels of self-direction can be a threat to learning and job performance. Learning agility is predicated on learning from experience, responding, reflecting upon, and trusting intuition where appropriate (Hallenbeck, 2016). Promoting learning agility can encourage humans to do what they do best.

Technology Development

Within the VHRD literature, technology development (TD) has been added as a fourth pillar of HRD in addition to training, organizational development, and career development (Bennett, 2014a). TD is defined in the field as "the integration of technology with HRD objectives and processes to improve learning capacity and performance" (Bennett & McWhorter, 2014, p. 581). Improving learning capacity through the use of technology implies not only individual learning but organizational learning, which is often embedded and preserved within intranets (Bennett, 2006a, 2006b, 2009). Learning capacity goes further than simple information processing; rather, it creates deep understanding through openness to diverse ways of viewing problems and to new possibilities, involving the human capacity to be curious and create work that is meaningful. Intranets that make up a large portion of IoPTS will be more organic and representative of an ecological system (Bennett & Bierema, 2010; Firestone & McElroy, 2003), supporting increased learning capacity. TD has at least two modes, including using technology to support and deliver HRD interventions and using HRD techniques to help with technology design and implementation, such as running a focus group or usability study (Bennett, 2014a). HRD offers techniques that help build IoPTS.

Design Thinking

In VHRD professionals become designers of environments that promote strong performance (Bennett, 2014a) and provide opportunities, access, and rich resources for learning and development. One way designers know they have been successful is when technology recedes into the background and becomes ubiquitous and natural. For business applications, the physical design is often less important than how a device functions within the organization (McEwen & Cassimally, 2014). Designing the ecology of an intranet includes the ability to imagine connections, user behavior, and downstream systems (Bennett & Bierema, 2010) that can function well in a given cultural milieu. As someone who has been involved in training since the 1990s, I have rarely seen off-the-shelf or computer-based training that did not need adaptation to the context in which new skills are to be performed. This principle is just as important for weaving in devices, people, and services into one system.

A useful new technique that may help adapt and design IoPTS to promote learning and innovation is Design Thinking (DT). Businesses have begun using DT to tackle complex problems, but nonprofits also use it for social innovations where important considerations include cultural context and human experience (Brown & Wyatt, 2010; Glen, Suciu, Baughn, & Anson, 2015; Gobble, 2014). It is a process best used when divergent thinking is needed, rather than incremental solutions, as it combines intuitive thinking and logic (Gobble, 2014; Brown & Wyatt, 2010). Brown and Wyatt (2010) provide three stages of DT. The first stage is inspiration, where groups are briefed about the problem to be solved and provided objectives, constraints, and measurements they must consider. This step often involves direct observation of the people affected by the problem, thus drawing on human empathy.

The second stage of DT is ideation that synthesizes insights and tests competing ideas. In this stage, it is critical that divergent thinking to create new and unusual ideas is not derailed. Premature judgment of ideas needs to be avoided, at least until there is a group sorting process of the ideas. The third stage is implementation of prototypes as well as a plan to communicate the innovation to stakeholders, often through storytelling. This stage is especially important for pitching new products to developing countries, because there is often a "lack of infrastructure, retail chains, communication networks, literacy, and other essential pieces of the system" (Brown & Wyatt,

2010, p. 35), which must be resolved for success. A crash course in design thinking is available online at Stanford University (see: https://dschool.stanford.edu/resources-collections/a-virtual-crash-course-in-design-thinking).

In summary, these techniques enhance learning and design in IoPTS. An Intranet–Internet–Intranet structure can create ecosystems that cross multiple locations and boundaries. Both VHRD and IoPTS are concerned with innovation and developing ecosystems that improve the organization's ability to meet its business objectives. Though many writing about IoPTS are concerned with architecture and programming protocols, there is a clear connection to learning for innovation. Additionally, IoPTS designers will affect the virtual systems in which modern employees learn and develop. The guidelines and implications bring the special characteristics of HRD into the conversation about IoPTS.

Conclusion

In concluding this chapter, it is clear that new and intriguing technologies are on the horizon. Fifth-generation, or 5G, connectivity will provide much greater planetary coverage of information and communication technology, which is already currently being tested for the potential to revolutionize download speed as well as advanced services, such as robotic surgical operations (Cheng, 2015). Internet linkages will become faster and reach a wider area of the world, bringing more users and devices online. One might argue that the sketch of a global brain might be in place in fifteen years, which mirrors human activity. Cyberspace "may be representative of the way humans think in the way that quantum physics is representative of the way bodies interact" (Glassman & Kang, 2010, p. 1413). IoPTS will continue growing and evolving, as will VHRD.

As more organizations adopt IOPTS, research is needed to understand how employee development is occurring in these new systems and how organizations respond to the challenges of constant connectivity and the overwhelming amount of data that results. As IoPTS expands, and, by extension, intranets of people, things, and services emerge, there will be many problems and opportunities to solve. One of the most important things is never to forget the humanity of the people now being webbed into IoPTS. This includes continuing to keep empathy for humans as a central tenet of design and staying true to ethical practices even if technology allows exploitation now and in the future. In keeping with Eloff et al. (2009), trust is paramount to security and privacy, but also to a reputation of success and goodwill in a technological ecosystem.

References

Ausburn, L. J., & Ausburn, F. B. (2014). Technical perspectives on theory in screen-based virtual reality environments: Leading from the future in VHRD. *Advances in Developing Human Resources*, *16*(3), 371–390.

Balaguera, H. U., Wise, D., Ng, Y. C, Tso, H., Chiang, W., Hutchinson, A. M., Galvin, T., Hilborne, L., Hoffman, C., Huang, C., & Wang, C. J. (2017). Using a medical intranet of things system to prevent bed falls in an acute care hospital: A pilot study. *Journal of Medical Internet Research*, *19*(5).e150. Retrieved January 26, 2018 from https://www.ncbi.nlm.nih.gov/pmc/articles/PMC5438463/.

Bashir, T., Ali, T. M., Asrar, M., & Babar, S. (2015). Performance and progress of OIC countries towards building technology development capacity. *Current Science*, *109*(5), 878–888. doi: 10.18520/v109/i5/878-888

Bennett, E. E. (2006a). Organizational intranets and the transition to managing knowledge. In M. Anandarajan, T. S. H. Teo, & C. A. Simmers (Eds.). *The internet and transformation of the workplace* (pp. 83–103). Armonke, NY: ME Sharpe.

Bennett, E. E. (2006b). *How organizational culture and change are embedded in an organization's intranet* (Unpublished doctoral dissertation). University of Georgia, Athens, GA.

Bennett, E. E. (2009). Virtual HRD: The intersection of knowledge management, culture, and intranets. *Advances in Developing Human Resources*, *11*(3), 362–374.

Bennett, E. E. (2010). The coming paradigm shift: Synthesis and future directions for Virtual HRD. *Advances in Developing Human Resources*, *12*(6), 728–741. doi: 10.1177/1523422310394796

Bennett, E. E. (2011a). Informal adult learning in simulated and virtual environments. In Information Resources Management Association (Ed.), *Gaming and simulations: Concepts, methodologies, tools and applications* (pp. 1914–1932). Hershey, PA: IGI Global. doi: 10.4018/978-1-60960-195-9.ch802

Bennett, E. E. (2011b, February). *Integrative informal learning in virtual HRD: The key to tacit knowledge?* Proceedings of the 2011 Academy of Human Resource Development Research Conference in the Americas, Chicago: AHRD.

Bennett, E. E. (2012). *A four-part model of informal learning: Extending Schugurensky's Conceptual Model*. Proceedings of the Adult Education Research Conference, Saratoga Springs, NY: AERC.

Bennett, E. E. (2014a). Introducing new perspectives on virtual HRD. *Advances in Developing Human Resources*, *16*(3), 263–280.

Bennett, E. E. (2014b). How an intranet provides opportunities for learning organizational culture: Implications for Virtual HRD. *Advances in Developing Human Resources*, *16*(3), 296–319.

Bennett, E. E., & Bierema, L. L. (2010). The ecology of virtual human resource development. *Advances in Developing Human Resources*, *12*(6), 632–647. doi: 10.1177/1523422310394789

Bennett, E. E., & McWhorter, R. R. (2014). Virtual human resource development. In N. E. Chalofsky, T. F. Rocco, & M. L. Morris (Eds.), *The handbook of human resource development: The discipline and the profession* (pp. 567–589). Hoboken, NJ: Wiley.

Bennett, E. E., & McWhorter, R. R. (2017a). IHRD and virtual HRD. In T. Garvin, A. McCarthy, & R. Carberry's (Eds.), *A handbook of international HRD: Contexts, processes and people* (pp. 268–294). London, UK: Edward Elgar.

Bennett, E. E., & McWhorter, R. R. (2017b). Organizational learning, community, and virtual HRD: Advancing the discussion. *New Horizons in Adult Education and Human Resource Development*, *29*(3), 19–27.

Brown, T., & Wyatt, J. (2010, Winter). Design thinking for social innovation. *Stanford Social Innovation Review*, 30–35.

Chapman, D. D., & Stone, S. J. (2010). Measurement of outcomes in virtual environments. *Advances in Developing Human Resources*, *12*(6), 665–680.

Cheng, R. (2015, September 9). *Verizon to be first to field-test crazy-fast 5G wireless*. CNET. Retrieved March 20, 2017, from www.cnet.com/news/verizon-to-hold-worlds-first-crazy-fast-5g-wireless-field-tests-next-year/

Cifolelli, K. (2016, September 20). *Using GPS or smart phone apps to monitor employee activity*. American Society of Employers. Retrieved from www.aseonline.org/News/Articles/ArtMID/628/ArticleID/947/Using-GPS-or-Smart-Phone-Apps-to-Monitor-Employee-Activity

Constantin, L. (2016, September 26). Armies of hacked IoT devices launch unprecedented DDoS attacks. *Computerworld*. Retrieved from www.computerworld.com/article/3124345/security/armies-of-hacked-iot-devices-launch-unprecedented-ddos-attacks.html

Deal, T. E., & Kennedy, A. A. (2000). *Corporate cultures: The rites and rituals of corporate life*. Cambridge, MA: Perseus Books.

Eloff, J. H. P., Eloff, M. M., Dlamini, M. T., & Zielinski, M. P. (2009). *Internet of people, things and services: The convergence of security, trust and privacy*. 3rd CompanionAble Workshop—IoPTS, Novotel Brussels—Brussels, 2 December, 8. Retrieved from http://hdl.handle.net/10204/4409

Fagan, M. H. (2014). Exploring a sociomaterial perspective on technology in virtual human resource development. *Advances in Developing Human Resources*, *16*(3).

Firestone, J. M., & McElroy, M. W. (2003). *Key issues in the new knowledge management*. Burlington, MA: Butterworth-Heinemann.

Gadallah, Y., elTager, M., & Elalamy, E. (2015). *A framework for cooperative intranet of things wireless sensor network applications*. The proceedings of the 2015 Eight International Workshop on Selected Topics in Mobile and Wireless Computing, Abu Dhabi, United Arab Emirates: IEEE, 147–154.

Germaine, M., & McGuire, D. (2014). The role of swift trust in virtual teams and implications for human resource development. *Advances in Developing Human Resources*, *16*(3), 356–370.

Glassman, M., & Kang, M. J. (2010). Pragmatism, connectionism and the internet: A mind's perfect storm. *Computers in Human Behavior*, *26*, 1412–1418.

Glen, R., Suciu, C., Baughn, C. C., & Anson, R. (2015). Teaching design thinking in business schools. *The International Journal of Management Education*, *13*(2015), 182–192.

Gobble, M. M. (2014). Design thinking. *Research Technology Management*, *57*(3), 59–61.

Greenberg, S. (2015). *The Internet of Things*. Cambridge, MA: MIT Press.

Hallenbeck, G. (2016). *Learning agility: Unlock the lessons of experience*. Greensboro, NC: Center for Creative Leadership Press.

Huang, W. D., Han, S., Park, U., & Seo, J. J. (2010). Managing employees' motivation, cognition, and performance in virtual workplaces: The blueprint of a game-based adaptive performance platform (GAPP). *Advances in Developing Human Resources*, *12*(6), 700–714.

IBM. (2015). *IBM analytics*. Retrieved from www.ibm.com/analytics/us/en/industry/

Kranz, M. (2017). *Building the Internet of Things: Implement new business models, disrupt competitors, transform your industry*. Hoboken, NJ: Wiley.

Kubiak, C., & Bertram, J. (2005). Network leadership's balancing act: Contrivance or emergence? *FORUM*, *47*(1), 8–11.

Langer, A. M. (2010). *Information technology and organizational learning: Managing behavioral change through technology and education* (2nd ed.). Boca Raton, FL: CRC Press.

Mani, G., Byun, B., & Cocca, P. (2013). *Enhancing communication and collaboration through integrated internet and intranet architecture.* The proceedings of SIGDOC'13, September 30–October 1, 2013, Greenville, NC: ACM.

Manyika, J., Chui, M., Bisson, P., Woetzel, J., Dobbs, R., Bughin, J., & Aharon, D. (2015). *Unlocking the potential of the Internet of Things.* Retrieved from www.mckinsey.com/insights/business_technology/the_internet_of_things_the_value_of_digitizing_the_physical_world

McEwen, A., & Cassimally, H. (2014). *Designing the Internet of Things.* Chichester, UK: Wiley.

McKendrick, J. (2015). In search of the true value in the Internet of Things. *Forbes.* Retrieved from www.forbes.com/sites/joemckendrick/2015/05/10/in-search-of-the-true-value-in-the-internet-of-things/

McLagan, P. A. (1989). Systems model 2000: Matching systems theory to future HRD issues. In D. B. Gradous (Ed.), *Systems theory applied to human resource development* (pp. 61–90). Alexandria, VA: ASTD.

McWhorter, R. R. (2014). A synthesis of new perspectives on Virtual HRD. *Advances in Developing Human Resources, 16*(3), 391–401.

McWhorter, R. R., & Lynham, S. A. (2014). An initial conceptualization of virtual scenario planning. *Advances in Developing Human Resources, 16*(3), 335–355.

Nafukho, F. M., Graham, C. M., & Muyia, H. M. A. (2010). Harnessing and optimal utilization of human capital in virtual workplace environments. *Advances in Developing Human Resources, 12*(6), 648–664.

Papert, M., & Pflaum, A. (2017). Development of an ecosystem model for the realization of Internet of Things (IoT) services in supply chain management. *Electron Markets, 27,* 175–189.

Poghosyan, G., Pefkianakis, I., Guyadec, P. L., & Christophides, V. (2016). Mining usage patterns in residential intranet of things. *Procedia Computer Science, 83,* 988–993.

Rabaey, J. M. (2015). *The human intranet: Where swarms and humans meet.* The proceedings of Automation & Text in Europe Conference & Exhibition, Grenoble, France: IEEE, 637–640.

Robinson, C., & Sebba, J. (2010). Personalising learning through the use of technology. *Computers & Education, 54,* 767–775.

Rowland, C., Goodman, E., Charlier, M., Light, A., & Lui, A. (2015). *Designing connected products: UX for the consumer of Internet of Things.* Sebastopol, CA: O'Reilly Media, Inc.

Schein, E. H. (2010). *Organizational culture and leadership* (4th ed.). San Francisco, CA: Wiley.

Schugurensky, D. (2000). *The forms of informal learning: Towards a conceptualization of the field.* NALL Working Paper #19–2000. Retrieved from www.nall.ca/res/19formsofinformal.htm

Swanson, R. A., & Holton, E. F. (2001). *Foundations of human resource development.* San Francisco, CA: Berrett-Koehler.

Thomas, K. (2014). Workplace technology and the creation of boundaries: The role of VHRD in a 24/7 work environment. *Advances in Developing Human Resources, 16*(3), 281–295.

Tilanus, P., Ran, B., Faeth, M., Kelaidonis, D., & Stavroulaki, V. (2013, June). *Virtual object access rights to enable multi-party use of sensors*. Proceedings of the IEEE 14th International Symposium and Workshops on a World of Wireless, Mobile and Multimedia Networks (WoWMoM '13), Madrid, Spain, 1–7.

Yang, M. (2013). The collision of social media and social unrest: Why shutting down social media is the wrong response. *Northwestern Journal of Technology & Intellectual Property*, *11*(7), 708–728.

Yoon, S. W., & Lim, D. H. (2010). Systemizing virtual learning and technologies by managing organizational competency and talents. *Advances in Developing Human Resources*, *12*(6), 715–727.

Part 3

IoPTS Workplace—Services

11 A SWOT Analysis Relating the Internet of Things to Designing Effective HR Performance Management Systems

Thomas Stephen Calvard

Introduction

In the history of work and human resources (HR), the New Lanark textile mill community managed by the entrepreneur Robert Owen in nineteenth-century Scotland is frequently looked back on as a pioneering and progressive community form of organization, given its emphasis on valuing employee education and creating fair working conditions for all (Donkin, 2010). In this utopian integration of the industrial and the social, Owen introduced a colored wooden block suspended near each worker's station called a 'Silent Monitor' to indicate their performance. On each of the four sides of the block was a different color (white, yellow, blue and black), and the color turned to the front reflected the assessed level of performance from the previous day, a record of which was also kept in a 'book of character' (Donkin, 2010).

Two centuries on from this historical example of New Lanark, organizations are still greatly invested in monitoring, managing and developing the performance of employees as successfully as possible. The purpose of this chapter therefore is to investigate how the emerging technological trend of the 'Internet of Things' (IoT) is likely to affect the HR processes and practices involved in employees' performance management, where the wooden blocks and paper ledgers of the nineteenth century are replaced by the digital, wireless, interconnected sensors and devices of the twenty-first.

IoT at its simplest reflects "the possibility of connecting various physical objects ('things') to the Internet . . . [that] can exchange information and interact with each other . . . [and] become 'smart things' that can behave autonomously [in ways] appropriate to the context and the situation" (Strohmeier, Franca, Majstorovic, & Schreiner, 2016, p. 5). The IoT vision for the next generation of the Internet becomes grander as more physical objects worldwide become digitally connected to the Internet and each other, and are able to intelligently and autonomously control and configure themselves and their environments (Li, Xu, & Zhao, 2015).

In the workplaces where technological trends such as IoT will continue to have an impact on employees, behind any broad discussion of talent management or HR strategy, there needs to be some consideration of the performance management systems and processes in place within organizations. Performance management concerns the "continuous process of identifying, measuring, and developing the performance of individuals and teams and aligning performance with the strategic goals of the organization" (Aguinis & Pierce, 2008, pp. 139–140).

Performance management is often viewed skeptically and narrowly in terms of 'performance appraisal', which is only a relatively nonstrategic meeting, typically once a year, to describe an employee's strengths and weaknesses (Aguinis & Pierce, 2008). Annual performance appraisal meetings with employees are now widely considered as outdated, inadequate and a bureaucratic waste of time (Ewenstein, Hancock, & Komm, 2016). The IoT can thus play a role in building more sophisticated, scientific, open, fair, continuous and inclusive performance systems with multiple raters, ratings, sources of data and feedback, with links to rewards at all levels, and adjustments to fit aspects of strategic and international business contexts (Ewenstein et al., 2016).

Some organizations are using more dynamic, continuous forms of performance coaching supported by technology in the form of apps and crowdsourcing to collect performance data in real time, for example (Ewenstein et al., 2016). In terms of IoT, the question becomes how various forms of digitally connected, data-driven objects can contribute usefully and appropriately to these processes, with advantages and drawbacks being anticipated and navigated accordingly.

Thus far, however, there is almost no work addressing the IoT in relation to HR practices and strategies, despite the broader applications of the IoT and the use of smart technologies in the workplace (e.g. Kim, Nussbaum, & Gabbard, 2016; Da Xu, He, & Li, 2014). One recent exception is work by Stefan Strohmeier and colleagues (2016), who conducted a Delphi study with 37 academic and practitioner experts in HR or human resource information systems (HRIS), which confirmed a range of general expectations that the IoT will lead to major changes. These included greater collection of employee data through sensors, more technically integrated interactions between novel objects and existing HR software and the continuing automation of administrative HR work and positions.

Given the limited work to date, this chapter aims to understand the potential positive and negative relationships between IoT and performance management, as well as constructive actions that HR functions can take to engage and address such relationships. To some extent, this requires creative theory building, drawing together some relevant strands of existing work concerning the IoT, performance management, electronic-HR (e-HR), digital sociology and urban informatics to extrapolate and imagine how the IoT might affect future work environments and HR practices.

Many frameworks around the IoT are emerging, with some expanding the acronym into Internet of People, Things and Services (IoPTS), as a reminder that as well as the 'things' or objects themselves, there are people interacting through them and services being provided across them (Eloff, Eloff, Dlamini, & Zielinski, 2009). Such frameworks can fragment the field, but where there are common and complementary factors, they are useful for guiding inquiry.

This chapter uses three IoT frameworks to guide its SWOT (strengths, weaknesses, opportunities, threats) analysis of the key factors affecting how effectively the IoT and performance management can fit together as part of a 'smart' HR performance management system. First, Eloff and colleagues (2009) propose a three-dimensional model of IoPTS based around configurations of different aspects of *privacy, trust* and *security* in any given system. Second, Wilson, Shah, and Whipple (2015) break down emerging IoT usage into four areas of *security, self-quantification, machine optimization* and *enhanced experiences*. Finally, Miorandi, Sicari, De Pellegrini, and Chlamtac (2012) propose four main IoT research areas: *security*; *computing, communication, identification; distributed systems;* and *distributed intelligence.* They also note six critical domains of IoT application: *smart homes/buildings, smart cities, environmental monitoring, health care, smart inventory/product management*, and *security and surveillance*.

Following a SWOT analysis guided by these frameworks, the chapter concludes with several implications for future HR research and IoT-supported performance management practice. The aim of the chapter is to argue that the IoT builds on existing strengths and weaknesses of technological and HR systems in organizations, but also extends toward opportunities and threats for HR and performance management along a longer-term horizon.

SWOT Analysis

This chapter has chosen SWOT analysis, over and above other frameworks, to unpack the IoT in relation to HR strategy, given the tool's exploratory, flexible and balanced nature in representing a current technological trend, as well as its heuristic value for guiding practical risk and value pursuits in organizations. SWOT analysis is a popular structured planning tool for assessing the strategic fit of an organization or other venture with its external environment (Chermack & Kasshanna, 2007). Surveys examining consultants' use of SWOT have criticized the framework for being too general as to verge on being meaningless, creating excessively long lists of factors, lacking in prioritization and not connecting properly with latter stages of a strategic implementation process (Hill & Westbrook, 1997).

However, the use of SWOT in the current chapter is justified precisely because these criticisms indicate oversimplifications or forms of misuse of SWOT (Chermack & Kasshanna, 2007) and even suggest constructive suggestions about how to deploy it more effectively. Weihrich (1982) has argued that SWOT can be applied most fruitfully when factors are clearly prioritized, it is mapped to features of the wider context, used in conjunction with other tools, used repeatedly over time and the dynamic interrelationships between specific factors in the SWOT quadrants are considered more systematically. Similarly, Chermack and Kasshanna (2007) argue that the effectiveness of SWOT depends on whether it is implemented in an open, unbiased fashion as part of a broader developmental process (not entirely unlike performance management itself).

This chapter will therefore continue by using SWOT to proceed with its project of identifying major inherent strengths and weaknesses (SW) of IoT and performance management practice internal to organizations and relating them to opportunities and threats (OT) in broader external environments. In turn, this allows discrete potential actions and points of guidance for HR and managerial decision makers to be derived.

SWOT can help to dictate or inform IoT/IoPTS strategy in HR by outlining a holistic set of practices and domains, negative and positive, as well as how practitioners can ensure strengths are 'matched' to opportunities, and weaknesses and threats 'converted' to strengths and opportunities, respectively (Piercy & Giles, 1989). In line with Eloff and colleagues' (2009) IoPTS framework, the SWOT here seeks to address all three dimensions of security, trust and privacy in relation to HR and performance management. Organizations need to match existing employee data *security* practices to opportunities to improve and convert them away from threats. Organizations should leverage employee trust as a strength where it already exists as a resource and build it up where it is weaker or lacking. Finally, existing privacy practices may serve as strengths, but could easily become threats if organizations do not anticipate technological change and manage risks and upscale proactively.

The following sections correspond to the four quadrants of the SWOT tool, and in each case three major factors are prioritized in relation to IoT and performance management. The SWOT analysis can thus help organizations avoid pitfalls in terms of understanding the current risks and limitations of IoT trends and developing the right capabilities and architecture for running IoT systems efficiently and effectively in the delivery of HR services. In particular, performance management HR practices can be enhanced via greater information processing to aid better-quality decision making, employee and line manager empowerment and more seamless interconnectivity across teams and distributed, diverse workforces. The SW aspect of the analysis helps to engage the *current* status of capabilities, whereas the OT aspect helps to trace possible *evolutionary trajectories* of change as HR strategy and IoT/IoPTS innovations become more entwined. In particular, this concerns the expansion of employee monitoring, the interconnectivity of employee performances on a larger scale and the increased interaction with digital objects and data to coordinate tasks more efficiently and effectively (Eloff et al., 2009). HR academics and practitioners should therefore be able to use the SWOT survey to make incremental adjustments to existing practices and systems, while proactively preparing for managing future risks and investing in future IoT-related opportunities.

Strengths

First, both IoT and performance management are embedded within a rich existing knowledge base and related trends, applications and paradigms that continue to affect workplaces. If they are considered entirely new or reduced to existing in a relatively isolated vacuum, then there is a risk that the strength that could be drawn from these existing connections might be overlooked. Performance management, for example, can and should be informed by related, long-standing areas of HR, organizational behavior (OB) and psychology literature on goal setting (Latham & Locke, 2007), feedback seeking (Ashford, Blatt, & Vande Walle, 2003) and conceptions of talent management (Dries, 2013). Indeed, as notions of performance and talent have evolved, a more comprehensive view of the wider system becomes important in terms of understanding and capitalizing upon the interplay between technologies, stakeholders and organizational practices in shaping forces of supply and demand in labor markets (Bersin by Deloitte, 2013).

Similarly, the IoT sits nested within a next-generation cluster of closely related technological developments or trends that are likely to mutually reinforce one another's development through their synergies and histories, spurring growth and innovation forward until at least 2025 (Pew Research Center, 2014). These trends include big data analytics, social media, cloud computing, machine learning, artificial intelligence (AI), biomedical engineering, wearable technologies and virtual reality (VR). In terms of wearable technologies, for example, health, safety and productivity aspects of performance have been usefully tracked via armbands, belts, visors, watches and other sensory devices in health care, sports, the military and many other industrial and organizational settings going back 50 years or more (Wilson, 2013). Building on existing devices and equipment is a strong way to keep developing IoT applications. These developments date back to some of the earliest trends in trying to improve workforce efficiency and motivation, particularly in terms of Taylorism, scientific management and 'time-and-motion' studies (Kanigel, 2005).

Second, IoT and performance management can act as mutually enabling strategic drivers for one another. Performance management is a significant part of the HR profession's platform for developing its strategic contributions to the performance of the organization as a whole (DeNisi & Smith, 2014). Although the precise nature of the strategic synergies between technology and HR strategies are still relatively elusive (Marler & Parry, 2016), the IoT and related digital, data-driven trends are likely to play a role in strengthening the capacity of HR in at least two ways—first, by helping HR to gather evidence more systematically to better support its decisions (Rousseau & Barends, 2011), and second, by more precisely accounting for how employees add value to an organization's balance sheet in conjunction with more fixed, tangible assets (Fulmer & Ployhart, 2014). A fairly recent example of this strength in action comes from the work of Alex 'Sandy' Pentland, his Human Dynamics Lab at MIT and the company he co-founded, Sociometric Solutions (Pentland, 2012). By using sensors built into sociometric badges worn by employees, these researchers have been able to track workers' commutes, financiers' trading patterns, call center employees' coffee break schedules and the conversational dynamics of team meetings to suggest interventions for improving productivity to the tune of millions of dollars in value added (Pentland, 2014).

A third and final strength factor concerns a renewed emphasis on the sociotechnical at work—the integration of the human and the physical or material in real time, with an emphasis on ergonomics and usability (Clegg & Walsh, 2004). A performance environment populated by various IoT devices and sensors would contain hardware, software and 'liveware' (employees, teams, managers), enabling customized, self-organizing opportunities for learning to occur in local, embodied and networked ways (Davis, Challenger, Jayewardene, & Clegg, 2014). For example, Italy's biggest grocery cooperative, Coop Italia, worked with Microsoft and other partners to adopt a 'supermarket of the future' IoPTS concept, using motion sensors to offer customers a more seamless, interactive and responsive shopping experience. This also stands to enhance employee performance, enabling employees to gain more rapid, richer insights into customer preferences and make more efficient, dynamic use of spare shop space (Ray, 2016).

To give another example, John Lanchester, the British novelist and journalist, in his account of using the 'Amazon Echo' device in his home, reports being pleasantly surprised by the life-enhancing, user-friendly benefits of the voice-activated technology, noting how enabling these features could be for those whose sight or mobility are restricted (Lanchester, 2017). Often when technology is discussed in HR terms in the workplace, it is reduced to automation, decreased headcount and other cost-savings benefits. With regard to the IoT, however, responsive devices that can connect more dynamically to the Internet and other objects open up the possibility of more affordances that interact with human capabilities more directly to enrich them (Want, Schilit, & Jenson, 2015). This could help challenge views of talent and performance as a competitive war and promote more creative, collaborative and inclusive performance systems. Furthermore, IoT devices that communicate with their own anthropomorphic voices can encourage greater engagement through their perceived social presence (Kim, 2016), and these strengths might dovetail with a performance management system in the form of an IoT-supported 360-degree feedback program, for instance.

Weaknesses

First, the IoT and wearable technology has so far really only shown growth in some domains and markets—such as health care devices, industrial sensors, and household appliances—and relatively slow or uneven growth and adoption at that (Bradshaw, 2017; The Economist, 2016). The IoT still seems to require something of a technological leap of faith beyond the success of smartphones and tablets, where the dream of living and working in a brave new world of densely interconnected infrastructure, standardization and measurement may defy fuller expansion and aggregation for some time to come (Bell, 2015).

Performance management is also struggling to reach a tipping point in progressing beyond outdated annual appraisals, on the one hand, and brutally disruptive 'forced ranking' performance management that promotes, develops or fires employees based on categorized performance rankings (Pfeffer & Sutton, 2006). Amazon, for example, still reportedly uses the latter approach, sometimes termed 'rank and yank', despite reports of its destructive effects on individual employees and organizational performance (Spicer, 2015). In sum, the IoT and performance management are unlikely to work strongly in combination until ineffectual elements in their respective marketplaces are eliminated and more interactive, user-friendly products and practices are adopted more widely.

Second, there is a general lack of digital skills and literacy among current generations of employees and managers. A recent survey of 268 HR professionals in the UK found only 15% or less of them reported team expertise in various digital skills (Patmore, Somers, D'Souza, Welch, & Lawrence, 2017). HR practices like performance management seem to be moving slowly along the digital adoption curve, largely due to reasons of inadequate retraining and slow updating and integrating of legacy systems into improved decision making and return on investment (ROI) (Patmore et al., 2017). The best computer or data scientists and start-ups are still often described as 'unicorns' to signify their rareness (McNeill, 2016). It's unclear as of yet how such rareness can shape or develop into connected workforces that collaborate more extensively on IoT-related innovations (Puthiyamadam, 2017). More broadly, uneven or weak digital skills and access could reinforce inequality-related issues arising from 'digital divides' along various socioeconomic and sociodemographic lines (van Dijk & Hacker, 2003).

Third, there are shortcomings inherent to the automation of IoT components of a digital ecosystem, particularly as they interact with any human and cultural shortcomings inherent to a performance management system, the two sets of shortcomings being likely to exacerbate one another to some extent. Since the first days of electronic computer terminals in organizations, for instance, there has been a sense that devices and automation present users with something of a confined and self-contained situation that can constrain their cognitive processes (Weick, 1985). So-called 'ironies of automation' can present themselves, where human operators are assisted by technology but face expanded challenges where the technology fails under more abnormal conditions and the operator is left with responsibility for diagnosing and recovering from the problem (Bainbridge, 1983). A related concept is that of 'automation surprises', where technology designers' intentions lead to unintended consequences for users, prompting new kinds of error, confusion and questions along the lines of 'what is this technology doing?' and 'why is this happening?' (Sarter, Woods, & Billings, 1997). Regarding IoT technologies, the media have reported everyday gripes with Amazon and Google voice assistants, such as automatically ordering unwanted products and responding to a child's misheard request by directing him to porn, much to the panic of his parents (Clark, 2016; Waters, 2017).

The same weaknesses can present in the workplace too, and at a more systemic level when they interact with human and cultural weaknesses of performance management systems. Common mistakes using talent analytics in performance management, for example, include systems overemphasizing certain metrics, ignoring nonquantitative aspects of performance and only holding lower-level employees accountable to the technology, not senior management (Davenport, Harris, & Shapiro, 2010). Examples of this might include Amazon's 'Anytime Feedback Tool', an internal platform that office workers can use to anonymously share praise and critique/blame regarding their peers. The tool has been criticized for being used as a hotbed of political scheming and sabotage that can ultimately lead to employees being unfairly eliminated for reasons unknown to them and that they are powerless to challenge (Stone, 2015). IoT technology can also be used as an appropriate means to inappropriate performance ends in relation to leaders and executives embracing a cult of extreme physical 'super' endurance, supported by wearable biometric devices and mind-boosting drugs (The Economist, 2015).

Opportunities

First, one key vision is the 'Industrial Internet' or Industry 4.0, often associated with General Electric (GE) and their large investments into infusing their logistics, operations, manufacturing and product development processes with digital sensors and analytics that connect tasks and equipment that were previously analog in nature (Iansiti & Lakhani, 2014). The potential for greater connectivity across tasks and equipment implies devices for measuring performance more accurately, reliably and holistically. Blurring boundaries and integrating manufacturing, IT and service skills more tightly together can better coordinate employee and business model performance, rather than employees working in functional silos or outsourcing capabilities (Kleiner & Sviokla, 2017). For the employees performing tasks using the digitally connected equipment, it can be providing them with rapid, personalized feedback on their productivity, error rates, safety and so on. For example, ABB, the multinational technology corporation, outlines an IoPTS case study on its website of 'Remote Support' and 'Remote Condition Monitoring' services, as applied to an SSAB steel factory in Finland (ABB, 2017). By using data from drives inside pumps, motors and industrial components ('things'), ABB and SSAB operations and maintenance planning teams ('people') were able to improve proactive problem resolution and prevention in disturbances and downtime of key processes ('service' and performance management).

Overall, an Industrial Internet means redefining employee production performance by linking it more closely to the coding and use of digital devices, data streams and platforms to cooperate and innovate in relation to diverse others (Kagermann, 2015). One image of this future employee—albeit a fanciful and provocative one—is as a sort of James Bond–type actor, whose performance is managed through the improvisational use of gadgets across a series of challenging projects or missions (Rose, 2014).

Second, there are possibilities inherent to improved machine learning and artificial intelligence (AI) capabilities of IoT devices. Networked objects can use algorithms and computational processing of large amounts of information from their environment to learn, adapt and make decisions more autonomously. This 'machine intelligence' can usefully "augment employee performance, automate increasingly complex workloads, and develop 'cognitive agents' that simulate both human thinking and engagement" (Briggs & Hodgetts, 2017, p. 35). This mirroring of performing employees by thinking, learning, performing devices could revolutionize performance management by putting humans and machines on a more equal and reciprocal footing in terms of how they mutually enhance and complement one another's performances. Given that technology is improving in its abilities to process language and neural-type connections, it is not too hard to envision AI that coaches and supervises employees, and vice versa (O'Reilly Media, 2017). Algorithms and devices are already being deemed effective performers in terms of hiring employees and detecting criminals (Datafloq, 2017; Kuncel, Ones, & Klieger, 2014), where humans may be freed up to work more effectively and complementarily on more socially and emotionally involving tasks (Beck & Libert, 2017). The opportunity is to develop *transhumanist* performance management practices that jointly appraise and develop humans and machines in how they doubly add value, through divisions of labor and interdependent forms of assistance, learning, care and improvement (Lorenz, Rüßmann, Strack, Lueth, & Bolle, 2015).

Third, larger-scale (inter)connectivity can be achieved, in spatial and geographical terms, to boost performance in aggregate, coordinating outputs across higher levels of analysis. To the extent that the IoT is able to grow on a larger scale, there is an opportunity for larger, smarter environments to develop, exercising greater capabilities than single devices or subsets of devices. One obvious level in question here is the city, or 'smart city' vision, where the technological solutions of IoT are used to securely manage a city's assets and the quality of life of its citizens and workers (Zanella, Bui, Castellani, & Vangelista, 2014). In terms of performance management, surveys of talented knowledge workers reveal that a desirable smart city location and community is key for attracting and developing employees (Thite, 2011).

Economic geographers and urban planners have long recognized this potential, but urban informatics and the IoT are bringing a digitalized version of the vision more sharply into view. Performance management systems can thus be improved by broadening their notions of performance beyond the internal environment of a single organization. Thus a wider IoT-supported architecture could help provide a useful emphasis on relatively neglected aspects of performance. These might include contributions to solving messy, high-level 'wicked problems' such as poverty and terrorism (Waddell, 2016), as well as interorganizational collaboration and boundary-spanning performance behaviors (Calvard, 2014). Employees have always been highly motivated by understanding how their performance has an impact on the bigger picture (Grant, 2007), and the IoT can only provide more data and transparency to helping employers and employees appreciate such impact. As well as cities, regional hubs, confederations, clusters and other centers of systemic, networked human and economic activity may well be able to take advantage of similar opportunities. Organizations and employees have a vested interest in understanding and acting upon IoT-type data generated on issues like parking, traffic, pollution, education, health care, crime, weather and utilities, all of which can affect their performance.

Threats

First, there is the sheer complexity of IoT objects (variety, dynamism) and the need to ensure their standardization and compatibility in informing performance standards and policies. Managing heterogeneous applications, environments and devices has been cited as a major IoT challenge, particularly in establishing interoperability standards and protocols at global or international levels, where consensus building and regulatory planning (e.g. for radio spectrum allocation) can be very slow, involving many stakeholders (Bandyopadhyay & Sen, 2011). The reality is that the IoT remains fragmented, with standards elusive across manufacturers, operating systems and levels of connectivity and programmability. Bigger firms remain relatively disinterested, with little immediate incentive to cooperate and surrender competitive advantages unique to their own products and services—in short, the IoT may fail to speak a common language (Newman, 2016).

In terms of HRIS and performance management, interoperability issues of the IoT will add to the typical implementation issues facing managers and employees of replacing existing legacy systems, customization across the organization, and training and support in new technological standards (Dery, Hall, Wailes, & Wiblen, 2013). Adoption and effectiveness of technologies can be highly uneven across employees in the organization, and at worst they may feel that the system is unfair or counterproductive (Stone, Stone-Romero, & Lukaszewski, 2003). There is a very real threat that IoT could expand and amplify the worse aspects of bureaucracy at work—the dehumanizing, absurd, frustrating and coercive webs of inflexible rules—as they are translated across great assemblages of objects and data (Stanley, 2015).

Second, employees might resist both the technological changes represented by the IoT and changes made to performance management processes.

Internet technologies can lead to unhealthy patterns of human addiction and dependence that negatively affect workplace performance (Griffiths, 2010). Heightened awareness and concern could invite more political responses, and even 'neo-Luddite' acts of resistance, such as attacks on drones, people wearing Google Glass products and taxi drivers rioting against Uber cars and drivers in France (Dillet, 2015; Hill, 2014). Regardless of how extreme the response, employees are likely to be ambivalent in general about heightened surveillance, monitoring and invasions of privacy.

Electronic performance monitoring can run counter to popular management rhetoric on employee empowerment, trust, flexibility and 'results only' work environments. Survey evidence shows employees feel negatively towards being closely monitored or recorded through devices, and more so if the monitoring is focused on individuals and is unpredictable in nature (Jeske & Santuzzi, 2015). Clearly a respect for ethical and legal boundaries, as well as social support, is needed to frame monitoring more positively. A name has been coined for users who exhibit misconduct in relation to Google Glass wearables—'Glassholes'. It serves as a reminder of the tensions and strains IoT could put on workplace relationships, as well as the risk of darker forms of counterproductive work behavior that show contempt for privacy and rights (Healey, 2015). A broader, critical perspective can recognize that power runs through both human employees and material objects in complex, interactive ways—leading to a 'government of things' presiding over their possible (inter)actions (Lemke, 2015).

Third, it's unclear whether or not the overall cybersecurity and safety of an IoT performance management system can be effectively and sustainably upheld. Security researchers have demonstrated how easily they can hack into objects, including a 2014 Jeep Cherokee automobile, prompting Fiat Chrysler to recall 1.4 million vehicles. The company had to post out USB drives with patches to block any further attacks on the infotainment systems of the cars and the Sprint network connecting cars and trucks (Greenberg & Zetter, 2015). In terms of workplace performance, hacking vulnerabilities through IoT-enabled objects could threaten trust in sensitive objects and information, enable counterproductive behaviors like theft or sabotage and pose serious risks to safety and control while employees work.

As Roman, Zhou, & Lopez (2013, p. 2270) note, "the threats that can affect the IoT entities are numerous, such as attacks that target diverse communication channels, physical threats, denial of service, identity fabrication, and others". Cybersecurity mechanisms therefore need to be correspondingly numerous and strong in their defenses against these attacks. Because of the dynamic and distributed nature of the IoT vision, traditional security methods are too static and generic. Flexible and improvisational countermeasures are needed, ones that take into account changing territories of trust and risk (Sicari, Rizzardi, Grieco, & Coen-Porisini, 2015). The main areas to attend to are access, authentication and identity management. Quick fixes are unlikely to be possible. Organizations will need to map out their performance systems by layers: how devices provide access to assets and which devices are vulnerable because of being left unattended or having low computing power. This means a systems approach, considering the types of vulnerabilities, threats, intruders and attacks that might be likely to occur in a given organizational context (Abomhara & Kien, 2015). Failure to do so is likely to invite an array of possible IoT abuses and threats, including blackouts, break-ins, lock-outs, thefts and other kinds of confusing and dangerous crisis (Dhanjani, 2015).

Regarding performance management, Dhanjani (2015) notes the threat posed from nosy or disgruntled employees, citing the example of the likely involvement of disgruntled Sony Pictures employees in leaking data (executive emails) in 2014 that was damaging to the company brand and reputation. Employees may be in a position to put colleagues and customers at risk, particularly if they have inside knowledge of IoT and performance systems, but also, depending on their role, they may themselves be vulnerable to 'social engineering attacks'—where threat actors rely on human deception rather than attacking the technology directly (Dhanjani, 2015). Performance management architects should look carefully at the design of jobs and roles that involve IoT cybersecurity risks, and assess and reward competent cybersecurity policy development and compliance, as well as IoT attack detection and prevention, where appropriate.

Discussion

Having presented the SWOT analysis and each set of factors in turn, this chapter now concludes by offering further implications and recommendations: three for future research on the IoT and performance management and three concerning future practice by HR, managers and employees. These recommendations should go some way toward 'joining up' the four areas of the SWOT, providing ways forward in terms of exploiting positive opportunities and converting negative concerns into more neutral and positive forces (Piercy & Giles, 1989). Positive and negative areas identified as surrounding the IoT/IoPTS aid in the crafting of corresponding policy recommendations around how to improve the security, trust, privacy and digitally distributed intelligence of HR's performance management, using research as evidence to inform practice.

Starting with future research, one recommendation is to give greater consideration to 'sociomateriality' in theoretically explaining and trying to account for sets of relationships and effects. Sociomateriality reflects a commitment to integrate, rather than separate, the technological and the social or organizational (Orlikowski & Scott, 2008). This move is given even greater urgency by the development of the IoT, where technological classes of material objects are fused even more richly and intimately with daily lives, relationships and practices. Research on components of the IoT and performance management (e.g. coaching, appraisals, leadership development) should therefore not overemphasize either technological determinism or unconstrained social construction at the expense of the other. Such research is likely to yield greater insights into how technological and social relationships are entangled and dynamically affect one another—understandings which will be important for organizations if they are to understand control, accountability and capacity (Boos, Guenter, Grote, & Kinder, 2013).

Second, theories of motivation and performance should be tested in conjunction with IoT technologies to see if traditional findings can be replicated with IoT devices and environments, or if they need to be modified. Goal-setting theory, for example, is starting to be tested and refined in relation to 'gamification' technologies, where performance-related objects and features like leaderboards and simulations are found to have positive motivational effects on task performance (Landers, Bauer, Callan, & Armstrong, 2015). Building on such research agendas will help ensure that performance management as a set of HR practices remains evidence-based in nature (Rousseau & Barends, 2011) and that decisions about incorporating IoT systems into the workplace are based on carefully formulated research.

Third, future research may benefit from focusing on transhumanism, in terms of the technological possibilities for boosting human performance by extending, transferring and improving various resources that go beyond the limits of the current physical and mental capabilities of individual employees. IoT environments might help employees to become ever smarter, fitter and healthier in various contexts (Bostrom, 2005). Future research might be able to further explore cases where the data and devices of the IoT present opportunities to transform performance in positive ways (e.g. in sports and medicine). In the music industry, the careers and performances of pop stars are now manufactured in highly digital, data-driven terms, going above and beyond the human pop artist themselves to ensure high levels of success (Colburn, 2017).

Turning to practice, perhaps the first and foremost priority for managers and HR to address is the digital (and statistical/analytical) skills gaps in their workforces. Future work skills, as predicted by panels, tend to prioritize a mixture of cognitive, social and technological capabilities (Davies, Fidler, & Gorbis, 2011). Managers and HR should think about how these three areas are integrated into their existing training needs analyses and programs to best adapt to trends like the IoT. Coding and programming devices have serious prospects for creating a new generation of blue-collar jobs (Thompson, 2017), so HR managers need to consider this in terms of recruitment and job design. Extending digital skills training to teams is also a good opportunity to integrate IT and technological functions with operations, HR and other areas of the organization in order to have more cohesive, value-adding discussions. Furthermore, the physical and material nature of IoT developments may lend itself well to more innovative training across space and objects that invokes design thinking, discovery and experiential learning methodologies, as opposed to more formal, traditional methods.

A second area for practice is to develop shared understandings around classifications of different objects or 'things' in the IoT. Some objects may be wearable, others not; some fixed in a local position, others more 'ambient' in their presence and sensory capacities; some more adaptive and programmable in their levels of machine learning, others more scripted and limited in functionality, and so on. Dodge and Kitchin (2009), for example, have categorized digital objects, by their permeability, reactivity and recording capacities. Their most sophisticated class are termed 'logjects' and are described as highly interoperable and have 'awareness' in terms of recording information from their environment for storage and future reuse (Dodge & Kitchin, 2009). If managers, HR and employees engage in this classification exercise as a practical change process, it will enable them to develop a common language around IoT-related performance management, developing clearer strategies about the status and use of such objects in existing task performance situations. The 'endpoints' or direct sensors in the proximal work environment can thus be traced back to functional hubs, and finally to more integrated and enhanced forms of performance management systems and services (e.g. dashboards, talent pipelines) in the cloud (Burkitt, 2014).

Finally, practice needs to address cybersecurity and ensure IoT performance management systems that are strong and resilient, avoiding the threat posed by various unwanted, invasive attacks. In terms of trust and fairness, this means having a system set up in ways acceptable to all users. In performance management, trust and confidence in the top management and the consistency of the system are intimately related (Mayer & Davis, 1999). On the IoT side, the reliability, dependability and trustworthiness of various technological layers are no less crucial in shaping employee perceptions of trustworthiness and risk. Thus managers are well advised to engage in 'trust management' (TM), taking a systematic and transparent approach to showing workforces how data are securely and robustly transmitted and fused across an IoT system according to clear, agreed-upon principles and goals (Yan, Zhang, & Vasilakos, 2014).

Conclusion

This chapter has presented a SWOT analysis outlining key factors with the potential to positively and negatively influence the success of an IoT-supported performance management system, also drawing implications for future research and practice at the junction of the two topics of the IoT and performance management. Almost no theory or research to date has explicitly linked the IoT as a technological trend with specific HR practices and strategies. Hopefully, as IoT products and services proliferate in households and industries, similar discussions on how to integrate them with various HR practices and workforce settings affecting employees will continue to be debated, explored and refined.

References

ABB. (2017). *Internet of Things delivers innovative remote services for drives maintenance planning*. (Webpage). Retrieved August 20, 2017, from http://new.abb.com/about/technology/iotsp/top-stories/customer-stories/innovative-remote-services-for-drives-maintenance-planning

Abomhara, M., & Kien, G. M. (2015). Cyber security and the Internet of Things: Vulnerabilities, threats, intruders and attacks. *Journal of Cyber Security*, *4*, 65–88.

Aguinis, H., & Pierce, C. A. (2008). Enhancing the relevance of organizational behavior by embracing performance management research. *Journal of Organizational Behavior*, *29*(1), 139–145.

Ashford, S. J., Blatt, R., & Vande Walle, D. (2003). Reflections on the looking glass: A review of research on feedback-seeking behavior in organizations. *Journal of Management*, *29*(6), 773–799.

Bainbridge, L. (1983). Ironies of automation. *Automatica*, *19*(6), 775–779.

Bandyopadhyay, D., & Sen, J. (2011). Internet of Things: Applications and challenges in technology and standardization. *Wireless Personal Communications*, *58*(1), 49–69.

Beck, M., & Libert, B. (2017). The rise of AI makes emotional intelligence more important. *Harvard Business Review*. Retrieved February 20, 2017, from https://hbr.org/2017/02/the-rise-of-ai-makes-emotional-intelligence-more-important

Bell, L. (2015, August 5). Wearables in the workplace? Not yet: IoT is just too complex. *The Inquirer*. Retrieved February 1, 2017, from www.theinquirer.net/inquirer/feature/2420475/wearables-in-the-workplace-not-yet-iot-is-just-too-complex

Bersin by Deloitte. (2013, December). *Predictions for 2014: Building a strong talent pipeline for the global economic recovery: Time for innovative and integrated talent and HR strategies*. Retrieved January 20, 2017, from www2.deloitte.com/content/dam/Deloitte/au/Documents/human-capital/deloitte-au-con-predictions-bersin-2014-1213.pdf

Boos, D., Guenter, H., Grote, G., & Kinder, K. (2013). Controllable accountabilities: The Internet of Things and its challenges for organisations. *Behaviour & Information Technology*, *32*(5), 449–467.

Bostrom, N. (2005). A history of transhumanist thought. *Journal of Evolution and Technology*, *14*(1), 1–25.

Bradshaw, T. (2017, February 9). Wearable tech groups press on despite not living up to hype. *Financial Times*. Retrieved February 10, 2017, from www.ft.com/content/9005134c-ee66-11e6-930f-061b01e23655

Briggs, B., & Hodgetts, C. (2017). Tech trends 2017: The kinetic enterprise. *Deloitte University Press*. Retrieved February 20, 2017, from https://dupress.deloitte.com/content/dam/dup-us-en/articles/3468_TechTrends2017/DUP_TechTrends2017.pdf

Burkitt, F. (2014, November 10). A strategist's guide to the Internet of Things. *Strategy+Business*. Retrieved February 20, 2017, from www.strategy-business.com/article/00294

Calvard, T. S. (2014). Difficulties in organizing boundary-spanning activities of inter-organizational teams. In J. Langan-Fox & C. Cooper (Eds.), *Boundary-spanning in organizations: Network, influence, and conflict* (pp. 116–142). New York: Taylor & Francis.

Chermack, T. J., & Kasshanna, B. K. (2007). The use and misuse of SWOT analysis and implications for HRD professionals. *Human Resource Development International*, *10*(4), 383–399.

Clark, P. A. (2016, December 30). Amazon Alexa helpfully tries to give porn to a child. *Yahoo! News*. Retrieved February 5, 2017, from https://uk.news.yahoo.com/amazon-alexa-helpfully-tries-porn-143018413.html

Clegg, C., & Walsh, S. (2004). Change management: Time for a change! *European Journal of Work and Organizational Psychology*, *13*(2), 217–239.

Colburn, R. (2017, February 23). Meet the 14-year-old pop star who's literally being created with internet data. *A.V. Club*. Retrieved February 24, 2017, from www.avclub.com/article/meet-14-year-old-pop-star-s-literally-being-create-250918?utm_content=Main&utm_campaign=SF&utm_source=Facebook&utm_medium=SocialMarketing

Datafloq. (2017, February 17). *How facial recognition plays a role in catching criminals*. Retrieved February 20, 2017, from https://datafloq.com/read/facial-recognitions-role-in-catching-criminals/2679

Davenport, T. H., Harris, J., & Shapiro, J. (2010). Competing on talent analytics. *Harvard Business Review*, *88*(10), 52–58.

Davies, A., Fidler, D., & Gorbis, M. (2011). Future work skills 2020. *Institute for the Future*. Retrieved February 21, 2017, from www.iftf.org/futureworkskills/

Davis, M. C., Challenger, R., Jayewardene, D. N. W., & Clegg, C. W. (2014). Advancing socio-technical systems thinking: A call for bravery. *Applied Ergonomics*, *45*(2), 171–180.

Da Xu, L., He, W., & Li, S. (2014). Internet of Things in industries: A survey. *IEEE Transactions on Industrial Informatics*, *10*(4), 2233–2243.

DeNisi, A., & Smith, C. E. (2014). Performance appraisal, performance management, and firm-level performance: A review, a proposed model, and new directions for future research. *Academy of Management Annals*, *8*(1), 127–179.

Dery, K., Hall, R., Wailes, N., & Wiblen, S. (2013). Lost in translation? An actor-network approach to HRIS implementation. *The Journal of Strategic Information Systems*, *22*(3), 225–237.

Dhanjani, N. (2015). *Abusing the Internet of Things: Blackouts, freakouts, and stakeouts*. North Sebastopol, CA: O'Reilly Media, Inc.

Dillet, R. (2015, June 25). French anti-Uber protest turns to guerrilla warfare as cabbies burn cars, attack Uber drivers. *Tech Crunch*. Retrieved February 4, 2017, from https://techcrunch.com/2015/06/25/french-anti-uber-protest-turns-to-guerrilla-warfare-as-cabbies-burn-cars-attack-uber-drivers/

Dodge, M., & Kitchin, R. (2009). Software, objects, and home space. *Environment and Planning A*, *41*(6), 1344–1365.

Donkin, R. (2010). The Silent Monitor. In *The History of Work* (pp. 87–102). London: Palgrave Macmillan.

Dries, N. (2013). The psychology of talent management: A review and research agenda. *Human Resource Management Review*, *23*(4), 272–285.

The Economist. (2015, December 16). Here comes SuperBoss: A cult of extreme physical endurance is taking root among executives. Retrieved January 5, 2017, from www.economist.com/news/business/21684107-cult-extreme-physical-endurance-taking-root-among-executives-here-comes-superboss

The Economist. (2016, June 11). Where the smart is: Connected homes will take longer to materialise than expected. Retrieved February 1, 2017, www.economist.com/news/business/21700380-connected-homes-will-take-longer-materialise-expected-where-smart

Eloff, J. H. P., Eloff, M. M., Dlamini, M. T., & Zielinski, M. P. (2009). Internet of people, things and services: The convergence of security, trust and privacy. 3rd CompanionAble Workshop-IoPTS, Brussels, 2 December.

Ewenstein, B., Hancock, B., & Komm, A. (2016, May). Ahead of the curve: The future of performance management. *McKinsey Quarterly*. Retrieved January 5, 2017, from www.mckinsey.com/business-functions/organization/our-insights/ahead-of-the-curve-the-future-of-performance-management?cid=other-eml-ttn-mkq-mck-oth-1701

Fulmer, I. S., & Ployhart, R. E. (2014). 'Our most important asset' a multidisciplinary/multilevel review of human capital valuation for research and practice. *Journal of Management*, *40*(1), 161–192.

Grant, A. M. (2007). Relational job design and the motivation to make a prosocial difference. *Academy of Management Review*, *32*(2), 393–417.

Greenberg, A., & Zetter, K. (2015, December 28). How the Internet of Things got hacked. *Wired*. Retrieved August 15, 2017, from www.wired.com/2015/12/2015-the-year-the-internet-of-things-got-hacked/

Griffiths, M. (2010). Internet abuse and internet addiction in the workplace. *Journal of Workplace Learning*, *22*(7), 463–472.

Healey, K. (2015, November 8). We are all glassholes now: Privilege, Silicon Valley and our new wearable tech problem. *Salon*. Retrieved February 4, 2017, from www.salon.com/2015/11/08/we_are_all_glassholes_now_privilege_silicon_valley_and_our_new_wearable_tech_problem/

Hill, K. (2014, July 15). The violent opt-out: The neo-Luddites attacking drones and Google Glass. *Forbes*. Retrieved February 4, 2017, from www.forbes.com/sites/kashmirhill/2014/07/15/the-violent-opt-out-people-destroying-drones-and-google-glass/#6426f32b3bb7

Hill, T., & Westbrook, R. (1997). SWOT analysis: It's time for a product recall. *Long Range Planning*, *30*(1), 46–52.

Iansiti, M., & Lakhani, K. R. (2014). Digital ubiquity: How connections, sensors, and data are revolutionizing business (digest summary). *Harvard Business Review*, *92*(11), 91–99.

Jeske, D., & Santuzzi, A. M. (2015). Monitoring what and how: Psychological implications of electronic performance monitoring. *New Technology, Work and Employment*, *30*(1), 62–78.

Kagermann, H. (2015). Change through digitization: Value creation in the age of Industry 4.0. In H. Albach et al. (Eds.), *Management of permanent change* (pp. 23–45). Wiesbaden: Springer Fachmedien.

Kanigel, R. (2005). *The one best way: Frederick Winslow Taylor and the enigma of efficiency*. New York: Viking Press.

Kim, K. J. (2016). Interacting socially with the Internet of Things (IoT): Effects of source attribution and specialization in human-IoT interaction. *Journal of Computer-Mediated Communication*, *21*(6), 420–435.

Kim, S., Nussbaum, M. A., & Gabbard, J. L. (2016). Augmented reality 'smart glasses' in the workplace: Industry perspectives and challenges for worker safety and health. *IIE Transactions on Occupational Ergonomics and Human Factors*, *4*(4), 253–258.

Kleiner, A., & Sviokla, J. (2017, February 1). The thought leader interview: GE's Bill Ruh on the Industrial Internet Revolution. *Strategy+Business*. Retrieved February 10, 2017, from www.strategy-business.com/article/The-Thought-Leader-Interview-Bill-Ruh?gko=9ae51&utm_source=itw&utm_medium=20170214&utm_campaign=resp

Kuncel, N. R., Ones, D. S., & Klieger, D. M. (2014). In hiring, algorithms beat instinct. *Harvard Business Review*. Retrieved February 12, 2017, from https://hbr.org/2014/05/in-hiring-algorithms-beat-instinct

Lanchester, J. (2017). Short cuts. *London Review of Books*, *39*(3), 22.

Landers, R. N., Bauer, K. N., Callan, R. C., & Armstrong, M. B. (2015). Psychological theory and the gamification of learning. In *Gamification in education and business* (pp. 165–186). New York: Springer International Publishing.

Latham, G. P., & Locke, E. A. (2007). New developments in and directions for goal-setting research. *European Psychologist*, *12*(4), 290–300.

Lemke, T. (2015). New materialisms: Foucault and the 'government of things'. *Theory, Culture & Society*, *32*(4), 3–25.

Li, S., Xu, L. D., & Zhao, S. (2015). The Internet of Things: A survey. *Information Systems Frontiers*, *17*(2), 243–259.

Lorenz, M., Rüßmann, M., Strack, R., Lueth, K. L., & Bolle, M. (2015, September). *Man and machine in industry 4.0: How will technology transform the industrial workforce through 2025?* Retrieved February 12, 2017, from www.bcgperspectives.com/content/articles/technology-business-transformation-engineered-products-infrastructure-man-machine-industry-4/?chapter=3

Marler, J. H., & Parry, E. (2016). Human resource management, strategic involvement and e-HRM technology. *The International Journal of Human Resource Management*, *27*(19), 2233–2253.

Mayer, R. C., & Davis, J. H. (1999). The effect of the performance appraisal system on trust for management: A field quasi-experiment. *Journal of Applied Psychology*, *84*(1), 123–136.

McNeill, D. (2016). Governing a city of unicorns: Technology capital and the urban politics of San Francisco. *Urban Geography*, *37*(4), 494–513.

Miorandi, D., Sicari, S., De Pellegrini, F., & Chlamtac, I. (2012). Internet of Things: Vision, applications and research challenges. *Ad Hoc Networks*, *10*(7), 1497–1516.

Newman, J. (2016, March 18). Why the Internet of Things might never speak a common language. *Fast Company*. Retrieved February 20, 2017, from www.fastcompany.com/3057770/why-the-internet-of-things-might-never-speak-a-common-language

O'Reilly Media. (2017, February). *Artificial intelligence now*. Free Ebook. Retrieved February 20, 2017, from www.oreilly.com/data/free/artificial-intelligence-now.csp

Orlikowski, W. J., & Scott, S. V. (2008). Sociomateriality: Challenging the separation of technology, work and organization. *Academy of Management Annals*, *2*(1), 433–474.

Patmore, B., Somers, J., D'Souza, D., Welch, D., & Lawrence, J. (2017, January 10). *The state of digital HR in 2017*. Retrieved February 1, 2017, from www.hrzone.com/resources/the-state-of-digital-hr-in-2017

Pentland, A. (2012). The new science of building great teams. *Harvard Business Review*, *90*(4), 60–69.

Pentland, A. (2014). *Social physics: How good ideas spread-the lessons from a new science*. New York: Penguin.

Pew Research Center. (2014, May). *The Internet of Things will thrive by 2025*. Retrieved January 20, 2017, from www.pewinternet.org/files/2014/05/PIP_Internet-of-things_0514142.pdf

Pfeffer, J., & Sutton, R. I. (2006). Evidence-based management. *Harvard Business Review*, *84*(1), 62–74.

Piercy, N., & Giles, W. (1989). Making SWOT analysis work. *Marketing Intelligence & Planning*, *7*(5–6), 5–7.

Puthiyamadam, T. (2017, February 8). How to build a connected workforce. *Strategy+Business*. Retrieved February 12, 2017, from www.strategy-business.com/blog/How-to-Build-a-Connected-Workforce?gko=71ef6&utm_source=itw&utm_medium=20170214&utm_campaign=resp

Ray, S. (2016, April 5). The supermarket of the future: Designing for humans. *Microsoft* [blog]. Retrieved August 15, 2017, from https://blogs.microsoft.com/transform/feature/the-supermarket-of-the-future-designing-for-humans/#sm.0008mvfaa9o4dl910ez2bluhrpe0u

Roman, R., Zhou, J., & Lopez, J. (2013). On the features and challenges of security and privacy in distributed Internet of Things. *Computer Networks*, *57*(10), 2266–2279.

Rose, D. (2014). *Enchanted objects: Design, human desire, and the Internet of Things*. New York: Simon and Schuster.

Rousseau, D. M., & Barends, E. G. R. (2011). Becoming an evidence-based HR practitioner. *Human Resource Management Journal*, *21*(3), 221–235.

Sarter, N. B., Woods, D. D., & Billings, C. E. (1997). Automation surprises. *Handbook of Human Factors and Ergonomics*, *2*, 1926–1943.

Sicari, S., Rizzardi, A., Grieco, L. A., & Coen-Porisini, A. (2015). Security, privacy and trust in Internet of Things: The road ahead. *Computer Networks*, *76*, 146–164.

Spicer, A. (2015, August 17). The flaw in Amazon's management fad. *The Guardian*. Retrieved January 28, 2017, from www.theguardian.com/commentisfree/2015/aug/17/amazon-management-fad-rank-yank-jeff-bezos

Stanley, J. (2015, April 7). The Internet of Kafkaesque things. *ACLU*. Retrieved February 15, 2017, from www.aclu.org/blog/free-future/internet-kafkaesque-things

Stone, D. L., Stone-Romero, E. F., & Lukaszewski, K. (2003). The functional and dysfunctional consequences of human resource information technology for organizations and their employees. In *Advances in human performance and cognitive engineering research* (pp. 37–68). New York: Emerald Group Publishing Limited.

Stone, M. (2015, August 15). Amazon employees reportedly slam each other through this internal review tool. *Business Insider*. Retrieved February 5, 2017, from http://uk.businessinsider.com/amazon-employees-reportedly-slam-each-other-through-this-internal-review-tool-2015–8?r=US&IR=T

Strohmeier, S., Franca, P., Majstorovic, D., & Schreiner, J. (2016, February). *Smart HRM: A Delphi study on the future of digital human resource management ('HRM 4.0')*. Retrieved January 5, 2017, from www.uni-saarland.de/fileadmin/user_upload/Professoren/fr13_ProfStrohmeier/Aktuelles/Final_report_Smart_HRM_EN.pdf

Thite, M. (2011). Smart cities: Implications of urban planning for human resource development. *Human Resource Development International*, *14*(5), 623–631.

Thompson, C. (2017, February 2). The next big blue-collar job is coding. *Wired*. Retrieved February 21, 2017, from www.wired.com/2017/02/programming-is-the-new-blue-collar-job/

van Dijk, J.A.G.M. and Hacker, K. (2003). The digital divide as a complex and dynamic phenomenon. *Information Society*, *19*, 315–326.

Waddell, S. (2016). Societal change systems: A framework to address wicked problems. *The Journal of Applied Behavioral Science*, *52*(4), 422–449.

Want, R., Schilit, B. N., & Jenson, S. (2015). Enabling the Internet of Things. *Computer*, *48*(1), 28–35.

Waters, R. (2017, February 10). My everyday grips with Google and Amazon voice assistants. *Financial Times*. Retrieved February 2, 2017, from www.ft.com/content/e6efb16c-eeb1-11e6-930f-061b01e23655

Weick, K. E. (1985). Cosmos vs. chaos: Sense and nonsense in electronic contexts. *Organizational Dynamics*, *14*(2), 51–64.

Weihrich, H. (1982). The TOWS matrix: A tool for situational analysis. *Long Range Planning*, *15*(2), 54–66.

Wilson, H. J. (2013). Wearables in the workplace. *Harvard Business Review*, *91*(9), 23–25.

Wilson, H. J., Shah, B., & Whipple, B. (2015). How people are actually using the Internet of Things. *Harvard Business Review*. Retrieved August 1, 2016, from https://hbr.org/2015/10/how-people-are-actually-using-the-internet-of-things

Yan, Z., Zhang, P., & Vasilakos, A. V. (2014). A survey on trust management for Internet of Things. *Journal of Network and Computer Applications*, 42, 120–134.

Zanella, A., Bui, N., Castellani, A., Vangelista, L., & Zorzi, M. (2014). Internet of Things for smart cities. *IEEE Internet of Things Journal*, *1*(1), 22–32.

12 Beyond the Consulting Room

The Internet of People, Things and Services and the Human Factors of Outpatient Support

James G. Phillips

These are exciting times for psychology. The Internet of Things, People and Services has created a previously unanticipated potential to monitor and control behaviors (Wilson, Shah, & Whipple, 2015). Hitherto therapeutic interventions tended to be by appointment in health professional offices. However this was not necessarily when a client was most "at risk". The enhanced connectivity promised by the Internet of Things (Kopetz, 2011) potentially confers the opportunity for psychologists to monitor maladaptive or inappropriate behaviors and deliver immediate, situated decisional support contingent upon actual needs (Gravenhorst et al., 2015). Even so, such behavior change support systems (Oinas-Kukkonen, 2010) require *user consent* (Eloff, Eloff, Dlamini, & Zielinski, 2009). To inform psychologists and system developers, the present chapter addresses issues arising from a study of how the Internet of People can assist healthcare and social service organizations in their efforts to improve the efficacy of therapeutic interventions. Although an eHealth perspective is adopted, considering issues related to the delivering of outpatient support within the addiction sector, many of the issues addressed might also occur in other sectors.

Internet of Things

The Internet of Things is anticipated to reduce energy and improve inventory, efficiency and delivery of services (Kaija, 2016; Kopetz, 2011). However, people are not objects, and their connectivity requires a degree of user consent (Eloff et al., 2009). This chapter considers variations in the extent to which people embrace the Internet and some of the complexity of interactions between humans and technology.

As background, consider the following example. A public transport company needs to enhance services without adding to road congestion and salary costs so they replace single-deck buses with double-decker buses. To encourage people to use the top deck, they want to provide immediate information to riders on seat availability, especially on seats available upstairs. The count of seats available can also inform the company on usage, guide further purchasing of buses and assist future timetabling and planning. Even so, there can be issues during implementation. How should the data be collected, and who should have access to it? These are common questions across multiple areas in the Internet of Things.

In our double-decker bus example, a count of occupants could be obtained by means of two sensors in the stairwell to count people ascending or descending. Alternatively, pressure sensors could note weights above a certain value on each seat (see Hooton, 2014). Each option needs to be considered within a context of computational loads and energy requirements and human factors because people are odd shapes, come in a range of sizes, put packages on seats and they move but have limited flexibility (Roebuck, 1995). (This illustrates how human impact on technology usage needs to be part of the equation as engineers design systems.) Unsurprisingly some engineers and organizations are considering implantable RFID tags to help locate and count people (Eloff et al., 2009; Warwick, 2002). Also see: www.npr.org/sections/thetwo-way/2017/07/25/539265157/wisconsin-company-plans-to-start-implanting-chips-in-its-employees.

The system in double-decker buses in the UK uses a low-resolution CCTV feed to count faces in seats (Hooton, 2014). This raises issues of privacy, trust and security in all applications of the Internet of Things. If a person is counted on the bus, should their commuter movements be linked to their personal demographic information or their online profile? And who should have access to their commuter movements—their family, employer, security forces or advertisers? Some people may welcome the implementation of technologies that reduce costs and make life easier (Wilson et al., 2015), but others may not and may wish to control the amount of information collected and how it is used (Weber & Weber, 2010). And others, inured to an increasingly information-rich environment, may simply not access the information. This chapter specifically explores the opportunities and risks of the Internet of People, Things and Services when trying to provide outpatient support when treating addicts.

Internet of People and Services

The Internet of People Things and Services (IoPTS) takes human computer interaction beyond the desktop Windows icon mouse pointer (WIMP) interface. The Internet can now augment reality, allowing people to be connected to services without the previously required desktop computer. In the IOPTS paradigm, a person with a mobile phone (or RFID implant) is now the pointer, and things denoted by a QR code, IP address or RFID patches perform the role previously occupied by icons within the interface.

The present paper takes an eHealth perspective, considering issues related to the delivering of outpatient support, specifically within the addiction sector, but many of the issues addressed might readily be applied to the marketing and customer service sector. In the present chapter we consider the human factor, namely the reliability and intermittency of the human as a pointer that might connect to eHealth services in the form of outpatient reminders and situated consumer warnings. As such, this chapter constitutes some basic work and early steps taken to transpose and conceptually extend previous work addressing target positioning and the predictability of cursor trajectories (Phillips & Triggs, 2001) into real-world appetitive behaviors.

Our early studies used emails as a method of assessing how people "connected" to the Internet. As will be outlined later, these studies indicated that people were selective in what they did when they connected to the Internet. People's interest was "directional" and thus might not always focus in the directions expected by management. For instance, people do not necessarily attend to work related processes when at work. In addition, people's responses to the Internet could be intermittent. People do not automatically respond to a received message. Unlike things, interactions with people occur with their *consent* (Whitworth, 2005), and this is illustrated by our study of email use.

Emails can serve as a method of logging aspects of work and patient self-management. Email can be a useful business tool supporting intraorganizational communication. For security and auditing purposes organizational Internet and email usage is recorded (Muhl, 2003), thereby documenting some aspects of employee work practices. Workplace email traffic can be analyzed (e.g. Murray, Gross, & Ayres, 1999; Renaud, Ramsay, & Hair, 2006), and so email traffic can serve a similar function within organizations to that of an event recorder in a Skinner box (see Shaffer, Peller, LaPlante, Nelson, & LaBrie, 2010).

Even when people are connected to the Internet, there seem to be delays in their responsiveness. People do not respond immediately to an organizational directive. The receipt of an email can create conflict. Within the context of other commitments, the recipient of an email has to decide whether to read and act upon the message (Baker & Phillips, 2007; Shirren & Phillips, 2011). As email tends to be rapid and has time stamps, there is pressure to respond to messages in a timely and appropriate manner (Romm & Pliskin, 1999). Nevertheless, the capacity to contact staff 24 hours a day 7 days a week contributes to workplace stress (Abdulaili, 2017). There are relationships between the amount of work-related email an individual receives and their stress levels (Renaud et al., 2006; Shirren & Phillips, 2011). It is likely that people have a *limited capacity* to respond to electronic communications. Indeed, our email research reveals a human *intermittency* in response to communications received over the Internet (Shirren & Phillips, 2011) that could pose problems when seeking compliance with health directives. The assumption that emails are an immediate and efficient medium of communication can be erroneous. Messages may be received, but a range of human factors influence whether they are read and acted upon.

Internet of People

Our studies of email use suggest that any online influence occurs within a context of user consent, attention and workload. These are important considerations when planning health interventions, as patient compliance is not guaranteed. Hence it may be more appropriate to talk about outpatient support than suggest online interventions will *directly* influence health behaviors. Instead, online health interventions are mediated by user consent.

Although there are exceptions (Warwick, 2002), people are not directly connected to the Internet *yet*. People are connected indirectly, the connection most commonly mediated by means of a smart phone, desktop, tablet or other device or some electronic transaction. A person may have a profile and a history of transactions, but at any particularly time they may not be connected. In other words a person's presence on the Internet flickers and is intermittently updated as devices are turned on and off or electronic transactions occur. For such reasons a person's presence on the Internet tends to be dynamic and changeable over time.

With IP locators and geospatial technology it is also now possible to determine where a person is and offer services as a function of their location (Mahmoud & Yu, 2006; Oh & Xu, 2003). As it is now possible to deliver location aware services, providers are now interested in whether a potential customer is nearing the point of sale (Aalto, Göthlin, Korhonen, & Ojala, 2004; Yang, Cheng, & Dia, 2008; Yuan & Tsao, 2003). Hence people no longer just register on the Internet on a dimension of time. People now register in space as well. People have history, their presence on the Internet can be intermittent and people are *mobile*. Their location changes. In the last few years we have sought to understand connectivity and intermittency of Internet access as well as consumer mobility.

Uptake and Connectivity

Our early studies involved self-report, but potentially better methods are available (Bentley, O'Brien, & Brock, 2014; Boase & Ling, 2013). For instance, we have been tracking Internet use within the education sector (Phillips & Jory, 2011; Phillips, Jory, & Mogford, 2007). As we have been using Blackboard's accounting application the data reflect a subset of work/study use and does not capture access to other applications such as entertainment. Hence the activity traces left by accounting software provide a sample of behavior (Shaughnessy, Zecmeister, & Zecmeister, 2006), but may overlook other features. For instance, the students may not actually look at the computer screen or may have other browsers open at the same time.

Although behavior can be tracked, tracking is only feasible when people use an identifiable account and leave some activity to trace. For instance, only a quarter of students that log in actually post on a discussion board (Phillips et al., 2007); the majority lurk and are not necessarily visible online (Preece, Nonnecke, & Andrews, 2004). Indeed, the vocal minority may sometimes lead people to misread group opinion (Janis, 1982) as sometimes occurs during elections (Mann, 1969). This missing data problem is not uncommon (Bentley et al., 2014; Howison, Crowston, &

Wiggins, 2011) and can cause cold-start problems if a personalized search engine (Resnick & Varian, 1997) lacks sufficient data (Montaner, López, & de la Rosa, 2003).

A stated aim of psychology is not just to describe, but explain, *predict and control* behavior. *Mobile phones now confer much of this capability.* For instance, a mobile phone with GPS can now detect a lack of activity and message and encourage people to exercise (e.g. Dantzig, Geleijnse, & van Halteren, 2013; Wilson et al., 2015).

A person that is connected to the Internet is potentially influenceable (Aral & Walker, 2012). Even so, a sent message does not automatically attract attention (Onnela & Reed-Tsochas, 2010; Wu & Huberman, 2007), nor does it automatically influence the recipient (Aral & Walker, 2012; Leskovec, Adamic, & Huberman, 2007). In the workplace most people receive more messages than they can comfortably deal with (Sumecki, Chipulu, & Ojiako, 2011). Our email diary study may offer insights as to some of the reasons why online communications do not automatically influence a recipient (Shirren & Phillips, 2011). This study indicated that messages are not necessarily read or acted upon. In our study of 39 employed individuals over a five-week period our participants received about 100 emails a week and deleted 40% of them. The majority of these messages (69%) were work related. On average our participants only reported opening and responding to 25% of workplace emails immediately (35% of personal emails immediately). In other words, even with 24/7 coverage there is liable to be an asynchrony of interaction with a human. People behave as if they are intermittently connected to the Internet, and even a response to a direct query may require time, and this may cause problems developing outpatient support.

In addition, human behavior does not occur in a constrained and impoverished environment like a Skinner box. Humans have an appreciably greater range of options in their behavioral repertoire (Givon, 1984), and this capacity for choice (Hernstein, 1961) extends to the Internet and can cause problems for *naming architecture* (Kopetz, 2011). The use of multiple devices, IP addresses, aliases and proxies can map one individual into many accounts and impair the capacity to track online behaviors (Kollock, 1999). In addition, as the Internet overcomes any problems posed by distance, it allows multiple service providers access to an individual consumer. This means that even if a person is connected, they may switch from one service provider to another. These one-to-many and many-to-one mappings may cause missing data in a specific database and can also exacerbate problems tracking an individual (Kopetz, 2011) and in developing outpatient support systems.

To anticipate the use of services that incorporate geospatial data, we have extended this work on the Internet to include the times and places that people access products such as gambling, alcohol, caffeine and nicotine (Phillips, Hughes, & Ogeil, 2017; Phillips & Ogeil, 2011; Phillips, Currie, & Ogeil, 2016). In each case people make use of a limited number of physical providers, but more involved consumers make use of more providers more often. Nevertheless, the actual number of places people source a product like nicotine or caffeine is quite low compared to the much larger number of providers. For instance, although there are an estimated 43,000 liquor stores and 306,695 outlets selling tobacco in the United States, on average our alcohol- or nicotine-dependent participants reported consuming alcohol at two locations and purchasing tobacco from two sources. Apparently people have a relatively restricted range (Song, Qu, Blumm, & Barabási, 2010) and spend much of their time near a home base (and work) (Johnson, 2014). As there seems to be a more limited use of physical providers, this may assist systems seeking to provide services that incorporate geospatial information. Location-aware services can drain the batteries of mobile phones (Kopetz, 2011). Systems that check for a more limited subset of likely locations can reduce computational loads (Kopetz, 2011) and improve the capacity of a system to develop location-based reminders.

Opting Out of the Internet

For the Internet of Things to work and deliver services to people, they need to be connected, but there can be a *cost* for the individual. Users sacrifice some of their privacy to be part of a network (Hoffman, Novak, & Peralta, 1999; Weber & Weber, 2010). Personalized search engines (recommenders) (Resnick & Varian, 1997) have been developed to track the behavior of specific consumers (or their peers) to offer conceptually related products or products that their peers purchased (Schafer, Konstan, & Riedl, 2001). Some of the reasons users opt out or disconnect that cause problems for online interventions will be outlined.

Users sacrifice their time reading and acknowledging messages (Shirren & Phillips, 2011), and they may also incur financial costs receiving messages. These consumer costs may not have been anticipated by legitimate providers (Eadington, 2004), but regrettably influence consumer choice (Griffiths, 2010; Kim, Jeong, Kim, & So, 2011) when online trust is eroded (Riegelsberger, Sasse, & McCarthy, 2005). Indeed there are already a number of joke "apps" (Savic, Best, Rodda, & Lubman, 2013) that cause problems for designers of legitimate health applications for the treatment of addicts.

Privacy was defined at one time as the "right to be let alone" (Warren & Brandeis, 1890), but in many cases mobile phone owners are incurring financial costs to receive advertisements and inducements. Systems developers acknowledge this issue, but often fail to appreciate the real cost to the user. For instance, computer users find their experience disrupted by often inexplicable warnings, inconvenient reboots and seemingly endless system updates (Fagan, Khan, & Buck, 2015; Modic & Anderson, 2014; Whitworth, 2005), and oftentimes these fraudulent requests mimic genuine messages (Griffiths, 2010).

Consumers have certainly been concerned about these issues. Consumers may respond negatively to behaviorally targeted advertisements (Alnahdi, Ali, & Alkayid, 2014; Moore, Moore, Shanahan, Horky, & Mack, 2015).

We have documented consumer concern, finding that gamblers report more problems with spam (Phillips, Ogeil, & Blaszczynski, 2012).

Indeed some groups of consumers may exhibit a preference to opt out of the network (or at least be anonymous). In our study of technology preferences gamblers seemed to prefer prepaid mobile phones and Internet cafes where there was less potential for the network to determine their identity and the nature of their transactions (Phillips, Sargeant, Ogeil, Chow, & Blaszczynski, 2014).

Ignoring the Internet

Corporate advertisers are interested in the prospect of using the Internet to influence consumers (Leskovec et al., 2007). Psychologists have sought equivalent technology (Gainsbury & Blaszczynski, 2011; Marsch, 2012; Wiederhold, 2015) for therapeutic interventions. Initially researchers sought to monitor people's emotions (e.g. Gee, Coventry, & Birkenhead, 2005; Suffoletto et al., 2014), but some are now considering methods of delivering interventions "on site" and in "real time" (Gustafson et al., 2011; Heron & Smyth, 2010; Suffoletto et al., 2014). There is considerable potential for online interventions (Blankers, Koeter, & Schippers, 2011; Danielsson, Eriksson, & Allebeck, 2014; Gainsbury & Blaszczynski, 2011). Even so, clients are not constrained in Skinner boxes. Outpatients will be in open environments with a range of other behavioral options available, and this may cause problems of uptake and compliance (e.g. Forsström, Hesser, & Carlbring, 2016; Palmer du Preez, Landon, Bellringer, Garrett, & Abbott, 2016). There appear to be organismic variables that influence whether people attend and respond to advertisements or consumer assistance.

Although we have been interested in the use of behavior change support systems (Oinas-Kukkonen, 2010) to influence behavior, we suspect those people that most need assistance might be least able to benefit from it (Phillips, Ogeil, & Blaszczynski, 2013) and that online interventions may require more care and effort. For instance, in the laboratory intoxicated participants appear less able to respond to variations in the likelihood of success (Phillips & Ogeil, 2010), sleep-deprived participants are less responsive at low risk and less time pressure (Fraser, Conduit, & Phillips, 2013) and addicts are well known for their lack of self-control.

Even if people are sometimes not responsive, the mechanisms for online influence are quite real. Reputation systems have been developed that utilize peer ratings to support consumer choice (Kollock, 1999), but there remains the possibility that such recommendations are subject to manipulation (Lam, Frankowski, & Riedl, 2006). Lam et al. (2006) explained how a browser or product recommendations could be subverted by multiple hits of a specific type (shilling attacks). During attempted influence, multiple hits by an attacker on a site can change the relative balance of a profile of peer ratings or the popularity of a website. This alters strength of peer recommendations or the ranking and visibility of a website.

Studies have demonstrated the potential for online messages to influence people's behavior (Phillips, Laughlin, Ogeil, & Blaszczynski, 2011). For instance, Kramer, Guillory, and Hancock (2014) biased online news feeds on Facebook in an attempt to influence people's mood. Some participants received positive news. Other participants received negative news. Although the effects were potentially small, Kramer et al. (2014) demonstrated these biases in Internet newsfeeds could influence people's moods (see also Canetti, Gross, Waismel-Manor, Levanon, & Cohen, 2017).

Although there is now a real capability for service providers to contact consumers, the potential for a large number of unsolicited messages encourages the consumer to filter or ignore messages and feel aggrieved about system updates (Whitworth, 2005). The tendency of consumers to selectively expose themselves to information (Sears & Freedman, 1967) means that messages sent are not necessary read or acted upon (Shirren & Phillips, 2011). In other words, when discussing the Internet of People, one has to appreciate there are situations in which people may deliberately render themselves "offline" (Hancock et al., 2009). This can be illustrated by studies of the use of consumer protection systems.

Jurisdictions that have legalized online gambling require the provision of consumer protection systems (Auer & Griffiths, 2014; Haefeli, Lischer, & Schwarz, 2011; Wohl, Parush, Kim, & Warren, 2014). Such systems are in place (e.g. Playscan), but there are concerns that they will not be adopted by gamblers (Auer & Griffiths, 2013; Griffiths, Wood, & Parke, 2009; Palmer Du Preez et al., 2016). The New Zealand government had implemented pop-up messages and forced breaks in play on electronic gaming machines to curb problem gambling. Palmer Du Preez et al. (2016) interviewed 460 gamblers in the vicinity of gambling venues. The majority of gamblers (57%) were aware of pop-up messages, and many saw pop-up messages often (38%). From those gamblers who reported seeing pop-up messages, only half read the message content, and just a quarter believed that pop-up messages helped them control the amounts of money they spent on gambling.

In two studies we have considered a person's willingness to seek further information related to an issue such as gambling or smoking. In an online survey Phillips et al. (2012) determined whether participants were at risk of a gambling problem. When offered further information, participants with a greater risk of a gambling problem were more likely to access further gambling-related information. A follow-up study considered caffeine and nicotine use. When participants were offered further information, caffeine-dependent participants were more likely to access caffeine-related information, and the nicotine dependent were more likely to access nicotine-related information (Phillips & Ogeil, 2016). Of more interest, however, were those *factors that led people to "opt out" and not seek further information online.* Phillips and Ogeil (2016) found people were less likely to attend to offers of further information if they were *confident* about their decisions. It seems confident people may not look for further information online. In this case information was offered about nicotine or caffeine during an online survey, but the phenomenon has also been demonstrated in the laboratory.

Phillips and Landon (2016) examined use of online advice during a blackjack task. They found people were more likely to attend to online advice if they had been losing. Similar fluctuations in amenability have been documented previously. For instance, Isen, Clark, and Schwartz (1976) found people were more likely to comply to a request for assistance for a period of 20 minutes after they received a free gift. Such observations indicate the importance of delivering decisional support in a *contingent* manner. It is likely that attempted influence will be more effective when delivered at an appropriate time or place (Mahatanankoon, Wen, & Lim, 2005; Oh & Xu, 2003).

Earlier in this chapter it was suggested that there may be fluctuations in people's connection to the Internet. Meeker and Wu (2013) estimated that people check their mobile phones 150 times a day. The strength of this checking behavior is supported by observations that a high proportion of the community report phantom vibrations of their mobile phones (Laramie, 2007). Apparently this sort of checking behavior extends to a person's self-presentation and self-image (Bibby, 2008; Buffardi & Campbell, 2008; Ong et al., 2011) and the surveillance of others (Joinson, 2008; Tong, 2013). Even so, there are variations in the strength of checking behaviors. Some people check to excess (Foa & Kozak, 1994), whereas others do not check their online preferences enough (Everett, 2007). For instance, Everett (2007) found only 37% of 108 participants checked the electronic votes they registered. Such observations indicate that even if a system monitors a person's health, there is no guarantee that this information will be attended to by the user.

Mobile phones now potentially provide a means of delivering negotiated outpatient services (Gravenhorst et al., 2015) at times when a patient feels vulnerable. An increasingly Internet-connected world (Kopetz, 2011) now affords the capacity for immediate, situated outpatient support (Campbell, Caine, Connelly, Doub, & Bragg, 2015). Smartphones, recommender technology, location-aware capability and targeted advertising (Chen & Stallaert, 2014) confer a capability to deliver contingent outpatient support "on site" in "real time" (Heron & Smyth, 2010), but consumer acceptance may be a problem (Milward, Day, Wadsworth, Strang, & Lynskey, 2015; Moore et al., 2015). In their study of 398 treatment-seeking substance users, Milward et al. (2015) found 86% were willing to be contacted by their treatment provider via a mobile phone, but 46% felt the use of geolocation was unacceptable.

The Internet of People and a Model of Online Influence and Intervention

An online service provider seeking to influence people needs to realize that they offer their services within a context of competing providers. Any attempted online influence will actually be viewed by the recipient within the context of a number of "filters". These "filters" can be conceptualized as dynamic moving windows that block attempted influence (see Figure 12.1). Recipients may not want to attend to a specific message. Privacy concerns may constrain specific personal activities (e.g. personal messages, gambling). Mood and timing may also influence susceptibility to influence, as may situation and location. Attempted online influence will only occur if it can pass uninterrupted through these moving windows. A number of technologies are already seeking methods of targeting these moving windows. For instance, *attention and privacy* windows are targeted by personalized search engines (Schafer et al., 2001). The window of opportunity for online influence as a function of *time* or mood is being addressed by targeted advertising (Chen & Stallaert, 2014) and sentiment analysis (Balci & Salah, 2015; Colace, Casaburi, De Santo, & Greco, 2015). And a window of opportunity for influence as a function of *location* is being addressed by global positioning systems and personalized search engines (Montaner et al., 2003).

By way of illustration, consider some observations made while tracking student Blackboard use. In an unpublished study conducted by Phillips and Landhuis, students completed the Alcohol Use Disorders Identification Test and their Blackboard use was tracked. We were hoping to examine the breadth and depth of their searches on the study website. Students were certainly not expected to study 24/7, but we found that risky drinkers of alcohol were less likely to log in to Blackboard on Thursday, Friday or Saturday nights

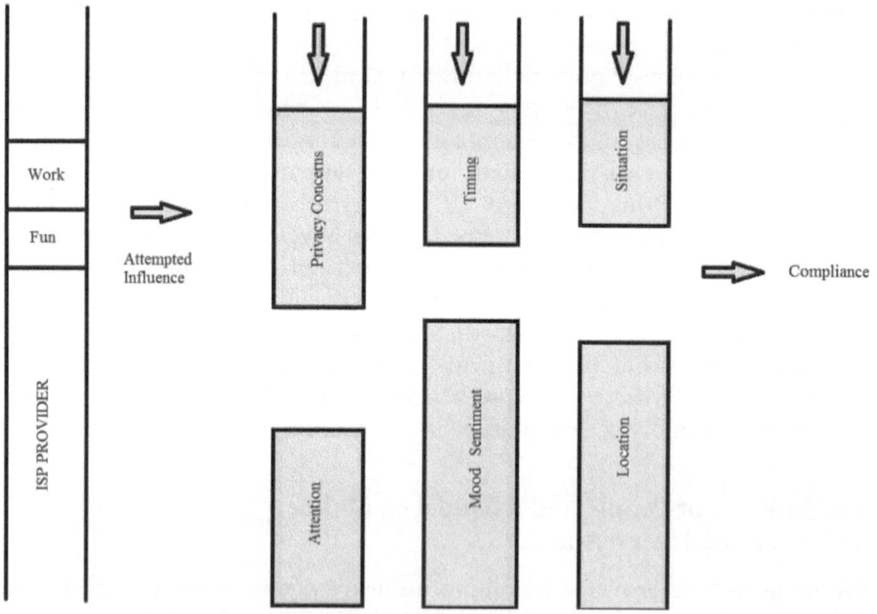

Figure 12.1 "Filters" as Dynamic Moving Windows Blocking Attempted Influence

and more importantly were less likely to log in Monday mornings, posing a potential problem of absenteeism. Such observations demonstrate the importance of people's interests and timing on the potential for online influence. If we were concerned about the amounts students drank or any pending assignments, we might consider 1) sending reminders on Thursday or Friday nights or 2) geofencing specific alcohol outlets and providing location-aware warnings to their mobile phones. Admittedly not all alcohol outlets could be targeted, but our research indicates people visit a limited number of outlets and that targeting a couple of local providers could be effective.

Conclusions

Given the wholesale consumer acceptance of the mobile phone, people are potentially contactable (and locatable) 24 hours a day, 7 days a week, and service providers are seeking to avail themselves of this capability. Whether in the form of behavioral advertising (Chen & Stallaert, 2014) or behavior change support systems (Oinas-Kukkonen, 2010), service providers can now seek to influence behavior "on-site" and in "real-time". This potential to technologically augment reality and make inducements and warnings contingent upon a person's interests or location means that the world is becoming a giant electronic Skinner box in which service providers seek to control people's behavior. The present chapter considers some of the mechanisms associated with the Internet of People and potential therapeutic interventions. Table 12.1 lists some of the problems that software designers will face when developing outpatient support systems and some potential solutions.

Table 12.1 Issues Faced by Health Promotion and Outpatient Support System Developers

Bad news	*Good news*
Limited digital franchise	Vulnerable people may be interested in health promotion systems
Health promotion systems require user consent	A section of the community (treatment seekers) are liable to consent
Healthy attitudes ≠ health behaviors	Healthy attitudes are likely to be correlated to healthy behaviors
People have a limited capacity to respond to the Internet	People do respond to the Internet
	People are not continuously engaging in unhealthy behaviors
	People may respond to health advice when they are unwell
There are many providers of tobacco, alcohol, gambling, etc.	People have a relatively restricted range
	Games and virtual reality can also be used for treatment purposes

Although the degree of digital franchise may vary, it is likely that there is a vulnerable cohort (e.g. people with low self-esteem) that may be interested in outpatient support systems. Even though systems trying to encourage healthy behaviors will require user consent, some cohorts are likely to consider using such systems (e.g. treatment seekers). There may be a disjunction between attitudes and behaviors, but there is at least some relationship between attitudes and behaviors. And although people have a limited capacity to process information received via the Internet, they will attend to messages at specific times (e.g. when they are losing or unwell). If the numbers of providers are posing problems for designers of location-based services, people have a relatively restricted range, and this could reduce the number of locations that require monitoring. Alternatively, persuasive games could be developed in simulations where the designer has more control of the environment (Chow, Susilo, Phillips, Baek, & Vlahu-Gjorgievska, 2017).

Sadly, disreputable operators attracted by borderless online environments and not hampered by a need for an appreciable physical land-based presence have inconvenienced the establishment of reputable online operators (Eadington, 2004; Owens, 2006). Similar issues have already occurred for therapeutic apps (Savic et al., 2013). This chapter has outlined some of the human factors limiting the Internet of People (connectivity) in the hope that this will help inform developers of sincere therapeutic interventions.

Acknowledgements

The author would like to thank Carla Bryant for pointing out issues associated with the occupancy counts on double-decker buses.

References

Aalto, L. Göthlin, N., Korhonen, J., & Ojala, T. (2004). *Bluetooth and WAP push based location-aware mobile advertising system*. MobiSys '04: Proceedings of the 2nd International Conference on Mobile Systems, Applications, and Services, 49–58.

Abdulaili, S. (2017, January 5). Does your boss keep emailing you 24/7? The French have a solution for you. *The Guardian*.

Alnahdi, S., Ali, M., & Alkayid, K. (2014). The effectiveness of online advertising via the behavioral targeting mechanism. *The Business & Management Review*, *5*(1), 23–31.

Aral, S., & Walker, D. (2012). Identifying influential and susceptible members of social networks. *Science*, *337*, 337–341.

Auer, M., & Griffiths M. D. (2013). Voluntary limit setting and player choice in most intense online gamblers: An empirical study of gambling behavior. *Journal of Gambling Studies*, *29*, 646–660.

Auer, M., & Griffiths, M. D. (2014). Personalised feedback in the promotion of responsible gambling: A brief overview. *Responsible Gambling Review*, *1*, 27–36.

Baker, J. R., & Phillips, J. G. (2007). Email, decisional styles and rest breaks. *CyberPsychology & Behavior, 10*(5), 705–708.

Balci, K., & Salah, A. A. (2015). Automatic analysis and identification of verbal aggression and abusive behaviors for online social games. *Computers in Human Behavior, 53*, 517–526.

Bentley, R. A., O'Brien, M. J., & Brock, W. A. (2014). Mapping collective behavior in the big-data era. *Behavioral and Brain Sciences, 37*, 63–119.

Bibby, P. A. (2008). Dispositional factors in the use of social networking sites: Findings and implications for social computing research. *Lecture Notes in Computer Science, 5075*, 392–400.

Blankers, M., Koeter, M. W., & Schippers, G. M. (2011). Internet therapy versus internet self-help versus no treatment for problematic alcohol use: A randomized controlled trial. *Journal of Consulting and Clinical Psychology, 79*(3), 330–341.

Boase, J., & Ling, R. (2013). Measuring mobile phone use: Self-report versus log data. *Journal of Computer-Mediated Communication, 18*, 508–519.

Buffardi, L. E., & Campbell, W. K. (2008). Narcissism and social networking web sites. *Personality and Social Psychology Bulletin, 34*, 1303–1314.

Campbell, B., Caine, K., Connelly, K., Doub, T., & Bragg, A. (2015). Cell phone ownership and use among mental health outpatients in the USA. *Personal and Ubiquitous Computing, 19*, 367–378.

Canetti, D., Gross, M., Waismel-Manor, I., Levanon, A., & Cohen, H. (2017). How cyberattacks terrorize: Cortisol and personal insecurity jump in the wake of cyberattacks. *Cyberpsychology, Behavior, and Social Networking, 20*(2), 1–6.

Chen, J., & Stallaert, J. (2014). An economic analysis of online advertising using behavioral targeting. *MIS Quarterly, 38*(2), 429–449.

Chow, Y.-W., Susilo, W., Phillips, J. G., Baek, J., & Vlahu-Gjorgievska, E. (2017). Video games and virtual reality as persuasive technologies for health care. *Journal of Wireless Mobile Networks, Ubiquitous Computing, and Dependable Applications, 8*(3), 18–35. doi: 10.22667/JOWUA.2017.09.30.018

Colace, F., Casaburi, L., De Santo, M., & Greco, L. (2015). Sentiment detection in social networks and in collaborative learning environments. *Computers in Human Behavior, 51B*, 1061–1067.

Danielsson, A. K., Eriksson, A. K., & Allebeck, P. (2014). Technology-based support via telephone or web: A systematic review of the effects on smoking, alcohol use and gambling. *Addictive Behavior, 39*(12), 1846–1868.

Dantzig, S., Geleijnse, G., & van Halteren, A. T. (2013). Toward a persuasive mobile application to reduce sedentary behavior. *Personal and Ubiquitous Computing, 17*, 1237–1246.

Eadington, W. R. (2004). The future of online gambling in the United States and elsewhere. *Journal of Public Policy & Marketing, 23*(2), 214–219.

Eloff, J. H. P., Eloff, M. M., Dlamini, M. T., & Zielinski M. P. (2009). *Internet of people, things and services: The convergence of security, trust and privacy*. 3rd Annual CompanionAble Consortium Workshop-IoPTS (Internet of People, Things and Services) 02 December 2009, Novotel Brussels, Brussels, Online proceedings retrieved from www.companionable.net/index.php?option=com_phocadownload&view=category&id=7:3rd-companionable-workshop-iopts-proceedings&Itemid=6

Everett, S. P. (2007). *The usability of electronic voting machines and how votes can be changed without detection* (Doctoral thesis). Rice University, Houston, TX. Retrieved from https://scholarship.rice.edu/handle/1911/20601

Fagan, M., Khan, M. M. H., & Buck, R. (2015). A study of users' experiences and beliefs about software update messages. *Computers in Human Behavior*, *51A*, 504–519.

Foa, E. B., & Kozak, M. J. (1994). DSM-IV and ICD-10 diagnostic criteria for obsessive compulsive disorder: Similarities and differences. In E. Hollander, J. Zohar, D. Marazzati, & B. Oliver (Eds.), *Current insights in obsessive compulsive disorder* (pp. 67–75). Chichester: John Wiley & Sons.

Forsström, D., Hesser, H., & Carlbring, P. (2016). Usage of a responsible gambling tool: A descriptive analysis and latent class analysis of user behavior. *Journal of Gambling Studies*, *32*(3), 889–904.

Fraser, M., Conduit, R., & Phillips, J. G. (2013). Sleep deprivation's influence on use of decisional support. *Ergonomics*, *56*(2), 235–245.

Gainsbury, S., & Blaszczynski, A. (2011). A systematic review of internet-based therapy for the treatment of addictions. *Clinical Psychology Review*, *31*(3), 490–498.

Gee, P., Coventry, K. R., & Birkenhead, D. (2005). Mood state and gambling: Using mobile telephones to track emotions. *British Journal of Psychology*, *96*, 53–66.

Givon, M. (1984). Variety seeking through brand switching. *Marketing Science*, *3*(1), 1–22.

Gravenhorst, F., Muaremi, A., Bardram, J., Grünerbl, A., Mayora, O., Wurzer, G., Frost, M., Osmani, V., Arnrich, B., Lukowicz, P., & Tröster, G. (2015). Mobile phones as medical devices in mental disorder treatment: An overview. *Personal and Ubiquitous*, *19*, 335–353.

Griffiths, M. D. (2010). Crime and gambling: A brief overview of gambling fraud on the Internet. *Internet Journal of Criminology*. Retrieved November 11, 2014, from www.internetjournalofcriminology.com/Griffiths_%20Gambling_Fraud_Jan_2010.pdf

Griffiths, M. D., Wood, R. T. A., & Parke, J. (2009). Social responsibility tools in online gambling: A survey of attitudes and behavior among Internet gamblers. *CyberPsychology & Behavior*, *12*, 413–421.

Gustafson, D. H., Shaw, B. R., Isham, A., Baker, T., Boyle, M. G., & Levy, M. (2011). Explicating an evidence-based, theoretically informed, mobile technology-based system to improve outcomes for people in recovery for alcohol dependence. *Substance Use & Misuse*, *46*(1), 96–111.

Haefeli, J., Lischer, S., & Schwarz, J. (2011). Early detection items and responsible gambling features for online gambling. *International Gambling Studies*, *11*(3), 273–288.

Hancock, J., Birnholtz, J., Bazarova, N., Guillory, J., Perlin, J., & Barrett, A. (2009). *Butler lies: Awareness, deception, and design*. CHI 2009, April 7th, Boston, MA, USA.

Hernstein, R. J. (1961). Relative and absolute strength of response as a function of frequency of reinforcement. *Journal of the Experimental Analysis of Behavior*, *4*, 267–272.

Heron, K. E., & Smyth, J. M. (2010). Ecological momentary interventions: Incorporating mobile technology into psychosocial and health behavior treatments. *British Journal of Health Psychology*, *15*, 1–39.

Hoffman, D. L., Novak, T. P., & Peralta, M. (1999). Building consumer trust online. *Communications of the ACM*, *42*(4), 80–85.

Hooton, C. (2014). *London buses to tell you how many people are sat upstairs*. Retrieved February 7, 2017, from www.independent.co.uk/news/uk/london-buses-to-tell-you-how-many-people-are-sat-upstairs-9556933.html

Howison, J., Crowston, K., & Wiggins, A. (2011). Validity issues in the use of social network analysis with digital trace data. *Journal of the Association for Information Systems, 12*, article 2.

Isen, A. M., Clark, M., & Schwartz, M. F. (1976). Duration of the effect of good mood on helping: 'Footprints on the sands of time'. *Journal of Personality and Social Psychology, 34*(3), 385–393.

Janis, I. L. (1982). *Groupthink: Psychological studies of policy decisions and fiascoes*. Boston: Houghton Mifflin.

Johnson, S. D. (2014). How do offenders choose where to offend? Perspectives from animal foraging. *Legal and Criminological Psychology, 19*, 193–210.

Joinson, A. N. (2008). *'Looking at,' 'looking up,' or 'keeping up' with people? Motives and uses of Facebook*. Paper presented at the 26th Annual SIGCHI Conference on Human Factors in Computing Systems, April 5–10, Florence, Italy.

Kaija, J. (2016). *A new age of industrial production the Internet of Things, services and people*. ABB. Retrieved from http://new.abb.com/docs/default-source/technology/a-new-age-of-industrial-production-iotsp.pdf

Kim, W., Jeong, O. R., Kim, C., & So, J. (2011). The dark side of the Internet: Attacks, costs and responses. *Information Systems, 36*, 675–705.

Kollock, P. (1999). The production of trust in online markets. In E. J. Lawler, M. Macy, S. Thyne, & H. A. Walker (Eds.), *Advances in group processes* (Vol. 16). Greenwich, CT: JAI Press. Retrieved June 10, 2016, from www.connectedaction.net/wp-content/uploads/2009/05/1999-peter-kollock-the-production-of-trust-in-online-markets.htm

Kopetz, H. (2011). Internet of things. In *Real-time systems: Design principles for distributed embedded applications* (pp. 307–323). New York: Springer. doi: 10.1007/978-1-4419-8237-7_13

Kramer, A. D. I., Guillory, J. E., & Hancock, J. T. (2014). Experimental evidence of massive-scale emotional contagion through social networks. *Proceedings of the National Academy of Sciences, 111*, 8788–8790.

Lam, S. K., Frankowski, D., & Riedl, J. (2006). Do you trust your recommendations? An exploration of security and privacy issues in recommender systems. *Lecture Notes in Computer Science, 3995*, 14–29.

Laramie, D. (2007). *Emotional and behavioral aspects of mobile phone use*. Retrieved August 14, 2015, from http://gradworks.umi.com/32/68/3268867.html

Leskovec, J., Adamic, L. A., & Huberman, B. A. (2007). The dynamics of viral marketing. *ACM Transactions on the Web, 1*(1), 1–39.

Mahatanankoon, P., Wen, H. J., & Lim, B. (2005). Consumer-based m-commerce: Exploring consumer perception of mobile applications. *Computer Standards & Interfaces, 27*, 347–357.

Mahmoud, Q. H., & Yu, L. (2006). Havana agents for comparison shopping and location-aware advertising in wireless mobile environments. *Electronic Commerce Research and Applications, 5*(3), 220–228.

Mann, L. (1969). *Social psychology* (ch. 7-Decision making). Sydney: John Wiley & Sons.

Marsch, L. A. (2012). Leveraging technology to enhance addiction treatment and recovery. *Journal of Addictive Diseases, 31*, 313–318.

Meeker, M., & Wu, L. (2013). *Internet trends*. Kleiner Perkins Caulfield & Byers. Slide 52. Retrieved August 17, 2015, from www.kpcb.com/file/kpcb-internet-trends-2013

Milward, J., Day, E., Wadsworth, E., Strang, J., & Lynskey, M. (2015). Mobile phone ownership, usage and readiness to use by patients in drug treatment. *Drug and Alcohol Dependence*, *146*, 111–115.

Modic, D., & Anderson, R. (2014). Reading this may harm your computer: The psychology of malware warnings. *Computers in Human Behavior*, *41*, 71–79.

Montaner, M., López, B., & de la Rosa, J. L. (2003). A taxonomy of recommender agents on the internet. *Artificial Intelligence Review*, *19*, 285–330.

Moore, R. S., Moore, M. L., Shanahan, K. J., Horky, A., & Mack, B. (2015). Creepy marketing: Three dimensions of perceived excessive online privacy violation. *The Marketing Management Journal*, *25*(1), 42–53.

Muhl, C. J. (2003). Workplace e-mail and internet use: Employees and employers beware. *Monthly Labor Review*, *126*(2), 36–45.

Murray, J., Gross, M. M., & Ayres, T. J. (1999). Human error in power plants: A search for pattern and context. In *Proceedings of the Silicon Valley Ergonomics Conference & Exposition* (pp. 187–191). San Jose, CA: San Jose State University.

Oh, L.-B., & Xu, H. (2003). *Effects of multimedia on mobile consumer behavior: An empirical study of location-aware advertising*. Twenty-Fourth International Conference on Information Systems, Seattle, Washington, December 14–17.

Oinas-Kukkonen, H. (2010). Behavior change support systems: A research model and agenda. *Lecture Notes in Computer Science*, *6137*, 4–14.

Ong, E. Y. L., Ang, R. P., Ho, J. C. M., Lim, J. C. Y., Goh, D. H., Lee, C. S., & Chua, A. Y. K. (2011). Narcissism, extraversion and adolescents' self-presentation on Facebook. *Personality and Individual Differences*, *50*, 180–185.

Onnela, J.-P., & Reed-Tsochas, F. (2010). Spontaneous emergence of social influence in online systems. *PNAS*, *107*(43), 18375–18380.

Owens, M. D. Jr. (2006). If you can't beat 'em, will they let you join? What American states can offer to attract internet gambling operators. *Gaming Law Review*, *10*(1), 26–32.

Palmer du Preez, K., Landon, J., Bellringer, M., Garrett, N., & Abbott, M. (2016). The effects of pop-up harm minimisation messages on electronic Gambling Machine behavior in New Zealand. *Journal of Gambling Studies*, *32*(4), 1115–1126.

Phillips, J. G., Currie, J., & Ogeil, R. P. (2016). Consumption and foraging behaviors for common stimulants (Nicotine, Caffeine). *Journal of Addictive Diseases*, *35*(1), 1–16.

Phillips, J. G., Hughes, B., & Ogeil, R. P. (2017). Alcohol consumption, dependence and foraging. *Journal of Substance Use*. Retrieved from http://dx.doi.org/10.1080/14659891.2017.1296038

Phillips, J. G., & Jory, M. K. (2011). Decisional style influences time management and the quality of work. In A. P. Varga (Ed.), *Time management* (pp. 41–66). New York: Nova Science Publishers.

Phillips, J. G., Jory, M. K., & Mogford, N. (2007). *Decisional style and eParticipation*. Proceedings of OZCHI2007, 139–141. Retrieved from http://portal.acm.org/dl.cfm

Phillips, J. G., & Landon, J. (2016). Dynamic changes in the use of online advice in response to task success or failure. *Behavior & Information Technology*, *35*(10), 796–806.

Phillips, J. G., Laughlin, A. L., Ogeil, R. P., & Blaszczynski, A. (2011). Effects of directional decisional support upon risk taking online. *Ergonomics Open Journal*, *4*, 47–54.

Phillips, J. G., & Ogeil, R. P. (2010). Alcohol influences the use of decisional support. *Psychopharmacology*, *208*(4), 603–611.

Phillips, J. G., & Ogeil, R. P. (2011). Decisional styles and risk of problem drinking or gambling. *Personality and Individual Differences*, *51*(4), 521–526.

Phillips, J. G., & Ogeil, R. P. (2016). Decision-making style, nicotine and caffeine use and dependence. *Human Psychopharmacology*, *30*(6), 442–450.

Phillips, J. G., Ogeil, R. P., & Blaszczynski, A. (2012). Electronic interests and behaviors associated with gambling problems. *International Journal of Mental Health & Addiction*, *10*, 585–596.

Phillips, J. G., Ogeil, R. P., & Blaszczynski, A. (2013). *Human factors limiting consumer benefit from decisional support*. Proceedings of 1st International Workshop on Behavior Change Support Systems, Sydney. Retrieved from ceur-ws.org/Vol-973/bcss2.pdf

Phillips, J. G., Sargeant, J., Ogeil, R. P., Chow, Y.-W., & Blaszczynski, A. (2014). Self reported gambling problems and digital traces. *CyberPsychology, Behavior and Social Networking*, *17*(12), 742–748.

Phillips, J. G., & Triggs, T. J. (2001). Characteristics of cursor trajectories controlled by the computer mouse. *Ergonomics*, *44*, 527–536.

Preece, J., Nonnecke, B., & Andrews, D. (2004). The top five reasons for lurking: Improving community experiences for everyone. *Computers in Human Behavior*, *20*, 201–223.

Renaud, K., Ramsay, J., & Hair, M. (2006). 'You've got e-mail!' . . . shall I deal with it now? Electronic mail from the recipient's perspective. *International Journal of Human-Computer Interaction*, *21*(3), 313–332.

Resnick, P., & Varian, H. R. (1997). Recommender systems. *Communications of the ACM*, *40*, 56–58.

Riegelsberger, J., Sasse, M. A., & McCarthy, J. D. (2005). The mechanics of trust: A framework for research and design. *International Journal of Human-Computer Studies*, *62*, 381–422.

Roebuck, J. A. (1995). *Anthropometric methods: Designing to fit the human body*. Santa Monica: Human Factors and Ergonomics Society.

Romm, C. T., & Pliskin, N. (1999). The office tyrant-social control through email. *Information Technology & People*, *12*(1), 27–43.

Savic, M., Best, D., Rodda, S., & Lubman, D. I. (2013). Exploring the focus and experiences of smartphone applications for addiction recovery. *Journal of Addictive Diseases*, *32*, 310–319.

Schafer, J. B., Konstan, J. A., & Riedl, J. (2001). E-commerce recommendation applications. *Data Mining and Knowledge Discovery*, *5*, 115–153.

Sears, D. O., & Freedman, J. L. (1967). Selective exposure to information: A critical review. *The Public Opinion Quarterly*, *31*(2), 194–213.

Shaffer, H. J., Peller, A. J., LaPlante, D. A., Nelson, S. E., & LaBrie, R. A. (2010). Toward a paradigm shift in Internet gambling research: From opinion and self-report to actual behavior. *Addiction Research and Theory*, *18*(3), 270–283.

Shaughnessy, J. J., Zecmeister, E. B., & Zecmeister, J. S. (2006). *Research methods* (ch. 6-Unobtrusive measures of behavior). Boston: McGraw-Hill.

Shirren, S., & Phillips, J. G. (2011). Decisional style, mood and work communication: Email diaries. *Ergonomics*, *54*(10), 891–903.

Song, C., Qu, Z., Blumm, N., & Barabási, A.-L. (2010). Limits of predictability in human mobility. *Science*, *327*, 1018–1021.

Suffoletto, B., Kristan, J., Callaway, C., Kim, K. H., Chung, T., Monti, P. M., & Clark, D. B. (2014). A text message alcohol intervention for young adult emergency department patients: A randomized clinical trial. *Annals of Emergency Medicine*, *64*(6), 664–672.

Sumecki, D., Chipulu, M., & Ojiako, U. (2011). Email overload: Exploring the moderating role of the perception of email as a 'business critical' tool. *International Journal of Information Management*, *31*, 407–414.

Tong, S. T. (2013). Facebook use during relationship termination: Uncertainty reduction and surveillance. *Cyberpsychology, Behavior and Social Networking*, *16*, 788–793.

Warren, S. D., & Brandeis, L. D. (1890). The right to privacy. *Harvard Law Review*, *4*(5). Retrieved January 30, 2017, from http://groups.csail.mit.edu/mac/classes/6.805/articles/privacy/Privacy_brand_warr2.html

Warwick, K. (2002). *I Cyborg*. London: Century.

Weber, R. H., & Weber, R. (2010). *Internet of Things: Legal perspectives*. New York: Springer.

Whitworth, B. (2005). Polite computing. *Behavior & Information Technology*, *24*, 353–363.

Wiederhold, B. K. (2015). mHealth sensors can promote behavior change and reduce healthcare costs. *Cyberpsychology, Behavior and Social Networking*, *18*, 559–560.

Wilson, H. J., Shah, B., & Whipple, B. (2015). How people are actually using the Internet of Things. *Harvard Business Review*. Retrieved December 20, 2016, from https://hbr.org/2015/10/how-people-are-actually-using-the-internet-of-things

Wohl, M. J. A., Parush, A., Kim, H. S., & Warren, K. (2014). Building it better: Applying human-computer interaction and persuasive system design principles to a monetary limit tool improves responsible gambling. *Computers in Human Behavior*, *37*, 124–132.

Wu, F., & Huberman, B. A. (2007). Novelty and collective attention. *PNAS*, *104*(45), 17599–17601.

Yang, W.-S., Cheng, H.-C., & Dia, J.-B. (2008). A location-aware recommender system for mobile shopping environments. *Expert Systems with Applications*, *34*, 437–445.

Yuan, S.-T., & Tsao, Y. W. (2003). A recommendation mechanism for contextualized mobile advertising. *Expert Systems with Applications*, *24*(4), 399–414.

13 An Examination of Online Repurchasing Behavior in an IoT Environment

Carol D. Portillo and Terri R. Lituchy

Introduction

The traditional purchasing environment has changed dramatically; the Internet offers consumers purchasing functions (research and purchasing) any time of day or night with a few clicks of a button or screen swipes. For retailers it provides the opportunity to reach consumers they would not have been able to reach via a physical store location. Although the Internet provides a wider reach, this method of purchasing has presented significant changes for the retail industry. Stores closing with the shift from physical stores to digital commerce and the transformative effect of e-commerce on pricing, product availability and shopping convenience are two common challenges (Dennis, 2017). Researchers have not reached a consensus regarding customers' acceptance of online shopping, and most of the research findings are mixed and inconclusive (Ashraf, Thongpapanl, & Auh, 2014). As the e-tail industry experiences heightened consumption and competition, further study of how to entice and retain online customers is needed (Wang, Minor, & Wei, 2011). This is especially imperative as the interconnectedness of devices in our homes, offices, transportation and health is continually creating new purchasing environments and opportunities.

The IoT is a global system of interconnecting private, public, academic, business and government networks (Ibarra-Esquer, González-Navarro, Flores-Rios, Burtseva, & Astorga-Vargas, 2017). With more than 5.5 million connected devices added every day, IoT is well on its way to involving more than 20.8 billion devices worldwide by 2020 (Weber, 2016). The Internet of Things is regarded as one of the disruptive technologies of this century, catching the attention of society, industry and academy by creating new business models to interact with consumers in the selling relationship (Ibarra-Esquer et al., 2017). The IoT already assists advertisers to obtain relevant information about consumers, their consumption habits and buying processes and frequency (Lemay, 2015). Advertisers have access to vast amounts of data that they use to try to improve the users' experience, thus leading to smarter purchases which can translate to time savings for online shoppers and more sales for retailers and the related supply chains. Thus, it is critical to explore and comprehend how different variables influence online repurchasing and more specifically how the interconnectivity of things, our home appliances, vehicles, smart phones, television and other devices will affect the way that consumers continue to make purchases via these networks. The topic of this chapter is to examine the impact of consumer demographics on online repurchasing behaviors in the IoT environment. As our lives are transformed by smart phones, tablets, notebooks, smart watches, wearables and office smart devices, the interconnectivity of these devices expands information gathering, enhances collaboration and affords creative learning spaces to better understand online repurchasing behaviors. In the retail industry a growing trend is the increase in a strong discovery process, as consumers go online seeking to compare items, prices and reviews before the purchase. Retailers need to position themselves not only in the retail space, but also in the search space (Dennis, 2017).

Literature Review and Research Model

A review of existing literature revealed that although researchers have begun to understand how and why consumers shop online, much information, including trait- and state-based antecedents to purchasing, is still needed. Despite efforts at exploring the marketing implications of this relatively new commerce avenue, online shopping research is lacking compared to offline consumer research (Kim & Eastin, 2011). Numerous studies have been published within the last five years focusing on the Internet or peripheral aspects of online purchasing such as web design, consumer interface, mobile purchasing and content. Many authors criticized the emphasis placed on web-based marketing and claimed many online businesses have fallen short in focusing their efforts on consumers (Luo & Lee, 2011). Gelard and Negahdari (2011) claimed the topic of online consumer behavior was still in the exploratory stage in both theory development and empirical investigations. The importance of socioeconomic user characteristics such as age, gender, educational level, place of residence and income on IT technology have been commonly employed in the field of marketing for purposes of market segmentation (Hernandez, Jimenez, & Martin, 2011). Consumer data collected by retailers are significant as they strive to identify the motivators attributable to online repurchasing. This research study centered on gender, digital experience (digital natives and digital immigrants), level of income and level of education to examine which of these is predictive of online consumer repurchasing behavior.

The research question is how online consumer repurchasing behavior might be adapting in the IoT world. Knowing this will facilitate the organizational adaptation of online retailers to improve product and service offerings, increasing not only online repurchasing but also customer satisfaction with the experiences of online shopping. In order to determine this adaptability, it is important to understand how socioeconomic variables influence the repurchasing behavior. The following literature review will discuss online repurchasing behavior and delve into gender, age, level of education and level of income as they pertain to online repurchasing behavior.

Online Repurchasing Behavior

The phenomenon of online repurchasing intentions is of significant interest in marketing, particularly in online retailing (Mpinganjira, 2014). In this study online repurchasing intention refers to the subjective probability that a customer will continue to purchase a product from the same online seller (Rau, 2015). Stiff competition in the online environment makes it difficult for firms to differentiate their offers using the traditional marketing mix elements of product, price, place and promotion (Mpinganjira, 2014). Compared with potential customers, repeat (i.e., experienced) customers are better at comprehending and evaluating the information and attributes of an online store due to their experience with the seller (Bolton, 1998; Kim & Gupta, 2009; Parasuraman, 1997).

Gender and Online Repurchasing Behavior

Prior research examining the effect of gender on willingness to shop online revealed that men are more likely to conduct online transactions than women (Brown, Pope, & Voges, 2003; Donthu & Garcia, 1999; Kim & Kim, 2004). Qureshi, Fatima, and Sarwar (2014) supported this finding in their study of 350 Pakistanis and found that females found it more difficult to adopt online shopping and female consumers perceive more barriers in online shopping than males. There are some studies where opposing or mixed conclusions were reported; however, these appear to be exceptions to the general pattern, such as the purchase of clothing by women (Goldsmith & Flynn, 2005). Contrary findings were presented by Krešić, Herceg, Lelas, and Režek, (2010) in their study of factors that influence milk purchasing. The researchers found there was a higher demand of women purchasing low-fat dairy beverages and even all dairy products in comparison with men, and conversely it was observed that men had higher loyalty toward purchasing favorite brands of milk beverages in comparison with women (Kurajdova & Táborecka-Petrovicova, 2015). The influence of gender upon decision making and shopping behavior has been a subject of special interest in the field of marketing and has also been analyzed with regard to the process of acceptance of new ITs (Venkatesh & Morris, 2000). The conclusion is that IT characteristics and use are evaluated differently, depending on the gender of the individual (Sun & Zhang, 2006). Despite the apparent differences in gender and IT acceptance, recent studies show that increased levels of technological experience narrow the gap between genders (Hernandez, Jimenez, & Martin, 2011). According to Naseri and Elliott (2011) core variables—that is, age, gender, income, education and occupation—have statistically significant impacts on the actual online shopping beyond the effects of other demographics, social connectedness and prior online experience variables.

Age and Online Repurchasing Behavior

Age has been a major factor in the study of online technology, and much of the previous research on age-related differences in technology usage has only investigated usage broadly—from a "used" or "not used" standpoint (Olson, O'Brien, Rogers & Charness, 2011). When we think of technology-savvy consumers, older adults typically are not described as such, but this is a common misconception (Olson et al., 2011). However, a better concept than chronological age to capture antecedent online repurchasing behavior is user experiences and preferences (Ramon-Jeronimo, Peral-Peral, & Arenas-Gaitan, 2013). Lack of user experience is generally found in older individuals (Hernandez et al., 2011). Additionally, when age increases, the adoption of new technology decreases, with familiar options tending to be preferred (Ramon-Jeronimo et al., 2013). Technology anxiety also increases with age (Meuter, Ostrom, Bitner, & Roundtree, 2003), and rapid evolution of online devices has challenged consumers to keep up in their technological adoptions. In the following section the constructs of digital natives and digital immigrants are discussed.

Digital native and digital immigrant are concepts representing information and communication technology (ICT) user experiences and preferences (Prensky, 2001a; Tapscott, 1998). Digital natives describe the kindergarten through college-level students who are the first generation to spend their entire lives surrounded by and using computers, video games, digital music players, video cams, cell phones and all the other toys and tools of the digital age (Prensky, 2001a; Smith, 2012). Researchers (Twenge, Campbell, Hoffman, & Lance, 2010; Zandt, 2010; Dagnaud, 2011; Gansky, 2011) have found that digital natives are dependent on technology. Prensky (2001a, 2001b) suggests that the digital native culture is physically different from prior ones because of the rich tacit knowledge interwoven through global digital connectivity. Hart, Gray, Chinburg, Saffarian, and Hart (2011) describe the digital native as always knowing a media-rich technical environment since birth. Given a preference, they will most often select technology-based tools as communication foundations. Digital natives utilize technology for simple tasks such as note taking to more complex tasks such as banking.

Characteristics of digital immigrants include the following: first, digital immigrants always retain their own "accent" more or less, and some of them tend to resist new information technologies and devices (Tilvawala, Sundaram, & Myers, 2013). For instance, adoption rates of new technology tend to be slower for digital immigrants versus digital natives (Davis, 1989). Second, digital immigrants tend to use traditional and formal communication channels and tools such as postal mail, phone or face-to-face meetings (Fernandez-Villavicencio, 2010; Kolikant, 2010). For example, many digital immigrants prefer taking notes on paper and printing out their emails rather than working on the computer screen. Third, digital immigrants are labeled the "single-threaded animal" and are generally focused on one task at a time, (albeit) done properly (Bayne & Ross, 2007; Prensky, 2001b). For instance, digital immigrants may not be as skilled at multitasking as digital natives and prefer to complete tasks in a step-by-step manner. Last but not the least, in the view of digital immigrants, utilitarian needs may play a more important role than hedonic needs; in addition many digital immigrants are gradually and slowly realizing the entertainment function of social media (Zhao, Xu, Sun, & Zhu, 2014). Although this research shows a demarcation between digital immigrants and digital natives when it comes to adopting and using technology, other research has shown that digital immigrants fare better than digital natives in particular online tasks. Ransdell, Kent, Gaillard-Kenney, and Long (2011) found that older adult cohorts (digital immigrants) showed greater external locus of control (LOC), a marker of social reliance, compared to younger cohorts who showed greater knowledge application skill and were more self-reliant than younger students (digital natives).

Income Level and Online Repurchasing Behavior

The relationship between income and online shopping repurchasing intentions is generally that as income increases, repurchasing increases (Punj, 2011). However, income has many aspects. Regarding online shopping adoption consumers with lower income are most cost sensitive and perceive more barriers to adopt online shopping due to high product/services cost (Qureshi et al., 2014). A study of 503 Chinese consumers supported this positive correlation, as those with higher income levels were more likely to shop online (Gong, Stump, & Maddox, 2013). A study conducted with online grocery shoppers versus in-store shoppers also supported these findings showing significantly higher income for online grocery shoppers than in-store grocery shoppers (Alamelu & Meena, 2015). The outcomes are consistent with empirical evidence indicating that consumers who shop online tend to have higher income than shoppers in general (Donthu & Garcia, 1999). An interesting viewpoint via a study by Comor (2000) considered income from the perspective of time savings, asserting that better-paid individuals tend to work longer hours and have higher incomes and thus utilize the Internet in order to gain free time (Comor, 2000). Conversely, consumers with less income have more time but are less motivated to purchase online (Comor, 2000). Low income levels may also be associated with fewer information technology and devices, but with the increase usage of mobile devices at all income levels this gap is likely narrowing (Pew Research Center, 2017).

Level of Education and Online Repurchasing Behavior

Many studies examined education as a predictor of online purchasing either as a standalone variable or combined with other demographic variables. Often coupled with gender, education is a good predictor of online purchasing (Qureshi et al., 2014); however, when combined with other demographic variables such as age, income and marital status, the findings are inconsistent (Gong et al., 2013). Qureshi et al., (2014) found that gender and education level of consumers significantly influence his or her perception regarding online shopping barriers. A study by Punj (2011) supported these findings linking education to saving time and found that consumers with more education believed that shopping online tended to save them time. A study of 15,510 online shoppers found they were generally highly educated, young, affluent and professionals regardless of the types of the products they purchase (Naseri & Elliott, 2011), supporting the positive correlation between online shopping and level of education. Inconsistent findings between level of education and online purchasing were discovered by Hu and Jasper (2015) for share of book purchases at the mall where two consumer characteristics, income and education level, had negative impacts. In addition, contrary to findings in studies of online shopping for other discretionary, higher-need items, such as apparel, electronics and books, the incidence of online grocery shopping appears to be unrelated to either age or education levels (Alamelu & Meena, 2015).

Based on the previous discussion, it is hypothesized that:

H1$_{a.}$ Women make more online repurchases than men.

H2$_{a}$. Consumers born before 1980 (digital immigrants) are less likely to make online repurchases versus digital natives (those born after 1980).

H3$_{a.}$ Consumers with a higher level of income make more online repurchases than those with lower levels of income.

H4$_{a.}$ Consumers with higher levels of education make more online repurchases than consumers with lower levels of education.

Method

Population and Sample

The population was composed of online consumers who had made a minimum of two online purchases of a product over the past three calendar months. The sample was derived from the third-party survey provider Pollfish. Participation in the online survey was entirely voluntary according to the consent provided by Pollfish. Respondents were presented a qualifying question as to whether they had made two or more purchases over the past three calendar months. This was important as the study focused on intent to continue to repurchase online. Based on the G*Power calculation tool version 3.1.9.2 the minimum number of participants for this correlation analysis was 279. This is based on an effect size f^2 of 25, an error probability of .05, a power of .80 and 12 predictors. The third-party survey provider Pollfish collected 279 usable surveys.

Research Study

A nonexperimental, correlational research study was chosen due to the lack of control over the conditions of the study and importance of generalization (Koksal, 2013). Nonexperimental research designs typically are in the form of survey questionnaires, descriptive research and comparative approach (Hsu, 2005), and the goal of a nonexperimental strategy is to gain the ability to generalize findings from a sample to the population (Prowse, 2010; Yin, 2009). The survey utilized was composed of a combination of survey questions from research studies by Walters (2014) and Obeidat (2015) and included a total of 13 questions. The questions used were determined to be reliable and valid as deemed by the aforementioned researchers. The survey comprised multiresponse questions to avoid acquiescence bias, which is a pervasive problem in survey research that could translate to social media (online) measurement as well (Kuru & Pasek, 2016). When questions are presented with agree/disagree (AD) or yes/no response options, some respondents select the "agree" (or "yes") option disproportionately more frequently than the "disagree" (or "no") option (Kuru & Pasek, 2016). Therefore, a mixture of true/false, multiple choice, Likert scale and open-ended questions were used in the survey. Questions 1 through 6 asked about the demographic variables, including gender, age, level of income and level of education questions, and questions 7 through 12 were related to repurchasing online intentions. Two open-ended questions at the end of the survey provided the opportunity to gather additional information on intent to repurchase in the respondent's own words. The open-ended questions were 1) what is the one main reason that you will continue to make online purchases? and 2) what is the main reason that would prevent you from continuing to make online purchases? The survey administrator Pollfish provided a link to qualified respondents to complete the survey. To qualify to participate, respondents were asked if they were over the age of 18 with survey question 1 asking "Are you at least 18 years of age or older?" Respondents that qualified based on age were able to continue to the online purchasing qualifying question.

Operational Definition of Variables

The variables examined were gender, digital native or digital immigrant, level of income and level of education and intent to continue making online repurchases. Age was provided by respondents in question 3 asking

"How old are you?" where respondents were able to select their current age from the following categories: 18–24, 25–34, 35–44, 45–54, 54 and older. Also collected was year of birth, which was used to determine whether the respondent was a digital immigrant (those born before 1980) or digital native (those born after 1980) where digital immigrant was coded as 0 and digital native coded as 1. Gender was captured in question 4 by asking, "Are you female or male?" Female was coded as 0 and male coded as 1. Respondents were asked to provide their highest level of education in question 5 which stated "What is the highest level of education you have completed?" Respondents were provided five category choices of middle school, high school, university, post-graduate and vocational technical college. Current level of income was asked in question 6 where respondents were asked to choose from the following seven income levels: high i, high ii, high iii, middle i, middle ii, lower i, lower ii and prefer not to say. Coding for these categories were as follows: high i = $100,000—$149,999, high ii = $150,000—$199,999 per year, high iii = $200,000 or higher per year, middle i = $50,000—$74,999 per year, middle ii = $75,000—$99,999 per year, lower i = $25,000—$49,999 per year and lower ii = less than $25,000 per year. In both questions respondents were given the opportunity to choose "Prefer not to answer" to avoid any discomfort. Intent to repurchase was captured by question 7 with a Likert-scale question asking "I will definitely continue to buy products online in the near future" in addition to the two open-ended questions discussed previously.

Data Analyses

The statistical analyses utilizing SPSS 24.0 were used to compute data gathered based upon the nature of the study which tested differences among more than two groups, namely gender, digital immigrant and digital native, income and level of education on the single continuous variable of intent to repurchase online. A correlational analysis utilizing Spearman's rho was conducted to determine correlation between the independent variable of intent to continue to repurchase online and the four dependent or predictor variables. A cross-tabulation analysis was performed to aggregate and jointly analyze the distribution of the interrelationships within the variables, along with a nonparametric procedure Kruskal-Wallis test to examine the hypotheses on the sample mean and assess for significant differences on the continuous dependent variable of intent to repurchase online by the four dependent variables. Cronbach's alpha reliability analysis was not necessary due to the ease of readability of the survey which was verified by the Flesch-Kincaid readability tool. The survey was submitted and collected within a 24-hour turnaround. Data collected for the research were verified as being accurate by the third-party provider Pollfish. After the data from the surveys were collected Pollfish provided a readout of all data in an Excel format which was sent to the researcher via email. The data were entered by the researcher into the statistical analysis program SPSS 24.0 to perform the following data analysis: data descriptives, correlational analysis Spearman's rho, cross-tabulation and the nonparametric Kruskal-Wallis test. Interpretational analysis was used to find common constructs, identify discrepancies, gain insights, find themes and determine patterns that can be used in the development of a deeper understanding of online repurchasing behavior and the demographics of the online repurchaser. Coding categories were developed for the two open-ended questions and used to help identify patterns for continuing and not continuing online repurchasing.

Results

Demographics

The survey included 279 participants residing in the United States who have made two or more online purchases via the Internet over the past three months. The subjects were 140 (50%) females and 139 males (49.8%). Age ranges and associated percentage make-ups were as follows: 18–24 (12%), 25–34 (34%), 35–44 (27%), 45–54 (16%) and 54 and older (9.6%) with the majority of respondents being from the 25–34 and 35–44 age brackets. Regarding digital immigrant and digital native as a categorical breakdown of age, a majority of the survey respondents were in the digital native category with 155 or 55% respondents being born after 1980. The digital immigrant category totaled 124 or 44%. Regarding level of income, the majority of respondents (29.7%) fell between the $25,000 and $49,999 income category with the majority of male respondents (31.8%) in the $25,000—$49,999 category. Female respondents had two equal categories at 36 or 27.7% in both the $25,000—$49,999 category and $50,000—$74,999 category. Level of education was categorized into the following five classifications: middle school, high school, vocational or technical college, university and post-graduate. The majority of female and male respondents had a high school education at 43%

Correlational Analysis

Correlational analysis was performed using Spearman's rho statistical analysis. This specific study explored the independent variable of intent to continue to repurchase online and four dependent or predictor variables. The predictor variables were analyzed and the results indicated that gender, being a digital immigrant or digital native and highest level of education all had a negative correlation with intent to repurchase online. Gender had the highest significance with digital native/digital immigrant next highest. Females were more likely to continue to make online repurchases versus males, and digital immigrants (those born before 1980) were also more likely to make online repurchases. Level of income indicated a positive correlation with intent to repurchase online, whereas highest level of education was negatively correlated with middle school education as the highest response and university second highest with intent to repurchase online. However, middle school responses totaled only 2 or less than 1% of responses.

A cross-tabulation analysis was also performed to aggregate and jointly analyze the distribution of the interrelationships within the variables. The test showed digital immigrants with a higher correlation than digital natives and their intent to repurchase online. Females showed a higher correlation than males with intent to repurchase. Level of income revealed the highest correlation for the $125,000 to $149,999 income category, whereas highest level of education at the middle school level exposed the highest correlation; however, this was based on only two responses. University level of education displayed the highest correlation with adequate responses. The significance level for all dependent variables was found to be greater than .01, which is not significant and therefore directs to retain the null hypothesis.

Hypotheses Testing

The hypotheses are worded as rejection supported so that if the null hypothesis is rejected, then the alternative hypothesis is accepted; if the null hypothesis is accepted, then the alternative hypothesis is rejected and is supportive of the research question. Each of the hypotheses was tested utilizing a nonparametric Friedman test to examine the differences between each of the respective dependent variables and the independent variable. See Table 13.1.

> **H1$_{a.}$** Women make more online repurchases than men.

As seen in Table 13.1 Kruskal-Wallis shows a significance of $r = -.062$ between gender and intent to repurchase online, resulting in rejecting the hypothesis that females make more online repurchases than males.

> **H2$_{a}$.** Consumers born before 1980 (digital immigrants) are less likely to make online repurchases versus digital natives (those born after 1980).

Kruskal-Wallis in Table 13.1 shows a correlation of $r = -.050$; therefore, the hypothesis is rejected.

> **H3$_{a.}$** Consumers with a higher level of income make more online repurchases than those with lower levels of income.

Kruskal-Wallis (shown in Table 13.1) shows a correlation of $r = .041$ between level of income and intent to repurchase online; therefore, the hypothesis is rejected that consumers with a higher level of income make more online repurchases than those with lower levels of income.

Table 13.1 Kruskal-Wallis Test of the Model

	Intent to Repurchase	N	*Mean Rank*	*Chi-Square*	*df*	*Asymp. Sig.*
Gender	No I will not	3	210.00			
	Not sure	5	182.10			
	More than likely	18	140.25			
	Most likely	50	137.84			
	Definitely	203				
	Total	279		5.02	4	.285
Digital Immigrant/ Digital Native	No I will not	3	115.00			
	Not sure	5	208.00			
	More than likely	18	161.50			
	Most likely	50	132.67			
	Definitely	203	138.59			
	Total	279		7.461	4	.113
Level of Income	No I will not	3	113.50			
	Not sure	5	95.60			
	More than likely	18	147.17			
	Most likely	50	136.13			
	Definitely	203	141.80			
	Total	279		2.304	4	.680
Level of Education	No I will not	3	173.67			
	Not sure	5	162.10			
	More than likely	18	130.33			
	Most likely	50	120.53			
	Definitely	203	144.61			
	Total	279		5.339	4	.254

H4$_{a.}$ Consumers with higher levels of education make more online repurchases than consumers with lower levels of education.

Kruskal-Wallis (Table 13.1) shows a correlation of r = .086 between level of education completed and intent to repurchase online. The hypothesis that consumers with a higher level of education make more online repurchases than those with lower levels of education was not supported.

Discussion

The purpose of this study was to examine online repurchasing behavior in an IoT environment. The independent variables of the study included gender, user experience (digital immigrant and digital native), level of income and level of education. The dependent variable was the intent to continue to make online repurchases. The nonexperimental quantitative research study included a statistical analysis of the data collected from an online survey of 279 respondents. The results of this study supported findings by Kwarteng and Pilik (2016) who found no significant association between gender, age, level of income or level of education and use of Internet shopping. Women are an attractive and growing market segment (Brennan, 2015; Krotz, 2012); therefore, insignificant findings regarding gender seem problematic. Recent research suggests that attitudinal variables, rather than gender are stronger predictors of repeat purchase intention; for example, positive post online purchase experiences (Pham & Ahammad, 2017) and trust and satisfaction (Hsu, Chang, & Chuang, 2015).

In their study on age and mobile commerce transactions Chan and Chong (2013) found no difference between younger and older consumers and their propensity to conduct mobile commerce transactions. The findings are counterintuitive to expectations regarding age. One would surmise that older adults born before technology was present would use the Internet less than those born with technology. There was a moderate negative correlation between being a digital immigrant or digital native and the intent to repurchase online, meaning that being a digital immigrant or digital native does not influence online repurchasing behavior. This finding was very similar to the finding for gender and indicates that when a person decides to continue making online purchases being a digital immigrant or digital native (a categorical factor of age) does not have any influence in that decision. This may seem counterintuitive when one understands the differences in Internet usage between digital immigrants and digital natives as supported by Hoffman, Lutz, and Meckel (2014) who found that digital natives were found to be more savvy Internet users and digital immigrants more passive Internet users. It must be remembered that the average age of e-shoppers is continuously rising, because individuals who at the end of the last century were 30 are 40 today (Hernandez et al., 2011). Consequently, life stages, which would until recently have been considered to be far removed from more technologically inclined generations, currently comprise individuals who may have been interacting with the Internet for several years and thus gained considerable familiarity, and moreover, users who have replaced them (i.e. those who are 20 to 30 years old) possess a broad digital culture (Hernandez et al., 2011).

There was a positive correlation between level of income and the likelihood of online repeat purchasing. This makes intuitive sense since higher income provides the means to purchase more or to have the access to online purchasing technology. However, the finding had a weak significance, which infers, it is not a strong determinant of online repurchasing behavior. In other words, one cannot say for sure that the more income an online consumer earns, the more they will continue to shop online. However, IoT is making it easier for consumers at all income levels to comparison shop, leading to more informed purchase decisions, more pricing comparisons and overall increased product research (Dennis, 2017).

A moderate negative correlation was demonstrated between highest level of education and the likelihood of repeat online purchasing, indicating that as education increases, the likelihood of continuing to purchase online will decrease. However, the findings related to the research questions were insignificant. Similar studies found no significant association between education and online purchasing. Anitha (2017) found the major reasons for the preference of online purchase dimension show no significant association with the education of the respondents.

The ultimate purpose of this research study was to examine the tenets of online repurchasing behavior relative to gender, age, level of income and level of education to examine consumer online repurchasing behavior within the IoT phenomenon. With more than 20 billion devices expected to be interconnected by 2020 (Weber, 2016), the importance of how consumer repurchasing behavior will change is important to retailers using IoT as part of their retail strategy. This is apparent with online retailers such as Amazon and Wal-Mart offering online grocery shopping and clothing retailers such as Stitch Fix offering personalized clothes shopping delivery.

Some limitations of the study include sample size, usage data, limited geography and common method bias. An extension of this research would be to advise online retailers on how demographic variables can be applied to online repurchasing. The findings suggest that online retailers do not necessarily have to provide either gender- or age-specific campaigns in order to increase the likelihood of online repurchasing. Annual household income is not a strong predictor, so it is likely that online retailers would not gain significant advantage through differentiation on this variable. Results on education are consistent with the other study variables so that online retailers would find slight advantage in creating online campaigns targeting different levels of education.

As we move into an IoT world user involvement will become more important as two-way communication between consumer and product enables an improved experience (Chang, Dong, & Sun, 2014). IoT can provide services so products can easily communicate with and interface with each other, enabling consumers to access more and enhanced functions. This allows for real-time information gathering by retailers as data between consumers and products are communicated in a convenient and timely manner. An opportunity for future research is to study user experience variables to identify trends and patterns that would increase online repurchasing behavior and thus drive online revenue. Variables such as trust, security and privacy will be increasingly important (Eloff, Eloff, Dlamini, & Zielinski, 2009). IoT is transforming retailers as machine-to-machine technology permeates the workplace. This will facilitate collaboration and efficiency increasingly through video collaboration robots (Corsello, 2013) to offer better service to consumers. The skills of retailers in understanding the consumer will evolve as the IoT continues to increase.

References

Alamelu, R., & Meena, L. (2015). Store and online grocery shopping: A customer value perspective. *TSM Business Review*, *3*(1), 54–68.

Anitha, N. (2017). Factors influencing preference of women toward online shopping. *Indian Journal of Commerce & Management Studies*, *8*(1), 38–45.

Ashraf, A., Thongpapanl, N., & Auh, S. (2014). The application of the technology acceptance model under different cultural contexts: The case of online shopping adoption. *Journal of International Marketing*, 22(3), 68–93.

Bayne, S., & Ross, J. (2009). *The 'digital native' and 'digital immigrant': A dangerous opposition*. Paper is presented at the Annual Conference of the Society for Research into Higher Education (SRHE) December 2007. Retrieved September 25.

Bolton, R. N. (1998). A dynamic model of the duration of the customer's relationship with a continuous service provider: The role of satisfaction. *Marketing Science*, *17*, 45–65.

Brennan, B. (2015, January 21). Top 10 Things Everyone Should Know About Women Consumers. Retrieved January 26, 2018, from https://www.forbes.com/sites/bridgetbrennan/2015/01/21/top-10-things-everyone-should-know-about-women-consumers/#facee766a8b4

Brown, M., Pope, N., & Voges, K. (2003). Buying or browsing? An exploration of shopping orientations and online purchase intention. *European Journal of Marketing*, *37*(11–12), 1666–1684.

Chan, F. T. S. & Chong, A.Y-L. (2013) Analysis of the determinants of consumers' m-commerce usage activities. Online Information Review, 37 (3), 443-461,

Chang, Y., Dong, X., & Sun, W. (2014). Influence of characteristics of the Internet of Things on consumer purchase intention. Social Behavior and Personality: An international journal, 42, 321-330. DOI: https://doi.org/10.2224/sbp.2014.42.2.321

Comor, E. (2000). Household consumption on the internet: Income, time, and institutional contradictions. *Journal of Economic Issues*, *34*(1), 105–116.

Corsello, J. (2013). What the Internet of Things will bring to the workplace. *Wired*. Retrieved from www.wired.com/insights/2013/11/what-the-internet-of-things-will-bring-to-the-workplace/

Dagnaud, M. (2011). *Génération Y. Les jeunes et les réseaux sociaux, de la dérision à la subversion*. Paris: Presses de Sciences Po.

Davis, F. D. (1989). Perceived usefulness, perceived ease of use, and user acceptance of information technology. *MIS Quarterly*, *13*, 319–340.

Dennis, S. (2017, June 12). *Retail's single biggest disruptor: Spoiler alert: It's not E-commerce*. Retrieved December 15, 2017, from www.forbes.com/sites/stevendennis/2017/06/12/retails-single-biggest-disruptor-spoiler-alert-its-not-e-commerce/#5ad64b9c227b

Donthu, N., & Garcia, A. (1999). The internet shopper. *Journal of Advertising Research*, *39*(3), 52–58.

Eloff, J. H. P., Eloff, M. M., Dlamini, M. T., & Zielinski, M. P. (2009). *Internet of people, things and services: The convergence of security, trust and privacy*. 3rd CompanionAble Workshop—IoPTS, Novotel Brussels. Retrieved from http://hdl.handle.net/10204/4409

Fernandez-Villavicencio, N. G. (2010). Helping students become literate in a digital, networking-based society: A literature review and discussion. *The International Information & Library Review*, *42*(2), 124–136.

Gansky, L. (2011). *The mesh: Why the future of business is sharing*. Bucharest: Publica.

Gelard, P., & Negahdari, A. (2011). A new framework for customer satisfaction in electronic commerce. *Journal of Applied Sciences Research*, 7(11), 1952–1961. Retrieved from http://t063.camel.ntupes.edu.tw/ezcatfiles/t063/download/attdown/0/A%20New%20Framework%20For%20Customer%20Satisfaction%20In%20Electronic%20 Commerce.pdf

Goldsmith, R. E., & Flynn, L. R. (2005). Bricks, clicks, and pix: Apparel buyers' use of stores, internet, and catalogs compared. *International Journal of Retail & Distribution Management*, *33*(4), 271–283.

Gong, W., Stump, R., & Maddox, L. (2013). Factors influencing consumers' online shopping in China. *Journal of Asia Business Studies*, *7*(3), 214–230.

Hart, M. L., Gray, D. M., Chinburg, S., Saffarian, M., & Hart, W. (2011). *Technical knowledge among undergraduates: Perception versus reality.* Conference Participants, 125. Retrieved from http://lupus.northern.edu/academics/Documents/ceib/2011proceedings.pdf#page=125

Hernandez, B., Jimenez, J., & Martin, M. J. (2011). Age, gender and income: Do they really moderate online shopping behaviour? *Online Information Review*, *35*(1), 113–133.

Hoffmann, C. P., Lutz, C. & Meckel, M. (May, 2014). Content Creation on the Internet: A Social Cognitive Perspective on the Participation Divide. Paper presented at the 64th Annual Conference of the International Communication Association (ICA) Seattle, WA.

Hsu, M. H., Chang, C. M., & Chuang, L. W. (2015). Understanding the determinants of online repeat purchase intention and moderating role of habit: The case of online group buying. *International Journal of Information Management*, *35*, 45–56.

Hsu, T. C. (2005). Research methods and data analysis procedures used by educational researchers. *International Journal of Research & Method in Education*, *28*(2), 109–133.

Hu, H., & Jasper, C. (2015). The impact of consumer shopping experience on consumer channel decision. *Academy of Marketing Studies Journal*, *19*(1), 213–224.

Ibarra-Esquer, J., González-Navarro, F., Flores-Rios, B., Burtseva, L., & Astorga-Vargas, M. (2017). Tracking the evolution of the Internet of Things concept across different application domains. *Sensors*, *17*, 2–24.

Kim, E. Y., & Kim, Y. K. (2004). Predicting online purchase intention for clothing products. *European Journal of Marketing*, *38*(7), 883–897.

Kim, H. W., & Gupta, S. (2009). A comparison of purchase decision calculus between potential and repeat customers of an online store. *Decision Support Systems*, *47*, 477–487.

Kim, S., & Eastin, M. (2011). Hedonic tendencies and the online consumer: An investigation of the online shopping process. *Journal of Internet Commerce*, *10*, 68–90.

Koksal, M. S. (2013). A comprehensive research design for experimental studies in science education. *Ilkogretim Online*, *12*(3), 628–634.

Kolikant, Y. B. D. (2010). Digital natives, better learners? Students' beliefs about how the internet influenced their ability to learn. *Computers in Human Behavior*, *26*(6), 1384–1391.

Krešić, G., Herceg, Z., Lelas, V., & Režek, J. (2010). Consumers' behaviour and motives for selection of dairy beverages in kvarner region: A pilot study. *Mljekarstvo*, *60*(1), 50–58.

Krotz, J. (2012, January 02). If You Want to Sell Online, Target Women. Retrieved January 26, 2018, from http://www.foxbusiness.com/features/2012/01/04/if-want-to-sell-online-target-women.html

Kurajdova, K., & Táborecka-Petrovicova, J. (2015). Literature review on factors influencing milk purchase behaviour. *International Review of Management and Marketing*, *5*(1), 9–25.

Kuru, O., & Pasek, J. (2016). Improving social media measurement in surveys: Avoiding acquiescence bias in Facebook research. *Computers in Human Behavior*, *57*, 82–92.

Kurzweil, R. (2005). *The singularity is near: When humans transcend biology*. New York: Viking Press.

Kwarteng, M., & Pilik, M. (2016). Exploring consumer's propensity for online shopping in a developing country: A demographic perspective. *International Journal of Entrepreneurial Knowledge*, *1*(4), 90–103.

Lemay, T. (2015). *The Internet of Things: How it transforms e-commerce*. Retrieved from www.mazeberry.com/en/blog-internet-of-things-how-it-transforms-ecommerce/

Luo, S., & Lee, T. (2011). The influence of trust and usefulness on customer perceptions of E- service quality. *Social Behavior & Personality: An International Journal*, *39*(6), 825–838.

Meuter, M. L., Ostrom, A., Bitner, M. J., & Roundtree, R. (2003). The influence of technology anxiety on consumer use and experiences with self-service technologies. *Journal of Business Research*, *56*, 899–906.

Mpinganjira, M. (2014). Understanding online repeat purchase intentions: A relationship marketing perspective. *Management*, *19*(2), 117–135.

Naseri, M., & Elliott, G. (2011). Role of demographics, social connectedness and prior internet experience in adoption of online shopping: Applications for direct marketing. *Journal of Targeting, Measurement and Analysis for Marketing*, *19*(2), 69–84.

Obeidat, M. S. (2015). *Consumer attitude toward online shopping in Jordan*. Wilmington University (Delaware), ProQuest Dissertations Publishing, 3680582.

Olson, K., O'Brien, M., Rogers, W., & Charness, N. (2011). Diffusion of technology: Frequency of use for younger and older adults. *Ageing International*, *36*, 123–145.

Parasuraman, A. (1997). Reflections on gaining competitive advantage through customer value. *Journal of the Academy of Marketing Science*, *25*, 154–161.

Pew Research Center. (2017, January 12). *Mobile fact sheet*. Retrieved December 15, 2017, from www.pewinternet.org/fact-sheet/mobile/

Pham, T. S. H., & Ahammad, M. F. (2017). Antecedents and consequences of online customer satisfaction: A holistic process perspective. Technological Forecasting and Social Change, 124, 332–342. https://doi.org/10.1016/j.techfore.2017.04.003

Prensky, M. (2001a). Digital natives, digital immigrants. *On the Horizon*, *9*(5), 1–6.

Prensky, M. (2001b). Digital natives, digital immigrants part 2: Do they really think differently? *On the Horizon*, *9*(6), 1–6.

Prowse, M. (2010). Integrating reflexivity into livelihoods research. *Progress in Development Studies*, *10*(3), 211–231.

Punj, G. (2011). Effect of consumer beliefs on online purchase behavior: The influence of demographic and consumption values. *Journal of Interactive Marketing*, *25*, 134–144.

Qureshi, H., Fatima, R., & Sarwar, A. (2014). Barriers to adoption of online shopping in Pakistan. *Science International*, *26*(3), 1277–1282.

Ramon-Jeronimo, M., Peral-Peral, B., & Arenas-Gaitan, J. (2013). Elderly persons and internet use. *Social Science Computer Review*, *31*(4), 389–403.

Ransdell, S., Kent, B., Gaillard-Kenney, S., & Long, J. (2011). Digital immigrants fare better than digital natives due to social reliance. *British Journal of Educational Technology*, *42*(6), 931–938.

Rau, P. (2015). *Cross-cultural design: Applications in mobile interaction, education, health, transport and cultural heritage*. Switzerland: Springer International Publishing.

Shin, J. I., Chung, K. H., Oh, J. S., & Lee, C. W. (2013). The effect of site quality on repurchase intention in internet shopping through mediating variables: The case of university student in South Korea. *International Journal of Information Management*, *33*(3), 453–463.

Smith, E. E. (2012). The digital native debate in higher education: A comparative analysis of recent literature. *Canadian Journal of Learning & Technology*, *38*(3), 1–18.

Sun, H., & Zhang, P. (2006). The role of moderating factors in user technology acceptance. *International Journal of Human-Computer Studies*, *64*(2), 53–78.

Tapscott, D. (1998). *Growing up digital: The rise of the net generation*. New York: McGraw Hill.

Tilvawala, K., Sundaram, D., & Myers, M. (2013). *Design of organizational ubiquitous information systems: Digital native and digital immigrant perspective*. Proceedings of the Pacific Asia Conference on Information Systems (PACIS), Jeju Island, Korea, 171.

Twenge, J. M., Campbell, S. M., Hoffman, B. J., & Lance, C. E. (2010). Increasing, social and intrinsic values decreasing generational differences in work values: Leisure Twenand extrinsic values. *Journal of Management*, *36*(5), 117–1142.

Venkatesh, V., & Morris, M. G. (2000). Why don't men ever stop to ask for directions? Gender, social influence, and their role in technology acceptance and usage behaviour. *MIS Quarterly*, *24*(1), 115–139.

Walters, C. (2014). *Using conjoint analysis to identify the determinants of female consumers' online website purchase choices*. Northcentral University, ProQuest Dissertations Publishing, 3671967.

Wang, Y. J., Minor, M. S., & Wei, J. (2011). Aesthetics and the online shopping environment: Understanding consumer responses. *Journal of Retailing*, *87*(1), 46–58.

Weber, R. (2016). Internet of Things becomes next big thing. *Journal of Financial Service Professionals*, *70*(6), 43–46.

Yin, R. K. (2009). *Case study research: Design and methods* (4th ed.). Thousand Oaks, CA: Sage.

Zandt, D. (2010). *Share this! How you will change the world with social networking*. San Francisco: Berrett-Koehler Publishers.

Zhao, Y., Xu, X., Sun, X., & Zhu, Q. (2014). An integrated framework of online generative capability: Interview from digital immigrants. *Aslib Journal of Information Management*, *66*(2), 219–239.

14 Leading the Digital Supply Chain

David B. Kurz

Background: Navigating Technology Disruptions Transforming the Supply Chain

The volatile, uncertain, and complex business environment and its threatening impacts on organizations has almost become cliché in professional circles recently (Bennett & Lemoine, 2014). Doomsday scenarios illuminate the harsh competitive consequences awaiting organizations if they fail to successfully navigate the disruptions of the new digital platforms, social media, and the Internet of People, Things and Services (IoPTS). Supply chain leaders, the managers and executives tasked with planning, sourcing, manufacturing, and delivering products and services, have to be practical. They are expected to deliver products and services on time and in full, concurrently seeking ways to manage cost and working capital. Upon discovering methods of making their value chains more effective, supply chain leaders are frequently expected to return gains back to the organization, likely to functional areas outside of their own. This chapter explores supply chain leadership with a practical discussion of some workforce changes needed to realize the full potential of IoPTS transformations.

The modern supply chain is now often described as the "digital supply chain", which represents the manifestation of a wide range of current and emerging technologies and process innovations, as well as shifts in talent. Before the term "digital" began being applied to the supply chain, some recognizable shifts were already taking place in strategic discussions among leaders tasked with keeping their operations competitive (The Center for Global Enterprise, 2016). Well-worn industry buzz phrases such as "demand-driven" or "end-to-end" are now augmented or replaced with discussions of digital. Practical supply chain leaders, who may have been at times accused of being slower to adopt new ideas, are increasingly using the term "transformational" to describe their strategies. It may be the case now where the hype has finally caught up with our supply chain reality.

In supply chains largely run on efficiency improvements and cost reduction, there is an increasing awareness that incremental improvements are no longer sufficient. To remain competitive, supply chain leaders are being asked to deliver step-changes in performance and to manage trade-offs between conflicting operational goals.

The challenge is, and has been, how to deliver high-performance segmented supply chains while concurrently balancing growth, cost, risks, and service quality. IoPTS and adjacent technologies are critical enablers to these needed gains in supply chain effectiveness (Tavana, 2014). Digital supply chains, it appears, could be the answer to the ever-present dilemma of making performance trade-offs.

The key to unlocking this potential, or, perhaps, suffering its competitive consequences, reside in our workforces. In John Gattorna's book, *Dynamic Supply Chains*, he asserts, "managing supply chains actually involves understanding the interaction between human behavior, information technology and infrastructure. Unfortunately, this is the antithesis of what actually happens in business today" (Gattorna, 2015, p. 18). There is a high probability that organizations investing in IoPTS will fail to realize performance benefits if they neglect to make commensurate investments in their people (Sanders, 2014). Like so many other meaningful shifts, pivots, and transformations we encounter in organizational life, realizing gains comes down to our people and how well we develop and support them.

The IoPTS Enabled Digital Supply Chain; How It Is Different and the Business Imperative for It

Supply chain leaders care deeply about things that help them (Camerinelli, 2009):

- Satisfy customer demand
- Manage and reduce supply chain costs
- Better manage inventories

Supply chain leaders know this list implicitly and deal with the daily struggles of the inherent conflicts and trade-offs between these three critical performance areas. Supply chain leaders ideally will be interested in which digital strategies will improve performance across these domains and, subsequently, the people capabilities that enable them. We know from practice that IoPTS technologies play a central role in effectively managing supply chain performance trade-offs (Pettey, 2015). The following are some examples of potential performance measures that are central to guiding digital process improvement.

Satisfying Customer Demand

Supply chain leaders grapple daily with the challenge of satisfying their firm's customers. "Perfect order performance", or the percentage of orders delivered on time and in full, which also meet the quality expectations of customers, is a key performance measure that is the essence of customer satisfaction. Another key customer satisfaction performance measure often cited as a "force multiplier" for the supply chain is "demand forecast accuracy", or the difference between the forecasted and actual customer demand for your products.

Perfect Order Performance

For supply chain leaders, the ability to deliver the correct products perfectly, in full, without damage, and within the expected time frames, is the main proxy for customer satisfaction. Some organizations have recognized the need to keep a close watch on customer attitudes and sentiments and have begun adding new analytic-driven metrics to augment net promoter scores (NPS) in their performance scorecards (Ventura Research, 2015). The firm's supply chain functional ability to meet and exceed customer expectations is widely regarded as a critical factor for supporting revenue and market share growth. Generating demand for the company's products is only one side of this equation—being able to deliver effectively in response to that demand is another equally important one. Digital supply chain technologies, in particular IoPTS and their processes, continue to play a central role in improving a firm's perfect order performance.

Driving Improvements in Demand Forecast Accuracy

Considered by some as the holy grail of supply chain measures, supply chain leaders often strive to improve the accuracy of their forecasted customer demand. There are clear business gains available to the firm that can more accurately predict which products, packaging, configurations, distribution centers, and transportation networks have the optimal chance of delivering a perfect order to customers. The ability to plan manufacturing runs, manage inventory levels, assess warehousing capacities, and optimize transportation networks depends on accurate planning. Getting it right yields the three-way-win of customer satisfaction, cost management, and working capital efficiency. The challenge of improving demand forecast accuracy has become an issue of data availability and latency. Delays in operating information may create a bullwhip effect, leading to longer lead times or costly excess and obsolete inventories.

How the Digital Supply Chain Can Improve Perfect Order Performance and Demand Forecast Accuracy

Digital technologies, such as the ones driving IoPTS changes, are powerful enablers of improved supply chain performance. IoT, in particular, has already enabled massive improvements in managing supply chain performance, even in its most basic forms, such as sensors enabling inventory tracking. Sensor technologies are not new. What is different in the IoPTS world is the sheer volume and variety of data being captured and analyzed in near-real time and how the data are being utilized with powerful data analytics and artificial intelligence and machine learning (AI/ML). Data science, AI/ML, and analytics have exploded to the point where the promise of detailed real-time knowledge of demand and inventories is within reach. It is now possible to know how much of an item is available, how much is desired by customers, and where it is in the supply chain rapidly enough to make business decisions that immediately affect performance. Products are now transparently visible on their retailer shelf, in their warehouse or factory, railcar, or container. The ability to make informed trade-off decisions with this accurate and up-to-the-minute information is crucial to realizing supply chain performance benefits.

What to Expect Next From the Digital Supply Chain

Perfect order and demand forecast accuracy are key supply chain performance measures, which can be improved by new digital technology and processes. Sensor technologies allow companies to expand their information sets deeper and wider into their value chains. Being able to track products manufactured beyond their delivery to the customer will provide opportunities to improve consumer insights and therefore increase customer satisfaction. Firms have not historically been able to obtain data related to the sales and inventory levels of their products sold to customers and business partners without complex negotiations to share information. Developing detailed consumer insights, profiles, and consumption profiles about end-user consumers is often still beyond the grasp of many firms.

Near-real-time data about both customers and consumers is essential for accurate demand forecasting, but has been very difficult to obtain. IoT technologies and analytics have the potential to break down barriers to accessing data across the value chain and bring supply chain performance to a new level, a level that more accurately predicts demand and customer behavior.

Customer Sensing and Demand Shaping

Using technology to better understand customers doesn't stop with IoT. Although physical sensors provide valuable data about product inventories, consumption, and trends, the digital supply chain is not limited to physical features alone. Savvy supply chain leaders are beginning to join marketing analysts in mining social media data to understand and engage customers. Social media is an important source of information about what people are saying about products. Leaders should be considering, planning, or implementing customer and consumer social media sentiment analysis programs designed to capture and analyze data expressed on various platforms. Customer product reviews and commented images of products, both positive and negative, may yield important insights about how people feel about the firm's products. Negative comments captured, logged, and processed are now an important source of product quality information that, if acted upon, may provide advance warning and head off costly warranty claims. Likewise, consumer raves about forthcoming product releases may provide the firm with insights about how to forecast an initial manufacturing run. The digital supply chain leader seeks to improve the accuracy of demand forecasts by including customer sentiment analysis, predictive analytics, and downstream usage data in their planning algorithms.

The Market Signal Focus of the Digital Supply Chain Leader

The *market signal focus* is an external perspective, as opposed to an internal one, and has been mentioned as a key direction for the digital supply chain (Cecere, 2014). By expanding supply chain data to include unstructured customer sentiments, competitor analysis, and consumer trends, as well as data about our supply chain ecosystems of value chain partners and their business health, firms will have access to an unprecedented volume of information supporting supply chain decisions. Accessing the right data and structuring them properly to facilitate analysis and planning algorithms is a key challenge. This is where the people side of the equation must be addressed. The real challenge in improving the all-important demand forecasting lies within the organization itself. Firms must strategize to engage the right functional players to share, collaborate, and build consensus for digital-enabled demand plans.

The Consensus-Driven Demand Forecast and Plan

The most serious challenge in creating an accurate and actionable demand forecast does not concern technology, data, and processes. Functions inside a firm are often structured in silos, and people behave in ways that are driven by individual goals, measures, and objectives. The marketing function is tasked with generating brand awareness, product awareness, promoting new product launches, and assessing the portfolio mix, among other things. World-class product company marketers have already been listening to consumers and sensing markets to assess market opportunities. The sales function, which is often the closest to actual customers of the firm, is able to observe and drive demand generation activities to realize increased revenues and satisfy the buyers of the firm's products. New product development also senses customer needs and works to design and engineer the next product launch to market. Supply chain leaders need to become more integrated with these outside functions if they hope to influence and better meet customer demand. The following are two case examples that will help illuminate some of these integration challenges on firm's and their leadership implications.

Two Digital Supply Chain Integration Case Examples

To illustrate the challenge and opportunity presented by digital supply chain transformation, this chapter explores the issues faced by two top-ranked supply chain organizations of long-established global consumer products manufacturers. The firms studied have global operations with annual sales in the billions of U.S. dollars and are selling in multiple categories in hundreds of countries worldwide. Both organizations are well regarded for supply chain excellence by industry analysts and have developed productive partnerships with leading process consulting firms and supply chain technology firms. As these organizations are leading supply chain innovators, they may serve as exemplars for the implementation challenges digital technology and process improvements encountered as they are rolled out to the workforce.

Case Company One: Global Consumer Products Manufacturing Company

The global supply chain function of the first case company recently defined several significant strategic initiatives, including customer focused innovation; improving its supply chain agility; becoming more analytics driven; building better alignment with overall business strategy; and the integration of planning processes to enable end-to-end performance improvements. These strategies are an excellent list of what world-class supply chains undergoing transformations should be striving for. A core concept among them is the enablement of a true end-to-end supply chain driven by integrated planning and execution that balances consumer demand and supplier response. An end-to-end supply chain, in this case, pertains to cross-functional and collaborative planning tools and processes that are intended to improve the firm's responsiveness. This organization reportedly made multiyear investments in technical tools, such as custom algorithms to better understand and predict demand patterns and IoPTS technologies to reduce information latency of data, including for inventory and stock levels. The firm also pioneered the use of control tower technology to allow the aggregation of stock and profitability information across regions. The net impacts of these investments were designed to improve decision-making quality and speed in managing the supply chain.

Case Example One: The Legacy Hypothetical Scenario

The case begins with a sales representative who has just negotiated a trade promotion with a retail customer, a large grocery retail store chain in Belgium. The promotion is scheduled in the next 30 days, and the customer needs to be supplied with an additional 10,000 cases of a small consumer packaged product. Under legacy processes and technologies, managers responding to the upcoming delivery would predictably react in the following way: first, planners would check to see if 10,000 cases were available in a warehouse in the customer's distribution region. If they were not, or if they were short by a number of cases, a manufacturing order would be sent to the firm's regional plant to request production of the required number of cases. Meanwhile, unknown to the planner, an existing oversupply of 20,000 cases of the same item might happen to be sitting in another warehouse just across the border in France.

In this hypothetical scenario, warehouse systems and stock on hand are not integrated, and without stock tracking via IoT and process technologies the excess inventory would be virtually invisible to the planner, setting off a chain of events that would add to excess inventories taking production capacity of product SKUs actually needed offline and leading to missed promotional stocking promise dates or excessive shipping costs. The legacy process would therefore lead to poor performance in both key metrics of inventory-holding costs and reduced customer service.

A New Digital Technology–Enhanced Process

The case company made a multiyear investment in developing and implementing sophisticated demand sensing tools partnering with a leading Enterprise Resource Planning (ERP) software vendor, and worked with supply chain consultants on processes designed to enable more accurate demand forecasts. The new technologies, including IoT tracking and real-time visibility of raw materials, work in process (WIP), finished goods, stock, and safety stock levels across regions, provides an opportunity to overcome inefficient decisions and actions when compared with the legacy environment. With real-time insights into excess stocks of the promotional SKU within reach, it is possible to make faster decisions on how to meet customer demands through the transfer of inventory from a nearby region, rather than contribute to lower performance. This amplification of excess inventory, caused by the latency of information, is often called the bullwhip effect.

Human Factors Limiting Performance

Human behavioral issues such as trust, communication, and collaboration are critical factors in enabling new IoPTS strategies to achieve their performance objectives. Leadership development interventions that address these factors must accompany sizable shifts in IoPTS strategies in order for firms to capture their full performance improvement potential. In the previous case scenario, planners and analysts close to the development of the new technologies and processes learned to trust and collaborate across roles and functions in the pursuit of optimal enterprise performance. Marketing, sales, planning, manufacturing, and distribution functions were transformed to allow for shared information, agree to prioritization strategies, and decision making about customer service/profitability trade-offs. The functions could essentially place faith in the collaborative, constrained demand-planning forecast. For those associates outside of this circle of cognoscenti, however, trusting the centralized demand planning numbers was a struggle.

The Need for Organizational Learning of Integrator Behaviors

Critical behaviors are needed to facilitate the scaling of digital and supply chain performance transformations. Firms, however, must approach developing the behaviors as an organizational learning challenge requiring intervention (Argyris & Schön, 1978). In our case example, the firm identified a key set of behavioral enablers that allowed for faster and more impactful deployment of the new systems. The underlying driver of this is that employees should feel empowered and encouraged to act on behalf of the end-to-end organization, rather than acting narrowly within self-interest–driven individual metrics. To realize this goal of developing the ideal enterprise-driven actor, a set of supporting dimensions contribute to this end state: trust in the alignment of forecasted plans with the holistic goals of the firm, a firm belief in the benefits of collaboration, and a mind-set that allows for functional boundary-spanning behavior.

Case Company Two: Global Consumer Packaged Foods Manufacturer

The second case example company has made significant public statements about its supply chain talent development strategies and goals. In public forums such as supply chain conferences, the case company's global supply chain leaders spoke of the challenges the organization faced as it set its growth strategy and pondered the talent needed to support them. The company's vision statement aimed to double the size of the company's revenues in 10 years. The key for the supply chain was to enable exponential growth without an accompanying increase in supply chain cost, infrastructure, or people. The case firm realized that the main barrier to achieving this goal was its managers' leadership capabilities. The leadership skills required to create exponential performance improvements lay hidden in the firm's ability to successfully integrate its operations across its enterprise.

Key Dimensions of Digital Supply Chain People Performance

In both case examples in this chapter, the firms' recognized that leadership behaviors were critical to unlocking more integrated supply chain performance. Employee attitudes, beliefs, and actions are magnified under a more digitally integrated supply chain. This next section will outline the key digital supply chain leadership attributes that drive performance.

The Digital Supply Chain Leader

To better define the role of the digital supply chain leader, the following categorizes leadership attributes into organizational strategies and measures, employee attitudes and beliefs, and lastly, capabilities. The integrated digital supply chain, such as the one our case study companies have developed, requires collaboration among cross-functional employees to a higher degree than previously. Digital supply chain leaders need to promote meaningful disciplined collaboration among employees. Productive and focused disciplined collaboration is a key behavior that will allow for more integrated performance improvements across functions and disciplines (Hansen, 2009).

Organizational-Level Strategies and Measures

Supply chain leaders must evaluate where new talent demands have surfaced due to the requirements of digital transformation. The following are some suggested strategies:

1. Ensure talent recruiting and development programs are digital-ready.

    a. In the digital world, both now and in the future, there is and will be increased pressure on organizations to attract and retain the right talent needed to compete. Attracting and developing a workforce that is ready for a more analytics-driven approach to operating and making decisions must become a core capability of the firm. Supply chain managers must develop a nuanced understanding of the needs, types, and ranges of digital talent. Recruiting a true data scientist, then mistakenly placing this person in a purely technology environment to perform routine analysis is one notable mistake (Provost & Fawcett, 2013). Similarly, promoting a junior data analyst into a strategic role that requires a senior data scientist is also problematic. Finding new blends of data science talent working alongside supply chain domain experts is a developing strategy that has paid dividends for digitally savvy supply chain leaders. (Kranz, 2017)

2. Ensure that performance and compensation metrics are aligned or shared within the supply chain (plan source, make, deliver), as well as cross-functionally with the marketing, sales, product development, and finance.

    a. The digital supply chain is highly integrated. Therefore, the talent management practices of the leading firms must reflect this by minimizing information and practice silos.
    b. Recognize that associates in the supply chain may not be able to visualize all possible benefits of integration and collaboration by

themselves. Interventions must be developed that will overcome this limitation and the barriers to transparency.

(Ramanathan et al., 2011)

3. Ensure that supply chain leadership promotes alignment of its own digital strategies with the overall corporate strategies.

    a. In the digital supply chain, strategies must align with and serve organizational strategy. New, digitally enhanced business models must be surfaced and developed in concert with supply chain leaders.
    b. Supply chain leaders must be able to interact in peer-to-peer relationships with a range of senior organizational leaders from all functions.

Individual Attitudes, Beliefs, and Behaviors

In addition to organizational-level leadership characteristics, developing an integrated digital supply chain places demands on a higher level of individual and networked performance. Networked performance is the ability of individuals to raise the performance levels of those around them in the organization. To achieve the objective of greater integration, leaders should be concerned with developing a leadership mind-set as an attitude with integrator behaviors, mutual gains approach capabilities, and data-driven problem-solving capabilities.

The Supply Chain Leadership Mindset

When the second case company's supply chain leaders were confronted with supporting an aggressive organizational growth strategy, they realized that old leadership mind-sets could not create the kind of innovative cultural change needed.

The new mind-set reflected a clearer sense of collective leadership responsibility. Reacting to problems within one's own function, and overlooking the upstream causes and downstream impacts of individual actions, would not create a cohesive supply chain to support growth without lock-step increases in cost, complexity, and infrastructure. This distributed, or shared, leadership capability is one that cultivates the sense that all employees are empowered and encouraged to step across their individual defined task thresholds in the pursuit of improved collective performance (Conger & Riggio, 2012; Prokesch, 2010). A supply chain manager with a leadership mind-set is not afraid to challenge assumptions about how things are done no matter how established the routine or who manages the process. Supply chain leaders who believe it is their primary role and responsibility to satisfy the firm's customers are better able to make integrated performance decisions. The leadership mind-set represents a shift away from local and individual efficiencies to a broader view of overall effectiveness that balances cost and performance.

Digital Supply Chain Integrators

Certain workforce behaviors are likely to promote and unlock end-to-end supply chain performance. These behaviors reflect spanning organizational boundaries, cross-functional disciplined collaboration, and problem solving seeking greater organizational outcomes. Firms that are able to build and expand these behaviors in their workforces will benefit from the competitive advantages offered by the digital supply chain more fully. The following are some of the key behaviors that will help firms become more integrated in their supply chain functions:

1. Reaching across functional boundaries to seek information and understanding.
2. Proactively seeking the prevention of problems at their source irrespective of the originating function.
3. Creating and leading effective boundary-spanning problem-solving teams.
4. Placing performance of the organization ahead of individual or unit performance, in spite of low organizational support or conflicting metrics.
5. Exhibiting leadership that demonstrates and encourages network performance, which is the behavior of taking action to raise the performance levels of those around you. It goes beyond individual task performance (Corporate Executive Board, 2014).
6. Effectively using influence and negotiating capabilities that seek *mutual gains* (Susskind & Movius, 2009).
7. Building relationships with value chain partners which are collaborative, based on mutual gains, and are measured by shared performance metrics (as opposed to lowest cost transactions).

IoPTS Impacts on the Supply Chain Function

Table 14.1 illustrates some of the key focus areas affected by the ongoing shift to the IoPTS environment. The focus areas of leadership, operations, people, and technology are then summarized by the current state of traditional supply chain organizations, a targeted digital supply chain future state, and the transformational leadership approaches needed to facilitate their transition.

In Table 14.1 the shift from a traditional supply chain to a digital one is shown to have implications across a number of different and integrated domains. At a strategic level, the traditional supply chain has historically been focused on internal performance in achieving high levels of order accuracy while managing inventory levels and operational costs. The digital supply chain adds to these traditional performance goals by further integrating the supply chain into the firm's business strategy. This integration is intended to tap into new processes and business models that will potentially open up new sources of revenue while increasing customer satisfaction. Rather than

Table 14.1 IoPTS, Supply Chain, and Leadership

IoPTS Environmental Impacts	*The Traditional Supply Chain*	*Digital Supply Chain Transformational Leadership*	*The Digital Chain Supply*
Leadership Focus	Manage to traditional metrics; strategies target internal SC performance	Vision and strategy formed by digital unconstrained by current operations	Supply chain integrated into business strategy driving top-line and bottom-line performance improvements
Operational Focus	Perfect order targets met while inventory levels managed and balanced	Integrated vision; supply chain as a source of competitive advantage, new digital processes and business models	Supply chain helps drive customer satisfaction and revenue increases through sensing and stimulation actions
People Focus	Individual functional performance measures; plan, source, make, deliver	Sponsorship of organizational behaviors interventions and rewards; digital talent strategy development and execution	Cross-functional collaboration that improves internal and external enterprise performance Digital-savvy workforce
Technology Focus	Forecast accuracy—manual processes	Strategic investment in digital supply chain technologies	Sophisticated use of IoT, sensors, data, analytics, artificial intelligence, and machine learning

simply delivering an operationally efficient supply chain, the digital supply chain leader will position their function as integral to the firm's competitive advantage.

To further illustrate the leadership actions needed to enable digital transformation, Figure 14.1 is a conceptual model that takes the focus areas in Table 14.1 and places them in a process orientation. The implication is that digital supply chain transformation requires key leadership actions to enable it. Deliberate, focused, transformational leadership is needed to set the firm's digital supply chain vision and strategies, develop and drive integration and innovation, and develop talent and make critical technology investments. Digital supply chain transformation will not happen on its own.

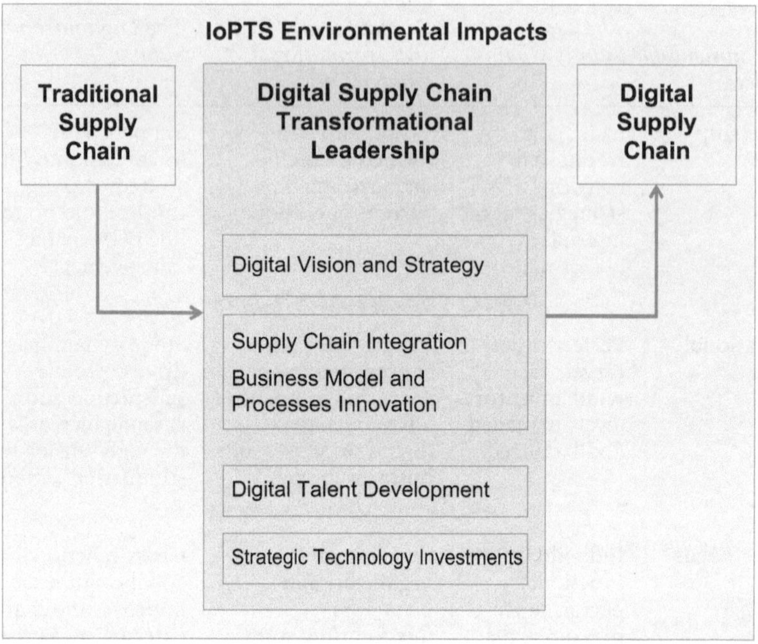

Figure 14.1 IoPTS Digital Supply Chain Environmental Impacts

Developing Digital Supply Chain Leaders

The argument made in this chapter is that the digital supply chain, led by technologies such as IoT and advanced analytics, will require enhancements in the management layer's mind-set and attitudes, integration behaviors, and skills in order to realize its competitive advantages. The changes required are more in the realm of organizational behavior (OB) change guided by intervention than they are of leadership training. OB interventions have traditionally been limited to corporate communications efforts such as face-to-face workshops or training sessions, town hall meetings, and internal media announcements.

The second case company's supply chain leadership development program resembled an OB platform intervention designed to drive the digital supply chain behaviors and skills needed to execute the firm strategy.

For example, some of the case company's leadership development program design requirements were:

- The ability to scale and reach large numbers of people quickly. Face-to-face training sessions for thousands of global associates are expensive, time consuming, and can be inconsistent in message and delivery. Media-based experiences delivered via the Web may overcome this issue.

- Teamwork and collaboration must be supported and encouraged through practice. Individuals viewing media pieces in isolation are unlikely to change their behavior. Videos from senior leaders sharing the firm vision and strategy may help build awareness, but they will not likely change the way people act. The ability to interact with a smaller group of participants as a team was required. The teams needed be able to work together online in real time, as well as asynchronously.
- The experience should be purposefully designed to promote and practice cross-functional supply chain problem solving. This means creating and guiding work teams in a structured dialog and using a set of action learning tasks and activities that have a pace, rhythm, and have weekly deadlines for sharing results with a larger cohort. The platform should be a social media learning management tool that can be easily modified to drive weekly supply chain challenges in assigned learning teams. This method connects participants in ways that builds participant confidence through experience and practice in cross-functional collaborative problem solving. Behaviors are more likely to change if participants can experience the power of finding firsthand solutions as a team based on real issues facing their own supply chain.
- The experience should allow for the efficient delivery of core leadership perspectives on the transformation of the supply chain and how it supports organizational strategy. Short (two- to five-minute), well-edited video clips of senior organizational leaders can be prepared to clarify digital supply chain change imperatives and show how they will help the firm achieve its objectives. All managers and associates should be called upon to take leadership actions to initiate change.
- Guided, paced, smaller cohorts of participants are given scaffolded daily activities to build and sustain knowledge, awareness, and, ultimately, change their feelings and perceptions. E-learning technologies and design approaches abound. The effectiveness of the intervention rests on the quality of the program's design. A traditional e-learning design that mimics compliance and skills-based training modules is unlikely to have the desired behavioral change impact. A set of new design principles that is more strategic, based on adult learning theory, change management theory, and a practical recognition of the constraints of daily work demands is needed to increase the chances of the intervention's success.

The innovation and opportunity this example represents for digital supply chain leadership is not about learning technology or platforms, but how the design builds integrative mind-sets and capabilities. By bringing participants together to practice integrated supply chain problem solving for regular intervals over multiple weeks, a collective belief in the power of integrative collaboration had a chance to develop in a sustainable way. Participants demonstrated abilities by finding solutions to complex problems beyond their individual capacities to solve.

Implications—IoT and the Workplace

Companies that regard the digital supply chain as digitizing current processes run the risk of being outmaneuvered by more nimble firms who are able to design their supply chains from a "zero base". Modern firms will "digitalize", that is they will reinvent their value chains from the ground up, potentially creating new business models enabled by technologies such as IoT, blockchain, 3-D printing, AI, and driverless vehicles and customer-focused data. Digital firms will deploy test-and-learn strategies while gathering and analyzing data with speed and flexibility. Failures will be assimilated and rapid iterations will uncover value far greater than our human workforces will find alone. It remains to be seen if the value chains of the future will become socially constructed by a mix of traditional and new firms or will become tightly controlled by digital natives.

Technologies such as IoT and blockchain have the potential to overcome traditional barriers to information sharing, trust, and security while providing transparency and new levels of supply chain integration able to deliver more value to customers and consumers. Mistrust, silos, and protective ownership over data in the highest margin segments of the value chain, particularly those closest to customer and consumers, pose threats in known and unknown ways.

Digital supply chains that are integrated, more transparent, and better able to meet customer demand will win in the transformed marketplace. It may not be possible to predict accurately where value will shift in this transformation, though our workplaces of the future must include agile data listeners, analysts, modelers, process innovators, and influencers. Digital natives, companies that grew up with technology as central to their business strategy, may have less of a challenge in becoming integrated and promoting winning workplace behaviors because technology is part of their core strategy.

At Amazon's headquarters in Seattle there is a building named "Day One". There are no marble floors or designer furniture and fixtures. Instead, the walls are rough concrete, the furniture is made of plywood, and the chandeliers are made of duct-taped work lights. Jeff Bezos says, "That is why it is always Day One" at Amazon (Bezos, 2017). Traditional incumbents leading supply chains should take note of this mind-set. The supply chains that survive and improve their performance relative to their peers will have leaders and associates with digital DNA. Firms that do not possess this mind-set will need to adopt organizational learning strategies to become the next closest thing.

References

Argyris, C., & Schön, D. (1978). *Organizational learning: A theory of action perspective*. Reading, MA: Addison Wesley.

Bennett, N., & Lemoine, G. J. (2014). What VUCA really means for you. *Harvard Business Review* (January–February), 27.

Bezos, J. P. (2017). 2016 letter to shareholders. *Amazon.com*. Retrieved from Amazon.com

Camerinelli, E. (2009). *Measuring the value of the supply chain: Linking financial performance and supply chain decisions*. Surrey, England: Gower Publishing, Ltd.

Cecere, L. M. (2014). *Supply chain metrics that matter*. Hoboken, NJ: John Wiley & Sons, Inc.

The Center for Global Enterprise (2016). *Digital supply chains: A frontside flip*. Retrieved from www.thecge.net, The Center for Global Enterprise: 38.

Conger, J. A., & Riggio, R. E. (2012). *The practice of leadership: Developing the next generation of leaders*. Hoboken, NJ: Wiley.

Corporate Executive Board. (2014). Executive guidance: Reframing leadership in the new work environment. Retrieved January 28, 2018 from www.cebglobal.com/top-insights/executive-guidance/editions/archive/eg-2014-annual.html

Gattorna, J. (2015). *Dynamic supply chains: How to design, build and manage people-centric value networks*. Upper Saddle River, NJ: FT Press.

Hansen, M. T. (2009). *Collaboration: How leaders avoid the traps, create unity, and reap big results*. Boston: Harvard Business Press.

Kranz, M. (2017). *Building the Internet of Things: Implement new business models, disrupt competitiors, and transform your industry*. Hoboken, NJ: John Wiley & Sons, Inc.

Pettey, C. (2015, April 9). Five ways the Internet of things will benefit the supply chain. Retrieved January 28, 2018, from https://www.gartner.com/smarterwithgartner/five-ways-the-internet-of-things-will-benefit-the-supply-chain-2/

Prokesch, S. (2010). The sustainable supply chain. *Harvard Business Review*, *88*(10), 70–72.

Provost, F., & Fawcett, T. (2013). *Data science for business*. Sebastapol, CA: O'Reilly Media, Inc.

Ramanathan, U., Gunasekaran, A., & Subramanian, N. (2011). Supply chain collaboration performance metrics: A conceptual framework. *Benchmarking: An International Journal*, *18*(6), 856–872. doi:10.1108/14635771111180734

Sanders, N. (2014). *Big data driven supply chain management: A framework for implementing analytics and turning information into intelligence*. New Jersey: Pearson Education.

Susskind, L., & Movius, H. (2009). *Built to win: Creating a world-class negotiating organization*. Boston: Harvard Business Press.

Tavana, M. (2014). *Handbook of research on organizational transformations through big data analytics*. Hershey, PA: IGI Global.

Ventura Research. (2015, June 29). Big Data analytics will displace Net Promoter Score (NPS) for measuring customer experience. Retrieved January 28, 2018, from https://blog.ventanaresearch.com/2015/06/29/big-data-analytics-will-displace-net-promoter-score-for-customer-satisfaction-index

15 A Framework to Reduce IoPTS Security Breaches in the Smart Workplace

Erika Pleskunas and Murugan Anandarajan

Introduction

The threats of security breaches are increasing as workplaces become smarter. Analysts expect the demand for smart workplace technology to grow by over 45 percent annually through 2019, becoming one of the most rapidly growing technology markets (Bersin, Mariani, & Monahan, 2016). The smart workplace is characterized by connectivity, collaboration and mobility through the Internet of People, Things and Services (IoPTS). In an IoPTS world, devices are wirelessly connected via smart sensors. The IoPTS uses the cloud to connect intelligent "things" (technologies) that sense and transmit a large amount of data, creating services that would not be available without this level of connectivity and analytical intelligence. With the IoPTS in the smart workplace, the roles of humans change as technology takes over the more routine work and processes.

Ultimately, IoPTS in the smart workplace assigns values to everything it measures, providing real-time data and insight into a broad array of facts about the behavior of people or other technologies (Rajagopalan, 2016). As the IoPTS becomes more and more pervasive in the workplace, the volume and detail of corporate data will continue to increase. With the increase in data collections comes an increase in the likelihood that these data can be breached. For example, data breaches reported during 2015 leaked over 736 million records, which was a 24 percent increase compared to 2014.

The next section will describe the IoPTS-enabled workplace. This is followed by a description of the IoPTS service architecture and the potential risks that could affect an organization. Lastly, there is a description of the IOPTS security policy framework and conclusions.

IoPTS-Enabled Workplace

Although the Internet is powered by humans inputting data, in an IoPTS setting, the role of humans changes to the point that machines can replace them in many operations. What makes the IoPTS so powerful is the ability to both create and communicate data. The models and algorithms are stored in IoPTS technology and the data pass through them for analysis. These analyses make it possible to identify and examine patterns as data are created in real time. The IoPTS-enabled workplace can have different focuses such as people-centric, environment-centric and process-centric. These are discussed next.

People-Centric IoPTS

People-centric IoPTS technology uses the predictability of humans and turns employee behaviors and interactions into data. With IoPTS technology, human actions can be monitored, measured, analyzed and reconfigured. Examples of this kind of technology include sociometric badges. Using the data collected from these devices, organizations can assess which aspects of work were positive or negative.

Environment-Centric IoPTS

Environment-centric IoPTS technologies aim to identify environmental risks and reduce energy usage. For instance, pocket-sized environmental sensors can monitor radiation, water quality, hazardous chemicals in the air and countless other environmental indicators. These sensors allow for a better understanding of surroundings and provide solutions for environmental problems.

Process-Centric IoPTS

Process-centric IoPTS technologies primarily refer to the ways in which technology is used from the time of production through consumer acquisition. Included in this category is automation of product control; the rotation of products in shelves and warehouses is monitored and controlled, thus restocking processes become automated. Automation of manufacturing and management of the production line uses RFID, sensors, video monitoring, remote information distribution and cloud solutions for production line monitoring. This results in improved product quality assurance processes because decision makers have access to real-time data.

IoPTS Service Architecture and Risks

Certain unique characteristics give IoPTS technologies value and make them different from traditional technologies. First, there's the underlying technology, which includes the various wireless radios that allow these devices to connect to the Internet and to each other. These include more familiar standards like Wi-Fi, low-energy Bluetooth, NFC and RFID. Then there are the items such as motion sensors, door locks or light bulbs. In some cases, there may also be a central hub that allows different devices to connect to one another. Finally, there are cloud services, which enable the collection and analysis of data so people can see what's going on and act upon the data via their mobile apps (Cha, 2015). These technologies allow for both human-to-machine and machine-to-machine interactions. In broad terms, the process of IoPTS data collection and analysis can be described by a three-layer process. This is illustrated in Figure 15.1.

First, in the sensor layer, the sensors in the technologies, such as the RFID tags and intelligent sensors, gather a wide variety of information such as location, environmental conditions or movement. Second, IoPTS gateways, which act as a bridge between the devices and the Internet, collect and transmit data to the external Internet infrastructure. The data then go from the gateway to the cloud infrastructure where they are stored and processed. Lastly, in the application layer, the data go to the end-user mobile apps or other devices where the data collected from the cloud can be viewed. Examples of this process are workplaces with temperature sensors, where a gateway helps to connect the temperature sensor network to the Internet through the cloud. The cloud or server processes data about the connected devices, allowing end users to interact with the cloud through a mobile app. Users send requests to the cloud, after which the cloud will identify the device and send a corresponding request to the appropriate sensor network using gateways. Then, the temperature sensor will read the current temperature in the room and will send the response back to the cloud. After the cloud identifies the user requesting the data, it pushes the request to the application. Lastly, the user sees the data on his or her device. The same general process applies to all IoPTS devices. For example, when using IoPTS to monitor manufacturing processes, sensors would monitor assembly lines and once the data are processed by the cloud and requested by the user, they will be requested from the cloud and back to the mobile device, after which the results can be monitored by the assembly line manager and business decisions can be made.

There are many benefits with IoPTS technology in the workplace. The major benefit is higher productivity and efficiency at a lower cost. Sensors

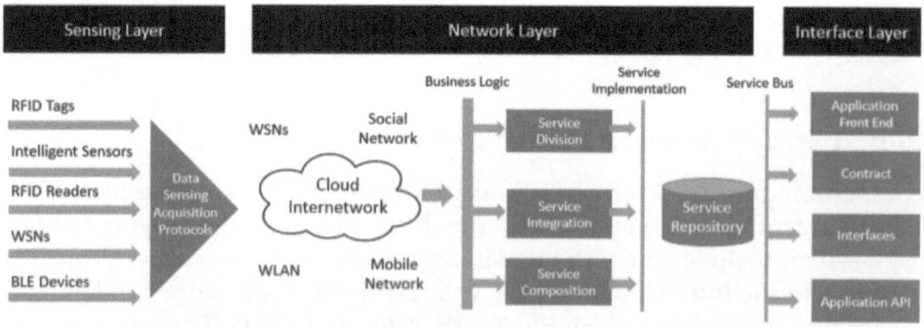

Figure 15.1 IoT Service Architecture

can be attached to any consumer product to give the organization information about how the product is used and how it can be tailored to better suit its users (Marr, 2015). The IoPTS generates data that otherwise would never exist. When the data collected from multiple devices can be viewed on a centralized platform through IoPTS, more insight is provided to more people and, in turn, better business decisions can be made (Burns, 2017). Everyday products that normally perform one function will become more valuable, as organizations will be able to sell not only a product with its primary function but also sell the data that it generates. For example, John Deere tractors have sensors that give farmers information about which crops to plant in which areas (Marr, 2015). The better business decisions from this vast data lead to more profits for the organization. Organizations can also see monetary benefits in more direct ways, such as when they use IoPTS technologies that reduce energy consumption using heating and ventilation systems that are only used during work hours. However, the IoPTS includes security risks at all these levels. The potential risks are summarized in Table 15.1.

The first risk of IoPTS in the smart workplace is the initial investment involved. When IoPTS becomes mainstream and the number of connected devices is in the billions, centralized systems experience bottlenecks. This means that there will be a high cost to maintain cloud servers that can handle such large amounts data (Banafa, 2017). IoPTS requires the creation of a risk management protocol, which comes with a high cost in terms of time and money (Mock & Paden, 2013). These risk management protocols must be a continual process, as technologies become more advanced and the risk management becomes even more important. For an organization to take on the implementation of IoPTS, it must look at its strategic goals and assets to determine if it can handle the risk of IoPTS. Smaller organizations have a tougher time adapting because of the high cost. This means it is more of a risk for smaller companies to use IoPTS when viewed from a financial perspective.

As IoPTS devices collect data about employees, the employees potentially suffer from risks. This is partly because companies will have difficulties understanding how to best manage the data collected by these devices, and these data are often about the employees. The information that can be stolen includes anything that an employee would have on an electronic device—health information, conversations with employees, bank information, etc. These security breaches are potentially the most dangerous risk involved with IoPTS technologies in the workplace. What makes IoPTS technologies especially vulnerable to security issues is that these devices are fundamentally different in the way they operate when compared to the basic Internet architecture. They are also neither standardized nor regulated, and the risks have not been fully comprehended (Bizarro & Masin, 2015). The diversity of the devices and software makes it difficult to take preventative measures, usually resulting in action after security breaches occur (Camhi, 2016).

Table 15.1 Security Threats in the IoPTS Architecture

Security Threat	*Description*
Remote configuration	Fail to configure at interfaces
Misconfiguration	Misconfiguration at remote IoT end node, end device or end gateway
Security management	Logs and key leakage
Management system	Failure of management system
Unauthorized access	Due to physical capture or logic attack, the sensitive information at the end nodes is captured by the attacker
Availability	The end node stops work because it is physically captured or attacked logically
Spoofing attack	With malware node, the attacker successfully masquerades as IoT end device, end node or end gateway by falsifying data
Selfish threat	Some IoT end nodes stop working to save resources or bandwidth and cause failure of the network
Malicious code	Viruses, Trojans and junk message can cause software failure
Transmission threats	Threats in transmission, such as interrupting, blocking, data manipulation, forgery, etc.
Routing attack	Attacks on a routing path
Sensitive information leakage at border	The sensitive information might be not protected at the border of layers
Identity spoofing	The identities in different layers have different priorities
Sensitive information spreads between layers	Sensitive information spreads at different layers and cause information leakage
Privacy threats	Privacy leakage or malicious location tracking
Services abuse	Unauthorized users access services or the authorized users access unsubscribed services
Identity masquerade	The IoT end device, node or gateway is masqueraded by the attacker
Service information manipulation	The information in services is manipulated by the attacker
Repudiation	Deny the operations have been done
Denial of services (DoS)	An attempt to make a IoT end-node resource unavailable to its users
Replay attack	The attack resends the information to spoof the receiver
Routing attack	Attacks on a routing path
Data breach	Release of secure information to an untrusted environment
Public key and private key	The compromise of keys in networks
Malicious code	Virus, Trojans and junk message can cause software failure

Lastly, society can experience the risks that come with IoPTS in the workplace. The organizations using IoPTS store external information on their IoPTS devices, creating a risk for people who are outside of the company. For example, if a healthcare company were to use smartphones as the main device for emails, those emails stored on the phone could have confidential information, such as a health history. If this data were to be stolen, this could affect insurance companies, hospitals or any other people or institutions that have a stake in the information that was breached. The next section provides a data governance framework that can help employers manage risk.

IoPTS Security Policy Framework

Although laws mandate that companies follow certain guidelines for employees' personnel files and notice for security breaches, management also needs to approach IoPTS security in a way that expresses its importance and instructs organizations, employees and the general public about what they need to do to achieve safety. Without a proper management policy, security technologies will be useless. The IoPTS policy framework described next provides a list of management policy tactics to prevent security weaknesses. The major components of the framework (see Figure 15.2) are discussed in the following section.

Data Collection

There should be limits to the quantity of personal data collected; all data should be acquired lawfully and should be collected with the knowledge and consent of the employee. This is especially difficult to follow with IoPTS technologies in the workplace because there is a risk of unintentionally collecting more data than necessary to accomplish the end goals of the devices. With more data than ever being collected, it is easy for companies to capture

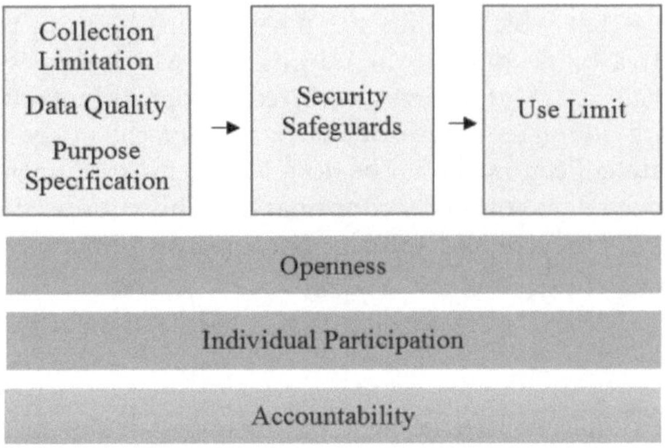

Figure 15.2 A Framework to Reduce IoPTS Security Breaches in the Smart Workplace

irrelevant data. However, there are ways in which companies making wearables or other IoPTS devices can help reduce privacy risks that occur from collecting too much data. Some of these precautions include providing notice to the employees that the organization is collecting data, creating limitations for the use of the data, not sharing with others inappropriately and specifically assigning privacy responsibility in formal job descriptions. This ensures that someone in the organization fully understands the data collection processes and policies. The Federal Trade Commission and other regulators are pushing IoPTS device manufacturers to establish privacy and security regulations for the whole wearable device industry, therefore providing extra protections to employees.

Data Quality

High-quality personal data comprise an important component of the framework. This is defined as data related to operations, decision making and planning and that is accurate, complete and current (Redman, 2008). As data volumes increase from the growing use of IoPTS in the workplace, the question of internal data consistency becomes even more critical. Thus data quality and security are intertwined. The NIST Smart Grid Interoperability Panel Privacy Subgroup (National Institute of Standards and Technology. 2016)) researched the ways in which smart meters and other smart grid devices create privacy risks. The group described the vast capacity of IoPTS devices to collect, store and use personal behavioral data, thus necessitating the needs to limit data only to that which are necessary to accomplish the end goal of the devices, thus facilitating a more efficient process for generating quality data.

Specification of the Purpose of Data Collection

It is important that the purposes for which personal data are collected should be outlined prior to collection, and the use of that data must be limited to only that which fulfills the purpose. In the past, personal data were primarily a by-product of the purpose for which they were collected (Moerel & Prins, 2015). However, with technological innovations like the IoPTS, data are no longer a by-product, but rather, the purpose of the data collection. Data collection should be done to meet a specific goal, resulting in purpose-driven data collection coordination. This coordination, although it is necessary for ethical and security purposes, in some ways defeats the benefits of Internet of Things technologies.

Data Use

Personal data should neither be exposed nor used for purposes other than those specified. IoPTS devices have countless security vulnerabilities, and research from Hewlett Packard (HP) revealed that 80 percent of connected devices were vulnerable to security risks because of unencrypted communications and inadequate authentication (Bell, 2014). HP researchers examined 10 devices for security vulnerabilities and found that 8 of them potentially could allow hackers to access personal information such as the user's name, address, health records and credit card details. HP concluded that a major reason for increased security risks was that device demand was so high that manufacturers rushed them to market without adequate testing for potential security breaches. Additionally, many large organizations implementing IoPTS solutions use legacy systems so the interfacing between old and new is often difficult, with the security mechanisms often being mismatched. Although the initial costs may be much less to use the legacy systems, many of them use sensors with weak security protocols inadequately designed for the IoPTS. With IoPTS, information moves in many directions as the back-end systems aggregate and analyze massive amounts of data, resulting in many more points of communication. Consequently, the older security framework of shared-system accounts and passwords no longer provide enough security in the IoPTS workplace (Saif, Peasley, & Perinkolam, 2015).

Security Safeguards

Personal data should be protected by security safeguards against risks such as loss, unauthorized access, modification or disclosure of data. Security is fraught with issues. One issue, particularly for smaller companies, is the tendency to try to save money by scrimping on security measures and policies. Recent research found that many of the top 30 fitness devices did not have either a privacy policy or accurate policy descriptions for the use of the data which would be collected (Bracy, 2013). A second issue is the concept of "multiple points of vulnerability" in IoPTS. There are many more points of communication encompassing the IoPTS product—embedded software, data inside the device, communication channels, data aggregation platform and data centers for analysis of sensor data—so potential security breaches have more ways to occur. Additionally, the sheer volume of connections inherently creates more opportunities for security breaches. The third issue is that there is currently no general agreement on how to define and implement IoPTS security because these technologies are so new and there is not yet a standard for security. The fourth issue is that devices in the IoPTS are very different from previous technologies, so security must be viewed from new and often completely different perspectives. Lastly, there is no "silver bullet" that can effectively eliminate all threats. By the very nature of IoPTS devices, there will always be the risk of security breaches.

Openness About Data Policy Practices

There should be a general openness within an organization about developments, practices and policies with regard to personal data. Employees should be aware that data are being collected, and they should know the main purposes of their use. The data controller should be readily available to address questions and concerns. One of the three main challenges of IoPTS is the potential for unexpected uses of data because so much is collected. This is an issue that can be mitigated by having data collection policies and procedures and to provide training on them (Higman & Pinfield, 2015).

Individual Participation

Individuals should have the right to obtain their personal data from a data controller within a reasonable time, at a low cost and in an easily understood format. They should be given reasons if a request is denied, and they should be able to challenge this denial. Lastly, they should be able to challenge the type and quantity of data collected about them and, if the challenge is successful, the data should be erased. The right of individuals to access and challenge their personal data is widely accepted to be one of the most important privacy protection safeguards as it keeps the data collection transparent (HG.org, 2017). This can be accomplished by having a team that is dedicated to data maintenance and control who provide services to employees seeking the data being collected about them, as well as employees knowing their rights or where to seek information about them (HG org, 2017).

Data Accountability

The data controller has a critical role and should be accountable for complying with the measures stated earlier (Murray & Kelleher, 2017). This role functions as the central gatekeeper because IoPTS technologies connect multiple organizations and information flows across multiple external devices and databases. Parties outside of the organization may not have robust security systems, so every party connected, even if indirectly connected, is at risk (Saif et al., 2015). Therefore, companies should not assume that customers or other stakeholders will take responsibility for maintaining data security and preventing breaches. In other words, organizations should behave as if the responsibility for security was solely theirs. Companies should be aware of data trails—where the data are going and who has access to them, while also making sure there are standards for how each of the stakeholders holding the information secures it.

Discussion

The information in this chapter is useful for governments, organizations and individuals because each entity plays a role in making the smart workplace safer. Just as IoPTS is a complex network with benefits and challenges, the management of it also will be complex with positive and negative effects.

Regardless of the risks, a survey by Information Systems Audit and Control Association (ISACA) discovered that 63 percent of businesses think that the benefits of IoPTS will outweigh the hazards (Bizarro & Masin, 2015). Borne (2014) lists six benefits as 1) tracking behavior for real-time marketing, 2) enhanced situational awareness, 3) sensor-driven decision analytics, 4) process optimization, 5) optimized resource consumption and 6) instantaneous control and response in complex autonomous systems.

The government is a major influence for regulation and dispersion of funds for IoPTS devices, and also plays a major role in the future of IoPTS technology and governance in the smart workplace. Although research has shown that businesses will be the top adopter of IoPTS solutions, governments will be the second-largest adopters (Meola, 2016). The first area in which the government plays a role is through providing funds for research, cybersecurity and other cost-based purposes. The government spent $8.8 billion on the Internet of Things in fiscal year 2015, mostly for defense spending (Ravindranath, 2016). These funds were used for a variety of purposes, such as the recent expansion of government programs to protect users of IoPTS technologies. Because IoPTS devices are used across borders, it is also necessary for other countries to put funds towards IoPTS-related projects. The UK, for example, spent over $60 million in 2014 to fund IoPTS research and created an umbrella program. This program has been the catalyst for a variety of projects, including creating a research hub focused on security and trust in new technologies (Lohrmann, 2015). Additionally, the judiciary branch of the government can help by making judicial rulings that favor consumers.

Organizations can also play a role in making the smart workplace safer and more secure. First, as the initial implementers of these technologies, it is crucial that the organizations understand how the IoPTS devices are working and the precautions they can take. Some examples of these precautions include understanding the types of data they are producing, what terminologies and coding languages are used and how their systems are set up to accept and analyze the many types of data (Bresnick, 2015). Additionally, they need to make sure that the massive amounts of data are capable of being stored by the current infrastructure. Organizations need to also train their employees about precautions and how to properly use these devices. This may be accomplished by setting standards that employees need to follow, such as setting unique passwords for their devices or moving from two-step verification to two-factor authentication that is easy to use (Apple, 2017). This could also mean simply developing trust with the employees and taking any necessary steps to ensure that their rights are protected. Lastly, organizations have the funds and power to influence how IoPTS is implemented into society. This means that organizations can work with other institutions, such as universities and other NGOs, to research privacy and to donate money to these other institutions researching these issues. By engaging in conversations about standards, companies can influence regulators and build recognition in the field (Deichmann, Roggendorf & Wee, 2015). Organizations have an especially influential role now, because the IoPTS is still being shaped.

Individuals using these devices can influence how IoPTS develops in the workplace. Individuals need to be educated on the basics of how these devices work, where the potential security risks exist and how these risks can be prevented. Second, individuals need to know their rights. Should there be a security breach or a question about the information an employer is collecting, an employee must know how he or she can protect her privacy. Lastly, open communication and trust within an organization are important to ensure that all parties are aware of the data being collected by these IoPTS devices. All should approve of usages beforehand and know how to address issues arising from usage outside the organization. If individuals understand security risks and the precautions that need to be taken, they can shape how the IoPTS evolves. IoPTS is a world of "ginormous data" (Modell, 2013) with ginormous connectivity; there are ginormous benefits and ginormous challenges. This chapter offers a discussion and framework on how we can manage in this ginormousness to work in a smarter and safer workplace.

References

Apple. (2017, September 20). *Switch from two-step verification to two-factor authentication.* Retrieved November 18, 2017, from https://support.apple.com/en-us/HT207198

Banafa, A. (2017, March 14). *Three major challenges facing IoT.* Retrieved November 2, 2017, from https://iot.ieee.org/newsletter/march-2017/three-major-challenges-facing-iot

Bell, L. (2014, July 31). *80 percent of IoT devices are vulnerable to data theft, says HP.* Retrieved September 18, 2016, from www.theinquirer.net/inquirer/news/2358141/80-percent-of-iot-devices-are-vulnerable-to-data-theft-says-hp

Bersin, J. Mariani, J. & Monahan, K. (2016, May 24). Will IoT technology bring us the quantified employee? *The Internet of Things in human resources.* Retrieved February 9, 2017, from http://dupress.com/articles/people-analytics-internet-of-things-iot-human-resources/#end-notes

Bizarro, P. A., & Masin, B. (2015). Preparing for enterprise security risks of the 'Internet of Things'. *Internal Auditing, 30*(4), 5–9.

Borne, K. (2014, August 6). *14 benefits and forces that are driving the Internet of Things.* Retrieved November 18, 2017, from https://mapr.com/blog/14-benefits-and-forces-are-driving-internet-things/

Bracy, J. (2013, November 20). *Are notice and consent possible with the Internet of Things?* Retrieved November 5, 2017, from https://iapp.org/news/a/is-notice-and-consent-possible-with-the-internet-of-things/

Bresnick, J. (2015, November 9). *Four big data governance tasks to prep for the Internet of Things.* Retrieved September 18, 2016, from https://healthitanalytics.com/news/four-big-data-governance-tasks-to-prep-for-the-internet-of-things

Burns, M. (2017, July 27). *3 ways the Internet of Things will change your workplace in 2017.* Retrieved November 2, 2017, from www.digitalistmag.com/iot/2017/07/27/3-ways-internet-of-things-change-workplace-in-2017-05238505

Camhi, J. (2016, September 16). *Risks in the connected workplace*. Retrieved November 2, 2017, from http://blog.nasstar.com/connected-iot-workplace-risks/

Cha, B. (2015, January 15). *A beginner's guide to understanding the Internet of Things*. Retrieved September 18, 2016, from www.recode.net/2015/1/15/11557782/a-beginners-guide-to-understanding-the-internet-of-things

Deichmann, J., Roggendorf, M., & Wee, D. (2015, November). *Preparing IT systems and organizations for the Internet of Things*. Retrieved September 2, 2016, from www.mckinsey.com/industries/high-tech/our-insights/preparing-it-systems-and-organizations-for-the-internet-of-things

HG.org. (2017). *Data protection law*. Retrieved November 18, 2017, from www.hg.org/data-protection.html

Higman, R., & Pinfield, S. (2015). Research data management and openness: The role of data sharing in developing institutional policies and practices. *Program, 49*(4), 364–381.

Lohrmann, D. (2015, October 24). *Governments need an Internet of Things strategy*. Retrieved November 5, 2017, from www.govtech.com/blogs/lohrmann-on-cyber security/governments-need-an-internet-of-things-strategy.html

Marr, B. (2015, August 17). *3 ways the Internet of Things will change every business*. Retrieved November 2, 2017, from www.forbes.com/sites/bernardmarr/2015/08/17/3-ways-the-internet-of-things-will-change-every-business/#489589231981

Meola, A. (2016, May 31). *The US government is pouring money into the Internet of Things*. Retrieved September 18, 2016, from www.businessinsider.com/the-us-government-is-pouring-money-into-the-internet-of-things-2016-5

Mock, T., & Paden, K. (2013, October 23). *Organizational risks and the Internet of Things*. Retrieved November 2, 2017, from https://er.educause.edu/blogs/2015/10/organizational-risks-and-the-internet-of-things

Modell, B. (2013, December 12). *Move over big data, here comes 'Ginormous Data!'*. Retrieved November 18, 2017, from https://blog.cdw.com/data-center/move-over-big-data-here-comes-ginormous-data

Moerel, L., & Prins, C. (2015, June, 2). On the death of purpose limitation. Retrieved September 18, 2016, from https://iapp.org/news/a/on-the-death-of-purpose-limitation/

Murray, K., & Kelleher, D. (2017). *Duties of data controllers*. Retrieved November 18, 2017, from http://ictlaw.com/data-protection/duties-of-data-controllers/

National Institute of Standards and Technology. (2016). NIST framework and roadmap for smart grid interoperability standards: Release 2.0 (pp. 1–227). Retrieved January 28, 2018, from www.nist.gov/sites/default/files/documents/smartgrid/NIST_Framework_Release_2-0_corr.pdf

Rajagopalan, R. (2016, February). *Wearables: Are they fit for the workplace?* 1–2. Retrieved September 18, 2016, from www.cognizant.com/InsightsWhitepapers/Wearables-At-Work-Are-They-Fit-for-the-Workplace-codex1542.pdf

Ravindranath, M. (2016, June 1). *Report: Federal 'Internet of Things' spending up by 20 percent*. Retrieved September 2, 2016, from www.nextgov.com/cio-briefing/2016/06/report-federal-internet-things-spending-20-percent/128740/

Redman, T. C. (2008). *Data driven: Profiting from your most important business asset*. New York, NY: Harvard Business Press.

Saif, I., Peasley, S., & Perinkolam, A. (2015, July 27). *Safeguarding the Internet of Things: Being secure, vigilant, and resilient in the connected age*. Retrieved September 2, 2016, from https://dupress.deloitte.com/dup-us-en/deloitte-review/issue-17/internet-of-things-data-security-and-privacy.html

16 IoPTS and the Future Workplace

A Global Perspective

Murugan Anandarajan and Claire Simmers

Introduction

The future workplace will be much more progressive than ever before. Employees will most likely have greater flexibility concerning when and where tasks are completed. As choice will be at the core of the model of the way we work, there will be even more flexibility for workers. People will begin to cowork, and there will be an increasing weight on making the environment a participative society. Enterprises will focus on collaboration as a major driver of performance and this will be a core competency for every employee. These trends will affect the future workforce in terms of cross-cultural work forces, global interdependencies, skilled workers from emerging countries improving productivities from within their own borders, remote workers increasing flexibility to meet labor needs, cultural diversity contributing towards business success, human employment toward creativity and social skills and the need for a more enlightened approach to management.

For this to become a reality, IoPTS should be mainstream within workplaces across the globe. However, IoPTS is still in its infancy in multiple countries, as many of the required factors are in the early stage of development; thus, it is posited that each country will have its own unique set of IoPTS capacity and readiness characteristics. The purpose of this chapter is to develop an IoPTS adaption score to classify national progress in adopting and using IoPTS. The first step is to identify a set of measures to assess IoPTS progress and then to evaluate and classify the adaption capacity and readiness of each country's IoPTS infrastructure. This chapter is organized as follows. In the next section, a conceptual framework is developed. This is followed by the IoPTS assessment scorecard. The chapter concludes with implications and limitations of the framework.

Literature Review

Two concepts are described in the literature as important for institutions to drive adaptation to change: adaptive capacity and adaptation readiness. Adaptive capacity focuses on the theoretical potential for adaptation and refers to a system's ability or potential to adapt based on the existence of a variety of social, political, economic, technological and institutional factors. However, adaptive capacity alone may not lead to adaptation. The concept of adaptation readiness goes beyond adaptive capacity and focuses on whether supportive measures and conditions for adaptation actually exist (Ford & King, 2015). Adaptation readiness captures what is actually being done to plan and prepare for adaptation by assessing the strength and existence of governance structures. It determines preparedness to support adaptation action and effectively develop, implement and monitor adaptation interventions. Adaptation readiness assessments therefore aim to examine preparations for adaptation, providing an indication of the likelihood that adaptation will occur and identifying where intervention will enhance preparedness (Ford & King, 2015). As such, the concept of readiness captures what is being done, or has been done, to prepare to adapt.

The concepts of adaptive capacity and adaptation readiness are applied to IoPTS as illustrated in Figure 16.1. It is proposed that both IoPTS adaptive capacity and IoPTS adaptation readiness are needed for adaptation to occur. A high adaptive capacity on its own may not lead to adaptation if the resources to adapt are not available or if few evident steps have been taken. Likewise, high adaptation readiness may not lead to adaptation if the political and social impetus for adaptation is absent or disrupted.

The next section provides an evaluation framework and recognizes the need for institutional resources, structures, processes and actions that determine both capacity and readiness to develop, implement and monitor adaptations.

IoPTS Adaptive Framework

Tilleard and Ford (2016)'s research on climate change is used as a framework for the proposed model to evaluate IoPTS adaptive capacity and adaptation readiness. Although the existence of both adaptive capacity and adaptation readiness will not always translate into adaptation, when

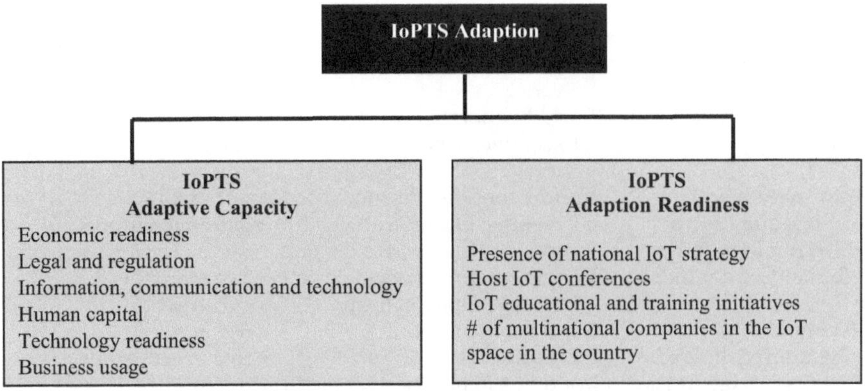

Figure 16.1 Conceptual Framework

combined they give a more comprehensive basis for evaluating the IoPTS adaptation landscape. Next the indicators for a country's IoPTS adaptive capacity are discussed, followed by the indicators for a country's IoPTS adaptive readiness.

Indicators for Country's IoPTS Adaptive Capacity

Building upon empirical scholarship examining determinates of actual adaptation (Moser & Ekstrom, 2010; Smith, Vogel, & Iii, 2009), it is possible to identify a number of factors that are required to build a sound national infrastructure that is favorable to IoPTS. These factors include government spending, R&D, technology, country risk, knowledgeable workforce and political instability. Gathered also was a list of potential factors widely recognized as having significant impacts on a country's e-strategies (ITU, 2010). The six indices of a country's IoPTS adaptive capacity include 1) economic readiness; 2) legal and regulatory; 3) information, communication and technology; 4) human capital; 5) technology; and 6) business usage. The indicators making up the indices were selected based on publically available datasets. The indices, descriptions and items are discussed next. Table 16.1 provides the source of the items and scoring scale.

Economic Readiness Index

Based on the literature, we gathered a master list of potential factors and scores from various databases. The Economic Readiness Index is made up of seven subdimensions. These are described here:

Fiscal freedom: The fiscal freedom component is a composite measure of the burden of taxes as a percentage of gross domestic product (GDP).

Table 16.1 Adaptive Capability Scoring

Index	*Source*	*Scoring*
Economic Readiness Index	Economic Readiness Index	0–100
Legal and Regulatory Index	World Economic Forum, Executive Opinion Survey	1 = not developed at all 7 = extremely well developed
Information and Communication Technology Index	World Economic Forum, Executive Opinion Survey	1 = not at all 7 = extremely successful
Human Capital Index	World Economic Forum, Executive Opinion Survey	1 = extremely poor 7 = excellent
Technology Readiness Index	World Economic Forum, Executive Opinion Survey	1 = not at all 7 = to a great extent
Business Usage Index	World Economic Forum, Executive Opinion Survey	1 = not at all 7 = to a great extent

Business freedom: Is an overall indicator of the efficiency of government regulation of business.

Labor freedom: Is a measure that considers various aspects of the legal and regulatory framework of a country's labor market.

Monetary freedom: Combines a measure of price stability with an assessment of price controls.

Trade freedom: Is a composite measure of the extent of tariff and non-tariff barriers that affect imports and exports of goods and services.

Investment freedom: In an economically free country, there would be no constraints on the flow of investment capital.

Financial freedom: Is an indicator of banking efficiency as well as a measure of independence from government control and interference in the financial sector.

Legal and Regulatory Index

The Legal and Regulatory Index, composed of four items, assesses the extent to which the national legal framework facilitates ICT penetration and the safe development of business activities, taking into account general features of the regulatory environment (including the independence of the judiciary and the efficiency and effectiveness of the law-making process), as well as more ICT-specific dimensions (laws related to ICTs).

Information and Communication Technology Index

The ICT dimension assesses the individual efforts of the main social agents, individuals, business and government to increase their capacity to use ICTs as well as their actual use of the technologies. The measure is composed of five items, including household with PC, importance of ICT to government's vision of the future, government success in ICT promotion, impact of ICTs on access to basic services and ICT use and government efficiency

Human Capital Index

The Human Capital Index gauges the ability of a society to make effective use of ICTs attributable to the existence of basic educational skills captured by the quality of the educational system, the level of adult literacy and the rate of secondary education enrollment. The measure is composed of three items: quality of management schools, quality of educational system and quality of math and science education.

Technology Index

The Technology Index measures the presence of conditions that allow innovation to flourish including variables on the overall availability of technology, the demand conditions for innovative products, the availability of venture capital for financing innovation related projects, and the presence of a skilled labor force.

Business Usage Index

The Business Usage Index captures the extent of business Internet use as well as the efforts of the firms in an economy to integrate ICTs into an internal, technology-savvy, innovation-conducive environment that generates productivity gains. The measure is composed of five items, including households with Internet access, individuals using the Internet, B2B Internet use, B2C to Internet use and Internet access.

Indicators for Country's IoPTS Adaption Readiness

The concept of readiness captures what is being done, or has been done, to prepare a country to adapt an IoPTS environment. There are a number of precursor factors which, when in place, help a country to increase readiness for IoPTS. These are national IoPTS policy initiatives, nationwide IoPTS educational initiatives, influx of multinational corporations into the country working on IoPTS initiatives and the hosting of IoPTS conferences. These initiatives are briefly described next.

National IoPTS Policy Initiatives

National policy initiatives are government procedures to set principles and rules that guide decisions and achieve rational outcomes. National policies to promote IoPTS may include IoPTS promotion policies, IoPTS policies and IoPTS legislation. In other words the government needs to create conducive environment for its growth.

Nationwide IoPTS Educational Initiatives

Education is an essential driver of personal, national and global development. However, reducing the gaps in school enrollment rates and total years of schooling is insufficient. Nations must also aim for quality in their educational systems—a key challenge (Jung-Wha, 2014). Information and communication technologies can stimulate the expansion of educational opportunities and improve educational quality at the national and global level by offering a variety of innovative learning channels. A country's lack of skilled IoPTS professionals who can design, program, install, configure and maintain IoPTS devices and architectures can seriously hamper IoPTS adaption and development.

Influx of Multinational Corporations Working on IoPTS Initiatives

Multinational corporations (MNCs) looking for new markets, skills and talent will continue to expand. Nations often offered incentives to attract MNC investments and in turn, sought technology transfer and training.

MNCs often asked for intellectual property protection and introduced globally established corporate governance norms and management practices (Solomon, 2005).

Hosting of IoPTS Conferences

At a conference, innovative ideas are discussed and new information is exchanged among experts. The purpose of the conference could be one of the following: an academic conference, a business conference or a trade conference. Hosting international conferences is a way to create international exposure for the nation and adds to building a value-added global network. They also provide access to new knowledge and professional discourse.

Classifying Adaptive Capacity and Adaptation Readiness

Although the conceptual difference between adaptive capacity and adaptation readiness is clear, the separation becomes more difficult when classifying the data into the appropriate dimensions and indicators. The data were put in categories to reflect the broader conceptual understanding of the two terms. There were no direct overlaps in dimensions and indicators of adaptive capacity and adaptation readiness even though they may appear similar. Table 16.2 provides a breakdown of the adaptive capacity scores by country. Shaded cells indicate countries with an above-average score for each of the

Table 16.2 Adaptive Capacity Indices

Country	*ERI*	*LRR*	*ICT*	*HCI*	*Tech*	*BUI*
Singapore	6.14	5.94	6.12	5.98	5.50	5.73
United Kingdom	5.57	5.76	5.41	4.92	5.29	6.24
Canada	5.58	5.54	5.32	5.37	4.99	5.85
Germany	5.33	5.32	5.40	5.11	5.43	5.67
Estonia	5.58	5.07	5.84	4.70	4.98	5.95
Japan	5.29	5.40	5.37	4.58	5.44	5.91
Malaysia	5.34	5.19	5.58	5.19	5.42	5.19
Iceland	5.22	4.87	5.49	4.94	5.05	6.31
United States	5.46	4.75	5.27	4.84	5.70	5.85
Australia	5.71	5.06	5.16	4.82	4.91	5.80
France	4.72	4.66	5.11	5.10	5.02	5.33
Saudi Arabia	4.75	4.67	5.57	4.12	4.87	4.79
Turkey	4.80	3.88	4.74	3.58	4.60	4.30
Indonesia	4.41	4.10	4.28	4.56	4.80	3.37
Philippines	4.73	3.66	4.11	4.47	4.58	3.67
Morocco	4.68	3.65	4.47	3.94	4.04	3.68
Brazil	4.22	3.29	4.11	3.30	4.24	3.99
Pakistan	4.14	3.36	3.52	3.69	4.02	2.68
Egypt	4.37	3.02	3.84	2.20	3.38	3.56
Zimbabwe	2.78	2.91	3.29	4.19	3.48	2.46
Venezuela	2.57	1.74	3.41	3.27	3.08	3.49

Table 16.3 Scores and Ranking by Country

Country	*Capability Score*	*Ranking*	*Readiness Score*	*Ranking*
Singapore	5.90	1	2.50	1
United Kingdom	5.53	2	2.25	3
Canada	5.44	3	1.75	6
Germany	5.38	4	1.75	6
Estonia	5.36	5	1.25	14
Japan	5.33	6	2.00	5
Malaysia	5.32	7	1.50	9
Iceland	5.31	8	0.50	19
United States	5.31	9	2.50	1
Australia	5.24	10	2.25	3
France	4.99	11	1.75	6
Saudi Arabia	4.80	12	1.00	17
Turkey	4.32	13	1.25	14
Indonesia	4.25	14	1.50	9
Philippines	4.20	15	1.50	9
Morocco	4.08	16	1.50	9
Brazil	3.86	17	1.50	9
Pakistan	3.57	18	0.75	18
Egypt	3.40	19	1.25	14
Zimbabwe	3.19	20	0.50	20
Venezuela	2.93	21	0.50	21

capacity indices. To identify high and low capacity countries, we developed an aggregate adaptive capacity score, calculated as the average across the six indices for each country. Similarly an aggregate adaptive readiness score was calculated across the four indicators for each of the countries. The scores are summarized in Table 16.3.

Results

The adaptive capacity and adaptation readiness scores were compiled for each country. The grouping space was then split so that countries were assigned as below or above the average aggregate score allowing division into four groups: 1) countries with below-average adaptive capacity and adaptation readiness; 2) countries with above-average adaptive capacity and below-average adaptation readiness; c) countries with above-average adaptation readiness and below-average adaptive capacity; and d) countries with above-average adaption readiness and adaptive capacity. Results are presented in Figure 16.2.

There is a large variation in adaptive capacity across the countries—the mean aggregate index score is 4.89—yet countries score as low as 2.93 (Venezuela) and as high as 5.9 (Singapore). As might be expected, the developing countries located in the lower-left quadrant tend to have lower adaptive

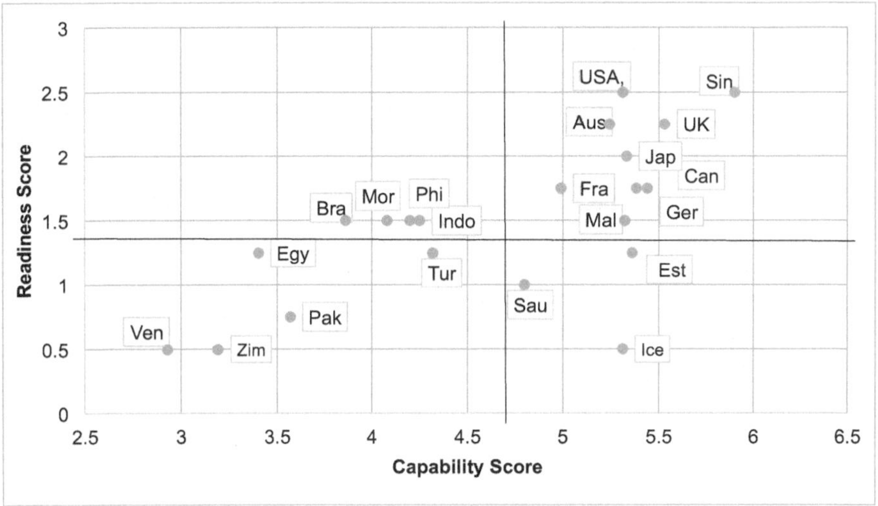

Figure 16.2 Adaption Score

capacities and the mostly developed countries located in top-right quadrant tend to have higher adaptive capacities.

Adaptation readiness is geographically more evenly spread than adaptive capacity, with high adaptation readiness documented in developed countries just above average adaptive readiness in Brazil, Morocco, Philippines and Indonesia. This reflects the different focus and resourcing requirements for capacity and readiness. Adaptive capacity is more focused on general levels of development and financial resources, which the developing countries often lack compared to those developed countries, whereas adaptation readiness is targeted to adaptation and places less emphasis on resources.

Discussion

Understanding a country's IoPTS readiness is vital for the effective implementation of the future global workplace. We envisage the future workplace to be transnational in nature, meaning that employees can be located anywhere in the world. For such a workplace to succeed, a country needs a strong IoPTS infrastructure. The scores developed in this study capture the country's readiness to provide a viable workplace IoPTS infrastructure.

Despite the limitations of the study, it makes a contribution to our knowledge of how nations might prepare for the workplace changes happening because of the IoPTS. The study results suggest that adaptive capacity varies substantially across the countries in the analysis. Not surprising, developed countries have higher capacities to adapt to IoPTS than developing countries.

The approach discussed in this chapter provided a starting point for identifying priorities for adaptation and a systematic and standardized means for assessing and monitoring change over time. Specifically, the results of the study can help in the research and policy debate in a number of areas, such as allocation of adaption funds, prioritization of projects and the monitoring and evaluation of projects. In addition the framework proposed in this chapter provides a basis for developing indicators. This can serve as a tool to communicate what is being done or not done for adaption. The Internet of Things is here and will continue to grow, and these innovations will change workplaces around the globe. Identifying factors that will increase adaptive capacity and readiness will contribute to a more equitable and widespread participation in the benefits of IoPTS, as well as increase awareness on how to counter the challenges of IoPTS.

References

Ford, J. D., & King, D. (2015). A framework for examining adaptation readiness. *Mitigation and Adaptation Strategies for Global Change*, *20*(4), 505–526.

ITU. (2010, November–December). *National e-strategies for development, global status and perspectives 2010*. Retrieved November 19, 2017, from http://itunews.itu.int/en/76-National-e-Strategies-for-Development-Global-Status-and-Perspectives-2010.note.aspx

Jung-Wha, L. (2014, September 16). *Why we must invest more in education*. Retrieved November 19, 2017, from www.weforum.org/agenda/2014/09/invest-in-education-income-inequality/

Moser, S. C., & Ekstrom, J. A. (2010). A framework to diagnose barriers to climate change adaptation. *Proceedings of the National Academy of Science*, *107*, 22026–22031.

Smith J. B., Vogel J. M., & Iii J. E. C. (2009). An architecture for government action on adaptation to climate change: An editorial comment. *Climate Change*, 95, 53–61.

Solomon, A. (2005). *Technology futures and global power, wealth, and conflict*. Washington, DC: Center for Strategic & International Studies.

Tilleard, S. & Ford, J. (2016). Adaptation readiness and adaptive capacity of transboundary river basins. *Climatic Change*, *137*(3–4), 575–591.

Index

Note: Page numbers in italics indicate figures and those in bold indicate tables.